Investment
Project Design

Founded in 1807, John Wiley & Sons is the oldest independent publishing company in the United States. With offices in North America, Europe, Australia and Asia, Wiley is globally committed to developing and marketing print and electronic products and services for our customers' professional and personal knowledge and understanding.

The Wiley Finance series contains books written specifically for finance and investment professionals as well as sophisticated individual investors and their financial advisors. Book topics range from portfolio management to e-commerce, risk management, financial engineering, valuation and financial instrument analysis, as well as much more.

For a list of available titles, visit our Web site at www.WileyFinance.com.

Investment Project Design

*A Guide to Financial
and Economic Analysis
with Constraints*

LECH KUROWSKI
DAVID SUSSMAN

WILEY
John Wiley & Sons, Inc.

Published by John Wiley & Sons, Inc., Hoboken, New Jersey.
Published simultaneously in Canada.

For general information on our other products and services or for technical support, please contact our Customer Care Department within the United States at (800) 762-2974, outside the United States at (317) 572-3993 or fax (317) 572-4002.

Wiley also publishes its books in a variety of electronic formats. Some content that appears in print may not be available in electronic books. For more information about Wiley products, visit our web site at www.wiley.com.

See the web site www.wiley.com/go/investmentprojectdesign for additional information.

Library of Congress Cataloging-in-Publication Data:

Kurowski, Lech.
  Investment project design : a guide to financial and economic analysis with constraints/ Lech Kurowski, David Sussman.
    p. cm. – (Wiley finance series)
  Includes bibliographical references and index.
ISBN 978-0-470-91389-5 (cloth)
  1. Capital investments—Evaluation. 2. Investment analysis. 3. Industrial development projects—Finance. 4. Infrastructure (Economics)—Finance. 5. Project management—Finance. I. Sussman, David (David Louis) II. Title.
  HG4028.C4K867 2011
  658.15′2–dc22

                                                                      2010037958

10 9 8 7 6 5 4 3 2 1

To
Zosia Kurowska and Claire Sussman
for their lifetimes of support

Contents

Acknowledgments

The foundation for our approach to project design and appraisal consists of ideas and concepts developed from our own work over the course of the past 25 years, and interactions with fellow consultants and others with whom we have collaborated, who graciously shared their knowledge and experiences through informal discussions and communications and formal presentations, and who have added immeasurably to the scope and depth of our effort. Their knowledge and experience in their respective areas of expertise has fused with that of the authors, so it is possible to identify only approximately the areas of contribution of each of the following individuals, to whom we are deeply indebted (listed in alphabetical order):

Jadranko Bendekovic, the economic viewpoint, particularly the value-added approach; Janusz Lukasik, forecasting and the basic idea for the expansion project case study; Andrzej Mlotkowski, project planning, implementation, and contracting; Joseph Moongananiyil who coordinated the work of the staff of the Enterprise Development Institute in Ahmedabad, India, with whom the authors communicated on a wide variety of topics; Klaus Pertz, financial analysis; Reino Routamo, concepts of futuristic forecasting and the basic idea for the yarns case study; Maria Elena Scaffo, market analysis and finance; Aleksander Sulejewicz, who contributed widely to the chapter on economic analysis; Robert Youker, who greatly influenced the presentation on project implementation and management; and Allan Young, project finance, financial planning, and risk. Jerzy Kurowski is responsible for much of the preparation of graphical materials. Michael Lisk, production editor at Wiley, was instrumental in integrating, organizing, and adding to the coherence of the manuscript.

Although this edition owes much of its usefulness to contributions of the aforementioned individuals, the authors are solely responsible for any errors and omissions.

Symbols and Most Frequently Used Acronyms

The symbols described below are consistent with international usage. They are, however, used in different contexts and consequently might have slightly different meanings in the main text. The exact meaning is indicated by the subscript—for example, $i_{(disc)}$ and $i_{(infl)}$ indicate the discount rate and the inflation rate, respectively, whereas "i" alone is used to mean interest rate.

Financial Symbols

BEP	breakeven point
COPS	cost of products sold
COT	coefficient of turnover (working capital)
df	discount factor, expressed as percentage
EBITDA	earnings before interest, taxes, depreciation and amortization
F	fixed cost (total)
f	fixed cost of production, subscript denotes related resource
FC	factory costs
FV	future value
i	rate (interest, profit expectations, inflation), expressed as percentage
I	investment
IN	inventory
IRR	internal rate of return
j	used as subscript; depending on context, describes year number, product number, input number, and so on
MIRR	modified internal rate of return (expressed as percentage)
n	number of periods, products, and so on
NCF	net cash flow
NPV	net present value
P	production
p	market price (product, input, etc.)
PC	production costs
PV	present value

Q, q	quantity, unit quantity (e.g., consumption of resource per unit of production)
R	project revenues (sales)
ResV	residual value
RoI, RoE	return on investment, return on equity
T	tax rate (corporate, income) (expressed as percentage)
V	value
v	unit variable cost
WACC	weighted average cost of capital (expressed as percentage)
WCap	working capital
WiP	work-in-progress
w_j	weight of factor j

Economic Symbols

ADJ	adjustment value (difference between adjusted value and original value)
AF	adjustment factor (expressed as percentage)
AU	accounting unit
AV_j	values adjusted for distortions of factor j
C_c	market cost of capital
CF	conversion factor (expressed as percentage)
CIF	cost, insurance, and freight
CRI	consumption rate of interest
EDR	economic discount rate
EIRR	economic internal rate of return (expressed as percentage)
FE	foreign exchange
FOB	free on board
FX	foreign exchange
GDP (GNP)	gross domestic (national) product
I	investment (or capital consumption when indicated)
M	imports
MI	material inputs
MPS	marginal propensity to save
MV	market value
NFIA	net factor income from abroad
NNI	net national income
OER	official exchange rate
RP	repatriated payments
SCF	standard conversion factor (in some methodologies, equal to OER/SER)

SER	shadow exchange rate
SP_j	shadow price (for factor j)
SWR	shadow wage rate
VA	value added
VDR	value with distortions removed
VEF	value at efficiency priced
W	wages and salaries
WTP	willingness to pay
X	exports

Introduction

Accumulating capital assets and applying them to provide future benefits is a practice that dates from antiquity. Over 250,000 years ago, ancestors of our species *Homo sapiens* invested their time and energy to fashion simple tools to improve the quality of their lives. Yet, even today, how capital resources are applied—decisions about when, where, and how they should be committed—presents its challenges and does not always produce expected results.

The central theme of this book—designing the project to be compatible with its operating milieu so that it is profitable and sustainable while providing goods and services demanded by clients—derives in part from our many years as consultants to industries around the world, where we have witnessed an inordinate quantity of idle and rusting, sometimes never used, capital facilities, almost invariably the result of poor planning. With about 90,000 failures occurring annually in the relatively propitious U.S. business environment alone, it's clear that investing has always been a hazardous undertaking. Our planet is littered with remnants of investment ideas gone awry, projects that failed mainly because some critical design factor was improperly assessed.

Aside from the imponderable external factors that can sweep aside "the best-laid schemes o' mice and men," such as political and economic upheavals, one of the main deficiencies in project planning is that there is usually not enough of it, with decisions often made on the basis of anything from intuition to inadequate analysis. The recent meltdown of the financial sector in the United States and around the world is symptomatic of worldwide economic strains that are inimical to the interests of capital investors. We believe that the approaches we provide for designing, analyzing, and appraising a project can increase confidence in the investment decision in the minefield of the contemporary investment environment. Preinvestment study of appropriate breadth and depth, using these guidelines, vastly improves chances for a successful outcome.

A second motivation for the book involves potential benefits of a more holistic view of a project's business environment than has been the case traditionally. Benefits for private and public investors are ordinarily measured against corporate financial goals and objectives. As lines of demarcation between private and public enterprise are blurred in the global economy through subsidies and other public support to major enterprises, and as some enterprise is either totally or partially nationalized, benefits can be additionally measured from the perspective of society—benefits to citizens from public investment and conformance with public goals of private investment—and at the same time enhance prospects for successful investment if project outcomes complement overarching social goals as enunciated by administrative, legislative, and judicial decision makers. We attempt to show how the economic perspective—a much broader view of the enterprise environment than is traditionally considered by investors—reduces risk and enhances prospects for a successful enterprise. This theme has been developed comprehensively in Chapter 5.

Our intention is to provide guidelines for steering along the hazardous road to success faced by private and public investors and their collaborators. While others have addressed the subject, we propose a more comprehensive framework of analysis for *any* project involving capital investment—large or small, in private and public sectors—one that clears up a number of important misconceptions about financial aspects of design and appraisal, and that aligns the project more compatibly with features of its operating environment than has heretofore been the norm.

Unanticipated impediments to the success of investment projects have included mismatches between internal characteristics of the enterprise, its personnel, and other project needs, and external aspects of the operational setting such as market dynamics, supply constraints, or environmental impacts. Often there is a failure to consider alternatives that would constitute more profitable applications of the time, energy, and other resources applied to the contemplated project.[1]

Maintenance and improvement of current material standards of living around the world requires new investment. In fact, at both macro (economy) and micro (enterprise) levels, new investment is needed just to maintain the current level of production capacity, which is diminished by technological obsolescence over time. Capital is also needed to accommodate advances in technology and for improving efficiency of existing production units. The question of whether a project is worthy of investment takes on ever-greater significance as capital accumulation for new projects is impeded by consumption demands of a growing population and by reticence of prospective investors and lenders in the face of increasing global uncertainties (e.g., depletion of critical resources and political instability).

An investment project becomes part of the economic, social, and ecological system within which it is intended to function and prosper. It affects the preexisting system of supply and demand and thereby alters its characteristics. Project success depends upon the degree of satisfaction that it provides to sponsors and collaborators, and also to the wider community that provides its market, its workers, and those whose lives are affected by its presence. A useful analogy for analyzing the relation between the project and its operational setting is the strategy of a biological organism seeking to survive and grow in its habitat.[2] The enterprise seeks to earn its living by forging a useful link between resources and consumers, while at the same time fulfilling its own objectives. It has internal characteristics that interact with components and systems in the operational setting. Its health and well-being depend upon compatibility with friendly forces and building defenses against those that are hostile.

As the project faces the general hazards of doing business, producing goods and services for public consumption, one design aspect too often overlooked is the fact that even in situations where the project is designed for finite life, the investment milieu of which the project is a part has no temporal boundary. In other words, benefits in the form of capital accumulation resulting from the project are generally intended for reinvestment: Culmination of the project after successful operations will provide opportunities to consider new projects. For this reason, even from the perspective of capital accumulation, the issue of sustainability is relevant. Successor opportunities in future reinvestment rounds will demand resources, so it is prudent to design the project so that it relies to the maximum extent on sustainable consumption.[3] Many studies show that it is not only environmentally beneficial but also good business to investigate the benefits of renewable, recycled, reduced, and reused resources in both the manufacturing process and in goods and services produced for industry and for public consumption.

Capital investment has not only shaped the modern world, but undoubtedly has contributed much to public welfare around the globe. Events of the early twenty-first century have demonstrated that the system of capital allocation is far from perfect. Excesses in capital markets have caused enormous disruptions in the global economy, which may never regain the footing that existed prior to the onset of massive defaults in credit markets.

Although the proximate cause of the disruption appeared to be unprecedented wide-scale risky behavior of market participants, including excessive leveraging, a more fundamental explanation lies in the strains that existed in the global economy. The world's wealthiest country continued to pile up massive trade and fiscal deficits that were being financed and otherwise accommodated by the rest of the world, a situation that was clearly unsustainable. Europe was striving to integrate countries with widely disparate political structures and standards of living into an economic union. Asian countries were struggling to apply their newfound export wealth to transition into well-rounded, industrialized economies. All of this in the face of declining stocks of fossil energy, which has supported an aura of prosperity in the industrialized countries for over a century.

Aside from macroeconomic policies (or rather, the lack of them) that led to the disaster, clearly the declining fortunes of industrial enterprises throughout the world were indicative of widespread miscalculations at the micro, or enterprise, level. Planners of investment projects apparently failed to take into account the macroeconomic forces that would overwhelm the management capacities of their organizations. Circumstances and events external to these enterprises were apparently not sufficiently investigated and their consequences not adequately considered in their plans so that calamity could be averted.

This work is an attempt to provide, for sponsors of investment projects in the public or private sector, suggestions for improving the quality of their investment decisions. Analysis of socioeconomic impacts leads to better use of scarce resources and, concomitantly, more balanced economic development. For this reason, a more extensive and intensive investigation of both internal capacities and features of the external project environment is proposed, with details of how to execute the design and analysis of the project so that the investment decision is predicated on a sound footing of information and risk assessment. Project implementation is also covered, so that the hazards of delays in start-up and the risk of cost overruns are averted.

The methods described herein are relevant to the design, analysis, and appraisal of industrial, commercial, and infrastructure investment projects in private and public sectors. They are applicable to revenue-generating and nonrevenue projects, as well as projects of virtually any scale.

This volume is structured somewhat differently from others on the subject. It is intended more as a guide to project design and analysis rather than to provide a definitive framework for conducting an investment study. Design/study is presented as a continuous process, rather than consisting of discrete stages, to conform more closely to practice. Mobility of production factors, particularly capital and labor, is more important than ever to take into account. Project design is necessarily less tidy than in the past, responding to increasing complexity of doing business in most parts of the world.

Confronted with resource constraints, global competition, and an increasingly crowded world, investment analysis demands greater attention to the *wider domain*[4]—the operational environment, including infrastructure, beyond the edges of the project proper and its commercial setting—which is a major theme of this work. The proposed methods of design and analysis are considered to be applicable in virtually any investment environment, in both industrialized and developing countries.

There is a tendency to cloud distinctions between the project's components and characteristics, its impacts and constraints, as either *internal* or *external.* It is difficult to conceive of any project feature that is purely within one or the other category. A decision to appoint a manager cannot be totally separated from the availability of personnel within the population, or from the institutions that provided his training and experience. The terminology employed (e.g., *internal*) is a way of conforming to familiar semantics while at the same time alluding to the unavoidable conjunction of what is internal and external to the project.

Investment, in this context, refers to projects that increase the stock of fixed capital/assets—that is, capital applied to new production or to expansion, modernization, or other forms of rehabilitation of production units, and not investments in marketable securities of existing enterprises, although the methods of investment appraisal are similar.[5]

The order of the chapters only loosely relates to a sequential design and appraisal process. In practice, the design can commence at any point and proceed through a wide variety of sequential and iterative stages. Chapters are independent, but inextricably linked. In the interest of maintaining continuity within each chapter, ideas that are important but peripheral to the main line of thought are added as appendixes and referenced in the text.

In addition to the main text chapters, two case studies are integral parts of the presentation. They are referenced at appropriate points in the text, covering supplementary topics: "Cambria Yarns Project" and "Victoria Coke Project." These are available on our web site, www.wiley.com/go/investmentprojectdesign. The case studies underpin discussions and expositions on methods of design and analysis. The Cambria Yarns Project (CYP) is a new investment undertaken to exploit export opportunities for processed high-quality yarns rather than currently exported raw material. The case is analyzed for its commercial viability and also its impacts upon the national economy. Results of the financial analysis are integrated and labeled (e.g., Income Statement—CPY) at appropriate points in the text of Chapters 2–4, and results of economic analysis are included in Chapters 5 and 6.

The second case, the Victoria Coke Project (VCP), is an example of a rehabilitation project that results in restoration of capacity and operating efficiencies. It is undertaken as a joint venture between foreign and domestic partners. A predominant feature is the special methods of incremental financial analysis appropriate for this type of project. The issue of asset valuation and how it affects negotiations on share distribution is another aspect of the case. Results are completely contained on the web site. The project name is sometimes in the abbreviated form, VCP.

Chapter 1, "Investment Environment," covers the framework for project design and development: the commercial and wider domains in which the enterprise is to be created and operated; design impacts of infrastructure and resource constraints; the rationale for strategic orientation, regardless of project size and complexity; and methods of developing strategies.

Chapter 2, "Preparing Pro-Forma Financial Statements," deals with methods for generating income, cash flow, and balance projections as the basis for estimating performance indicators. In this chapter and the next, the main elements of analysis and results for the Cambria Yarns Project (see our web site) are interwoven into the text at appropriate points.

Chapter 3, "Financial Indicators and Criteria," explains the derivation of performance indicators from financial statements and criteria for stakeholders related to opportunity cost of capital and to inflation, exchange rates, and risk; methods of analysis appropriate for projects of existing enterprises; and valuation of the enterprise in connection with joint venture and takeover negotiations.

Chapter 4, "Financing the Project," reviews sources of equity, debt, and other capital to cover the cost of project assets and implementation, and both conventional and innovative financing schemes, including private-public partnerships.

Chapter 5, "The Economic Perspective," regards the project's impacts on the regional, national, or international economy as a means of assuring compatibility with the host environment, including those directly related to operations and those that are external (i.e., social and economic effects that arise from the existence of the project but are unrelated to its commercial performance). Quantitative costs and benefits are identified and valued in terms of an economic accounting unit.

Chapter 6, "Economic Cost/Benefit Analysis," is a guide for systematically compiling quantitative and qualitative effects of the project. A social discount rate is applied as a hurdle or challenge as part of the appraisal process; an alternative approach to economic assessment, value-added, is also discussed, and correspondences between the two methods identified. Analysis and results of the Cambria Yarns Project are included as appropriate in the text, including distribution impacts of savings/investment and direct consumption among social groups.

Chapter 7, "Investment Decisions under Uncertainty and Risk," views the project design as a forecast, replete with uncertainties and associated risks in virtually every one of its design dimensions. Methods of identifying areas of uncertainty and assessing qualitative and quantitative risk are presented, as well as implications for stakeholders.

Chapter 8, "Project Appraisal," discusses methods of arriving at an investment decision based upon a comparison of project performance characteristics that derive from design and analysis, the criteria of each type of participant—investor, financier, guarantor, regulator, licensor—and special concerns of foreign investors. Issues that may be of concern to each type of participant are identified, and discussion of appraisal reporting is included.

Chapter 9, "Implementation Planning and Budgeting," explains the development of a preliminary implementation plan as prerequisite to decision making and detailed planning. Activation of enterprise functions in the pre-production phase (e.g., market development and procurement) constitute part of the implementation plan and costs. Project management and contractual alternatives are discussed.

"Cambria Yarns Project" describes the background and essential features of a project to convert domestically produced cotton into mainly exportable processed cotton yarn. Analyses of financial and economic viability of the project are integrated into the text at appropriate points. External agricultural impacts are internalized in the economic analysis (see our web site).

"Victoria Coke Project" describes an example of rehabilitation of a company suffering from deterioration of its production facilities, and from excessive use of production factors. Techniques of financial analysis for joint venture partners are covered (see our web site).

Note: All of the tables of the Cambria Yarns Project are included in the text, some in abbreviated form, which illustrate the structure of analysis. Complete Excel tables from which they were extracted can be found at our web site. Tables for the Victoria Coke Project are found only on the web site.

A comprehensive discussion of market issues is also included on our web site: "Market Research and Marketing."

NOTES

1. William R. Easterly, *The Elusive Quest for Growth: Adventures and Misadventures in the Tropics* (Cambridge, MA: MIT Press, 2002). Easterly discusses why and how much capital investment in the developing countries has been wasted as a result of the failure of international investment promotion agencies to foster policies that would incentivize engagement in productive and profitable lines of market activity.
2. Biological organisms acquire their strategies through the process of evolution; natural selection molds both the organism and the manner of accommodating to its environment. However, strategic development among biological organisms is not very efficient. Essentially random mutations are tested against the prevailing environment and, if found wanting, are quickly obliterated. We see the vestiges only in fossilized remains of experimental organisms that took the wrong turn. Investors do not have the luxury of trial and error in strategic development for the enterprise, as the process would be unacceptably costly.

3. This begs the question: What is sustainable? In general, to be sustainable, employment of a resource does not diminish the possibility of consumption in the future. These are only a few possibilities: products designed for easy disassembly for recycling and reuse; products made from recycled and renewable materials; nonpolluting disposal (e.g., decomposition into environmentally harmless substances); energy conservation in buildings, manufacture, and product consumption; use of renewable energy sources—solar, wind, geothermal, tidal, hydro, biomass.

4. The term *wider domain* is used to indicate elements of the project's external environment beyond those traditionally considered as relevant to its design and analysis. This is explained in some depth in Chapter 1.

5. Investment that adds to the stock of productive assets is more assuredly a contributor to economic well-being than is investment in financial markets where the primary emphasis is on the price of assets rather than what they produce. Increments of productive assets (physical and intangible) increase national wealth and are conducive to improvement in the standard of living of the society as a whole.

CHAPTER 1

Investment Environment

The investment project creates an enterprise that functions in an environment comprising internal characteristics and external surroundings. Design of internal characteristics is essentially within the province of project personnel, but external features are variously susceptible to influence: Some are clearly independent of the existence of the project, others can be moderately affected, and some can be readily adjusted to serve project needs. Being aware of its features is the first step in assuring mutual compatibility between the investment environment and the project, which is essential to success.

A project is considered to be a set of coordinated activities intended to achieve a specific outcome, with a beginning and an end. The project starts when the investment idea attracts serious attention, progresses through preinvestment phases of study, design, analysis, and appraisal; then, if acceptable for investment, through commitment of resources and implementation, in which the enterprise is either created or modified, and production facilities assembled, constructed, installed, and then commissioned for operations. The decision to invest in the project is predicated on results of appraisal of the projected relationship between the investment and the excess of benefits over costs to be derived during the operations phase, as described in Chapters 2–4 (financial) and 5 and 6 (economic).

The enterprise commences operations as resources are consumed to produce goods and/or services (hereinafter referred to as *products*) provided to consumers; there follows a decommissioning phase, if applicable, or perhaps renewal in the next investment cycle. The project conception and design, and its appraisal, are inevitably predicated on forecasts that are inherently uncertain; thus, consideration of associated risks is an indispensable dimension of the planning process.

SYSTEMATIC PROJECT ANALYSIS

The investment project is most effectively studied and designed as a system, or perhaps a primary system with interacting subsystems. The enterprise in its environment is modeled as a whole rather than an assemblage of individual elements or parts. The description of system elements, structure, and processes, and their interactions, yields insights into their functions and dynamics, providing a basis for refining project design toward attainment of objectives and goals. This requires specifications of system elements and plans to effectively mobilize resources necessary for their proper functioning (e.g., energy, materials, labor, information, technology, finance) and creative conceptions about how they can be employed so that they are mutually reinforcing.

Design/study follows a logical, but not necessarily linear, sequence, often through several iterations, consisting of the following elements:

- Goals and objectives—what is to be accomplished, and why, by individuals and organizations involved.
- Criteria of acceptability for stakeholders—investors, lenders, guarantors, regulators, licensors.
- Alternatives—the range of choices for design of the system and its components: product; enterprise organization and staffing; location; site selection and layout; plant and ancillary facilities; process; machinery and equipment.
- Impacts of each alternative—resources consumed and generated and other tangible and intangible consequences.
- Quantitative and qualitative forecasts of impacts to the planning horizon.
- Benefits and costs to be counted—elements to be included in assessing profitability and other indicators of performance, and their individual, organizational and/or geographical range of relevance.
- Unit of measurement for meaningful aggregation of impacts, and identifying impacts that can only be assessed qualitatively.
- Determining quantitative performance indicators and nonquantifiable measures of project impact (e.g., commercial, economic, social).
- Assessing risk—decisions predicated on uncertainty in forecasts and their possible negative impacts on performance.
- Appraisal—comparing performance indicators and other impacts with criteria of stakeholders, considering risk of failure to meet criteria.
- Recommending a course of action as the most favorable among alternatives.

For practical reasons, it is necessary to select only those aspects of the project with the most significant impacts for detailed analysis. Some impacts are best estimated in aggregated form using accepted rules of thumb. However, details can be important: What appear as minor factors at the outset can loom large when they become problematic.[1]

A fundamental concept for all types of projects is *incremental analysis*, the difference between the situation for stakeholders *with the project* and *without the project*. This is not the same as after versus before the project. For a new investment the without-project situation is usually relatively straightforward. It is concerned with the current disposition, and effects for stakeholders, of resources that will be transferred or otherwise dedicated to the project. For a project undertaken by an existing enterprise, the without-project situation involves the operational scenario if the project is not undertaken. In either case, the incremental impact is the difference between the with-project and without-project situations. This concept is further explained in Victoria Coke Project case study, on our web site and in Chapter 3.

PROJECT ENVIRONMENT AND STRATEGY

An investment project becomes part of a system of supply and demand for goods and services, and also an integral part of socioeconomic and ecological systems within which it is to function and prosper. Its success depends upon how well it accommodates to its operating environment, as well as the degree of satisfaction that it provides to its clients and to the wider community that provides its market, its workers and those whose lives are affected by its presence. Whether the project is undertaken in an industrialized or developing country or a country in transition, the analogy of a biological organism employing a strategy to survive and grow in its habitat, or environment, described in the Introduction, is applicable.

In some environments, demonstration that the project will serve socioeconomic goals and objectives and be compatible with the host ecology is required. Public interest is expressed through fiscal, administrative, environmental, and other conditions imposed by governing bodies requiring that the investment project employ scarce resources efficiently for local, regional, or national development. Government initiatives that encourage or compel adherence to public goals with incentives and restrictions enter into analysis and appraisal of the project.

The strategic plan might include factors involving corporate social responsibility (CSR) as a means of enhancing corporate image and reception of the project by the host community. For further discussion see our web site—Corporate Social Responsibility.

Project Domains

The relationship between the project's commercial domain and the wider domain with which it interacts is illustrated in Figure 1.1. The commercial domain comprises markets and suppliers, financiers, competitors, technologies, and internal project characteristics designed to produce desired benefits for investors. The wider domain is project-specific, encompassing the political, social, economic, and environmental milieu in which the enterprise is to function. It can be delimited geographically as the community (e.g., city), the region, the country, or the international setting, and operationally as the scope of major interactions between the project and external factors. In reality these domains are not so clearly demarcated—they are unified by interactions and mutual repercussions. As one example, aesthetics and culture (a feature of the wider domain) may affect the market—what people are willing to consume (a characteristic of the commercial domain).[2] A partial listing of elements of the commercial and wider domains for consideration is provided in Appendix 1.1.[3]

That project stakeholders are obliged to consider the commercial domain is obvious, certainly for private-sector projects and often in the

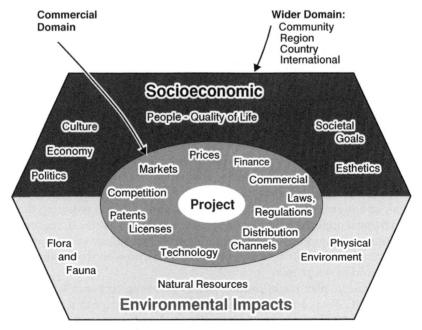

FIGURE 1.1   Commercial and Wider Domain

public sector as well. Investors, guarantors, and lenders are interested in how a project will fare—securing market share and operating with sufficient financial returns. Why there should be interest in the wider domain is often ignored.

All dimensions of the wider domain have consequences—the economy, culture, nature of the political arena, consumption of natural resources (renewable and nonrenewable), the physical environment, flora and fauna, aesthetics, and the general quality of life of the affected population. Strains at the local, regional, national, and international levels are an important consideration for the project, needing markets with people willing and able to consume the output of the enterprise and to supply needed inputs. As the project is imposed on commercial and more extensive systems, its repercussions create ripples that are reflected back, sometimes in amplified form. In recent years the scientific community has discovered the phenomenon of chaos in complex systems such as weather or economies, in which small perturbations in one corner of the world can have major consequences in another—prototypically the butterfly flapping its wings in an African village causing a tsunami in Asia.

Although red flags of warning concerning resource constraints have been hoisted for centuries,[4] human ingenuity has usually found a way to circumvent these problems. However, until the human population stabilizes (perhaps at 10 or 12 billion by the end of the twenty-first century, according to some forecasts), by definition a decreasing quantity of Earth's surface and natural resources is allotted to each on average, a factor that may warrant examination in regard to project viability.

There are other pragmatic reasons for maintaining an interest in the wider domain. International agreements have lowered barriers to trade and to mobility of production factors. For this reason alone, elements of the wider domain, within and without host country borders, affect project viability. Differences in environmental protection, labor conditions, and human rights provisions among countries, coupled with global mobility, have a significant bearing on the nature of existing and future competition.[5] The project may benefit from heightened awareness by licensing authorities of external benefits attributable to the enterprise.

External effects, regarded as problematic by the larger community, also have to be identified and their long-term consequences for the enterprise taken into account. As information concerning consequences of resource consumption and applications becomes more widespread, the market will increasingly reflect impacts that presently do not affect the bottom line (profit) but that do have an impact upon interests of direct stakeholders and the broader community. To ignore these factors is to add to project risk. Better to account for these external impacts, derive the advantages of beneficial effects, and protect against unanticipated consequences of real or perceived undesirable impacts.

Industrial policy embodied in measures such as incentives, quotas, and protection may reflect the host government's strategic policies regarding the general business environment. Macroeconomic policies and actions may be relevant: for example, fiscal (liberal or conservative), monetary (tightening or relaxing), and foreign trade (export/import financing by the banking system, import quotas and other protective barriers, export/import duties, promotion facilities). Design of project and marketing strategy are affected by entry/exit barriers to participation, restrictions on foreign participation, policy on repatriation of earnings, and exchange controls. For example, the existence of exchange controls (usually responsible for local currency overvaluation) may render export difficult or impossible.

The wider domain has more direct significance. As an example, the state of flora and fauna may have implications for stability of needed inputs. A lake supplying cooling water to the project, if contaminated, can lose required qualities and consequently its usefulness for the project.[6] Reliability and loyalty of workers are enhanced when health and quality of life are maintained at acceptable levels. Generally favorable economic conditions provide a healthy environment for the enterprise to survive and grow.

International and domestic terrorism is increasingly a factor with the potential to affect project outcomes, so that consideration of prevention and/or mitigation strategies is sometimes appropriate. For further discussion see our web site—Domestic and International Terrorism.

Size is a determinant of the degree of investigation: For relatively small projects, with little or no regional or national impact, assessing compatibility with concerns of the local community is probably as far as appraisal goes in the investment decision process. For an export project, the international economy and national parameters such as trade balance and exchange rates are relevant.

The extent of analysis has to serve the interests of stakeholders but also reflect the larger implications for sustainability of operations and public interest. A major issue is whether there is any conflict, at present and in the long run, between basic project (corporate) objectives and development objectives in the operational socioeconomic environment.[7]

At the micro (project) level, sponsors' primary concerns for the project as a business opportunity, where commercial profitability is of paramount importance, invariably need to be supplemented with some concern for wider impacts, if only to satisfy licensors and regulators. When the project is either large enough or otherwise strategically significant, macro-level appraisal may be warranted, considering its contribution to regional, national, and perhaps international income, distribution effects, and job creation.

Examination of the wider domain can lead to alternative project config-urations that benefit investors. For example, the cost of pollution abatement or mitigation can be weighed against adverse impacts if such measures are not taken. Enterprises have been held legally and financially accountable for contamination even when in compliance with emissions regulations.[8] Projects planned for 10 to 20 years or longer can anticipate more stringent regulation and consider including anticipated compliance requirements in the initial investment cost.

Infrastructure Investment Projects

Infrastructure can most generally be considered as the entire range of ele-ments of the wider domain, as previously described, or more commonly as service components of the project's external environment, provided by enti-ties created with private investment, public-private partnerships (PPPs), or by the government. The complex of services is usually the cumulative effect of investments over an extended period of time—Rome was not built in a day.

Some infrastructure projects are designed as revenue generating, some completely supported by fees charged to users, and others with varying degrees of subsidization for consumers of services produced. Government subsidies can be provided for the investment and/or more directly to the consumer in the form of a price per unit of service lower than production cost. Other projects provide services without direct cost to consumers, such as roads and bridges that are free of user tolls.

Private investors regard infrastructure projects as any other investment, with acceptability based on criteria such as risk-adjusted cost of capital, payback, and breakeven. The public side of PPPs or strictly government projects, whether or not revenue generating, considers the economic con-sequences to a much greater degree. In fact, economic impact may be the primary criterion from the government's point of view.

For relatively small infrastructure projects (small to medium enterprise, or SME), such as technical services or local transportation, the approach to project design and analysis is similar to that for a manufacturing or service project. For large projects, such as hydroelectric, fuel-powered, or nuclear electricity generating stations, a very significant difference is financing (see the section on build-operate-transfer [BOT] financing in Chapter 4). Power plants may require investment in billions of U.S. dollars, so the financing arrangements are considerably more complicated than for SMEs.

The sheer size of these projects frequently requires government involve-ment. In smaller economies the investment is usually too great for the local private sector. Governments intent on economic development look upon the provision of infrastructure services as a means of attracting domestic and for-eign investment. Under government sponsorship there is greater likelihood of subsidized prices (e.g., utility service rates) for industry as an inducement for investment.

Government sponsorship also reflects growth-oriented economic policy, particularly in developing countries. For the production of consumer and industrial goods, in principle governments have the option of direct investment (as in former centrally planned economies) or indirectly influencing investment by the private sector, the approach now followed by all but a few command economies. In this way, governments promote investment by creating a supportive environment, in which the barriers for entrepreneurs are lowered, and prospects for meeting criteria enhanced, with adequate and reasonably priced (or publicly supported) infrastructure.

Physical infrastructure (e.g., transportation, communications, energy) is the most important. Some projects produce commercial services, with any of the structures previously discussed. For self-supporting revenue projects, calculation of expected return is identical to that of industrial projects. If services are provided with some degree of subsidization or free of charge (i.e., nonrevenue), the design might be oriented to cost minimization and the economic perspective, which in effect weighs the cost of subsidies against the benefits provided to consumers and to the economy in general.

Need alone is not a sufficient criterion for selection of a project within existing constraints (financing is usually the most apparent). Less developed countries often also are confronted with an *implementation constraint* (alternatively, *absorptive capacities constraint*).[9] Meaningful financial and economic analysis requires realistic assessments of benefits and costs under prevailing conditions. If the government is the sponsor, performance indicators for the project under consideration are compared with alternative uses of available capital to determine whether the project is a good use of public funds. Accurate estimation of benefits is the difficult part. Use of public funds imposes a need to analyze the effect on targeted beneficiaries, which is a function of numbers, income level, and social status. To avoid political bias, uniform standards for benefits and costs are applied across the country. In appraising alternative road projects, for example, cost savings accruing to users (per mile or kilometer) would be valued by the same or similar standards. For example, savings in fuel and maintenance would be the same for a project in one province or another, except for local adjustments (less developed regions might have slightly lower prices and wages).

The history of applying public funds for infrastructure projects across the world is not very encouraging. Large quantities of public funds have been expended on politically inspired projects of dubious utility, while socially valuable projects have often been set aside for lack of funding. Even in advanced economies, so-called pork-barrel projects are often added to completely unrelated legislative actions, sometimes in the dead of night to avoid public scrutiny. But that is another story.

Infrastructure as a Design Constraint

The enterprise to be created by the project exists in an environment in which it requires supportive services—infrastructure—to function and prosper. The surrounding community (local, regional, and national) has provided services whose costs are either shared or, in some instances, completely covered with public funds, a form of private/public synergy. The greater the proportion of required infrastructure provided by the community, the less the burden on the project to augment services to the point that they provide a healthy and adequately supportive environment. Interacting with public officials and community leaders is one way to smooth the way. In fact, in many communities, public works projects have been implemented for the sole purpose of attracting a desired industry.

Infrastructure is a public good that affects the capacity of industry in general, and the project in particular, to operate effectively. It often requires commitment of public funds, which is not always the first priority of budget authorities. Although there is ample evidence that infrastructure investment is a factor in the level of productivity, when the host economy is under stress the tendency is to divert funds to consumption rather than investment.

This is a problem even in industrialized countries. In the United States, "on average since 1980, the growth of infrastructure investment has lagged behind overall economic growth. The result has been slow degradation of infrastructure, a worsening infrastructure deficit and mounting investment needs."[10] In a 2006 study, Rodriguez[11] found that a measure of "core infrastructure" which included highways, mass transit, airports, electrical and gas facilities, water, and sewers had a highly significant effect on both labor and multifactor productivity: "The decline in U.S. infrastructure investment after 1970 had led . . . to a decline in TFP (total factor productivity) growth of 0.8 percent a year—a very large effect."

Where infrastructure development requires commitment of public funds, government authorities tend to respond to what appear to be more pressing problems on their hands, to apply resources to the squeaky wheel, which becomes infrastructure only under dire circumstances such as the collapse of a bridge, a rail catastrophe, or a road washout from heavy rains or flooding.

The complex of infrastructure services, their availability, and the cost to the project is a key factor in location, best selected to optimize project performance. Services might be provided by private, private-public (PPP), or public entities. Private infrastructure investment is invariably for-profit, but its services are not necessarily more expensive than revenue-generating public services. Public services provided at no cost to the project (funded from taxation and other government sources) are usually the most desirable but subject to uncertainty if public coffers are stretched tight.

Project investment and operating costs would be much higher in some locations as compared with others in the country, the difference usually attributable to infrastructure—typically, access to no-cost or low-cost services. For this reason projects are rarely implemented in the desert (unless there are natural resources to exploit). In fact, a salient feature of location analysis is cost minimization, with the cost of transportation for inputs and outputs of primary importance. In light of the possibility of changes in the energy outlook, prudence suggests at least consideration of a futuristic view concerning transportation. Some analysts believe that the system of energy generation and consumption will undergo a virtual metamorphosis, with far less international, and even interregional, movement of goods and services.[12]

Infrastructure is a significant factor in site selection. Many projects of existing companies are essentially design replicas of plants already in existence. These can be considered black boxes that need connections to supporting supplies of nutrients—utilities and other services that derive from local infrastructure—with availability, cost minimization, and reliability the major criteria. They may also require connections to sites and other facilities for disposal of effluents and wastes. For an assembly plant, transport costs of components from upstream affiliates or suppliers are a major consideration in site (or location) selection.

Profitability is directly linked to the existence of infrastructure services. Without this kind of public support, project capital would be needed to create the facilities and services needed for profitable operation—roads, power supplies, water wells and treatment plants, housing facilities for workers if not otherwise available at the project site. It is no wonder that profitability of a project with the benefit of services provided with public support is more favorable than a similar project in a location where such facilities are unavailable. This explains, to some extent, why investments flow to favorable areas with well-developed infrastructure, unless high product value justifies expensive modes of transportation (e.g., gold and diamonds mined in Russian Siberia are transported by air, which would not be possible in the case of most of the other minerals waiting to be exploited there, were cheaper transportation available).

Cost structure is fundamental to a profit-oriented project but is important in any case, even for nonrevenue public service projects. Infrastructure services represent a significant part of the cost of operations in any case: The question is, what part of the bill, and how much, does the project have to pay? Projects to develop or expand the capacity of infrastructure are usually too large for an individual manufacturing project to handle. A power plant has to be large enough to exploit economies of scale—for example, 1,000 megawatts—while an individual energy user such as the project would rarely require more than 50 to 100 megawatts. Unless there are fortuitous conditions (e.g., a fast-flowing river with potential to build a dam and generating station that would serve project needs, or wind conditions at or near the site that justify erecting wind turbines), construction and operation of a small diesel generating station might be a solution, but the energy generated would usually cost considerably more than energy from the grid. Particular attention to cost and reliability has to be applied to those infrastructure services, usually including energy, transportation, and communications, which are essential for efficient operations.

As the buildup of infrastructure in an area has occurred over an extended period of time, expecting rapid response of the government to project needs is probably unrealistic. Appeals for government-funded infrastructure improvements in a given location have to be timed to account for lengthy delays involving legislative hearings and debate, the funding cycle, and implementation. Infrastructure needs involving SME projects might be much more quickly and securely implemented by the private sector. In some cases cooperative agreements can be drawn with other entities (enterprises, investment groups, or individuals) in appropriate fields to secure creation of needed service facilities.

Of primary concern from the project's point of view:

- Capacity of existing infrastructure to support project activities and to accommodate future growth—what issues need to be addressed?
- Capital investment and operating costs necessary to attain a level of infrastructure capacity and reliability that allows for unfettered project operations.
- Willingness of the community (local, regional, national) to expand capacity in accordance with the needs of the project at public expense; what is the funding gap between public support and project need (cost to project to provide needed infrastructure if not provided with public funds)? Consider possible reversion to community control at termination of the project (alternatively, consider cooperative agreements with private services providers).
- The funding gap, if any, between the cost of maintenance and repair of infrastructure and what will be provided by the community (costs that will have to be borne by the project).

Analysis of existing infrastructure service systems takes into account current capacities in relation to existing demand versus project needs, and reliability of the community to continue current levels of service. In all cases it is advisable to consider the *aggregated contemporary* (all existing sources or demands) and *temporal* (cumulative demands and impacts over time) relations. Some other possible issues of concern regarding infrastructure components (other than capacity, maintenance, and repair) are:

- Solid waste management: disposal fees and outlook; indiscriminate dumping, pollution.
- Liquid waste management (nonseptic): disposal system—are lakes, rivers, and other waterways being contaminated or untreated wastes spread on land?
- Drainage and flood protection (storm drains, swales, dams, outlets—rivers and streams, lakes, etc.): designed for extreme events?
- Sewerage: pretreatment requirements, characteristics of effluents of other users.
- Water supply (waterways, groundwater, drilled and surface wells): treatment (primary, secondary, tertiary), quality (minerals, organics, radiations—e.g., radon, radium, uranium, etc.).
- Fuel supply (sources of gasoline, diesel, natural gas, propane): domestic supplies or imported; foreign exchange requirements.
- Transportation (roads and parking areas, railroads, and airports [passenger, freight]): traffic bottlenecks, safety.
- Communications (telephone, cellular, wireless, Internet): status of technology.
- Public facilities (recreation [parks, playgrounds, open space], cultural, educational, personal services): open access for project personnel?
- Housing (private residences, apartments, condominiums, hotels): to acceptable standards for project personnel, hospitality?
- Law enforcement (civil and private organizations): crime rate, respect for statutes and laws, impartiality of justice system.
- Financial: banks, securities exchanges, financial services.
- Technical services (private and public organizations): personnel qualifications; availability of materials, supplies, and equipment.
- Public health facilities (hospitals, clinics, private practitioners): endemic illnesses, state of medical practice and technology.
- Natural resources (mineral deposits, forests, watercourses, vistas, open space): overexploited to detriment of project interests?
- Educational and research institutions (colleges, universities, technical schools, laboratories): quality of training available to project personnel, research facilities, availability of consulting services for industry.

The project benefits from availability of skilled workers supplied locally, reducing or eliminating the costs of in-house education and training.

In the knowledge-based economy that extends to the developing countries, economists now include knowledge as a variable in the *production function* (describing relationships affecting efficiency of resource utilization) along with other factors, such as labor, capital, materials, and energy.[13] In addition to creating opportunities for transforming production factors into new products and processes, knowledge investments increase productivity of the other factors of production. For these reasons, project interests are served by collaborating with institutions that prepare highly qualified personnel and that conduct research related to project needs, promoting allocation of public funds and applying project funds to the extent necessary and practicable.

Infrastructure capacities as they relate to project needs have to take into account demands of other government, commercial, industrial, and public users, which may be affected by factors in the host environment: uncontrolled migration, excessively high population density, unauthorized or illegal settlements in areas not presently served.

SWOT analysis (strengths, weaknesses, opportunities, and threats) can be applied to those infrastructure elements that are critical to project operations, although a liberal approach to what is to be included in detailed analysis is prudent to avoid unforeseen potholes in the road. An example applies to the transportation system of the Cambria Yarns project. This essentially qualitative assessment is useful to deal with organizational issues related to infrastructure and also for pinning down related capital and operating expenditures.

Strengths

- Restricted access road to port, well engineered for safety and speed.
- Private haulers with sufficient capacity who have been in business for a minimum of 15 years, with good records for safety and timely deliveries.
- Efficient containerized port facilities.

Weaknesses

- Existing provincial and national fuel tax revenues consumed in maintenance of existing road system, limiting capacity of these government entities to expand the transportation infrastructure.
- Seventy-five percent of local (municipal) transportation and public utility budget spent on maintaining the existing system, so little available for new capital needs; local roads in need of repair.

Opportunities

- Try to employ good relations with local officials to promote use of local infrastructure budgets for leveraging additional private and public

investment in transportation infrastructure. Encourage private trans-
porters to develop partnerships with local government to provide better
and more restricted access routes from plant to turnpike.

- Initiate ongoing discussions between national government and neigh-
boring country (location of port facilities) to improve rail line to
port city.
- Growing level of industrial activity in country favors greater attention
of authorities to transportation infrastructure.

Threats

- Inconsistent and subjective local and interstate enforcement of traffic
safety laws and regulations.
- Heavy fines levied for violations of load and vehicular safety inspections,
inhibiting expansion.

Resource Constraints

The enterprise, and the project from which it derives, requires a flow of feed-
stock in the form of people, materials, machines, equipment, and other types
of capital to maintain its vitality and to allow it to grow. The design has to
include the system of procurement for all major inputs, along with product
specifications, sources, and supply channels. Logistical planning for acquisition of resources has to be applied both to the implementation project and
for the operating enterprise. The supplies program for the implementation
project (see Chapter 9) involves a sequence of purchasing, transportation,
and storage (inventory management), many of them one-time or intermittent
events. For the operating enterprise, an optimal plan for providing a continuous flow of materials and supplies has to be developed, taking into account
trade-offs such as price, quality, order quantity, warehousing requirements,
and reliability.

Logistical issues associated with maintaining the flow of required inputs
involve extended and complex supply chains in the global economy. For critical inputs it is advisable to develop details of the supply chain from point
of origin (source) to the enterprise gate, including transportation and handling sequences, storage nodes, and price buildup (e.g., markups, taxes and
duties, commissions, and handling fees). Selection of production scale has to
be commensurate with any constraints on the supply of resources. Where a
potentially significant impact is indicated, design of the supply chain should
be predicated on application of supply optimization tools and techniques
that include consideration of management (coordination), transaction, and
transportation costs.[14]

An overriding issue in the selection of sources of supply is make-or-buy. Availability and cost from prospective suppliers, particularly for imported items, can be compared with cost and reliability of including production as part of the project, or backward integration (bringing an existing supplier into the project fold). Make-or-buy can be decided independently of the basic project design, unless there is a capital constraint. Decisions on make-or-buy depend on exploiting cost differentials. Within a particular country, usually economies of production scale adjusted for transportation cost and supply security considerations would indicate the better alternative.

Extended supply chains in the globalized market rely heavily on low transportation costs, which in turn depend on inexpensive energy. However, fossil fuel costs are subject to increasing demand in the face of nonrenewable supply, a factor to be taken into account in designing the system for supplying inputs to the project.[15]

International trade has mushroomed since World War II, and particularly in the past few decades,[16] as a result of production factor cost differentials, mainly labor, which is not as mobile as capital. For some inputs, labor-intensive elements can be outsourced to lower-labor-cost countries (these conditions are by no means static; labor cost differentials are subject to change as working conditions improve in low-labor-cost countries). This applies mainly to assembly-type industries (garment, automotive, and others) with clearly identifiable production components that are assembled into the final product (consumer or industrial markets).

The automotive industry provides a good illustration: Volkswagen assembles one of its models in its factory in Wolfsburg (Germany). Wiring (as a fully assembled component) for this car is made in Jelenia Gora (Poland). All the subcomponents to produce the wiring bundle are outsourced—for example, all individual wires of different colors and diameter are imported, in this case, from Tunisia, already precut to the length according to Volkswagon's design and requirements. Wires travel some 1,500 kilometers from Tunisia to Poland and then 500 kilometers from Poland to Germany. Still, the transportation cost is lower than differences between labor costs in Germany and in suppliers' countries.

The relationship between material and labor costs varies by industry and the host environment. Together they usually make up the largest portion of production costs. Project inputs can be in the form of solids, liquids, gases, and any combination thereof, each presenting its particular issues of transportation and handling. Resources needed for production and other enterprise functions include raw and semiprocessed materials, parts, components, subsystems, and services (e.g., infrastructure, professional). A plan is needed for supply of any and all materials and services necessary for the production schedule.

Optimizing design of the supply chain for each major input can be approached by analyzing a discrete set of potential sources. Variables for each are compared, such as price buildup, optimal order quantity (see Chapter 2) and related ordering cost (may differ for domestic vs. foreign suppliers), technical specifications (quality), and reliability (price, flow).

Price forecasts differ for various types of suppliers. For example, unless moderated by international markets, supply price from an emerging market may be affected by projected changes in the country's currency exchange rate, which usually means that the price received for exports to an industrialized country will decrease as the local currency strengthens. Although quality standards are specified (see Chapter 9, the subsection "Standards"), the specifications from various sources may differ, with attendant benefits or disadvantages for the production process. Political or economic instability in a supplier country might threaten reliability of supply. Production standards in the supplying country are a factor (e.g., labor, environmental): If below international norms, compulsory adjustments could threaten reliability of supply. For raw materials, the extent of ore deposits may be a factor to consider (resource depletion).

Each of the factors can be assigned a weight and then each potential supplier rated on a point scale. Weights and points can be combined to optimize the selection.

Some resources require special considerations. One important factor is price elasticity for resources with little or no slack (current demand equal to or exceeding a relatively fixed supply). Superimposing the project's demand on the existing market may have a significant impact on prices. Intrusion of another major user could easily create a spike in prices if demand exceeds available supply.

For produce from agriculture, marine, or animal husbandry, if existing surpluses are insufficient to satisfy the project production schedule, new cultivation may be required, either integrated with the project or through grower contracts. Even if the input is currently, or has been, produced in the host environment, feasibility testing of production at the scale required by the project may be required (i.e., experimental production under representative conditions and pilot plant verification in some cases). It is very risky to base the project plan on availability of a crop that has not been previously produced in the area without experimental plantings on a commercial scale and testing of the crop to ensure its adequacy for the production process.

Sustainable yields and the cost of collection are major issues for marine inputs. The capacity of collection facilities (e.g., the fishing fleet) is determined by existing demand: It may be necessary for the project to provide its own facilities (marine vessels and staff) to augment harvesting capacity. Yields may be at or close to sustainable levels, so that additional harvesting under prevailing conditions is not possible in the medium to long term. Harvesting levels may be controlled by domestic or international agreements; where quotas and control do not exist, prudence suggests independent analysis of sustainable yields in the light of project demand. Commercial farming of necessary marine inputs is one possible solution.

For required minerals, an existing survey, or one commissioned by the project, should provide details of the location, size, quality, uniformity of deposits, and composition. Processing details should be examined for the specific ore as mining, refining, and associated costs differ depending on composition and deposit characteristics. Pilot plant processing may be required to verify the suitability of minerals as input for the production technology selected.

Commodities such as metals, fuels, agricultural products, and livestock trade internationally. Prices generally fluctuate widely, depending on a host of economic and demand conditions (weather in case of agricultural production), usually too complex to analyze. Historical prices and trends may indicate a pattern, or perhaps can be analyzed statistically to determine a range of possible prices that can be considered in the project design. Some risk can be avoided if substitutes can be identified with more reliable pricing histories. Plastics, for example, have replaced metals in some products, but the market effect has to be carefully assessed. Another approach is to plan on futures trading to lock in prices, but there are associated costs that have to be taken into account (see Chapter 7).

Scarce capital can be allocated using an indicator such as net present value ratio (NPVR) as discussed in Chapter 3. From the economic viewpoint, shadow prices (see Chapter 5) reflect scarcity, but a similar approach can be employed at the project or enterprise level: What is the effect on the corporate objective(s) of applying some quantity of scarce capital to this project or to an alternative? A capital constraint can be relaxed with additional sources, but capital markets also reflect scarcity. Paying higher prices is one possible approach—for example, issuing a class of equity with preferential conditions (e.g., voting rights, dividends), preferred or convertible shares on favorable terms for investors, or tapping into debt markets employing one of the innovative financing schemes discussed in Chapter 4.

Strategic Project Planning

A *strategy* is a plan, or road map, for survival and progress toward the goal of project sponsors.[17] A good understanding of the current situation is essential for deciding how the project is to move from the status quo to the desired goal, both of which are states, or sets of conditions, that prevail at a given point in time. The overall strategy is the plan to make the transition

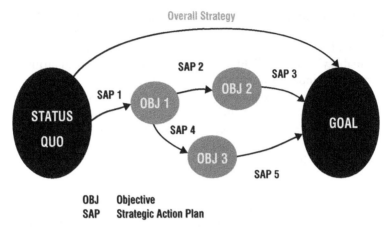

FIGURE 1.2 Strategy, Goals, and Objectives

from the status quo to the goal, which should define the desired state of the enterprise at some point in the future—for example, market share and profitability. *Objectives* are intermediate states. Objectives and goals are achieved through *action plans*, one or more actions or activities that will facilitate the transition. A particular objective may have precedent objectives, those that must be achieved before actions can be initiated to move toward the objective desired. The relation between strategies, goals, and objectives is illustrated in Figure 1.2. An example of precedent objectives is demonstrated by objective 3, which requires attainment of other objectives, namely carrying out strategic action plans (SAPs) 1 and 4, as prerequisites.

To put this in more concrete terms, consider a strategy for building market share for toothpaste. Objective 1 is attainment of brand recognition, and objective 3 is gaining the loyalty of young families with children in the household. The action plan for attaining objective 1 (SAP 1) includes a campaign to deliver small free samples through retail outlets in the target market area. For objective 3, the central theme of the action plan (SAP 4) is mass media advertising directed toward households with young children. The expenditure for each action plan is determined in accordance with quantitative targets.

During the project planning phase, and even after launch, the strategic concept may be in flux, evolving as more information feeds back into the decision process. Strategic decisions take into account the project as a system interacting with its internal and external environments; strategic features may change at irregular intervals as information and insights are clarified.[18]

Formulating a project strategy is one of the primary aspects of project design, relevant to enterprises large and small, its extent and complexity scaled to needs, commensurate with the range of project interactions.[19] If the project is undertaken by an existing enterprise, the project strategy should complement and be coordinated with the corporate strategy.

Importance and Utility of a Strategy For an operating entity such as an organism or enterprise, a strategy is the fundamental operational plan for securing survival and growth. In the private sector, strategic positioning is intended to achieve and maintain competitive advantage. For public-sector projects, strategies are directed toward optimizing the use of resources in the public interest. As a general principle, the strategic goal of the enterprise is attained through pursuit of a series of intermediate steps—long- and short-term intermediate objectives—with plans of action for their attainment. A core strategy[20] serves as a framework for functional strategies covering operational components—for example, marketing, production, procurement, human resources, research and development, corporate planning. Centralized coordination minimizes cross currents and inefficiencies. A strategy is fundamental to the design of the project, the framework for choice of design parameters—location, product features, capacity and production technology, and procurement channels. From the earliest stages, a preliminary or conceptual strategy serves as a guide to project configuration, such as setting up a joint venture with a foreign partner to secure export markets or achieving brand loyalty through outstanding product services. Alternative strategies for marketing and other project functions can be evaluated for compatibility and consistency with the core strategy.

Some Strategic Principles The strategy is intended to engender mutually reinforcing relationships between the enterprise and its external environment. A few principles are relevant for all types and sizes of projects:

- *Compatibility.* Design the project to be well integrated, and compatible, with the commercial and wider domains, so that enterprise creation and operations are supported, rather than opposed, by its external environment.
- *Focus.* Apply resources to strengths and avoid unpromising expenditures on weaknesses—in other words, focus on achievable objectives. Resources are best applied to areas of advantage, such as secure markets, competitive production, or superior technical skills.
- *Risk balance.* The adopted strategy entails risks associated with most, if not all, project elements, which can be managed (i.e., avoided, mitigated, or spread). The design is adjusted so that high risk associated

with some features (e.g., market, supply, technology, political environment) is reduced, perhaps by reallocating resources, while the risk of more secure features may be somewhat elevated. If project features are regarded as links in a chain, the weakest determines the chain's strength. Balancing risk in this way improves the overall strength of the chain. The area of greatest risk governs overall project risk (see Chapter 7, "Investment Decision under Uncertainty and Risk").

- Cooperation. A mutually beneficial strategy of cooperation with other individuals and entities avoids expenditure of time and resources to create all the facilities and skills required. Where possible, it is usually more productive than confrontation. The collaboration may be in the form of informal agreement, contractual joint venture, acquisition, or merger. Outsourcing of necessary components and services is advisable if the decision is based upon true competitive advantage rather than unsustainable exploitation of low-cost production factors, but for critical project inputs some form of cooperative venture with suppliers might offer greater security and price stability.

Formulating the Project Strategy   Attainment of project goals in a dynamic operating environment is best served by finding the optimal combination of technical and economic features to produce the desired output, such as maximizing profitability and terminal value (at the planning horizon), or achieving or bettering cost and technical efficiency benchmarks at acceptable levels of risk.[21] Strategic orientation is conducive to selecting this best course of action. Project sponsors, designers, and management are encouraged to think dynamically, to study sources of inevitable change to be encountered, and to develop capacities and resources that are essential for survival and growth in a competitive environment.

The strategy encompasses offensive and defensive features, and temporal dimensions. Product and marketing innovation are overt attempts to reform the playing field. Building internal capacities—identifying and developing skills to match or better those of the competition—has more of a defensive nature. The strategy also identifies what must be done on a temporal scale: Quickly adjust the corporate culture to the needs of the market; enhance staff capacities over the next two years; increase production capacity to match anticipated market share within three to five years.

Design of the enterprise is predicated on its interdependence with its operational environment (Figure 1.1). Within the wider domain, the enterprise is viewed as an economic and social entity or organism that mediates the relationship between consumers and resources. As part of this environment it competes with other producers for resources (from suppliers) and consumers. Mutual dependence requires that the enterprise be designed to adapt to environmental change and to results that do not follow precisely according to plan, and to influence or control change to exploit opportunities and minimize threats by being capable of assimilating and acting upon information about the forces underlying the process of change.

Project planners, once having formulated the strategy—what seems to be the best course of action—will almost inevitably be faced with new information that demands strategic rethinking. What appears to be the optimal plan at the outset may cease to be so tomorrow. As then General Dwight Eisenhower once said, "Plans are nothing, planning is everything." The corollary, "Strategy is nothing, strategic thinking is everything," emphasizes the dynamics of the environment. The strategic plan conceived during the planning phase will be influenced by the course of events, competitive reactions, and unanticipated environmental phenomena. Almost invariably, the strategy that is actually applied will differ from the original conception during planning and implementation and also during the operations phase.

So both project planners and the designed enterprise have to be adaptable to change, which for the enterprise can be promoted by staffing it with competent and flexible people and allocating resources to research and development (R&D).

Capacities that provide competitive advantage have to be identified—for example, product innovations, superior product quality, competitive costs, outstanding product services, or efficient distribution channels—that utilize existing and future market forces to advantage. To survive and grow in a competitive environment the enterprise needs to possess, acquire, or develop skills that confer advantage and provide for better performance than competitors, which may be vested in individuals or in organizational subdivisions. They are advantageous only to the extent that competitors are not easily able to replicate them.

Process of Strategy Development   A basic iterative process for developing the strategy consists of the following eight stages:[22]

1. Identify the vision, purpose, or mission of the project, its *raison d'être*, describing what needs are to be satisfied—that is, what markets are to be served (demographic, social, geographic)—and why the need for project output (goods and/or services) either exists or can be created.
2. Define project goals (increased earnings, improved market position, more efficient modus operandi, enhanced public image) and intermediate objectives necessary for their attainment.
3. Determine the project scope (products, markets, plant locations and capacities, distribution network) most conducive to achieving goals.

4. Consider positive and negative aspects associated with the overall plan and with each specific goal and objective:
   - Internal capacities (strengths, weaknesses).
   - External environment (opportunities and threats).
   - Competitor characteristics (strengths and weaknesses).
   - Skills required vis-à-vis actual or potential competitors.
   - Main advantages and constraints (e.g., resources, political, social, ecological).
5. Specify the approaches, or strategies, necessary to meet each project objective and goal:
   - Promising strategic options and preferences (e.g., low production cost, differentiation, plant location), rationale, and risks.
   - Cooperation: collaboration, joint venture, merger, acquisition.
   - Strategic mix: coordination between central strategy and substrategies related to project functions (e.g., management, administration, marketing, production, supply, finance, personnel management).
   - Strategic plan for project implementation (design, construction, and commissioning).
6. Identify and describe specific action plans necessary to achieve each objective and goal, for each functional area.
7. Define the system for implementing the strategy:
   - Coordinating and adapting strategic elements.
   - Assignment of responsibilities to functional areas and individuals.
8. Assess the overall strategic plan and associated risks (e.g., political, social, financial, environmental) in regard to the mission and goals, and decide whether the plan can be successfully carried out by the organization.

Comparative analysis of alternatives can be carried out essentially in one of two modes: If differences in alternative strategies are mainly in the details, variations can be considered within the structure as outlined; if the fundamental conceptual options differ considerably, better to analyze them independently and then compare assessments of each game plan to determine which is most promising.

Investment Cycle Capital investment has a cyclical character. The project is usually a component of an investment portfolio in which investments are planned, implemented, and carried out, then either terminated or liquidated, with residual capital reinvested in new projects. The investment cycle has relevance for project design and for longer-term planning, to contemplate postproject reinvestment possibilities at the planning horizon. Figure 1.3 illustrates project timelines and the investment cycle.

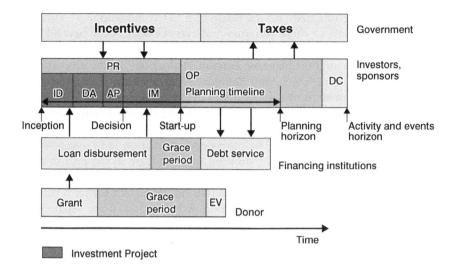

ID   Identification
DA   Design and analysis
AP   Appraisal
IM   Implementation
PR   Project promotion
OP   Operations
DC   Decommissioning, if applicable
EV   Evaluation

Planning timeline: Investors and other stakeholders consider activities within their particular time frame in assessing whether to participate in the project (this is the basis for appraisal).

Activities and events timeline: The full scope of activities envisioned as a consequence of investment in the project.

FIGURE 1.3 Project Timelines and Investment Cycle

Stakeholders have preferences that affect the time frame during which activities and events are counted in appraisal of the project from their individual perspectives, considering only those that occur up to the point in time relevant to their objectives and goals. For this reason, the *planning timeline* and its termination point, the *planning horizon*, differ for each of them. In any case, the timeline necessarily includes the investment period and a period of operations. Within the time frame up to the *activities and events horizon* are included all of the contemplated consequences of investment: the implementation project, operations, and possibly decommissioning after operations are terminated (see the subsection "Decommissioning" later in this chapter). Some of these activities and events might occur beyond the planning horizon of a particular stakeholder.

At a point beyond the planning horizon, *evaluation*[23] of the investment, its operational performance, and conditions prevailing at that point will most likely determine future undertakings by each stakeholder, all of whom have the opportunity to improve their investment decisions with feedback on their appraisal methods.[24] This can be considered the termination of the current investment cycle. The purpose of evaluation is to assess what has transpired as a result of the decision to participate in the project and to plan for the future, the next investment cycle. Investors might conduct their evaluation at the planning horizon (see Figure 1.3), or earlier if results do not meet expectations; lenders, during or at the end of the repayment phase; the government, when the consequences of its participation (e.g., providing services or incentives) are apparent. For investors, such evaluation leads to a decision on the future direction of the enterprise, examining the effectiveness of the project and where to go from there—to continue existing operations, expand, change direction, or liquidate. For lenders, evaluation provides feedback intended to improve their ability to select projects and to rate the capacities of their credit officers. Governments use this information to update their development plans. A donor usually allows the project time to achieve the objectives and goals of the grant (a grace period) before assessing the project in relation to possible additional support or to improve project selection processes.

Completion of one cycle of planning, implementation, operations, and project evaluation after the plan has been executed leads to another, building on the experience of previous cycles.

The *investment cycle* is the description of the sequence of phases (and stages of development) from conception to the project's activities and events horizon. At the decision point the project is appraised, based upon the information developed during the design and study process and the criteria of participants. During the *investment phase* the project is implemented—the organization, facilities, supplies, and distribution channels are set up to begin production. Production and marketing plans are executed during the *operations phase*. Evaluation at the planning horizon gives rise to ideas about new opportunities and commencement of the next cycle.

For investors/sponsors, the planning timeline comprises the *investment project*, all or part of the *operations phase*, and possibly *decommissioning*. In most cases, the planning horizon is not commensurate with the expected life of the project, as investors and other stakeholders limit their planning to a time frame within their respective comfort zones—that is, where the determinant of the *planning horizon* is essentially the tolerance for risk associated with forecasts of future developments. In assessing the project, performance indicators are predicated on projections only up to that point in time, and what is to occur beyond is essentially ignored.

The investment project includes stages of identification, design and analysis, appraisal, and implementation. Appraisal (see Chapter 8) is the process of comparing project design features and indicators of performance with criteria of stakeholders. Only when all necessary participants are convinced that their particular criteria are satisfied should the project be implemented. Project promotion—essentially a search for collaborators and funding, and securing tentative approval of relevant institutions and individuals (as distinguished from *product* promotion)—is an indispensable activity that commences at the conception stage and continues throughout the project, as long as needed to assure financial and other support necessary for its completion.

Bankers and other lenders are primarily interested only as long as credit that they have extended remains outstanding.[25] They supply credit during the implementation phase, may grant a period of grace during which only interest payments are normally due, expect the debt to be serviced according to a predetermined schedule, and essentially lose interest when the full amount of debt is repaid.

The project may require approval of government investment planning agencies, which are usually interested in the degree of conformance of project characteristics with their development plans (e.g., improving the economy of a particular region, technological advance, or employment creation). Governments may provide incentives in the form of capital or operating subsidies, guarantees, or tax holidays. A government's time frame for contributions and receipts in the form of direct and indirect taxes, as well as satisfaction of other nonmonetary criteria, determine its planning horizon.

The project may have the good fortune to receive a grant from a donor with interests in its projected outcomes—government agencies, nongovernmental organizations (NGOs, sometimes also called Civil Society Organizations), foundations, or private individuals. Eligibility requirements for a grant usually include submission of a proposal that is prepared according to guidelines issued by the grantor, which is then reviewed against other solicitations.

PROJECT DEVELOPMENT PROCESS

A well-designed project plan is a road map to successful investment. Without it the likelihood of taking a wrong turn is greatly elevated. Even for investors with extensive experience, many projects fail to meet expectations as a result of problems arising from one or more flaws in the project plan.

Compilation and analysis of relevant information, and then appraisal against criteria of investors and other stakeholders before committing capital to the project, determines whether it is a worthwhile investment. Promotion is usually needed either to attract investors or to acquire the necessary resources and other support. Project implementation—enterprise organization, construction, and plant commissioning—requires planning and management to develop an enterprise ready to carry out production, sales, and distribution.

Each investment project has unique characteristics that determine issues of concern. Objective and comprehensive study of how the project is to function in its environment in the short and long term helps to identify those issues that should be scrutinized and to identify appropriate project development activities and events pertaining to each project phase.

The project development process (PDP) comprises preoperational planning activities that first provide a basis for the investment decision, and then an investment phase during which the plant is constructed and commissioned and the enterprise organized. The planning process involves stages of design and analysis, increasing in depth as the project passes through progressively more rigorous screening. Although described as a linear progression of steps, in practice the process is iterative. In seeking an optimal project configuration, accumulated information at later stages is selectively fed back to earlier designs and decisions that are then modified in the light of that information. In fact, the sequence can be initiated almost at any point; only as information and ideas take shape can the entire project configuration crystallize.

Preinvestment Phase

At this point in the development process, quality of the project concept (see the later subsection "An Investment Opportunity") is of paramount concern (in the investment phase, time is of the essence to ensure that investment and cost projections are within acceptable bounds). Investors are well advised to avoid short-circuiting design and analysis, moving directly from project identification to a loan application. The time and effort expended in studying project alternatives to find the optimal design usually pays for itself many times over.

A project idea is conceived, from inspiration or perhaps from a general study of business opportunities in a country or region. Once the idea is germinated, investigation of its viability as an investment opportunity can begin. The project design normally goes through a number of iterations prior to becoming a reality.

In the course of investigating, designing, and promoting the project, each participant—investor, commercial bank, development finance institution, equipment and material suppliers, prospective clients, export credit insurance agency, consulting firm, licensing authority—is a potential font of ideas and information.

The preinvestment phase commences with an opportunity identified. For an existing enterprise, the process may be initiated as part of the normal investment cycle, responding to a need for restructuring or rehabilitation, or to alter the trajectory of the existing enterprise. In any case, a perceived investment opportunity is developed starting with a preliminary profile of the project, which is progressively transformed to a comprehensive design that is feasible and optimal as the project passes through screening stages.

Project sponsors have something else to do, equally important as coming up with the project idea. As the project develops, a promotion effort is required to identify participants—investors, financiers, guarantors, suppliers—and their criteria of acceptability. Promotional effort is usually required throughout the preinvestment phase and may even extend to the investment phase.

Project Identification Identification of investment opportunities is the starting point. Project ideas can arise within the enterprise, from business associations or promotion agencies, or from special studies conducted for identifying opportunities within a country or region. Initiatives leading to promising ventures (commercial, industrial, infrastructure) that will satisfy needs of potential consumers can be undertaken by private and public investors or groups or by promotion agencies that identify opportunities at the sector or enterprise level, usually by disseminating project profiles. Figure 1.4 illustrates the project identification process.

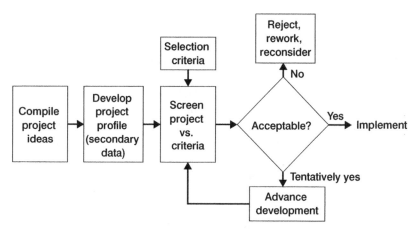

FIGURE 1.4 Project Identification Process

An Investment Opportunity   At the outset, promising ideas have to be separated from unreasoned speculation.[26] Features to be examined in the process of identification include the following.

At the micro level:

- A *project (business) concept*—described in strategic terms considering the project's commercial environment and the wider socioeconomic and environmental domain (see the subsection titled "Strategic Project Planning"). The concept includes a *product or service* for which a need exists or can be created, and a *strategy* for production, marketing, and distribution that justifies prediction of survival and growth of the enterprise in its environment.
- *Investors*—willing and able to provide the necessary equity. Their history and qualifications must be adequate to organize the project and to qualify for any additional financing required.
- *Market*—people willing and able to buy or otherwise consume. In some cases, susceptibility of potential consumers to psychological transformations is necessary to engender a need for the product. Consideration of market includes determining a point in the product life cycle conducive to acceptance by sufficient numbers of consumers and a *market environment* supportive of the establishment of a new enterprise.
- *Resources*—available as needed for proper creation and functioning of the enterprise. These include managerial capacity and other labor; finance; raw materials and intermediate goods and services; a technology appropriate to the environment; land in a suitable location.

At the macro level:

- *Business climate*—a stable political environment; supportive industrial policies and practices; transparent, efficient, and even-handed legal and regulatory mechanisms.
- *Business cycle*—favorable for cyclical industries[27] if in the ascendant state.
- *Economic status and trend*—growing GDP and national income. A state of secular economic decline in the country or region does not generally bode well for a new business entrant, although economic adversity can enhance demand for low cost, basic goods.

Generation and Sources of Ideas   Investment ideas arise from individuals —entrepreneurs, industrialists, enterprise managers—and from investment groups, business and trade associations, and commercial organizations (e.g., chambers of commerce) that have either performed general investment opportunity studies or have accumulated ideas from members' experience. Information is usually preliminary or tentative.

Another type of source consists of broad-based sector studies, usually conducted under the auspices of international development organizations— for example, strategic sector studies sponsored by the Asian Development Bank.[28] They generally include a review of current economic conditions in potential host countries or regions, including structural problems faced in manufacturing or services and recommendations that can be very useful in project design.

Government investment promotion agencies (e.g., ministry of industry) and national development banks identify promising sectors through geographical area studies, resource-based studies, and industrial plans. They are conducted in both emerging economies and industrialized countries, and directly or indirectly identify possible projects that can then be subjected to further screening and promotion. These investment idea sources include:

- *Periodic reports* of industrial planning agencies on national or regional development plans, identifying industries to be promoted, incentives (e.g., tax breaks, subsidies, repatriation of profits), and special procedures for easing the permitting process for targeted industries.
- *Sector studies* of economic development agencies or educational institutions in areas of particular interest to government.
- *Local resource studies* by industrial promotion agencies. (A caveat: Sources of raw materials are relevant only if quality standards are compatible with product specifications acceptable to local or export market.)
- *Studies of natural resources* for potential exploitation. Such studies usually include information on quantity of deposits, quality, exploitation potential, and constraints (e.g., accessibility, environmental impacts). They may include analysis of the general level of demand, domestic and international, for the resource per se or for products for which the resource is a major component. A regional study might include a broader range of information in addition to data on natural resources (e.g., industrial profiles, infrastructure capacities, human resource availability, economic conditions).

Once interest is expressed in a particular project, a preliminary profile is prepared (often by the promotion agency) to quantify parameters, as the first step in developing the project idea into a proposal. Thereafter, the project requires study of increasing depth according to the level of interest of potential investors (see the "Preinvestment Studies" section later in this chapter).

One of the common sources of investment ideas is to follow the lead of others, a "me too" approach that is appealing for its simplicity. If one enterprise is successful producing widgets, then another will likely follow in its footsteps. This may be true if there is unmet demand and if the project is able to emulate the successful operating modes of its antecedents.

A much better approach is to study the characteristics of the environment to decide what needs exist or can be created for goods and services. Existing enterprises look toward expanding product lines. New investors survey the field for niches to fill. Innovators assess how their technology fits into the lifestyles or operating modes of clientele with no prior experience in using the product or service. Each sector of the economy—consumers, industry, agriculture, commerce—is scanned to detect what needs exist for different or additional goods and services. Some of these ideas can be rejected out of hand because it is fairly obvious that a key element is either missing or will not function in the environment.

Other sources of ideas include the following:

- Export potential predicated on international competitiveness, more promising without need for protection and/or subsidies.
- Unsatisfied or potential domestic demand based on projected demographic changes (e.g., population growth, age and income distribution, purchasing power, consumption patterns), nationally or by region.
- Gaps in backward and forward linkages for existing enterprises (i.e., vertical integration): currently procured inputs or products for which the enterprise is a consumer, or to exploit possible advantages that the enterprise might enjoy (quality, price, or security of supply) over downstream producers (alternatively, merger or acquisition involving existing suppliers or clients).
- Changing market conditions, such as demand/supply relationships, strengths and weaknesses of competition.
- Problems/constraints in economic development arising from shortages of essential facilities, services, infrastructure, or materials.
- Possibilities for import substitution of consumer or industrial goods. However, protections (if present) easily evaporate, particularly when provided for infant industries, so the question must be asked, how will the enterprise function in the absence of such supports?
- Incentives offered by government agencies—tax holidays, subsidies, grants for development in sectors or regions. (Caution: These must not be the sole basis for embarking on a business venture.)
- Technology developments: modernization of production and/or products; peripheral equipment for a product innovation (e.g., external

computer data storage media). Joint venture is a way to enter the business when the production technology is not otherwise accessible.

■ Favorable costs of production factors.

■ Substitutes for expensive or scarce products.

■ Government policy initiatives (e.g., self-sufficiency in food production, energy generation).

■ Replication of successful projects of another country in similar circumstances. Nuances of difference, including culture, have to be examined to ascertain if the experience is relevant.

■ Delivery of an existing product at lower cost or a better product at the same price.[29]

■ Review of international standard industrial classification (ISIC) lists or other lists of classified products.

Terms of reference for a study commissioned by the enterprise to identify investment opportunities should include at least the following items:

■ Scope of opportunities to be investigated, including any or all of the possibilities listed earlier.

■ Geographical area of interest.

■ Socioeconomic environment, consumer demographics, disposable income.

■ General business climate—economy and trends, government policies on commerce and industry.

■ How information is to be presented—graphs, tables, formats, summaries.

■ Accuracy and precision of surveys and secondary information.

■ For each identified opportunity:
  ■ Estimates of capital investment and performance indicators.
  ■ Supply of major inputs—sources, quantities, qualities, prices.
  ■ Demand for outputs—unfilled or to be created.
  ■ Location analysis and site availability.
  ■ Infrastructure requirements and availability.

Investment Profiles An outline of the project, necessary for seeking partners and for other promotional purposes, contains all available information in concise form. For a potential stakeholder to seriously consider a project idea, a minimal amount of conceptualization is necessary, which usually can be developed from available data. A profile contains a skeleton description of an investment opportunity based on secondary information that outlines the basic business concept, technologies, markets, and preliminary estimates of investment and profitability.

Selection Criteria   At the preliminary stage of project identification, selection is primarily an issue for prospective investors. Before other stakeholders enter the picture and more extensive project appraisal is undertaken, investors have to identify those projects that are to be pursued further. Preliminary *criteria* have to be defined, such as minimum size and growth rate of the market; minimum or maximum level of investment; leveraging potential; and approximate targets for a limited range of performance indicators. Minimum conditions may be specified regarding availability of local resources (quantities, qualities, and prices), availability of appropriate technology, the state of the economy in the region or country, infrastructure adequacy, and conformance of the project idea with industrial policy. In later stages, preliminary criteria are supplemented with definitive performance benchmarks, such as hurdle rate (return on investment), payback period, and breakeven.

Screening   Profiles and opportunity studies are screened to sort out the most promising. The cost of investigation increases rapidly as projects are selected for more advanced study. Interesting opportunities can be classified systematically—for example, (1) worth further study if preliminary assessment reveals no obvious pitfalls and if there appears to be either an unfilled need for the product or service or one that can be created; (2) rejected outright because some feature will obviously not work in the environment (even these can be periodically reviewed to see if feasibility constraints have been removed); (3) recycled: projects that need some refining of major features before serious consideration; and (4) to be revisited at a later date: projects that are not currently timely but that could be implemented in the future after anticipated changes in the environment have occurred.

An effective method of screening is to rate projects according to the set of criteria using a point system. Each criterion can be weighted on a scale of 1 to 10 in terms of its significance or importance. Then each project can be rated for each criterion (on a scale of 1 to 5). The sum of products of category weights and ratings determines the points for each alternative. If a single project idea emerges for expansion of an existing enterprise, screening can be applied to alternative technologies and strategies, with the objective of utilizing planning resources in the most productive way.

Focusing attention on a limited number of project ideas with the greatest promise is a way to avoid wasting planning resources. Planners and investigators can do a better job when efforts are not diluted by having too much to do. There usually is a limit to the capital available for investment, so working on an excessively wide array of possibilities is unrealistic. Particularly where there are sufficient project ideas, it is better to quickly reject, or at least recycle, ideas that present difficult obstacles from the outset. These projects can be reconsidered at a later time. Meanwhile, attention can be focused, and resources concentrated, upon the project that appears to be most likely to succeed.

Design and Analysis   From the point that a project is selected for further development, it proceeds through a series of stages of design and analysis of more or less constant breadth and progressively greater depth (see the "Preinvestment Studies" section) as confidence in project viability increases. *Market research* addresses existing demand or the potential to create demand. The *marketing strategy* is an outgrowth of market study—how potential consumers will be attracted and how their needs can best be served. Together they provide information on expected sales revenues. *Engineering* defines the technology, production process and plant design, investment and operating costs, and human resource requirements. *Capital structure* defines the providers and proportions of debt and equity to finance the project. Analysis of *financial costs and benefits*, predicated on market analysis, engineering design, and capital structure, determines profitability for investors at market prices and other financial performance indicators. *Economic analysis* provides information concerning the project's social, economic, and environmental impacts.

A business plan (BP) is an outgrowth of study and the investment decision. The basic difference between the content of the BP and the design study is that the plan focuses on a specific approach to the business, whereas the study considers alternative configurations. In the project planning phase, the main utility of the BP is promotion—to attract investment capital and strategic partners, secure loans, and convince potential key employees of the viability of the enterprise. During the investment and operations phase the BP serves to communicate with enterprise personnel and other stakeholders, and as a management and planning tool. The BP basically demonstrates the viability of the business proposition. It builds on the information gathered from the study to answer all questions pertaining to finance, implementation, management, operations, and commercial viability. Appendix 1.2 is an outline of a typical business plan for a manufacturing enterprise.

Project Appraisal and Risk   Project characteristics and performance indicators are compared with criteria of stakeholders. Appraisal by an independent consultant may illuminate issues beyond those otherwise identified. Appraisal is discussed in detail in Chapter 8.

Underlying appraisal is the element of risk, which arises when decisions are made in the face of uncertainties concerning predictions of the project's future activities and events. Each stakeholder considers risk factors associated with features and characteristics of the project with respect to particular objectives and goals. Risk can be handled in several ways (see Chapter 7):

adding a premium to criteria, effectively raising the barrier; determining variability in project parameters and how they individually and collectively affect predictions of outcomes; spreading risk among stakeholders; insuring against risk via either contracts or derivative financial instruments (e.g., commodities futures related to inputs and outputs—see Chapter 7). As in any other type of measurement, predicted operational characteristics and performance indicators can only be assessed in the light of uncertainties in both the project feature and the measuring instruments employed.

Decision A decision to invest is predicated on a positive outcome of appraisal. It means that criteria are satisfied, and the project is accepted and will proceed to implementation and operations. It also means that, in the opinion of investors, this is the best use of marginal uncommitted resources. Projects that do not meet criteria may be rejected, recycled, or modified (as described earlier).

Implementation Phase

The commitment to invest precipitates preparation and execution of the implementation phase (Figure 1.3), which commences at the time of the decision to go forward with the project, and comprises the following activities (see Chapter 9):

- Creating and staffing the implementation team.
- Enterprise formation, or creation of a responsible management entity (for an existing enterprise): organization, staffing, design of operating systems.
- Construction project: project management, detailed design engineering, procurement of capital items and start-up materials and services, construction and installations, performance tests.
- Plant commissioning and start-up.

A critical aspect of project development is the implementation plan, which specifies how these activities will be carried out. A disciplined approach to planning avoids the pitfalls of delays and overruns. One systematic methodology is the Logical Framework Approach (LFA), which employs a standardized framework document to identify inconsistencies.[30]

Operations Phase

A successful PDP leads to project operations—commencement of production and sales—as the organization attempts to fulfill planned goals and objectives. Production and sales plans developed during the preinvestment phase are carried out during the operations phase. The quality of project study and design is a major determinant of success or failure—a plan based on inaccurate or inadequate information and assumptions is not conducive to success, no matter how well executed and operated. If operating forecasts or the strategies on which they were predicated turn out to be deficient, remedial measures (e.g., changes in financial structure, marketing approach, distribution channels) may be difficult and expensive.

Operating efficiency during the start-up period usually suffers from a combination of marketing and operational challenges. Marketing plans have to be fine-tuned to consumer needs, distribution, or product promotion. Workers' inexperience, problems with machinery and equipment, and uneven supply of all necessary inputs and factory supplies are early impediments to reaching production goals. Unforeseen operating problems may be related to errors and inadequate preparation during design and implementation phases. These factors have to be taken into account in formulating a realistic production plan.

At the planning horizon (the end of the relevant portion of the operations phase), stakeholders will face decisions concerning the future of the enterprise: whether to expand, rehabilitate, seek new markets and investment opportunities, or wind down operations. At the outset of the project, its future beyond the planning horizon can only be surmised, but it behooves sponsors and planners to try to keep one step ahead of the information at hand, at least to contemplate the future.

Decommissioning

It may be necessary to plan for decommissioning project facilities. A mining or energy project, for example, is often compelled by government authorities to clear the site and reclaim the land, returning it to its pre-project state or another state specified either by sponsors or by government authorities. Enterprises are usually required to safely dispose of hazardous materials. Plants may have to be dismantled and removed safely from the site. If the project has a defined life, some level of decommissioning may be required, with a plan required for financing and executing decommissioning as part of the overall project plan.[31]

PLANNING HORIZON AND PROJECT LIFE

The purpose of planning is to predict and control future events. The planning process integrates futuristic thinking and analysis of information and assumptions to define the means of achieving desired outcomes. The planning horizon defines the period of time selected as the basis for project assessment. It may be the span of time that investors plan to retain control of the enterprise, the limit of time for which forecasts are considered reliable, or the economic life of the project. Based on product life cycle, the span might vary from 5 years (e.g., pharmaceuticals) to 15 or 20 years (e.g., standard production machinery) to 50 years (e.g., infrastructure, power plants). Economic life[32] (the period of time that the project is expected to continue generating acceptable benefits for investors) is related to several factors:

- Technological life of major plant, machinery, and equipment.
- Product or industry life cycle.
- Extent of raw material deposits.
- Rate of technology advancement.
- Capacity of technology to adapt to change (e.g., demand, operating environment).
- Regulatory constraints on exploitation of natural resource reserves, cumulative emissions.

Unless the plan is to exit in a shorter time, the most solid basis for the planning horizon is the reliability of forecasts and associated risk, which increases for estimates further out in time. The length of time to the planning horizon will affect performance indicators. A longer time frame usually results nominally in more favorable results, although this effect is mitigated or even nullified by time-related risk enhancement. Investors are well advised to select a planning horizon consistent with their investment objectives and not necessarily tied to intrinsic project characteristics such as economic life of major assets. For some types of projects potentially affected by cutting-edge technology, the increase in uncertainty over time limits the practical planning span to five years or even less. Consequently, the planning horizon is shorter than the possible project life.

How the enterprise fares in the future will be somewhat related to its flexibility in adapting to change in the business environment. However, project planning is inherently limited to the fairly predictable future. Anticipated changes are either included in the project plan or, at the very least, subjected to sensitivity analysis to measure their potential effects on the project's outcome.

PROJECT SCOPE

What is the extent of markets, the feasible geographical range of operations, the location and capacities of sources of supply and infrastructure? The answers serve to define the project configuration that can be accommodated by the organization and its available resources; precisely what is to be done to plan, construct, operate, and (if necessary) decommission the enterprise; and what resources are to be employed in the process.

All of the functions of the enterprise and activities necessary for its creation have to be clearly identified. Facilities and activities within the scope of the project frequently extend beyond the plant site: effluents handling, treatment, and disposal; off-site transport and storage of inputs and outputs (including final products, by-products, wastes, and emissions); and offsite ancillary activities, such as housing, education, training, and recreation facilities. The project may also require primary offsite facilities such as marketing and distribution channels and public relations functions.

Defining the scope for expansion and rehabilitation projects can be particularly problematic. Resources associated with facilities and activities that are transferred from, or shared with, other enterprise functions not directly related to the project have to be identified and their costs and benefits allocated. To better understand the structure of the project, all facilities and activities within spatial and functional boundaries in each phase are identified—preinvestment, implementation, operation, and decommissioning (if applicable). One way is to break the project down into cost or profit units (centers) and then identify facilities and activities for each unit and for each phase. The process can be extended to several levels or stages of definition. For example, the production function can be divided into manufacturing, materials handling, and maintenance. Manufacturing, in turn, can be divided into machining, forming, forging, and quality control. This process provides a detailed conceptualization of the project and facilitates developing a preliminary implementation plan, which is a framework for estimating costs and benefits for each of the facilities and activities of functional subunits during each phase that can be aggregated to develop the complete picture.

During the planning process, functions may be identified that were originally not included in the project concept but that would logically fall within the project scope. Environmental analysis, for example, might lead to the inclusion of clean-waste technologies (e.g., closed-circuit processes) and environmental protection technologies (e.g., filters and systems for the removal of gases and particulates), either for business reasons or to comply with regulations. Upstream and downstream functions (e.g., agricultural production of project inputs that are not within the commercial scope) can be internalized to provide a more comprehensive and comprehensible economic analysis. At the study stage, make-or-buy decisions have an impact on the project's scope (outsource or manufacture). For very large projects that have regional or national impact, analysis might be carried out using a model (input-output, economic base, multiplier, regional growth[33]) in which the scope is virtually the entire economy.

PREINVESTMENT STUDIES

Preinvestment study of industrial and commercial ventures has not been the rule throughout the world since the dawn of the industrial age. Failure to meet expectations often results from what appeared to be insignificant factors. Even in industrialized countries, direct investment is often undertaken in haste, avoiding the trouble and cost of investigation, but increasing the risk of failure. The weak link in the chain defines the fragility of the entire venture.[34] Hence, the need to study—to design all of the links so that they are of adequate strength, and to identify those that may be most subject to internal weaknesses or susceptible to external threats.

A project study has to provide synthesis (integration of project components operating as a system) and simulation (modeling to determine performance characteristics), explaining its design, how it will be implemented, and how it will function in the commercial and wider domains. If executed with due diligence, the study provides a solid foundation for decision making and for detailed design if the decision is made to go forward with the project. To enhance confidence, preliminary uncertainties identified in interim stages of study have to be clarified in later stages. For coherence of presentation, treatment of major issues is contained in the body of the study report (see Appendix 1.3); supporting materials (e.g., statistics, results of market surveys, detailed technical descriptions and equipment lists, plant layouts) are better presented as separate annexes.

One of the first issues concerning the magnitude and depth of a preinvestment study is its cost. Cost is a function of project type, complexity, and scope, which determine the time and effort required to collect and assess the necessary information. As the need for more detailed information increases, so does cost. If the level of uncertainty demands study out of proportion to the scale of the investment, it should probably be abandoned from the start.

For small to medium projects, the expected range of cost of study is approximately 0.5 to 3 percent of investment (fixed assets plus preoperational expenditures), increasing from preliminary investigation to comprehensive analysis; for large projects the range is from about 0.5 to 1 percent of investment. The percentage for large projects is generally reduced as a result of economies of scale for the main study and for support studies (e.g., markets or technology selection). Study costs are usually capitalized as part of preoperational expenditures.

Consultants' fees are a function of stature (experience and reputation) and the effort required to complete the study.[35] The study agreement usually covers travel and per diem, communications, design, and office expenditures. Other factors that enter into consultant fees are related to the work plan: consultants' workload and level of interest in the project, and the competency of project personnel to support the study.

Feasibility and Optimization

Study of an industrial investment opportunity involves both a feasibility and optimization process. *Feasibility* refers to what *can* be done but not necessarily what *should* be done. Rather, the most favorable, or optimal, of feasible configurations is to be sought, considering criteria of stakeholders.[36] There may be a number of feasible alternatives, which first have to be identified and then analyzed comparatively to find the most favorable choice. Detailed investigation of the range of alternatives—such as choice of technology, equipment, capacity, location, financing—may be problematic if carried along to more comprehensive stages of study.

Early screening for feasibility of alternative configurations avoids inordinate expenditure of time and resources. If a clear advantage does not emerge in early stages it may be advisable to study more than one configuration in detail—for example, two or three possible locations, or two production programs with different technologies. Once selected, a particular configuration has to be explained and justified as the best (optimal) solution considering objectives and constraints.

Types of Studies

A study commences at the time that a preliminary profile or other description of the project has been considered, and it has been decided to investigate further. A general principle is that the *breadth*, or scope, of study content is defined early in the project development process, with research and analysis of all aspects pursued from the start through stages of development as confidence in the project increases, modified as warranted by progressive understanding of the project and associated features. Study and analysis generally increases in *depth* as more resources are provided with increasing confidence of sponsors, with information and analysis at previous stages built upon, rather than discarded and begun anew.

The process of design and analysis of an investment project can be described in discrete stages but only to illustrate the progressive advancement of the simulation and synthesis that represents the project in the minds of stakeholders. The process is usually a continuum without clearly defined stages. Alternative designs can be added or dropped from consideration at any stage, but to contain effort and cost, alternatives are investigated only to the point that it becomes clear that one or more configurations have superior characteristics. Interim reports may be necessary as the project progresses.

Ideally the project is studied without regard to the particular interests of various stakeholders, developing as complete a synthesis as possible within available resources. The following dilemma may surface for the designer: Professional judgment dictates the appropriate scope of study, but the client defines terms of reference that focus on a limited range of issues that are not considered sufficiently inclusive. The project can be declined (exited) or risks of an incomplete scope of responsibility can be explained (discontent voiced).[37]

The content and format of *study reports* respond to the particular needs and interests of stakeholders. Although it is costly and time-consuming (and avoided if possible), there may be a need for multiple reports as stakeholders commissioning studies have their particular areas of interest. For example, the financing institution may have its own report requirements that must be followed if the project is to be considered. Reporting requirements need to be sorted out as early as possible to avoid unnecessary duplication of effort.

Ultimately, stakeholders appraise the project. To support the decision process, and as a prelude to that eventuality, assessment of the strengths and weaknesses[38] of the business concept and alternative project configurations are included in the study report with increasing depth as the project progresses through stages of development.

The following breakdown of study stages is *for illustrative purposes only* and not intended to define discrete, indispensable steps in the process. In practice, these stages meld into a continuous process of refinement in project simulation and synthesis. The development of study and design of expansion and rehabilitation projects for an existing enterprise usually follows a similar pattern, except that recognition by management of the opportunity (or necessity) obviates the need for the most preliminary stages. An example of an expansion and rehabilitation project (Victoria Coke) is provided on our web site, www.wiley.com/go/investmentprojectdesign.

Opportunity Study   Promising ideas are refined with a preliminary or *opportunity study* outlining basic features. A study at this level is usually based upon sketchy, readily available secondary information, often derived from similar projects or from the sponsor's knowledge. Refinement of the *business concept*, explaining why the idea should work in the proposed environment and its basic operating characteristics, distinguishes project study from identification of opportunities. Alternative approaches are investigated regarding project variables, such as marketing (product, price, promotion, distribution), technology, location and site, and capital structure.

At this preliminary stage, information may be obtained from comparable existing projects, from commerce and industry organizations, from prospective equipment vendors and suppliers, and from trade statistics published by government commerce departments (e.g., import statistics of varying degrees of product specificity). Investment promotion agencies are potential sources (e.g., chamber of commerce, ministry of industry, regional and national development banks) that perform or sponsor specific project opportunity studies or general sector opportunity studies with the objective of stimulating industrial investment in a region or country. To be useful, these studies must contain a scope of information that reasonably explains the investment opportunity (a simple listing of product possibilities will usually not be very helpful). Information has to be more comprehensive than that developed during the identification stage (see earlier discussion).

Prefeasibility Study An intermediate stage of study is an effective means of clarifying the nature of the project before committing the considerable resources necessary for an investment decision, with the project idea elaborated in greater depth. Objectives of study at this stage are expanded from the preliminary (opportunity) stage to include the following:

- More rigorous confirmation of the logic of the business concept or project idea and strategy.
- Refined definition of the scope of the project.
- More thorough investigation of possible project alternatives and selection of the most promising for comprehensive study and analysis.
- Identification of critical features that may require in-depth study involving surveys, laboratory tests, or a pilot plant.
- More definitive calculation of financial performance indicators.
- Preliminary assessment of environmental, social, and economic impacts and their compatibility with standards and objectives.
- Identification of quantitative and qualitative stakeholder criteria.
- Preliminary assessment of projected performance versus criteria.

The project strategy, or corporate strategies in which the project has a role, are developed more fully and their logic tested. Alternative ways of approaching design features—product, technology, marketing and distribution, capital structure—are investigated. The strengths and weaknesses of each selected alternative configuration are compared in regard to implementation and operating characteristics. Feasibility of favorable alternatives is ascertained on the basis of available information.

At this stage the scope of the project is more clearly defined: Upstream and downstream linkages are identified, allocations of resources from other corporate activities are clarified, environmental impacts and mitigation measures are defined. Special support studies of critical features may be justified, such as laboratory tests of materials and components, pilot processes to test technical feasibility, or agricultural tests to confirm feasibility of commercial-scale production. Compatibility of the project with socioeconomic goals is investigated to an extent justified by the range and severity of impacts. Most information is derived from secondary sources, but compilation of primary data may be appropriate for the most critical factors (e.g., limited test marketing or survey for an innovative product).

Selection of the most promising alternative project configurations at an intermediate stage avoids inordinate costs of in-depth study required for an informed investment decision.

Feasibility Study   At the *feasibility* stage the study provides a description of the project sufficient in breadth and depth for an investment decision. At this point, alternatives have been investigated to sufficient depth for a recommendation and analysis of the most promising approach. A *feasible* project can operate successfully in its operating environment. External constraints that may exist are manageable. The study is a detailed analysis of the project—in effect, a descriptive synthesis that clearly and in detail illustrates how it will function in the commercial (if applicable) and wider domain. The depth of investigation in all areas (commercial, technical, financial, socioeconomic, environmental) provides information adequate for potential investors, financiers, guarantors, and licensing agencies to decide whether to go ahead with the project.

If the study process has been properly carried out, the term *feasibility study* is a misnomer—a better designation is *optimization study*, as the proposed project design should be both feasible and optimal (the best way). Some characteristics of a feasibility study are:

- Description of a clear project concept and underlying strategy—how the project will successfully be implemented and operate in its environment.
- Well-defined project scope, with all onsite and off-site functions and their interactions identified.
- Justification for project configuration selected vis-à-vis feasible alternatives.
- In-depth study of critical features, including acquisition and analysis of primary data from surveys, laboratory tests, or pilot-plants tests; studies by qualified professionals of features requiring scientific expertise; detailed analyses of data with error and confidence intervals indicated;

checks, when necessary, against alternative sources to assure data consistency; and defensible conclusions based upon data and consistent with analyses.

- Critical information from reliable sources (e.g., tenders for major equipment acquisitions and construction).
- Comprehensive project design describing how project components will interact successfully, of sufficient depth to prepare detailed engineering plans, to develop the organization and distribution channels and to set up operations once the project is approved.
- Assessment of commercial, environmental, social, and economic impacts and their compatibility with standards, objectives, and criteria of stakeholders.

There is not a standard format, approach, or pattern that will serve all projects (or all stakeholders) of whatever type, size, or category. The composition and features of significance vary from project to project. For most industrial projects, the range of features outlined in the subsection "Content of an Industrial Investment Project Study Report" later in this chapter should serve as a guideline for the ground to be covered.

Estimates of performance indicators are meaningful only for the *project scope* defined to include all essential components and related costs. The scope needs to be documented with descriptions of all functions including preliminary design drawings, schedules, and procedures, to provide quantitative and qualitative parameter values that can serve to derive indicators and as supporting structure for more advanced project development.

Through all stages of development, the study follows an iterative optimization process, including simulation of all project elements and their functions and linkages, with feedback influencing changes that are necessary to correct design deficiencies. In principle, analysis of risk factors underlies every dimension of the study. Sensitivity of risky elements is examined through the range of potential variation (see Chapter 7). Risks associated with performance indicators and other characteristics are identified. If, in the light of analysis, insoluble problems render the project fundamentally unviable, this view needs to be expressed and explained. A study that averts an unwise investment avoids misallocation of scarce capital.

Assumptions underlying analysis are clearly explained and justified, and the foundations upon which the design is constructed are understood by stakeholders, and particularly decision makers. Identifying and correcting unfounded assumptions is facilitated when they are explicit. Virtually any project can take on a rosy hue if assumptions are sufficiently optimistic.

Caveat: An equipment or technology supplier may provide a so-called feasibility study free of charge, essentially a proposal to supply equipment, emphasizing only those project features that support investment. As these studies are unrelated or ill adapted to the local business environment, they can be misleading and, if accepted at face value, result in an inappropriate investment decision. They may be no more than promotional instruments, describing operations under optimistic assumptions or ideal conditions and omitting risky or uncertain features. Production or sales estimates are based on conditions that might bear little relevance to the country in which investment takes place. Such expanded bids or sales supplements are offered widely, with only slight alterations specific to the operating environment for the prospective client.

Accepting a project on this basis might misdirect investment or lead to excess capacity. An investment proposal by an equipment supplier also has the disadvantage that typically no genuine alternative technology and equipment selection is considered. If equipment suppliers are to be the source of project proposals (not recommended in any case), they should at least be prepared under the same terms of reference to ensure that the so-called studies are comparable. The study must also relate to available production factors and local market and production conditions that permit a realistic assessment of potential benefits and costs.

The capital structure and commitment of investors and financiers are investigated at the earliest study stages and refined as the project nears the decision point, with detailed study proceeding only so long as there is reason to believe that financing will be made available when, and in the amounts, required. There is little sense in conducting a detailed feasibility study without reliable assurance that financing will be made available in the event of positive findings. Another factor is the cost of capital (see Chapter 4), which depends upon the capital structure and which has a direct bearing on project feasibility.

Support Studies   Project elements that are vital to success and for which there is an unacceptable degree of uncertainty (information is insufficient, irrelevant, or otherwise unavailable) may require special support studies, highly focused, of limited scope, and providing a detailed technical analysis of sufficient depth to provide the necessary level of confidence in the results.

These studies are performed by technical experts, usually members of consulting firms specializing in the area of interest, or by testing laboratories. They are intended to answer key questions concerning the project's viability. For a project planning to exploit natural resources, for example, an expert might be called upon to assess the magnitude and quality of reserves and to identify any problems associated with their extraction and use.

Some types of special studies that may be required include:

- Market research—demand projections, analysis of competition.
- Marketing study—strategies for access, securing share, and penetration.
- Raw materials and other intermediate inputs—supplies, current and projected price trends.
- Laboratory (quality of material and component supplies) and pilot-plant (production process) tests.
- Location studies—evaluation of alternatives against criteria, such as minimizing transport costs.
- Environmental impact assessment (EIA),[39] particularly for projects involving hazardous materials or operations with significant environmental impacts (e.g., chemical plants; paper and cellulose mills; petroleum refineries; iron and steel mills; nuclear, thermal, and hydropower plants; and infrastructure projects).
- Economy-of-scale studies—to determine optimal plant capacity, a function of investment and operating cost.
- Technology selection—capital versus labor-intensive alternatives and degree of automation.
- Equipment selection studies concerning performance specifications and costs, particularly for large plants.[40] Special tests may be required if design specifications significantly differ from actual operating conditions; design adaptations may be necessary to deal with local operating conditions or with quality of available inputs.

Support or functional studies are conducted at any stage of project development. Judgment is required in deciding at what point it makes sense to devote resources to a special study. As these studies are concerned with vital aspects of the project, they must be designed for sufficient depth, with conclusions clear enough either to remove the issue as a bottleneck to subsequent stages of development or to verify infeasibility of the project in its current configuration.

Content of an Industrial Investment Project Study Report   One of the first issues in determining the content of a preinvestment study report is the audience and its concerns. It makes no sense to produce a report that does not address issues of concern to the target audience; conversely, issues of *no concern* to the audience might be omitted (as potentially confusing), although discretion is necessary in deciding whether an issue has relevance even if it is not apparent to the stakeholder to whom the report is addressed.

The report content conforms to the project scope, describing the design features of all operating units and how they are to function and interact, internally and externally. At the same time, issues of particular concern to individual and institutional stakeholders have to be addressed; some may even insist on having information provided in a particular format. *There may be a need for more than one study report*, with each addressed to a particular audience or audience range. This does not mean that the range of issues studied is incomplete, only that some material may be either included in summary form or even omitted in a report for a particular stakeholder. A suggested comprehensive outline for an investment project study report for the general audience is provided in Appendix 1.3.

The *executive summary* is a synopsis of the project for decision makers, which identifies and provides concise analysis of critical issues presented in detail in the main body of the report, with emphasis on key indicators and major risks. The study content follows the project scope, describing the design features of all dimensions of the operating entity and how they are to function and interact, internally and with the external environment.

Information Flow for Investment Project Study   The general flow of information for the formulation and analysis of an investment project study is illustrated in Figure 1.5. Details of the content of each step are contained in Appendix 1.4. The process can be adapted for private-sector and public projects of virtually any size by adjusting the scope and depth of analysis as appropriate. The linearity of the diagram is only an approximation; in practice the process is iterative and can commence at almost any point.

As backdrop for all other aspects of project planning, an indispensable step is knowledge of markets, demand for goods and services to be produced, along with knowledge of the capacities and strategies of alternative suppliers. Market research should also provide projections of market share (proportion of demand to be captured by the project, i.e. sales projections) and penetration (rate of market acquisition).

A marketing strategy for approaching and attracting buyers or other types of potential consumers is part of project planning, geared toward potential consumers' willingness and ability to pay, but non-revenue public service projects also have to assure that the target population is ready and willing to consume the project's output.

Regardless of strategic purposes, in the final analysis, consumers are the focal point for all investment projects, whether responding to a business opportunity or providing a public service. Identifying the market and its characteristics, and how to promote and deliver the project output to potential consumers, are important, if not essential, aspects of a well-planned investment project, and vital for determining its features, e.g. scope, production program, technology and choice of location.

A more thorough discussion of these issues is included on our web site—Market Research and Marketing.

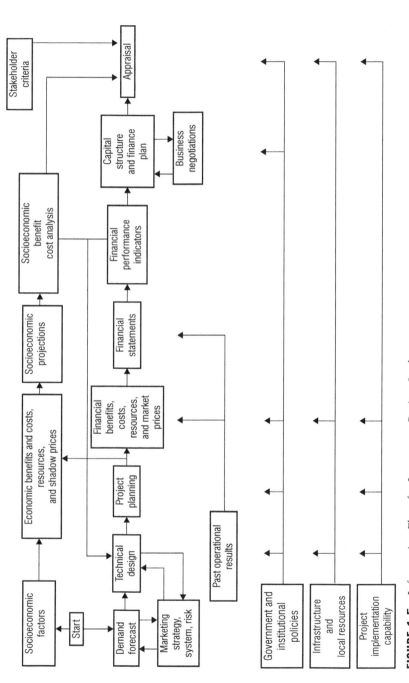

FIGURE 1.5 Information Flow for Investment Project Study
Source: Adapted from information flow diagram provided by Robert Youker.

The project plan is the foundation for financial analysis—estimates of revenues and costs and performance indicators. Formulation of the capital structure is an outgrowth of the identification of capital requirements and cost of capital, and is usually the subject of negotiations between financial institutions and venture partners.

For an existing enterprise, operating history is a useful backdrop for estimating the project's financial parameters and indicators and the implications of taking on the project for the organization (e.g., whether the project will strain the capacities of management or other resources). However, as a rule, extrapolation of historical operating data is not a reliable guide for predicting the future.

Characteristics of the external environment bear heavily on project formulation: Government and institutional policies have implications for engineering design (incentives related to location, technology choice); financial infrastructure determines, to a great extent, the project's capital structure (availability of equity, credit, subsidies, grants, tax policies, foreign direct investment policies); physical infrastructure capacities and policies influence design decisions (location, distribution channels); existing supply chains for local resources and their composition (quantities, qualities) affect production process and product design.

Analysis of economic, social, and environmental consequences parallels the development of market, technical, and financial analysis. Its purpose is to measure the impacts of the project on society, the economy, and the environment at the plant site, and to identify the need for accommodation and, in some cases, mitigation measures. Information is collected concerning elements of the wider domain (see Figure 1.1) and project activities that are linked economically or technologically. This information, combined with knowledge of resources to be generated and consumed, is the basis for some level of economic appraisal—anywhere from compatibility with the host operating environment for relatively small and environmentally benign projects to economic cost/benefit analysis (ECBA) with shadow (economic) pricing of inputs and outputs and measurements of other regional or national economic parameters and indicators (e.g., foreign exchange effect, shadow wage rate, efficiencies of resource applications) for projects with significant economic impacts (Chapter 5).

Overriding all of the information and analysis is the element of risk. Uncertainties and probabilities of occurrence related to markets, technical design, implementation, and financial and economic parameters are assessed quantitatively where possible, and qualitatively otherwise.

In the appraisal stage, characteristics and performance indicators are compared with stakeholder criteria, which have to be satisfied for key participants if the project is to go forward.

Conducting Studies

The expertise and composition of the team required to study and design the project depends on the complexity of the work to be done, employing specialists as required for investigations beyond the competencies of the team. The use of expert consultants can be expensive, but a wise investment if selected carefully on the basis of experience, ability, and need. Outside expertise, having no direct stake in the project, would be more objective in assessing project qualities than any of the potential stakeholders. An ounce of prevention is still worth a pound of cure.

A well-functioning design/study team under competent leadership, capable of coordinating disparate interests and viewpoints, is more likely to arrive at consistent, comprehensive, and logical conclusions concerning project viability.

The Project Design/Study Team   Members of the team are selected to cover major areas, depending on project features. Examples include:

- Project economics—commercial and economic viability and optimization (preferably covered by the team leader).
- Markets (market analyst or marketing expert).
- Process engineering and technology (a specialist in the related field).
- Construction engineering—industrial, mechanical, civil.
- Organizational economics and management (structure and personnel).
- Finance and accounting.
- Environmental impact assessment.
- Social and political analysis.

The team is complemented, as needed, with expertise provided by other specialists (e.g., specialty markets, science and engineering). For example, the inclusion of an ecologist and/or sociologist (anthropologist) might be justified for a large project with significant social impacts. The team leader's responsibility, beside a possible role as specialist, is to plan, organize, direct, and supervise all activities of the team until the design/study is completed.

Accuracy and Precision of Design   As the project progresses from conception through increasingly more refined stages of definition, the depth of analysis increases accordingly, with commensurate improvements in accuracy and precision of information and predicted results. Greater accuracy and precision implies greater cost. Rough approximations of the uncertainty or error to be expected in progressive stages of design development:

the combination of accuracy error (systematic error) and precision error (random error) is typically ±25 to 30 percent for an opportunity study based primarily on secondary information. For an in-depth study an error of ±10 percent might apply, a fairly tight level of uncertainty, which can be achieved only with reliable data sources. These error ranges apply most concretely to quantitative factors (e.g., size of the market, level of investment, cost of operations, return on investment), but qualitative aspects also contribute to error (e.g., uncertainties in personnel qualifications).

If errors are all on the same side (i.e., cumulative), the effect can be to produce a gross miscalculation of the anticipated performance of the project. However, errors generally tend to cancel one another, some on the high side and others on the low, so that the percentage can, in practice, be considered as applicable to each of the separate factors.[41]

However, these rough estimates of uncertainty are not a substitute for analysis of risk (probability of an undesirable outcome), which can be more accurately assessed with the more comprehensive approach related to uncertainties in specific parameters described in Chapter 7.

INVESTMENT PLANNING INFRASTRUCTURE

Assigning competent and qualified people to analyze and design the project is essential to successful investment. Availability of appropriately skilled designers and consultants in the host country is a function of the scope of industrialization, the quality of training and educational institutions, and the level of experience in the industry. For example, to assure international competitiveness, either a designer with experience in an export project, or consultants with appropriate competencies, are needed.

Savings in cost of implementation and more efficient operations usually justify expenditure on consulting fees in the preinvestment phase, and particularly if an ill-advised investment is avoided. A prudent approach is to develop the study in stages, with interim appraisals so that the high cost of a complete feasibility study is not wasted. Consultants can also pay their way by employing their expertise in negotiations with financiers and suppliers. With strong consultant services available to perform comprehensive and accurate investment studies, a good project can be approved on its merits, rather than relying on the creditworthiness of investors or on the collateral or other pledges to reduce lender risk.

Organizations and individuals either having direct experience or that have commissioned similar projects can be helpful in selecting qualified and competent consultants:

- *National and regional investment promotion agencies.* In many countries, government-sponsored development organizations (e.g., ministries, planning agencies) have primary responsibility for identifying and attracting investment projects. Ideas are documented in the form of project profiles or opportunity studies, and prospective sponsors or promoters are sought in-country and abroad. Some of these promotion agencies offer consulting services for preparing preinvestment studies and monitor projects during investment and operations phases.
- *National and regional finance organizations.* Development banks and some commercial banks offer consulting services for their clients. Although they consider investment projects as a rule from the point of view of creditworthiness of sponsors and collateral rather than performance characteristics developed through study, perceived risk reduction from employment of a competent and well-regarded consultant may be sufficient inducement for a commercial bank to support the project. It could also foster close cooperation between development and commercial banks, providing project sponsors access to the complementary services of each type of institution.[42]
- *National consultants.* In some developing countries, expansion and strengthening of consulting capacity has advanced through initiatives of regional and national authorities, which seek to stimulate economic growth by this means. The intervention usually targets development of management skills and technical expertise to foster an indigenous consulting capacity offering comprehensive services, thereby reducing the need for expatriate consultants. Government development agencies (e.g., ministry of industry and commerce) either support or provide consulting services in some countries. Universities also provide a consulting base, applying the skills of faculty in economics, business management, and engineering to form the nucleus of consulting services for local industries. Senior students are employed to carry out studies designed by faculty, receiving academic credits for their work and gaining professional experience.
- *International development organizations.* Organizations such as the Overseas Private Investment Corporation (OPIC) and other government-sponsored private investment promoters[43] either provide or finance consulting services for their clients: Food and Agriculture Organization (FAO), the International Labor Organization (ILO), the United Nations Industrial Development Organization (UNIDO), and the World Bank Group.
- *International consultants.* Availability, type of services, and qualifications of international consultants may be difficult to discern, a situation exacerbated by cultural factors and divergent views on the nature of

study required. For these reasons, clear and precise language and unambiguous conditions are essential in *terms of reference* (agreement to perform the study), to assure that the study addresses issues that are relevant to design and appraisal of the enterprise, provides supporting data and analysis, and proposes recommendations based upon the evidence. Especially close coordination between project sponsors and the international consultant in drafting the agreement provides a sound basis for determining consultancy fees and assurance that the study is consistent with project needs.

APPENDIX 1.1: ELEMENTS OF COMMERCIAL AND WIDER DOMAINS

Commercial Domain

Product

- Design features, technology.
- Substitutes.
- Packaging.

Markets

- Domestic and international.
- Structure, segments.
- Characteristics: cultural, social, economic.
- Purchasing power.
- Trends.

Prices

- Domestic and traded outputs and inputs.
- Market interventions (tariffs, quotas).
- Monopoly and monopsony (buyer's monopoly).

Competition

- Strengths and weaknesses.
- Production capacity.
- Market share.

Distribution Channels

- Structure.
- Price buildup.
- Strength.

Production

- Technology, automation, innovations in pipeline.
- Cost and trends.
- Materials.
- Raw materials, factory supplies, components, subsystems.
- Energy sources.
- Utilities (e.g., water, waste disposal, industrial gases).
- Recovery, reuse, recycling.

Infrastructure Services

- Communications.
- Transportation (vehicular, rail, air, marine).
- Water supply.
- Sanitation.

Finance

- Capital market for equity and credit.
- Short-term finance availability.
- Cost of capital.

Wider Domain

Socioeconomic

- General economic, macro-level conditions.
- GDP, national income, and growth rate.
- Personal income, disposable income.
- Economic cycles—frequency, intensity.
- Monetary and fiscal status and policies.
- Balance of payments and trade.
- Inflation.
- Foreign exchange rates, trends, interventions (e.g., currency controls).
- Employment.
- Investment policies and trends.
- Domestic and foreign investment.
- International trade—blocs, protection.
- Capital markets—domestic and international.

Culture and Society

- Social norms and mores.
- Kinship and family structure.

- Aesthetics.
- Value systems.

Social Goals and Objectives

- Work ethic.
- Thrift, spending, saving.
- Leisure-time behavior.
- Level of trust.
- Property rights.
- Attitude toward change.
- Social and religious organizations.

Political Status and Structure

- Form of government.
- Political leadership—structure and status.
- Political parties, orientation, membership.
- Legal framework, transparency, efficiency.
- Legislation and regulation of commerce and industry.
- Social legislation and labor laws.
- Status of labor unions.

Physical Infrastructure

- Roads, bridges, airports, seaports.
- Ecological.

Physical Environment

- Climatic conditions.
- Geology.
- Land features and sites.
- Land, air, and water qualities.

Natural and Other Resources

- Exploitable: location, type, quantity, quality.
- Other resources affected by the presence of the project.
- Cultural, historic, or scientifically significant sites.
- Flora and fauna, habitats.

APPENDIX 1.2: OUTLINE OF BUSINESS PLAN FOR A MANUFACTURING ENTERPRISE

Executive Summary

- Vision, mission, and goals.
- Key elements of project design for successful investment.
- Playing to strengths and overcoming weaknesses.
- Fending off threats and seizing opportunities.
- Summary of projected performance indicators.

Enterprise Description

- Sponsors.
- Organization—management team and key personnel.
- Production processes and technology.
- Investment plan—costs and schedule.

Products and Services

- Descriptions.
- Relation to rest of industry.

Market Analysis

- Segments and strategies.
- Demand.
- Competition, market share.

Strategy

- Basic strategic concept.
- Strengths and weaknesses vis-à-vis competition.
- Marketing strategy and sales forecast.

Management

- Key management personnel and responsibilities.

Financial Plan

- Basic assumptions and risk analysis.
- Capital structure, sources of finance.
- Pro-forma income, cash flow, balance sheet.
- Financial ratios, breakeven point.
- Projected financial indicators.

APPENDIX 1.3: OUTLINE OF DESIGN/ STUDY REPORT

Executive Summary

- Synopsis of the project for decision makers, with concise analysis of critical issues:
  - Project goals and strategy.
  - Scope.
  - Projected performance.
  - Analysis of critical risk factors.

Project Background and Concept

- History and sponsorship.
- Basic project (business) concept.
- Project and functional strategies.
- Role of the industry in the national economy.
- Market analysis and marketing concept.

Analysis of Market Research

- Description of product and/or services.
- Demand and growth rate forecasts, major determinants and indicators; reliability of market projections.
- Structure and characteristics of the market.
- Industry: growth rates, estimated future expansions, geographical dispersal, capacities and strengths/weaknesses of competitors, major problems and prospects, quality of products currently offered.
- Imports and trends, volume and prices.

Marketing Strategy, Sales Forecast, and Marketing Plan

- Description of the marketing concept, targets, and strategies for market segments.
- Location of markets and distribution issues.
- Competition—domestic and foreign.
- Sales program.
- Estimated annual sales revenues from products and by-products (domestic and foreign).
- Estimated annual costs of sales promotion and marketing (budget).
- Design of marketing organization and operating plan.
- Analysis of market risks.

Project Engineering

- Project scope (functions and activities).
- Engineering design (technology, process, plant):
  - Product analysis and specifications.
  - Technology description, rationale for selection (analysis of alternatives).
  - Technology acquisition and cost analysis, intellectual property.
  - Plant capacity (economy of scale).
  - Production program (products, by-products, wastes—including estimated annual cost of waste disposal).
  - Supplies program (sources, channels, reliability, cost)—domestic and imported material inputs and price trends: raw materials, processed industrial materials, components and subsystems, auxiliary materials, utilities (e.g., electricity, water, natural gas), factory supplies, spare parts, tools.
  - Plant design (analysis and layouts), including materials handling and storage.
  - Machinery, equipment and special tools—production, auxiliary, and service (quantities, specifications, installation details, costs).
  - Cost estimates for technology, machinery and equipment, installations.
  - Analysis of risks associated with technology, equipment selection, supplies, construction.

Organization, Human Resources, and Overhead Costs

- Enterprise structure (organization chart): functional divisions (e.g., management, production, sales, procurement, administration).
- Human resources requirements:
  - Classifications and skills, quantities, both domestic and expatriate.
  - Availability of human resources.
  - Estimated annual human resource costs, including wages and benefits, social services (e.g., housing, recreation, schools).
- Overhead costs
  - Cost or profit centers and identification of related cost elements.
- Analysis of organization and human resource risks.

Location, Site, and Environment

- Location analysis.
- Site selection.
- Site engineering:
  - Layout of civil engineering works, arrangement and description of buildings and construction features.

- Site preparation and development.
- Other site facilities (e.g., wells, substations, loading docks).
- Off-site construction and installations, special civil works.
- Identification of social and economic impacts.
- Environmental regulations and impact assessment (EIA).
- Cost estimates for site engineering works (domestic and foreign), environmental mitigation, social compatibility measures.
- Analysis of risks associated with location, site and environment, social impacts.

Implementation

- Construction project:
  - Planning.
  - Special studies.
  - Detailed design and engineering.
  - Project management and staff.
  - Implementation schedule.
  - Cost estimates for construction project (design, consultancies, studies, management).
  - Analysis of implementation risks.

Enterprise Formation

- Organization.
- Staffing.
- Legal procedures (e.g., charter, incorporation, licenses, registrations).

Investment

- Fixed assets.
- Preoperational expenditures.
- Initial and operational working capital requirements.

Project Finance

- Capital structure.
- Capital sources, disbursement schedule, domestic and foreign exchange.
- Cost of capital.

Financial Analysis

- Estimate of production cost and cost of goods sold.
- Financial statements (income, balance, cash flow).
- Financial indicators—static (payback period, ratios, breakeven).

- Financial indicators—dynamic (net present value, internal rate of return, dynamic payback).
- Financial criteria.
- Criteria versus indicators.
- Sensitivity and risk analysis—rates, inflation, exchange rates.

Economic Analysis (Economic, Social, and Ecological Impacts)

- Compatibility with host environment.
- Benefit/cost, value-added analysis:
  - Supplementary economic indicators (e.g., efficient use of scarce resources).
  - International competitiveness.
  - Foreign exchange effects.
  - Employment effects.
- Externalities (economic, social, ecological).
- Conformance with local, regional, and national objectives.
- Sensitivity and risk analysis.

Project Appraisal, Conclusions, and Recommendations

- Major strengths and weaknesses, opportunities and threats.
- Projected performance versus criteria.
- Recommendations (e.g., further study, risk alleviation, extension or contraction of scope, change in capital structure).

APPENDIX 1.4: INFORMATION FLOW DETAILS

See Figure 1.5 for a graphic depiction of the general flow of information.

Technical Design

- Product mix.
- Location, site.
- Size, scale, timing.
- Technology.
- Physical inputs.
- Physical outputs.
- Technical risk.

Socioeconomic Factors

- Economy and trends.
- Social milieu.

- Economic and technological linkages.
- Ecological setting.
- Shadow prices (regional or national parameters).

Economic Benefits and Costs: Resources and Shadow Prices

- Generated resources (products).
- Consumed resources (operations):
  - Land.
  - Labor.
  - Capital.
  - Foreign exchange.

Socioeconomic Benefit/Cost Analysis

- Economic internal rate of return, net present value, benefits/costs ratio.
- Foreign exchange impact.
- Efficiency of resource consumption.
- International competitiveness.
- Ecological benefits and costs.
- Socioeconomic sensitivity and risk.

Project Planning

- Strategies.
- Engineering.
- Procurement.
- Contracting.
- Construction.
- Start-up.
- Commercial (inventories, sales, etc.).
- Marketing.
- Organization and human resources.
- Training.

Financial Benefits/Costs, Resources, and Market Prices

- Sales revenues.
- Operating costs.
- Fixed assets.
- Working capital.
- Preproduction.
- Implementation project costs.

Financial Statements

- Income statements.
- Funds flow: sources, uses.
- Real and financial flows.
- Balance sheets.

Financial Performance Indicators

- Liquidity.
- Breakeven.
- Payback.
- Static indicators (rate of return, ratios).
- Dynamic indicators.
- Financial sensitivity and risk.

Capital Structure and Finance Plan

- Debt.
- Equity.
- Sources.
- Cost of capital.

Appraisal

- Strategies.
- Technical.
- Commercial.
- Managerial.
- Organizational.
- Financial.
- Economic
- Social.
- Ecological.
- Implementation plans.
- Risk assessment.

Past Operational Results

- Physical units.
- Financial statements.
- Financial analysis.

Infrastructure and Local Resources

- Institutional (private and public sectors).
- Internal.

Project Implementation Capability
- Planning.
- Scheduling.
- Construction and start-up.

NOTES

1. Two examples: Locally procured replacement nozzles for a grain processing plant were found to be inadequate because the alloy used in their fabrication could not bear the erosive effects of high-velocity flows; imports proved to be problematic because foreign exchange was not available. A plan to procure locally available coke for a steel plant was later undermined by unforeseen impurities that rendered the coke unsuitable for the process.
2. Aesthetics is now an aspect of the commercial domain, with investment potential, viz. landscape, cityscape, or other elements of cultural heritage, not to mention product design attractive to potential buyers.
3. No listing of this type can be complete; it should be considered as no more than a guide to possible issues to be addressed in designing the project. Some can be discarded out of hand as inapplicable for a given type of project. Others may gain in importance, as the project configuration is progressively refined.
4. In recent years, by Donella H. Meadows, Jorgen Randers, and Dennis L. Meadows, in their books *Limits to Growth: The 30-Year Update* (White River Junction, VT: Chelsea Green, 2004) and *Beyond the Limits* (1992).
5. After the end of the cold war, changes occurred in the world economy, characterized by the Washington Consensus, which essentially promoted standards for international trade and development. As a consequence of more liberal trade policies adopted by the industrialized countries, the significance of national borders is diminished, as capital and other production factors flow across them with more frequency and ease. Trade deficits are balanced with increased capital flows and, in the case of the United States, by external purchases of national debt. The structure of the labor force has changed dramatically, as outsourcing of services and manufacturing have given new impetus to emerging economies.
6. The Aral Sea, located in the Central Asian republics of Kazakhstan and Uzbekistan, was once the world's fourth largest lake, but is now only 30 percent of its original size. Excessive diversion of its feed waters for irrigation projects degraded the entire sea basin: It greatly reduced fish production, increased salinity and pollution, led to violent sandstorms, diminished fresh water supplies, and increased human health problems.
7. Recent economic developments indicate that corporate social responsibility, which includes environmental and ethical considerations, is positively correlated with corporate financial performance.
8. In the United States, courts have frequently overruled exclusions of the Comprehensive Environmental Response, Compensation and Liability Act of

1980 (CERCLA), which absolves property owners of liability if unaware of preexisting pollution. For example, Aviell Services was not allowed to recover unanticipated cleanup costs of a property it had purchased (see "Supreme Court Rules on Case Involving CERCLA Recovery Costs," *Pollution Engineering*, December 23, 2004, www.pollutionengineering.com/Articles/ Regulation_Update/f654f9afefd68010VgnVCM100000f932a8c0).

9. *Absorptive capacity* refers to productive use of investment funds, particularly in developing countries. Project implementation requires not only financial means but also competent contractors, capable of implementing the project on budget, on schedule, and to specified quality standards. A country lacking this capacity is less attractive for investment—one possible consequence is that the project would require foreign contractors, which would increase the investment and diminish the attractiveness of the project. An indicator of capacity deficiency is disparity among skills categories, with wages for scarce skills a multiple of those for nonscarce skills.

10. James Heintz, Robert Pollin, and Heidi Garrett-Peltier, "Infrastructure Investments and the U.S. Economy," http://www.infrastructureusa.org/wp-content/ uploads/2009/07/aam_investments.pdf.

11. Francisco Rodriguez, "Have Collapses in Infrastructure Spending led to Cross-Country Divergence in per Capita GDP?" background note for World Economic and Social Survey of the United Nations Department of Economic and Social Affairs, 2006, www.un.org/esa/policy/backgroundpapers/rodriguez_1.pdf.

12. See Jeff Rubin, *Why Your World Is About to Get a Whole Lot Smaller: Oil and the End of Globalization* (New York: Random House, 2009). Although the dire energy scenario depicted by Rubin is disputed by many analysts, depletion of easily mined fossil fuels will almost certainly raise the relative cost of energy, assuming it does not so adversely affect global economic activity that demand is significantly reduced.

13. Organisation for Economic Co-operation and Development, *The Knowledge-Based Economy* (Paris: OECD, 1996), www.oecd.org/dataoecd/51/8/ 1913021.pdf.

14. See Poirier (1999).

15. At least one analyst of global trade believes that the current system is unsustainable and that supply chains will become much shorter in the near future. See Rubin (2009).

16. From 1980 to 2009, global exports as measure in U.S. dollars increased by a factor of 6. See World Trade Organization (WTO) statistics database, http://stat .wto.org/Home/WSDBHome.aspx.

17. Just as an individual grows in intelligence, an enterprise can grow by doing things better, more intelligently, and using resources in more creative ways to produce more value-added. It is not necessary to utilize more resources to grow.

18. A strategic concept may appear cast in stone, with brick and mortar in place, but even then prudence demands that nothing remain sacrosanct if new information prescribes a change in direction.

19. An example of project and marketing strategies is provided in Cambria Yarns Project (see our web site).

20. For an existing enterprise, the basic project objective and strategy are coordinated with corporate objectives and strategies.

21. A number of models and systems have been developed to provide structure to the strategic planning process. Of greatest relevance to project planning are operations research, a discipline in which mathematical models are used to seek optimal decisions, applicable to some complex project design decisions (e.g., production, distribution, multicriteria optimization; analysis of political, economic, social, and technological (PEST) factors; brainstorming, which is a loosely structured group activity to promote creative thinking; scenario planning, meaning strategy derived from analysis of a limited number of scenarios concerning future developments and how they affect the project; force-field analysis, in which driving and restraining forces in the operating environment concerning cultural and economic factors are presented diagrammatically; and Kepner-Tregoe Matrix, a systematic approach to decision making, similar to SWOT analysis. Some models are more applicable to strategic dynamics of an operating enterprise: for example, real options theory is an approach to adapt management decisions to market developments.

22. Alternative processes for developing the strategy are primarily related to orientation or focus: concentration on issues arising from SWOT analysis; alignment of goals and organizational resources; organic development based on organizational culture, vision—in other words, doing what comes "naturally."

23. The term *evaluation* is distinguished from *appraisal:* evaluation is ex post, whereas appraisal refers to preinvestment assessment.

24. Evaluation by financial institutions such as the World Bank and its affiliates is intended to determine the effectiveness of the projects that they finance. It is normally conducted when the consequences of investment in the project have been sufficiently manifested. "The goals of evaluation are to learn from experience, to provide an objective basis for assessing the results of the Bank's work, and to provide accountability in the achievement of its objectives." (World Bank Group, Global Environment Facility, Monitoring and Evaluation, http://web.worldbank.org/.)

25. This is usually not true for development banks, whose mission is economic improvement. Their interest may continue beyond cancellation of debt, focused on evaluating their involvement in the project relative to their continuing efforts to stimulate economic progress.

26. Most of the characteristics of a business opportunity apply as well to a public-sector opportunity.

27. Cyclical industries generally provide durable products (that provide services for an extended period) for which demand varies according to the state of the economy. Examples are automobiles (products) and producer equipment maintenance (services).

28. These types of studies are conducted by a number of international finance organizations. As an example, see "Baseline Surveys and Sector Studies in Bangladesh's Engineering, Agribusiness, Textiles and Apparels Sectors," sponsored by the International Finance Corporation (IFC), Southeast Asia Enterprise Development Facility (SEDF): "To achieve higher growth IFC SEDF

intends to help the SMEs producing better quality products, attain more pro-
ductively, adhering to environmental and social compliance standards with
a better understanding of their markets." (www.dgmarket.com/tenders/np-
notice.do~3707369.)

29. This is the impetus for much foreign investment in Central and Eastern European
markets in the early twenty-first century.

30. The Logical Framework Approach (LFA), also called Objectives Oriented
Project Planning (OOPP), is a project design methodology that imposes a
logical discipline on the project design team. The idea is to devise a relatively
complete and workable project plan, so that implementation will proceed
without incurring delays and cost overruns. The technique employs the Logical
Framework document (*logframe*), a 4 by 4 matrix, each cell of which contains
text that describes the project's most important features. The logframe is intended to identify deficiencies in the project design. See *The Logical Framework
Approach, Handbook for Objectives-Oriented Planning*, 4th ed. (Oslo:
NORAD, 1999); or see *AusGUIDEline: The Logical Framework Approach*
(Australian Agency for International Development, June 2003), http://portals
.wi.wur.nl/files/docs/ppme/ausguidelines-logical%20framework%20approach.
pdf.

31. The nuclear power plant at Stade, Germany, was commissioned in 1972 and
shut down in 2003. A decommissioning project was undertaken that includes
completing dismantling of all facilities by 2015. The reason for the shutdown
was economic, as the plant produced only 630 megawatts, about half the capacity of most of Germany's other power plants, and also was subject to a state
levy on cooling water from the Elbe River. Decommissioning costs are in the
order of €660 million, considerably higher than initially anticipated. Had the
full amount of decommissioning costs been taken into account, it is likely that
the plant would have been considered commercially unviable at the time of
the initial investment. The high decommissioning costs would most likely have
resulted in unacceptable, or at least ambiguous (e.g., more than one IRR—see
Chapter 3), financial performance indicators.

32. The *efficient* (optimal) economic life minimizes long-run average costs of production. It is easier to estimate for smaller projects.

33. For example, see Robert L. Mansell and Robert W. Wright, "A Neoclassical
Model Evaluating Large-Scale Investment Impacts on the Regional Economy,"
Growth and Change 9 (1) (January 30, 1978): 23–30 First published online by
John Wiley & Sons, July 3, 2006. (http://onlinelibrary.wiley.com/doi/10.1111/
j.1468-2257.1978.tb00356.x/full.)

34. After a steel plant commenced operation it was discovered that plentiful domestically available coke contained impurities that were incompatible with the
quality specifications for the product for which the factory was built. A plant
was constructed to produce nonfoaming detergent soap for the local market,
neglecting the local preference for natural soaps with high foaming action. A
plant for producing high-quality wooden spindles faltered because it did not
have a sufficient source of convertible currency to purchase the necessary spare
parts.

35. As a rule of thumb, the range of effort required, from the opportunity stage to a comprehensive study, is from 2 to 3 person-months to 12 to 15 person-months, applicable for most medium-scale industrial investment projects.
36. The relationship between feasibility and optimality is further described in Chapter 5 in the section titled "Economic Pricing Principles."
37. The dilemma is expounded upon in D. L. Weimer and A. R. Vining, *Policy Analysis: Concepts and Practice*, 3rd ed. (Saddle River, N.J.: Prentice Hall, 1997), after A. O. Hirschman: voice (criticize), exit (decline), disloyalty (sabotage). The last option is not considered in the text!
38. See the section on SWOT analysis in Chapter 8.
39. Required by some international financial institutions as a condition for financing.
40. Equipment procurement—invitations for bids, evaluation, contracting, and delivery—is a critical factor for large investments, in which the structure and economics of the project depend heavily on the type of equipment, related production cost, and price.
41. The theoretical justification for this assertion is explained in Malinvaud, E., "First Order Certainty Equivalent," *Econometrica* 37 (4) (1969).
42. In some cases commercial banks co-finance projects in cooperation with development finance institutions.
43. See Directory of Development Organizations, http://www.devdir.org/.

REFERENCES

Malinvaud, E. 1969. First order certainty equivalent. *Econometrica* 37 (4) (October 1969): 706–718, http://www.jstor.org/stable/1910445.

Meadows, Donella H., Jorgen Randers, and Dennis L. Meadows. 2004. *Limits to growth: The 30-year update.* White River Junction, VT: Chelsea Green.

———. 1992. *Beyond the limits.* White River Junction, VT: Chelsea Green.

Norwegian Agency for Development Corporation. 1999. *The logical framework approach: Handbook for objectives-oriented planning,* 4th ed. Oslo: NORAD.

Poirier, Charles C., and Stephen E. Reiter. 1996. *Supply chain optimization: Building the strongest total business network,* 1st ed. San Francisco: Berrett-Koehler.

Rubin, Jeff. 2009. *Why your world is about to get a whole lot smaller: Oil and the end of globalization.* New York: Random House.

Shaw, David, Peter Roberts, and James Walsh, ed. 2000. *Regional planning and development in Europe.* Surrey, England: Ashgate.

Weimer, D. L., and A. R. Vining. 1997. *Policy analysis: Concepts and practice,* 3rd ed. Saddle River, NJ: Prentice Hall.

Preparing Pro-Forma
Financial Statements

Financial information derived from a preinvestment study is usually the primary basis for deciding whether to proceed with investment in the project: amounts and timing of capital required, sufficiency of available financial resources, revenues to be generated and costs incurred, risk-adjusted return on investment, and other financial indicators.[1] Although applicable analytical methods vary from one operational setting to another, the approaches described herein are intended to provide a comprehensive and adaptable analytical framework, but, perhaps more important, to highlight issues and viewpoints that are essential to properly assess the project, either as a commercial venture or, for public-sector projects, as a contributor to public welfare. For nonrevenue public-service projects, investment and operating costs are the basis for developing useful indicators, such as cost per unit of service rendered.

Assessment of the project as a commercial venture or as a provider of public goods and services is facilitated by preparation of a series of pro-forma financial statements derived from project design features. Capital and operations flows of resources and funds are organized into statements of projected income, cash flow, and balance of assets and liabilities, from which indicators of performance are derived to be compared with stakeholder criteria.

In virtually any investment environment, financial viability has to be maintained throughout the project life. While it has become quite common for enterprises that are considered "too big to fail" to be rescued with infusions of capital from public sources, this safety net is usually not available to smaller enterprises whose demise would not be perceived as producing so great an adverse affect on the host economy.[2] For these reasons, prospects for a successful venture by project sponsors and satisfaction of investment criteria are enhanced with close attention to financial analysis and assiduous monitoring of the market and engineering design information upon which it is predicated.[3]

Market, sales forecast, and engineering studies provide information related to plant capacity, revenues to be generated, and investment and operating costs—that is, estimates of quantities, values, and timing of resources (tangible and intangible) to be consumed and generated by the enterprise during construction, operations, and possible decommissioning phases. This information is used to prepare pro-forma financial statements, from which performance indicators are extracted. Market values of inputs and outputs (goods and services) are expressed in a common monetary denominator (currency). Indicators are compared with criteria of investors and other stakeholders. The analysis also provides a foundation for viewing the project in a broader public-interest context, as the flow of resources priced at market serves as a point of demarcation for economic and social valuation.

Because it is so thoroughly linked to other decisions, financial analysis is best commenced at the conceptual stage, helping to assess financial consequences of alternative configurations and strategies in the process of shaping and defining the project design until its final configuration has been decided. The likelihood of reaching meaningful and accurate financial conclusions is enhanced through a continuous flow of information between project personnel and other specialists (e.g., consultants and other investigators) at all stages of the design process.

Recognizing country-specific accounting practices, enterprise law, and tax codes as necessary background for the analysis is conducive to developing financial information compatible with the operating environment and comprehensible to decision makers. Normally, standards of the host country would be followed, but those of the country of a major foreign investor may be more appropriate. In any case, the standards to be applied should be identified and justified. This information is particularly relevant for multinational projects.

Major issues relate to the project configuration: Does the project create a new enterprise or is it an expansion of an existing operation? What are the contributions and special interests of joint venture partners? Is the amount of debt financing within the capacities of accessible individuals and institutions? Do sponsors have to seek equity capital from outside sources?

Financial gain (and avoidance of loss) is a common goal for investors and other stakeholders, although their expectations and methods of valuing benefits, costs, and associated risks may differ considerably. Investors and sponsors aspire to financial and economic gain, against the risk of capital loss: The promise of full recovery of the initial investment within an acceptable time frame is generally viewed favorably as minimizing risk. Bankers want to be assured that their loans will be adequately serviced, recovering principal and receiving interest payments and other charges; guarantors and insurers, that they will not have to compensate for nonperformance and default; licensors and regulators, that commitment of resources is justified in regard to public goals.

Major financial issues can be summarized as follows:

- Availability of capital (funds and resources) to cover fixed investment, preoperational expenditures, and working capital: Does the plan maintain liquidity throughout the project to the planning horizon?
- Appropriateness of the proposed capital structure and debt service plan: Are criteria of investors and lenders satisfied? Are funds available in required currencies to cover financial obligations over the life of the project?
- Projected financial performance indicators (periodic and cumulative, static and dynamic) that satisfy stakeholder criteria within acceptable levels of risk.

Postinvestment deviations from underlying design assumptions arise from unforeseen changes in the internal and external environments (e.g., design changes; unanticipated inflation and price escalations; changes in competition, supplies, markets, consumers, public policies) or from forecasting errors. Another type of risk is associated with the expected range of operational parameter values[4] on which forecasted financial indicators are based. Criteria can also be risk-adjusted, with stakeholders modifying their benchmarks according to the uncertainties involved; rather than accept a rate of return to be expected in a fairly stable economic environment, investors may raise the barrier by adding a premium to their expectation of return if warranted by the level of risk. Double-counting risk—applying adjustments to both indicators *and* criteria—may unnecessarily raise the barrier (see Chapter 7).

In this chapter and the next, two cases explain the process of financial analysis for a new investment and for modernization and expansion of an existing enterprise. Background for the new investment is provided on our web site (in the Cambria Yarns Project) and in the other aspects of analysis explained in the text (usually the case name is abbreviated as CYP). The modernization/expansion case is also completely described on our web site (the Victoria Coke Project).

ACCOUNTING SYSTEM

The quality of financial analysis and investment appraisal depends basically on reliability of information processed and on the soundness of the approach. Although accounting systems differ among countries, basic accounting principles are universal, involving revenues and expenditures and related flows of goods and services, cash flow, and balance of assets and liabilities. Consistency is essential (e.g., a cross-check between cash flow and balance sheet should reveal no discrepancy). Developing pro-forma statements and performance indicators requires systematic processing of data on investment and operations. Accounting systems serving various management purposes can be employed to a large extent but need some modification for application to project analysis.

Cost accounting in an operating enterprise is based upon *standards*, the values of resources normally consumed in producing a unit of output, which can serve as a measure of efficiency of the production process when compared with actual costs.[5] Production cost estimates for the project can be based upon standard costs if reliable information is available from secondary sources.

Although competition usually dictates sales pricing decisions, in some cases (e.g., public services or noncompetitive commerce) they can be predicated upon standard costs and their relationship to sales volume. Budgeted operating cost, as a function of planned capacity in each period, can similarly be estimated from standard costs, from which profit estimates are derived.

Classification facilitates identifying revenue and cost items for cash planning and budgeting. Revenues are estimates from the market and sales program; capital investment from plans for procurement of machinery and equipment, site development, construction, and project implementation; and operating costs from production process information and human resources requirements. Another level of classification separates operating departments, such as administration, marketing, sales, production, warehousing, and the like. Cost and profit centers can be utilized for organizing information, particularly for a project undertaken by an existing enterprise—the analysis can be set up to reflect the impact of undertaking the project by an autonomous division as a profit center. Allocation of indirect costs would have to be compared for enterprise operating units or divisions with and without project implementation.[6] Cost and profit centers are also useful for a fairly large and complex start-up project.

The method of accounting employed herein is designed to be essentially consistent with standard accounting practice for an operating enterprise and to conform as closely as practicable to international accounting standards. Modifications that are necessary in the context of investment project analysis and appraisal are applied consistently throughout.

In the accounting system of an ongoing enterprise, *production cost* ordinarily includes all expenditures for factors of production, whether or not they are applied to products sold (*product* is hereafter used throughout in lieu of goods and services), including those factors that affect product and material inventories. However, in the *planning process*, product inventory levels are estimated from an *assumed relationship of production and sales*; material inventories are estimated on the basis of the resulting production program. For this reason, in the methods described, a change (increase) in material inventory is added to *factory cost* (based upon total production, including units produced for inventory) to determine *production* cost (in an operating enterprise the increase would be deducted from production cost to determine factory cost). Production cost, in turn, is adjusted for both product and material inventories to determine *cost of product sold*. This classification is of particular importance for investment in existing enterprises and for start-up periods, when working capital has to be increased. In later periods production and sales volumes would ordinarily be essentially identical.

The relationship between production cost (PC), factory cost (FC), and cost of product sold (COPS), and material consumption and inventory is shown in Figure 2.1. Production cost includes cost of finished product (FP) sold in the period, plus changes in FP, work in progress (WIP), and material inventories. FC includes everything produced in the period, for sale or inventory. Cost of products sold is the cost only for products that are *sold* in the period, from production and possibly from inventory. Materials procured during the period flow into COPS and into changes in material inventories.

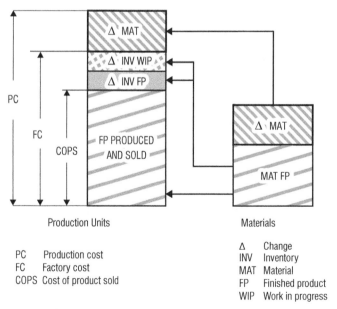

FIGURE 2.1   Relation of Production Costs (PC), Factory Costs (FC), and Cost of Products Sold (COPS)

Cost of products sold is FC adjusted for change in *product inventory*; if the change is positive, as shown in the figure, i.e. inventory increased (decreased), then COPS is less than (greater than) FC. Factory cost is PC adjusted for change in *material inventories*; if the change is positive, i.e. material inventory increases (decreases), then FC is less than (greater than) PC. Cost of products sold can also be calculated as PC adjusted for changes in product and material inventories, as shown later in Table 2.14.

In Figure 2.1, all inventory changes are shown as positive values; increases (decreases) tend to reduce (increase) FC relative to PC and COPS relative to FC. For example, if the change in FP (ΔINV FP) is negative (i.e., a decrease), COPS will tend to be greater than FC (depending on the change in WIP, ΔINV WIP). In other words, if some sales are drawn from inventory, COPS will tend to commensurately increase relative to FC.

Production cost is FC adjusted for change in material inventory; if the change is positive (increase in material inventory), PC is greater than FC; conversely, if some FC materials are drawn from inventory (a decrease), FC is greater than PC.

The relationship between the components of production cost, operating cost, factory cost, and cost of product sold is further explained in Figure 2.2. Production cost includes materials, labor, factory overhead, and

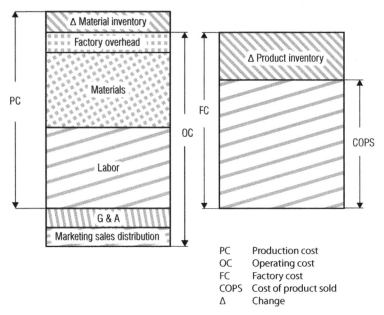

PC	Production cost
OC	Operating cost
FC	Factory cost
COPS	Cost of product sold
Δ	Change

FIGURE 2.2 Components of Cost

depreciation[7] of assets used in production of output for the period, including products for inventory and change in material inventories. Operating cost is FC plus general costs and administration (G&A) plus marketing, sales, and distribution costs.[8]

Why is it important to take into account these relationships? The buildup of inventories, which typically occurs in the early project stages, will usually materially affect the flow of funds, with a significant bearing on the project's financial aspects.

PROCESS OF FINANCIAL ANALYSIS

The project is simulated in all its phases to derive estimates of financial performance. Indicators are generated for comparison with criteria of decision makers regarding whether to accept, reject, or modify the proposed design. Part of the process involves progressive validation of the set of assumptions developed during the project's early formulation. Secondary data may need to be updated either by seeking alternative sources for verification or, in some cases, by using primary information from actual tender offers (capital equipment costs), market tests or surveys (demand and sales prices), or pilot simulations (production costs).

Figure 2.3 illustrates the general flow for financial analysis of the project. Although it appears in the diagram as a linear process, it is anything but linear. An important feature is the iterative nature of the process, whereby interim financial results feed back to impact the project design (e.g., market selection, physical plant). As information is gathered and refined, inevitably prior stages have to be revisited and revised. Ultimately all the following pieces of the puzzle have to fit into a configuration that delivers the product and satisfies criteria:

- *Revenues, operating costs*. Estimates of operating outputs and the revenue stream derive from market analysis, market penetration, sales projections, and cash/credit proportions; operating costs from estimated consumption of materials, labor, and supplies.
- *Investment*. Capital inflows follow from the engineering design—commitments for technology, plant, and machinery; construction and start-up costs; spares; human resources; and other capital inputs. The total investment package, consisting of fixed assets, preoperational expenditures (planning, start-up, and commissioning), and working capital margin[9] are covered with available capital—equity and debt, physical assets, and other in-kind contributions.

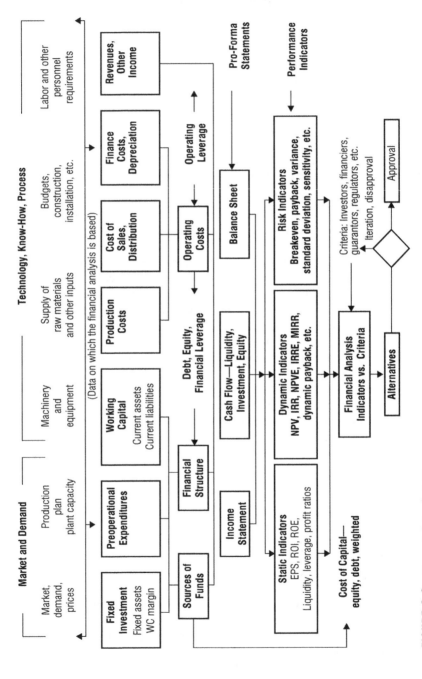

FIGURE 2.3 Financial Analysis Process

- *Capital structure.* Sources of finance to cover the total investment package are structured in accordance with agreements among investors, lenders, and other interested parties; proportions of equity and debt; distribution of ownership among partners; and shareholder classifications. A primary issue for lenders is *leverage*, the ratio of debt to equity, which is directly linked to risk for both lender and borrower (the project).
- *Operations.* Estimates of production costs, financing costs, and depreciation of assets are combined with sales to determine projected revenues and expenditures for all operating periods to the planning horizon. Operating leverage[10] is derived as a measure of how sales margin is translated into profit.
- *Financial statements.* Capital requirements and operating estimates (values of project inputs and outputs) are combined to develop a series of financial statements—income, cash flow, balance sheet—that describe the expected financial condition for each period to the planning horizon (see the "Financial Statements" section).
- *Financial performance indicators.* Static (usually for one period) and dynamic (for the project life, or to the planning horizon if different) indicators of performance are derived from one or more financial statements. They are expressed numerically as ratios, percentages, or another quantitative measure—for example, rates of return, leverage,[11] and turnover (rotations per period).
- *Risk assessment* weighs the likelihood of an undesirable outcome. Some indicators deal with risk inherently (e.g., breakeven). Quantitative assessment of risk associated with some indicators is determined by applying anticipated variations to underlying variables.
- *Cost of capital.* Once the capital structure is defined, the cost of capital is ascertained for each individual source of equity and debt. The cost of capital is either the return on capital in its most favorable alternative use (opportunity cost) or the actual cost of capital that is to be applied to the project. The weighted average cost of capital (see the "Cost of Capital" section in Chapter 4) serves as a benchmark for financial performance.
- *Criteria.* Stakeholders' quantitative criteria (benchmarks) are a guide to performance indicators to be determined, supplemented by special concerns surrounding critical design areas. Criteria are to some extent independent of financial analysis, generally based upon alternative uses of the investors' capital or on the aspirations of other interested parties. However, interpretation or adjustments may be necessary, such as in an inflationary environment where market rates may not reflect the actual cost of capital, or where criteria are adjusted to reflect the level of risk tolerance of the investor or other participant.[12] During the study stage, stakeholders' criteria weightings provide some indication of how resources should be applied to the study of project features.

- *Alternatives.* Consideration of alternative configurations is a means of optimizing project design. The project can also be considered in relation to alternative investments. When capital is scarce, a rationing process based upon benefits generated per unit of capital investment helps to determine which alternative appears most favorable from the financial (commercial) point of view.[13]
- *Financial appraisal—indicators versus criteria.*[14] Projected performance indicators are compared with criteria of stakeholders. If indicators equal or exceed criteria, the project is acceptable as a candidate for investment from the financial point of view.
- *Investment decision (approval, rejection).* Comparison of financial indicators with criteria is usually a major, but not the sole, element of the appraisal and decision process. Investor preferences, subjective evaluation, and socioeconomic and ecological impacts are other possible factors. If the project is approved, further development and planning are undertaken; if disapproved, the concept is discarded, or revisited and perhaps revised to make it more attractive. The project may be shelved rather than eliminated from further consideration as future external and internal developments alter its appeal as an investment opportunity.

FINANCIAL COSTS AND BENEFITS

During planning and construction phases, the project mobilizes financial capital to cover the cost of fixed and current assets, which are employed to generate benefits accruing to investors during the operations phase. The *net financial benefit* in each operating period is the difference between financial inflows (revenues, capital inflows, and other income) and outflows (operating expenditures, capital outflows, debt service, taxes).[15] Equity investors and lenders expect to recover their initial investments plus a return at least equal to or exceeding their respective hurdle[16] rates (capital recovery plus its rental cost). Theoretically, the enterprise created by the project should remain in operation so long as marginal benefits are higher than marginal costs,[17] although the planning horizon may be limited by stakeholder preferences.

Estimates of Financial Flows

Financial indicators are based on estimates of quantities and prices, or values, of inflows and outflows. Capital inflows include equity and debt and, for some projects, grants and subsidies. Some inflows that are counted in the analysis may be in forms other than money (e.g., know-how, goodwill, or in-kind contributions of assets such as land, equipment, and machinery); other inflows are revenues from product sales, earnings on possible project investments, and recovery of residual values (actual or simulated) of fixed and current assets at the planning horizon. Outflows consist of investments in fixed and current assets; other capital expenditures during planning, construction, and start-up; debt service; expenditures for production factors (goods and services) during the operations phase; taxes; and clearing any residual liabilities at the planning horizon.

Pricing Project Inputs and Outputs   Prices are used to express values of physical and intangible inputs and outputs, in terms of a common-value denominator—usually an accounting currency (local, foreign exchange):

- *Market prices* are determined by supply and demand relationships or by government control in some instances. For purposes of financial analysis, the actual price or cost is applied, taking into account delivery charges, tariffs, taxes, subsidies, and the like.
- *Absolute prices* reflect value in terms of a particular number of currency units, while *relative prices* express the value of one product compared with another. If the absolute price of one ton of coal is 100 monetary units and an equivalent quantity of oil has a price of 300 monetary units, the relative price of coal in terms of oil is 0.33, or, conversely, the relative price of oil is three times the price of coal.[18] Inflation or productivity changes may alter the level of absolute prices over the project life but do not necessarily imply changes in relative prices; the relationship between prices of two items may (and often does) remain unchanged despite variations in absolute prices.
- Values of inputs and outputs may be expressed in *constant* or *current* prices. Constant prices are those prevailing at the time of the analysis and assumed to last over the project's life. Some items are expected to escalate in price (rise or fall in relation to general price trends) during the project life, even when a constant pricing system is employed. In such a case, adjustments for escalations (expected change in relative price) in a limited number of items (e.g., main cost and revenue items) may be necessary. Current prices take into account general inflationary effects and are the nominal prices that are expected to prevail during each project period.

  Should financial analysis be performed at constant or current prices?[19] If there is little or no inflation, or if general inflation affects all inputs and outputs essentially in the same way so that relative prices remain unchanged, the analysis is best performed at constant prices. Current prices are important if inflation creates financing or other liquidity issues, if rates of inflation vary among project elements (see Chapter 3), or if there is significant exposure to a controlled currency market.

Differential inflation in local and foreign currencies affects relative prices of imports and corresponding domestic products. Working capital requirements are affected by inflation and escalation, particularly during production buildup to full capacity. Sales forecasts are affected by inflationary price changes. In hyperinflationary environments, performing the analysis using a stable currency is one solution. Periodic revaluation of fixed and current assets, if mandated by tax authorities, has to be included in the analysis to properly account for depreciation (and taxes). Because inflation is impossible to foresee for longer periods, most projects are analyzed in constant prices, as general inflation would have, ceteris paribus, a positive effect on nominal profitability (see Chapter 3 section "Inflation and Dynamic Criteria" and Figure 3.6).

▪ *Domestic prices* are applied to items procured in local markets and *foreign prices* (import or export) are used for traded items. Computations are performed by converting flows in all applicable currencies to any single *accounting currency*. Exchange rates for currencies used to designate values of items other than the accounting currency must be determined; if expected to vary over time, the problem is to predict the course of future exchange rate movements (see Chapter 5, the subsection titled "Shadow Price of Foreign Exchange"). Exchange rates can be estimated as the average expected to prevail over the project life, or by period if significant variations are expected (e.g., precipitate market correction for an overvalued currency). A factor of importance is the manner of performing financial analysis: If at constant prices, which is the most common practice, the exchange rate may usually be held constant if no relative inflation is anticipated between the accounting currency and foreign currency. Markets (eventually) generally adjust exchange rates to relative inflation between two currencies, so if the accounting (say, domestic) currency inflates relative to the foreign currency, at constant prices the escalation can be estimated (approximately) at the differential inflation rate. However, if there are other significant stresses in currency markets, other factors come into play concerning exchange rates, which may have to be taken into account.[20]

Inflows

For cash planning purposes (see the later subsection "Income Statement and Cash Flow Plan"), financial inflows consist of the revenue stream from sales of goods and services, equity contributions of investors, takedown of loan principal, and credits from suppliers. Values of in-kind contributions of assets also have to be counted, as they represent part of the capital dedicated to the project. Grants and subsidies are other possible inflows. The proportions of equity and debt are determined as part of the capital structure analysis.

The revenue stream is estimated from the sales program derived from market analysis (quantities and prices) and rate of expected market penetration. Other possible inflows are from investments that are considered within the scope of the project.

Outflows

Outflows consist of investment costs for fixed assets; preoperational expenditures; working capital (investment in current assets less short-term credits); operating expenditures for production, administration, marketing, distribution, and other planned operating divisions; and taxes. Servicing debt includes principal payments, interest charges, and other fees. Dividend payments are considered for liquidity purposes but *in general* are not relevant to rates of return (see Chapter 3, the section titled "Dynamic Indicators").

INVESTMENT COSTS

The *initial investment package* represents the value of assets initially committed to the project: Procurement of these assets generally involves cash outlays. *In-kind* assets (e.g., physical assets or intellectual property) might be considered as part of the investment package, but their value has to be determined according to some standard—in most cases not the original cost but rather replacement cost, liquidation value, or productivity in their best alternative uses. Differences between original (book value) and actual market value of assets at the time of project implementation (if lower) can be considered sunk (unrecoverable) costs. In some cases such in-kind assets would be entirely sunk costs if their productivity essentially depends upon implementation of the project (i.e., the opportunity cost is essentially nil).

The initial investment represents the total value of resources that must be committed when assets are mobilized to implement the project. During the operations stage, the value of investment will usually be affected by deterioration, obsolescence, or supply and demand factors (usually accounted through depreciation); it may change as a result of additional investments, financed either from commitments of new capital or from surplus generated by operations. Investment may be required for replacement of assets during the project life and also for decommissioning the plant at termination of the project. Costs of fixed assets and preoperational expenditures valued in the currency of origin have to be converted to a single accounting currency (see the earlier subsection "Pricing Project Inputs and Outputs").

Fixed Assets

Fixed assets are capital items committed to the project that are intended to remain in use over an extended period, usually for more than one year, and up to the shorter of the duration of the project or their economic life. Quantities are affected by downtime and production efficiency. The cost of fixed assets is generally covered with long-term sources of finance. Cost estimates cover procurement and delivery of the asset to the site (e.g., purchase price, packing, transport, taxes and duties, insurance). Technological usefulness of fixed assets is usually finite as they are depleted (i.e., "consumed") by wear and tear, obsolescence, and other factors. The value that they consequently lose over the life of the project represents a cost to the project (depreciation). Some of these assets may have to be replaced during the project life. Tangible and intangible fixed assets are differentiated to ensure that all fixed asset costs are included in the investment estimate and because rules for accounting for their costs (allowable methods of depreciation and/or amortization) differ in most countries.

Tangible (physical) assets include:

- *Land*. Most investment projects require acquisition of land for buildings and other facilities. Land is the only kind of fixed asset that is not consumed, except for mining and some types of agricultural projects where land may be deteriorated from operations. Depreciation of land is generally not allowed, but some countries permit depletion allowances for mining and other extraction processes.
- *Site preparation and development*. Normally investment involves preparation and development of the plant site (e.g., clearing, leveling, drainage, paving, and utilities such as water, gas, and electricity), rail spurs, roadways and other paved areas, and security facilities. Additional costs may be associated with acquisition of rights of way or easements from owners of adjacent properties or from planning authorities (public lands).
- *Buildings*. The project usually needs buildings to house manufacturing, stores, administration, and other enterprise functions; cost includes foundations, construction, and installation of services (electricity, plumbing, natural gas, air conditioning).

- *Plant machinery and equipment.* Production requires investment in machinery and equipment, usually a large proportion of the fixed assets committed to the project.
- *Installations.* Investment usually requires installation of machinery and equipment in the plant and other project facilities. Installation costs include moving and attaching to the foundation, electrical wiring, water and gas piping, and antipollution devices (e.g., filters, cyclones, hoods).
- *Other fixed assets.* Ancillary equipment, materials handling facilities, special tools, vehicles, and refrigerating and air-conditioning equipment are part of the fixed investment package.

Intangible Assets

Nonphysical assets are embedded in the design of other assets—for example, lump-sum payments for know-how or other proprietary knowledge, a license to use a patented machine or process, or payments for other intellectual property (e.g., copyrights, brand names). Service fees and other payments to owners for use or transfer of intellectual property, technical know-how, or other proprietary knowledge; access to technology (lump-sum payments or royalties); or use of trade or brand identification are considered either capital or operating expenditures depending on accounting standards in the host country. Payments linked to sales volume are usually operating expenditures, while one-time payments are treated as capital and amortized.

Depreciation

Depreciation amortizes the value of investment in assets over their economic life, justified by consumption of capital assets as they deteriorate from wear and tear or become obsolete during their employment in production. In most countries, tax authorities specify rates and methods of depreciation for various classes of assets. The amount allowed as an expense against revenue is normally intended to compensate for diminishing value as the capital asset is depleted. Depreciation is treated as expense.

Although depreciation does not involve cash flow directly, it does have an indirect effect, normally tax-deductible (in most countries) and reflected accordingly in the income statement to account for the portion of capital consumed during a period. The primary impact of depreciation as an expense item is tax savings.

Tax authorities may set depreciation rates according to estimated economic life of a class of assets (generally speaking, the point at which maintenance and repair costs are expected to become excessive in relation to output). Rates are sometimes set to encourage capital investment. For this reason, and the general inapplicability of the rate for an entire class of assets, technological life may be different from economic life prescribed by tax authorities, which may not be related to the actual depletion of the asset; when fully depreciated in economic terms, an asset can still be technologically useful.

When accelerated depreciation is permitted (depreciation charged at a rate greater than the asset's normal depletion), after-tax cash flow is *increased* (with *lower* profit and, consequently, lower taxes). It may be necessary to adjust the income statements with more realistic depreciation for a better estimate of profitability (however, the improvement in cash flow is the more significant impact).

To promote investment in capital goods, some countries insist on setting up reserves for depreciation, to be used to acquire a replacement when the capital item is at the end of its economic or technological life, in which case two types of depreciation accounts are maintained for the project—one for the expense and another for the reserve (shareholders' equity account). Setting up a reserve for depreciation presents a constraint on payment of dividends. In some countries the reserve is mandatory and tied to the allowable depreciation or some multiple thereof.

The principal depreciation methods are (1) straight-line to zero, (2) straight-line to salvage value, (3) declining balance, and (4) sum of the years' digits. Some other methods, with rates usually set by tax authorities, are depreciation fund, depletion per unit, and machine-hour rate. The choice of depreciation method is usually not within the discretion of the project, but when a choice is permitted, faster rates are generally advantageous, considering the beneficial effects on cash flow if there are profits to be offset. In some cases the enterprise is given a choice, but once selected the method usually has to be followed until the end of the asset's economic life.[21] The depreciation fund method is a sinking fund approach whereby an annual amount for a number of years (the economic life) is calculated at a specified rate of return so that the terminal amount matches the needed reinvestment in the asset. The depletion-per-unit method applies an estimate of the decrease in value of the asset per unit of production. The machine-hour rate method is a similar approach in which the asset is depleted for each hour of use based upon its expected life.

A comparison of straight-line-to-zero (SL), double declining balance (DDB), and sum-of-years'-digits methods (SYD) is shown in Figure 2.4. The book value (BV) for SYD is higher than DDB for the early periods (DDB has higher accumulated depreciation) but in general provides greater acceleration over most of the depreciation period. DDB provides greater acceleration than SL for all periods.

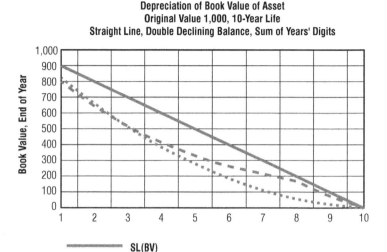

FIGURE 2.4 Comparison of Depreciation Methods

Residual Value of Assets

At the planning horizon, initial assets and those added as replacements or additions during the project life will have been depreciated so that the book value (original value less accumulated depreciation) will be less than the original value[22] and nonnegative (assets should not be depreciated to a book value below zero).

For purposes of analysis, residual values of assets at the planning horizon or at the time the asset is sold or otherwise taken out of service have to be taken into account as inflow for the project either at book or liquidation value, cost, or other appropriate basis. These residuals are part of the terminal value for the project, which has important financial implications. Even if assets are not actually liquidated, liquidation is simulated at the planning horizon as cash inflow (available to shareholders). Similarly, the liquidation value of working capital (current assets net of current liabilities) is treated as cash inflow at the planning horizon, even if operation is to be continued beyond that point in time (there may have to be adjustments if values of these short-term assets and liabilities are expected to differ from their nominal values at the planning horizon). If an asset is expected to be liquidated above book value, the gain is usually treated as taxable income;

liquidation below book value constitutes a loss. Other outstanding liabilities are similarly cleared at the planning horizon.

Depreciation—CYP   In this example, fixed assets and preoperational expenditures are depreciated on the basis of straight-line to zero salvage value (see Table 2.1), in accordance with regulations of tax authorities. Capitalized interest incurred during the construction phase is amortized as a component of preoperational expenditures. In Table 2.1 "T INV" is Total Investment for all periods and "T DEP" is the total depreciation for all periods. The difference between them is "RES VAL," residual value.

As a general rule, the residual value at the planning horizon consists of assets that can be sold (if the plan is to liquidate), including the land on which the project was constructed. There are other possibilities for an ongoing enterprise, but they cannot be reliably estimated during the planning stage—for example, replacement value or value in the most favorable alternative use. For the CYP, the residual value of fixed assets at the planning horizon is assumed at book value of fixed assets plus net working capital. The book value of long-term assets is determined as (all values in US$ thousands) *initial fixed assets* plus *replacements* plus *preoperational expenditures* (including capitalized interest) (36,050.4) minus *accumulated depreciation* (28,593.2) = 7,457.2. The total residual value also includes simulated liquidation of current assets and clearing all liabilities.

Contingencies

Contingencies are provisions for unforeseen expenditures and price increases, added to estimates of capital expenditures (fixed assets and preoperational expenditures) as a risk-avoidance measure to cover investment costs overruns. While costs can theoretically go up or down, contingencies are always added, covering the pessimistic scenario. *Physical contingencies* are intended to account for unforeseen physical requirements: change in design of some physical component, a needed component omitted, or some additional area required for special machinery for which capital costs may not have been included. *Price contingencies* are intended to account for unforeseen increases in cost of assets during the construction phase resulting from general inflation or price escalation for the particular item; as prices seem always to go in one direction (up), delay in implementation usually entails increased investment costs. Local currency devaluation during the implementation phase increases cost of imports (expressed in local currency).

Contingencies are, in a sense, factors of ignorance. It is one thing to be aware of what is not known with certainty, but to immerse the project in a sea of uncertainty does not solve anything and may well scuttle it. Better to

TABLE 2.1 Depreciation—CYP, US$(000)

	Years	%	Initial Value	3	4	5	...	9	10	T INV	T DEP	Residual Value
Civil works and buildings	25.0	4.0	2,243.7	89.7	89.7	89.7		89.7	89.7	2,243.7	718.0	1,525.7
Spinning machinery and equipment	10.0	10.0	20,435.2	2,043.5	2,043.5	2,043.5		2,043.5	2,043.5	20,435.2	16,348.1	4,087.0
Auxiliary equipment and utilities	10.0	10.0	8,699.0	869.9	869.9	869.9		869.9	869.9	8,699.0	6,959.2	1,739.8
Transportation and handling equipment	7.0	14.3	42.8	6.1	6.1	6.1		6.1	6.1	85.5	48.9	36.6
Office equipment[1]	5.0	20.0	170.1	34.0	34.0	34.0		34.0	34.0	340.1	272.1	68.0
Preproduction expenditure[2]	3.0	33.3	4,247.0	1,415.7	1,415.7	1,415.7				4,247.0	4,247.0	0.0
Total			35,837.6	4,458.9	4,458.9	4,458.9		3,043.3	3,043.3	4,247.0	4,247.0	
Cumulative depreciation				4,458.9	8,917.9	13,376.8		25,549.9	28,593.2	36,050.4	28,593.2	7,457.2
Depreciation of fixed assets				3,043.3	3,043.3	3,043.3		3,043.3	3,043.3			
Cumulative depreciation—fixed assets				3,043.3	6,086.6	9,129.8		21,302.9	24,346.2			

[1]Office equipment and transportation depreciated to zero value and replaced before planning horizon.
[2]Includes capitalized interests.

expend the effort necessary to predict the most accurate costs of assets, and only then to consider the need for contingencies. In the early planning stages, when not all costs are identified in detail, contingencies may be higher, and then gradually reduced as cost estimates are refined.

Plant and Equipment Replacement Costs

During the operations phase, the cost of assets that have reached the end of their economic lives and need to be replaced is included in expenditure estimates at the anticipated time of replacement. If the old assets are to be sold or otherwise retired, any residual value received is accounted either as return of capital or as profit (usually sale above book value is treated as profit and below as loss). Estimates include procurement, transport and handling, and installation and commissioning of equipment.

Fixed Asset Costs—CYP   A summary of fixed asset investment for the CYP during its two-year construction phase is shown in Table 2.2. A more detailed breakdown for each major item (e.g., civil works and buildings, machinery and equipment) and for each plant unit, showing quantities and prices, can be prepared in a format similar to that of Table 2.3, which can include installation details and costs and utility requirements (e.g., electricity, water supply, natural gas). In this example, it is assumed that equipment will have to be replaced when the asset is fully depreciated. Residual values at the planning horizon are estimated in this case as either book value or 10 percent of original cost, whichever is greater.

Preoperational Expenditures

During planning and implementation phases, some capital expenditures cover items in addition to fixed assets—part of the initial investment package financed with long-term capital. As enterprise assets, their costs are generally capitalized and amortized over a period of years that differs according to the tax laws of the host country; or they may be allocated to fixed assets and depreciated accordingly. Elements of preoperational expenditures include, but are not limited to, the following:

■ *Preparatory study*—expenditures for preinvestment studies at various stages of development, and support or background studies (e.g., market, production, financial and economic analysis, environmental impacts)
■ *Project implementation management*—costs associated with the management team responsible for implementation (covered in more detail in Chapter 9).

TABLE 2.2 Fixed Assets—CYP, US$(000)

Item[1]	Foreign Currency[2,3]		Domestic Currency		Initial Value	Depreciation Period, Years
	Year 1	Year 2	Year 1	Year 2		
Civil works, infrastructure, and buildings[4]	1,103.7		1,140.0		2,243.7	25
Spinning machinery and equipment[5]		20,435.2			20,435.2	10
Auxiliary equipment and utilities	8,226.8		472.2	8699.0	8,699.0	10
Transportation and handling equipment[6]	42.8				42.8	7
Office equipment[6]		12.4	157.7	157.7	170.1	5
Total years	9,373.3	20,447.5	1,612.2	157.7		
Total currency	29,820.8		1,769.9			
Total fixed assets	31,590.6					

[1] If necessary, details for each item can be included in a separate schedule with a similar layout.

[2] Import prices are CIF. The project is absolved of payment of import duties on capital items of 5 percent.

[3] Separate schedules can be prepared in similar format for each currency to identify foreign exchange requirements, but the value for all items must be converted to the accounting currency.

[4] Includes 678.5(000) foreign exchange and 120.5(000) domestic currency for infrastructure development.

[5] Transportation and handling to site are included in preproduction expenditures.

[6] Office equipment and transport replaced in years 7 and 9 respectively; residual values at 25 percent of original cost recovered in years 8 and 10 respectively.

TABLE 2.3 Sample Investment Cost Detail for Plant Unit

Plant Unit:				Currency and Unit:						
Unit Cost[1]				Total Cost				Utilities		
Item	Q	F	L	Inland	F	L	Year	Installation Details	Electricity	Water	Gas

Q = quantity, F = foreign exchange, L = local currency.
[1]Unit cost expressed in foreign exchange and local currency as applicable, to be converted to a single accounting currency.

- *Enterprise formation*:
  - Organization buildup—personnel appointed in advance of operations for activating the enterprise and related training (wages and salaries, benefits, travel) plus rents and other expenses.
  - Operations and training manuals.
  - Expenditures for equity and debt capital issues: underwriting and brokerage fees, prospectus, advertising.
  - Legal fees: charter, incorporation, registration, purchase agreements, loan applications, mortgage documents.
  - Licensing and patent fees.
  - Preoperational marketing and promotion: test marketing, setting up the marketing organization and program, promotion, creation of sales network.
  - Procurement system development—setting up supply chains.
  - Miscellaneous: insurance, rents, supplies.
- *Construction and commissioning project*:
  - Supervision and coordination of construction, erection, installation, testing, trial runs, start-up, and commissioning: consultant fees; wages, salaries, fringe benefits, and recruiting costs; consumption of production materials and supplies; utilities; and other start-up costs.
  - Detailed engineering: design of process, equipment, and civil works; tendering (bid process), negotiations, and contracting.
  - Financial costs during construction: interest and fees on loans during the implementation phase (may be capitalized).

- Insurance during construction.
- Technology acquisition and transfer costs.
- Temporary construction facilities: housing, offices, storage.
- Training: fees, travel, living expenses, salaries, and stipends of trainees.

Preoperational Expenditures—CYP   Preoperational expenditures for the two-year implementation of the Cambria Yarns Project are shown in Table 2.4.

Working Capital

Just as fixed assets require capital investment, so do current assets—for example, inventories, receivables, and other short-term assets (e.g., cash on hand)—that are employed to maintain operations at the planned level. Part of the capital need is offset with current liabilities, a form of short-term financing. Net working capital is the difference between them (current assets minus current liabilities). It is quite common for start-up enterprises to experience liquidity (short-term cash flow) problems resulting from insufficient planning for covering working capital—either not included or underestimated.

Current Assets   The financing of investment in current assets during operations is usually cyclical and relatively short, almost without exception less than one year. Inventories of materials, components, and other resources are converted through the production process (work in progress) into products (finished product inventory) that are sold, in some cases for cash and in other cases "on account." The latter are *receivables*, which constitute part of current assets, to be collected at some future time when funds are freed to be recycled into the process. Current liquid assets are cash and near-cash items (e.g., notes and marketable securities).

Inventories   Minimizing stocks of finished products, work in progress, and materials, which provide buffers (immunity to perturbations) for sales and production, reduces investment in working capital and consequently improves return on investment/equity. Additional costs of maintaining inventories are related to storage facilities and losses from deterioration, pilferage, and obsolescence. Just-in-time (JIT) inventory systems match delivery of materials and other production components with the production schedule so that little inventory is carried by the enterprise. However, JIT requires careful management to avoid stock-out situations that disrupt production or

TABLE 2.4 Preoperational Expenditures—CYP, US$(000)

Item	Year 1 Foreign Exchange	Year 1 Local Currency	Year 2 Foreign Exchange	Year 2 Local Currency
Management and administration				
Management salary and benefits	186.5		284.4	
Travel and installation of expatriate team			400.0	
Administrative salaries			69.9	
Local project staff		7.2		
Engineering and supervision				
Consulting fee	250.0			
Supervision			330.0	
Miscellaneous (communications, travel)			0.9	1.0
Installation of machinery and equipment				
Supervision			818.7	
Local labor costs				108.6
Miscellaneous materials and supplies				5.0
Training				
Fees			242.7	
Travel and allowances			28.0	
Other expenses				
Rented and leased equipment		10.0		10.0
Legal costs, communications, travel	10.0	10.0	10.0	
Transportation of machinery and equipment to site		3.0	12.0	
Materials consumed in test runs				
Raw cotton				106.8
Other materials			187.8	
Total	446.5	30.2	2,384.4	231.4
Total preoperational expenditures	446.5	30.2	2,384.4	231.4
Total foreign	2,830.9			
Total local	261.6			
Total	3,092.5			

sales (see the subsection "Optimal Investment in Working Capital" later in this chapter).

- *Production materials*—raw materials, semifinished products, components, subsystems, spares, and factory supplies. Inventory levels depend upon sources and supply chains; local and adequate sources and convenient transport tend to diminish quantities to be stocked. As much as six months' consumption or more may have to be maintained for imports, depending upon procurement lead time and customs practices. Other factors influencing size of inventories are reliability and seasonality of supplies, number of suppliers, possible substitutions, and expected price changes. A set of spare parts is usually included as part of the initial investment package.
- *Finished products.* Inventory level depends on the nature of the product and trade patterns. Shelf life is a factor—if short, generally low levels are advisable. Uncertainty or seasonality in demand tends to bias inventory toward larger quantities of finished products to avoid stock-outs and lost sales.
- *Work in progress.* Capital requirement depends upon the nature of the production process—time in process and integration of materials and other resources at each production stage. Work-in-progress capital requirements are relatively high for large capital equipment products (e.g., aircraft and ships, although capital inflows are usually synchronized with production progress) and small for industries such as food processing.

Receivables   Receivables are trade credits extended to clients. The amount to be financed is determined by credit policy, which may be guided by industry norms, and how well the policy is to be executed. Age of receivables, and corresponding level of credit outstanding, has to be managed, and the control system defined in the plan. The ratio *credit:gross sales* differs for industries and for companies within industries. The value of receivables to be included in working capital can be estimated as follows:[23]

$$AR_j = \frac{CT * R_j * PCS_j}{12} = \frac{R_j * PCS_j}{COT}$$

where AR_j = value of accounts receivable for period j
CT = credit terms, months
R_j = sales revenue
PCS_j = percentage credit sales
COT = coefficient of turnover ($12/CT$ = number of credit rotations in a year)

Cash, Bank Deposits, and Other Liquid Assets   Liquid assets are required as a buffer for ongoing operations. Requirements can be estimated as a percentage of current assets (e.g., 5 percent) or on the basis of total nonmaterial operating costs (depreciation not included) divided by the coefficient of turnover for these types of assets.

Current Liabilities   Current liabilities are short-term, cyclical obligations that arise primarily from credit purchases from suppliers (payables). The level depends upon suppliers' credit terms. Materials, components, subsystems, factory supplies, and services (e.g., utilities such as electricity, gas, water) are usually purchased on credit. Current liabilities also include short-term debt (e.g., overdraft) and other short-term obligations, the current portion of long-term debt, and advances from clients against future deliveries of goods or services. Accrued tax liabilities or wages payable are other components, usually inapplicable for project planning purposes.

Current liabilities offset current assets, an inexpensive way to reduce working capital required, a form of interest-free financing. Terms imposed by suppliers and other creditors, including penalties for late payments, have to be taken into account in planning. In the current liabilities cycle, advances and suppliers' trade credits are used to procure production factors, which are converted to products and then sold, with the receipts applied, in part, to cover payables, completing the cycle.

Net Working Capital   The amount of financing required to cover working capital is the difference between values of current assets and current liabilities. During any operating period, *changes* in current assets or liabilities have an impact on financial requirements. An increase in working capital corresponds to a cash outflow (use or application of funds) requiring financing. A decrease in working capital frees financial resources (source of funds). Financing is required to cover these short-term investments as current assets are built up in the form of inventories and receivables, particularly in the early stages of operations. Advances to suppliers and other deposits (e.g., opening letters of credit) against purchases of project inputs increase the amount of financing required.

Permanent and Cyclical Working Capital   Maintaining liquidity over the project life, or to the planning horizon if different, requires a sufficient level of working capital. Financing a minimum or buffer level of current assets with permanent capital (equity or long-term debt) avoids what would otherwise require virtually continuous cash management. The permanent portion (working capital margin) can be estimated at the base level of production or the minimum of a cyclical production pattern, to be committed for the project life. It can be included in the initial outlay and supplemented with additional infusions of short-term funds, or from funds internally generated during early operating periods as production increases toward full capacity.

Optimizing working capital investment is a trade-off: If it is too large, the result is high interest and inventory costs; if too small, lost sales (product inventory too low), penalties for late payment of short-term obligations, or liquidity crises.

Seasonal or cyclical peaks can be financed with short- or medium-term capital. Operations having cyclical characteristics generally require relatively higher levels of temporary working capital, obtained from flexible sources that allow repayment without penalty when not in use. Sources of finance to cover the cyclical portion need to be identified; however, if the cyclical portion is small compared with the base (permanent) level, it may be sufficiently accurate to base the estimate on average working capital requirements.

Estimating Working Capital

Working capital can be estimated systematically for each project period by determining the amount associated with components of current assets and liabilities, each of which requires an amount of coverage that can be expressed in terms of *number of days*. For example, stock of a material is maintained to cover a certain number of days of production, determined essentially by its consumption per unit of output. *Days coverage* is the normal period of rotation for the item—that is, the number of days that would deplete the inventory (down to the buffer level, if any) at the consumption rate. For example, if the inventory level is 1,000 units and the consumption rate in production is 50 units per day, days of coverage is $1,000/50 = 20$ days (for more comprehensive elaboration, see the later subsection "Cyclical Supply of Input"). The number of days selected is a function of variables such as procurement lead time (for inputs), shelf life, process cycle time, the cost of holding inventory, and setup and order costs (see Figure 2.9 later in this chapter).

Coefficient of Turnover The coefficient of turnover (COT) defines the number of rotations of the working capital item per period (year), determined by dividing the number of days per year by days of coverage.

$$COT = \frac{365}{DC}$$

where $DC =$ days coverage

For calculating the COT—that is, the number of rotations in a calendar year—the number of days can be taken as 365. A material with annual consumption of $10,000 with 10 rotations per year would require $1,000 in working capital (i.e., $10,000/10).[24]

Days coverage is selected on the basis of the rotation cycle for the item—inventory, receivables or payables. The amount of capital tied up increases with "days coverage." If a material input has a cyclical pattern of delivery and consumption, during each cycle the maximum amount is tied up at the time of payment for the order and reduces thereafter, as shown later in Figure 2.6. The average capital tie-up is less than the maximum and is a better basis for estimating financing costs. If the pattern is linear, the maximum is twice the average plus the buffer, or minimum level. For inventory items the maximum is also affected by payment terms for orders, as shown in the lower part of the figure.

Bases A *basis* is the starting point for determining the amount of associated working capital committed to the item, which is also a function of the COT:

$$WCap = \frac{\text{Basis}}{COT}$$

WCap is the amount of working capital required for the item (raw materials, receivables, inventories, etc.). Cost is the appropriate basis for the amount required for a material or component. Bases for other working capital items depend on their operating cycle: Annual credit sales is an appropriate basis for receivables;[25] the basis for product inventories is factory cost (this is the amount invested). Bases are selected so that changes in working capital items are accurately reflected in their cash flow impact. A suggested system of bases for working capital items is provided in Table 2.5. Variations

TABLE 2.5 Bases for Working Capital Items

Working Capital Item	Basis	Rationale
Finished products	Factory cost	Amount invested in inventory
Work in progress	Factory cost	Similar to finished products
Materials, spare parts	Cost of production materials and spares	Purchase price
Accounts receivable	Sales price	Effect on revenue stream
Accounts payable	Cost of purchased materials	Purchase price
Cash	Operating cost less materials	Items that may utilize cash reserves

may be warranted in some circumstances; for example, terms of payment can alter the amount tied up for an item (see Figure 2.6 later in this chapter).

Rule-of-thumb methods can be used to estimate working capital—for example, norms obtained from studies of similar industries, such as turnover as a percentage of sales revenue —but the models of Table 2.5 for determining working capital requirements should provide more accurate estimates.

Inventory (Material Items) Estimates of the value of working capital items for each period to the planning horizon are calculated using the following nomenclature:

- *Quantity* (*Q*) of an item in a period represents the level of production for products, or level of consumption or procurement of materials or other inputs.
- *Value* (*V*) can be at initial, constant, or current level; value for material items is determined as the product of quantity and price.
- *Basis* (b_j) is the unit value equivalent of a working capital item (see Table 2.5). In the formulas shown, a unit basis is employed to convert quantities into their respective values.
- *SB* is the initial or starting balance of a working capital item in the initial investment package and/or an asset of an existing enterprise immediately prior to the project start.

The method of determining inventory quantity and value for material items is similar to that for relating the production program to the sales program:

$$EQ_j \geq \frac{Q_j}{COT}, EQ_{j-1} - Q_j, N_j$$

$$\delta EQ = (EQ_j - EQ_{j-1})$$

$$EV_j = (EQ_j)(b_j)$$

$$\delta EV = (EV_j - EV_{j-1})$$

where EQ_j = ending quantity
Q_j = quantity consumed in production ($P_j * u$)
N_j = specified level of ending inventory based on other criteria (e.g., depletion of starting inventory or cyclical production program)
P_j = production level
u = units of material required per unit of production
EV_j = ending value
b_j = unit basis

δ = indicator of change

j = period (e.g., year) 1, 2, . . .

The working capital for the period (increment or decrement) is the change from the prior to the current period (see Table 2.8 later in this chapter).[26]

In an operating enterprise, either last in first out (LIFO), first in first out (FIFO), or average inventory valuation is employed for accounting purposes. For project planning purposes, with the exception of a situation in which there is a starting inventory, valuing inventory at the current price should give a sufficient approximation of the need for working capital.

If there is a starting balance of inventory with valuation considerably different from the bases of Table 2.5, the analytical model can be set up to exhaust the starting balance in the sales or production program first, using the value of the initial inventory.

In the most general case there is a starting balance with a basis different from that of the operating periods. An algorithm for this situation is presented in Appendix 2.2. An example of the treatment of starting balances of product and material inventories is provided on our web site: the Victoria Coke Project (VCP). If the inventory units are not identical to the items produced or consumed during the production phase, then their disposition is handled separately—in other words, finished product inventory that is not identical to what is produced is treated as a separate product.

Nonmaterial Items The values of nonmaterial working capital elements (e.g., receivables, payables) can be best approximated in aggregated form. In such cases estimates can be derived as follows:

$$EV_j \geq \frac{B_j}{COT}, N_j$$
$$\delta EV = \left(EV_j - EV_{j-1}\right)$$

where B_j = basis, period j

If a working capital item in the starting balance is to be incorporated into the operating plan over a number of periods, N_j can be used to specify the rate. For example, if there is a starting balance of receivables at a level of 30 to be collected uniformly over three periods, the ending balances for the next three periods can be specified as no less than 20, 10, and 0 respectively. The ending balance is B_j/COT for any period in which it is greater than the corresponding N_j.

Seasonal Sales and Production   Working capital for cyclical output, either seasonal (e.g., agricultural fertilizer) or longer, is determined for monthly or even shorter periods to more accurately determine working capital requirements. The principle is the same as for yearly calculations, but more detail is revealed concerning working capital fluctuations.

An additional criterion is the minimum or safety stock, determined on the basis of tactical considerations (e.g., avoidance of stock-outs resulting from fluctuations in the sales program). An example (not related to the Cambria Yarns Project) is shown in Table 2.6 and Figure 2.5. The minimum safety stock is determined to be 10 units. The plan is designed to maintain a constant level of production so that the sales program can be satisfied and the minimum level of inventory criterion is not violated.

The minimum stock may be financed as part of the initial investment package, while the cyclical requirement more appropriately would be financed with short-term capital. The average inventory is 201/12 or 16.7 units. If the minimum inventory of 10 units is financed with permanent capital, then short-term financing would be required to cover a maximum of 12 units (22 – 10) and an average of 6.7 units (16.7 – 10).

Cyclical Supply of Input   A cyclical pattern of supply for an input affects the requirement for working capital. Two situations can be distinguished—a supply pattern arising from the order cycle and a seasonal pattern.

TABLE 2.6   Cyclical Production and Sales Plan, Units Finished Product

Month	Sales	Production	Inventory
1	3	5	18
2	3	5	20
3	3	5	22
4	6	5	21
5	6	5	20
6	6	5	19
7	8	5	16
8	8	5	13
9	8	5	10
10	3	5	12
11	3	5	14
12	3	5	16
Totals	60	60	201

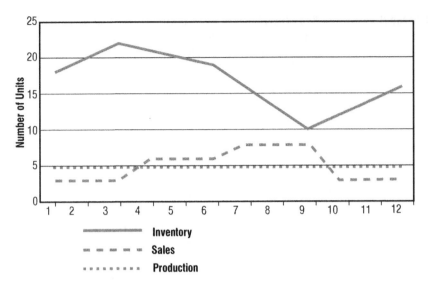

FIGURE 2.5 Cyclical Sales and Inventory

Order Cycle If the order and consumption pattern for the material is cyclical—for example, it rises to a peak when delivered and drops to a minimum just before the next delivery—the amount of investment varies over time. The number of days of coverage is tied to the order cycle (see Figure 2.9).

For a cyclical supply of inputs, the amount required for investment in inventory depends upon the order cycle and procurement lead time, which may have to be adjusted—for example, for imports, if a bank deposit is required to cover a letter of credit (LC) at the time of order. In the upper section of Figure 2.6, payment is made at the time of delivery. The order and consumption cycles are the same. The maximum investment is the minimum stock plus the value of order quantity, with the average value determined by:

$$AVG = \frac{MIN + MAX}{2}$$

In the second case, payment (e.g., coverage of the LC) is required at the time of order. The order and consumption cycles differ as a result of lead time. The maximum investment is the minimum stock plus the stock level at the lead time plus the order quantity. The average investment can be determined as before, but the value will be higher (higher still, if advances

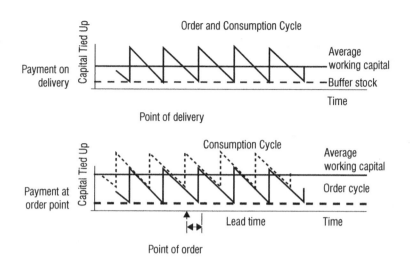

FIGURE 2.6   Cyclical Supply of Input

are required to secure delivery of the item). If the inventory is financed with a revolving credit line, the average investment may be a better basis for estimating the cost of financing, depending on the planned temporal pattern of the account balance.

Suppose it is estimated that the annual cost of coal consumed is $36 million; this is the basis for estimating the working capital requirements for coal. Sufficient coal will be inventoried to cover 60 days of production. If there are 240 *working days* per year, the number of rotations or cycles (COT) for the stock of coal is four (i.e., 240/60); the value of coal consumed per cycle is $36 million/4 = $9 million. If the buffer stock is to cover 20 production days (one-third of the cycle), the value of buffer stock is $\frac{1}{3}$($9 million) = $3 million. The maximum value of stock = $3 million + $9 million = $12 million and the average is ($3 million + $12 million)/2 = $7.5 million. The number of calendar days per cycle is 365/COT = 365/4 $\cong$ 91. The inventory cycle is illustrated in Figure 2.7.

In this example, if the $36 million basis for coal is divided by the COT, the result is $9 million. If the pattern of procurement and consumption in the production process is similar to the cycle in Figure 2.7, the amount of capital needed *on average* to cover the cyclical portion plus the buffer is $9 million/2 + $3 million = $7.5 million. If the procurement cycle is financed with either short-term debt (e.g., revolving credit line) or with internal funds, the average inventory investment is a better basis for determining the financing cost (interest charges on debt) of carrying inventory. The buffer stock,

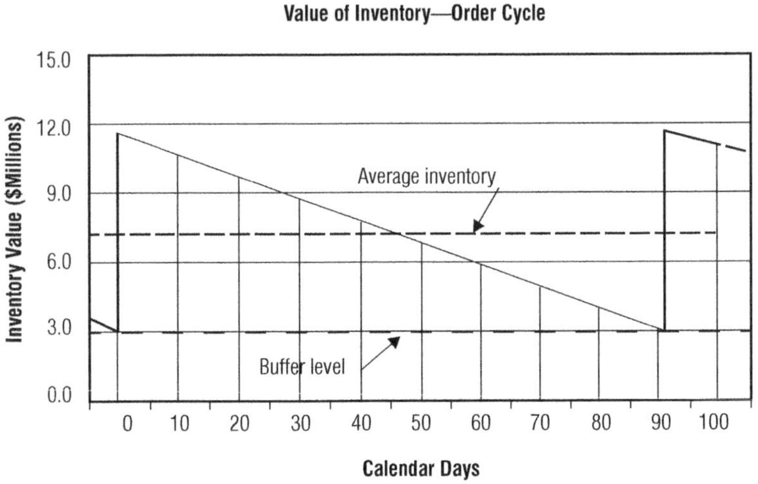

Value of Inventory—Order Cycle

FIGURE 2.7   Example of Cyclical Inventory with Buffer Stock

or base level, would normally be financed as part of the initial investment package with long-term capital.

Alternatively, if the *average days coverage* is applied, the COT would be $365/45.1 \cong 8$, and the amount calculated for WCap would be $36 million/8 = $4.5 million. If the buffer stock is added, the amount calculated for WCap is $7.5 million, the average shown in Figure 2.7. In other words, using average days coverage provides a better estimate for cost of financing.

This illustrates the need for caution in selecting the number of days of coverage and the amount of finance needed to cover inventory of the item. Using the combination of the basis and the number of days for the full inventory cycle overstates the average investment as related to financing costs, but it does reveal the maximum amount of capital investment required; the average number of days provides the average investment, but in some parts of the cycle the amount of investment (and corresponding requirement for finance) would be higher.

Seasonal Patterns   Some project inputs can only be obtained on a seasonal basis, which can dramatically affect the amount of working capital required. Supplies must be procured and stored during a relatively short growing season (or through some other supply mechanism) at relatively high levels to cover production needs over the year. Alternatively, input would have to be processed during the short time period when the seasonal input is available; consequently plant capacity would have to be adjusted and used only for a limited time during the year (e.g., sugar beet processing).

Sales may also be seasonal, requiring stocks of inventory to be built up during slack seasons—an issue significant for the plant capacity decision. For agricultural commodities that are available only during a relatively short harvesting season, estimates of working capital buildup should take into account the procurement and consumption cycle.

Example: Cotton Procurement Cycle for CYP　　As an example from the Cambria Yarns Project, the procurement cycle for raw cotton is predicated on the cultivation and harvesting cycle in the country. Cotton is harvested in the months of August through October. The project plans to purchase all cotton during those months and to maintain a minimum stock to cover 60 days of production at all times. As production during all months of the year will be essentially constant, the procurement and consumption cycle will be approximately as shown in Table 2.7 and Figure 2.8.

The parameters of this cycle are as follows (in metric tons): average inventory = 3,071.8; minimum = 945.2; maximum = 5,198.5; maximum − minimum = 2,126.6 (fractional amounts shown for consistency only).

The price of raw cotton is US$668 per metric ton (MT). Assuming that farmers are paid on delivery, the amount of working capital required to cover cotton purchases can be estimated as the product of quantity in stock and price. The minimum, maximum, and average amounts in thousands of dollars are US$631.4, US$3,473, and US$2,052, respectively.

TABLE 2.7　Raw Cotton Acquisition and Consumption Cycle, CYP

	Acquisition	Consumption	Inventory
Jan	0.0	472.6	3,780.7
Feb	0.0	472.6	3,308.1
Mar	0.0	472.6	2,835.5
Apr	0.0	472.6	2,363.0
May	0.0	472.6	1,890.4
June	0.0	472.6	1,417.8
July	0.0	472.6	945.2
Aug	1,890.3	472.6	2,363.0
Sep	1,890.3	472.6	3,780.7
Oct	1,890.3	472.6	5,198.5
Nov	0.0	472.6	4,725.9
Dec	0.0	472.6	4,253.3
Totals	5,671.0	5,671.0	3,071.8

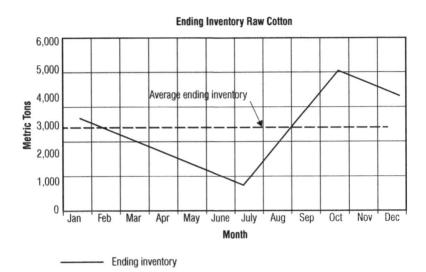

FIGURE 2.8 Cyclical Cotton Inventory, CYP

Net Working Capital, CYP The estimation of working capital requirements for the CYP is shown in Table 2.8a (working capital) and Table 2.8b
(working capital increments). Working capital increments affect cash flow,
an increase (decrease) as outflow (inflow). With the exception of raw cotton,
estimates are derived from the basis and the COT. For the working capital
estimate, investment in cotton inventory is predicated on the harvesting and
procurement cycle, using the average of the maximum and the base level.
This implies that the maximum financing required for cotton inventories
will be higher than the averages shown (see Table 2.7 and Figure 2.8).[27]
Internally generated surplus funds may be used to cover some increments of
working capital.

Optimal Investment in Working Capital Planning should be predicated on
the closest practicable approach to optimal order cycles for major inputs.
Cyclical order quantity is determined as the trade-off between inventory
carrying (or holding) cost and order cost. Unit holding cost increases with
order size (higher level of inventory on hand): financing, deterioration in
storage (short or fixed shelf life), obsolescence, reworking existing inventory
for design changes, internal handling, pilferage, and other storage costs.
Conversely, unit order cost (e.g., processing, shipping and handling) generally decreases (per unit ordered) with order size. The unit cost of inventory
is minimized in a range of order sizes, as shown in Figure 2.9. The frequency

TABLE 2.8a Working Capital Requirements—CYP, US$(000)

Foreign

WC Item	Days	COT		Year				
			2[1]	3[6]	4	5	6–10	
Product Inventories			0.0	65.6	71.0	70.5	70.5	
Finished product	15	24.3		42.8	46.3	46.0	46.0	
Work in progress	8	45.6		22.8	24.7	24.5	24.5	
Material Inventories			258.0	256.8	277.8	275.9	275.9	
Raw cotton	60	6.1						
Auxiliary materials[2]	90	4.1	164.7	164.8	185.8	183.9	183.9	
Factory supplies	40	9.1						
Spare parts	90	4.1	93.3	92.0	92.0	92.0	92.0	
Receivables	65	5.6		1195.2	2390.4	2390.4	2390.4	1260.9 *
Cash	10	36.5		26.4	42.2	37.0	34.3	
Less: Payables[3]	60	6.1		281.7	390.8	389.5	389.5	340.9 **
Totals			258.0	1262.3	2390.6	2384.3	2381.6	
Change			258.0	1004.3	1128.3	−6.3	−2.7	

Local

WC Item	Days	COT		Year			
			2[1]	3[6]	4	5	6–10
Product Inventories			0.0	275.2	307.9	305.1	305.1
Finished product	15	24.3		179.5	200.8	198.9	198.9
Work in progress	8	45.6		95.7	107.1	106.1	106.1
Material Inventories			646.0	1852.3	2087.3	2066.5	2066.5
Raw cotton[4,5]	60	6.1	631.4	1,838.6	2,072.7	2,052.0	2,052.0
Auxiliary materials	40	9.1	7.2	6.7	7.5	7.4	7.4
Factory supplies	40	9.1	7.4	7.1	7.1	7.1	7.1
Spare parts	90	4.1					

(Continued)

TABLE 2.8a (*Continued*)

Local

WC Item	Days	COT				
Receivables	65	5.6	1,060.0	505.2	505.2	505.2
Cash	10	36.5	20.8	25.9	25.8	25.8
Less: Payables	60	6.1	752.4	857.4	646.6	850.4
Totals		646.0	2,455.9	2,068.9	2,256.0	2,052.2
Change		646.0	1,809.9	−387.0	187.1	−203.7 ***
Totals		904.0	3,718.3	4,459.5	4,640.3	4,433.8
Change		904.0	2,814.3	741.3	180.8	−206.5

*FP + WIP + receivables financed with foreign loan year 3.

**Product inventory year 3.

***Material inventories: 904.0 year 3. 2,109.1 year 4.

[1]Current assets to be financed with permanent capital include the base level of raw materials stocks, inventory of auxiliary materials, spare parts, and factory supplies and receivables.

[2]Domestically procured auxiliary materials for 40 days; FP + WIP + REC financed with foreign loan, year 3, total 1,260.9.

[3]Imported spare parts are paid with LC so are not included in payables. Farmers paid in 30 days average.

[4]Average of minimum and maximum inventories based upon purchase and production cycle, adjusted for level of production. For example, year 3 level = (945.2 + 5,198.5)/2 × 0.668 × 0.917 (production level). Short-term financing or internally generated funds are required to cover difference between average and maximum levels.

[5]Year 2, 60 days inventory financed with permanent capital; base level of 945.2 MT × US$668/MT = US$631.4 (in US$000).

[6]Finished product, work in progress, and receivables are included in the initial investment package but expenditures occur in year 3 (first year of production).

TABLE 2.8b Working Capital Increments—CYP, US$(000)

	Year				
Change in Product Inventories	2	3	4	5	6–10
Foreign	0.0	65.6	5.4	(0.5)	0.0
Local	0.0	275.2	32.7	(2.9)	0.0
Total	0.0	340.9	38.1	(3.4)	0.0
Change in Material Inventories					
Foreign	258.0	(1.2)	21.0	(1.9)	0.0
Local	646.0	1,206.3	235.0	(20.7)	0.0
Total	904.0	1,205.2	255.9	(22.5)	0.0
Change in Receivables					
Foreign		1,195.2	1,195.2	0.0	0.0
Local		1,060.0	(554.7)	0.0	0.0
Total		2,255.2	640.4		
Change in Payables					
Foreign		281.7	109.1	(1.2)	0.0
Local		752.4	105.0	(210.8)	203.7
Total		1,034.1	214.1	(211.2)	203.7
Change in WC Cash					
Foreign		26.4	15.8	(5.2)	(2.7)
Local		20.8	5.0	(0.1)	0.0
Total		47.2	20.9	(5.3)	(2.7)
Percent foreign		55.9%	75.9%	98.5%	100.0%

of shipments is a factor; a shorter shipping cycle (low order quantity) has the effect of reducing inventory requirements and, consequently, holding cost, while a longer shipping cycle has the opposite effect. Transportation may be a significant factor in order cost: It may pay to ship by air instead of sea if carrying costs are reduced sufficiently.

Another optimization factor is the trade-off between carrying costs and stock-out costs, which result in losses in sales and profits. Risk of stock-out diminishes with increased investment in working capital, but increased investment lowers the rate of return. At the optimal point the investment in working capital is minimized, as shown in Figure 2.10. Stock-out cost decreases, and carrying cost increases, as working capital is increased. For this model, the optimal investment is the minimum total of stock-out plus carrying costs. Holding cost, order cost, and stock-out cost can be combined into a single model to determine the optimum order quantity.[28]

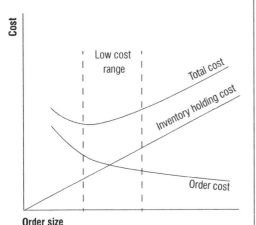

Economic Order Quantity

Cost

Low cost range

Total cost

Inventory holding cost

Order cost

Order size

Q - Size of order (in units)
C - Carrying cost per unit in inventory
O - Ordering cost per order
S - Total annual consumption in units

Estimation of Economic Order Quantity

$$\text{Total cost} = \frac{CQ}{2} + \frac{SO}{Q}$$

The function has a minimum, when

$$\frac{d(\text{total cost})}{dQ} = 0 = \frac{C}{2} - \frac{SO}{Q^2} = 0$$

Then $$Q^2 = \frac{2SO}{C}$$

and $Q = \sqrt{\dfrac{2SO}{C}}$ is economic order quantity

FIGURE 2.9 Economic Order Quantity

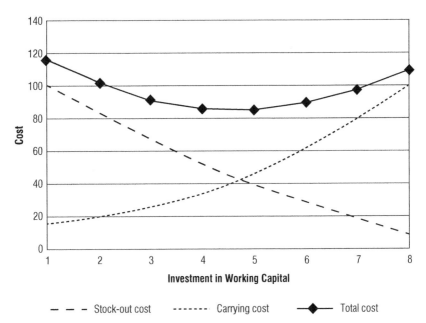

FIGURE 2.10 Working Capital Optimization

Decommissioning

Decommissioning or *end-of-life costs* are associated with retirement or dismantling of fixed assets or for reclamation, less any revenues from the sale of assets. A major cost item might be disposal of waste accumulations, particularly if they contain hazardous materials. These items are included in the financial plan with resources set aside to cover their costs. Tax consequences depend upon regulations in the host country.

Total Investment

Fixed capital is required to finance fixed assets, preoperational expenditures, and initial working capital. Additional capital may be required for replacement of assets during the operations phase, for working capital increments, and for decommissioning.

Total Investment, CYP The investment for the Cambria Yarns Project is shown in Table 2.9, including product inventories and receivables in year 3. The total amount (all in US$000) is US$39,555.9. Additional investments for replacements will be needed in year 7 for office equipment ($170.1) and year 9 for transportation and handling equipment ($42.8—see Table 2.2). Interest

TABLE 2.9 Capital Investment—CYP, US$(000)

	Year						
	1		2		3		
	F	L	F	L	F	L	Total
Fixed assets	9,373.3	1,612.2	20,447.5	157.7			31,590.6
Preproduction expenditures	446.5	30.2	2,384.4	231.4			3,092.5
Working capital[1]			258.0	646.0	1,004.3	1,809.9	3,718.3
Totals	9,819.8	1,642.4	23,089.9	1,035.1	1,004.3	1,809.9	38,401.4
Percent total investment		29.8%		62.8%		7.3%	
Total foreign exchange	33,914.0						
Total local currency	4,487.4						
Total F + L	38,401.4						
Interest during construction	1,154.5						
Total investment	39,555.9						

[1] Change in net working capital for period.

on the loan is capitalized in year 2 (see Tables 2.15b and Table 2.16 later in this chapter). The investment package includes working capital increments in year 2 (preproduction) and in year 3 (first production year).

PRODUCTION COST

The *cost of production* is the value of *resources consumed* in each planning period to comply with the production plan, which is based on the sales program and an estimate of production that flows into (or out of) inventory in each period. In this case, the ending inventory (EI) is estimated as the level of sales divided by the COT for the product, which is primarily dependent upon distribution channels and storage characteristics. This approach results in a level of inventory at the start of any period (carried over from the previous period) approximately sufficient to cover a sales rotation (turnover of product inventory). For example, if sales are 1,000 units per year with 10 rotations, the ending inventory is calculated as 100 (i.e., 1,000/10), so in the year the total production would be 1,100. If there is a starting balance of inventory at the start of the project, the situation is somewhat different (see Victoria Coke Project on our web site for a project with a starting balance and Appendix 2.2 for the case in which the starting balance includes inventory items valued differently from planned production items).

Production Plan—CYP

The production plan for the Cambria Yarns Project is shown in Table 2.10. It is derived from the sales program (Tables A1.6 and A1.7 in "Cambria Yarns Project," on our web site) and product inventory policy (see the subsection "Working Capital" under "Investment Cost" earlier in this chapter).

Fixed and Variable Costs

Production cost and *cost of products sold* are calculated for each of the planning periods, taking into account the level of capacity utilization, broken down at least into the main cost items (raw materials, factory supplies, personnel, overheads, etc.).[29] The *cost of products sold* is the basis for determining profit for each operating period. The relationship between the two is a function of the *change* in inventories (product—finished goods, work in progress, and materials) during each period, as shown later in Table 2.14 and depicted earlier in Figure 2.2.

TABLE 2.10 Production Plan—CYP (in Metric Tons)

	2	3	4	5	6	7	8	9	10
					Year				
Sales Ne 30/1	0.0	2,641.0	3,136.0	3,136.0	3,136.0	3,136.0	3,136.0	3,136.0	3,136.0
EI FP 30/1	0.0	110.0	130.7	130.7	130.7	130.7	130.7	130.7	130.7
Change		110.0	20.6	0.0	0.0	0.0	0.0	0.0	0.0
EI WIP 30/1	0.0	58.7	69.7	69.7	69.7	69.7	69.7	69.7	69.7
Change		58.7	11.0	0.0	0.0	0.0	0.0	0.0	0.0
Production 30/1		2,809.7	3,167.6	3,136.0	3,136.0	3,136.0	3,136.0	3,136.0	3,136.0
Sales Ne 40/1	0.0	1,132.0	1,344.0	1,344.0	1,344.0	1,344.0	1,344.0	1,344.0	1,344.0
EI FP 40/1	0.0	47.2	56.0	56.0	56.0	56.0	56.0	56.0	56.0
Change		47.2	8.8	0.0	0.0	0.0	0.0	0.0	0.0
EI WIP 40/1	0.0	25.2	29.9	29.9	29.9	29.9	29.9	29.9	29.9
Change		25.2	4.7	0.0	0.0	0.0	0.0	0.0	0.0
Production 40/1		1,204.3	1,357.5	1,344.0	1,344.0	1,344.0	1,344.0	1,344.0	1,344.0
Total Production		4,014.1	4,525.2	4,480.0	4,480.0	4,480.0	4,480.0	4,480.0	4,480.0
Percentage of full production		0.896	1.010	1.000	1.000	1.000	1.000	1.000	1.000

Coefficients of turnover:

	FP	WIP
Days	15	8
COT	24	45

Proportion of inventory change to production:

	Year			
	3	4	5	6–10
Finished product (FP)	0.039	0.007	0.000	0.000
Work in progress (WIP)	0.021	0.003	0.000	0.000
Total	0.060	0.010	0.000	0.000

EI = ending inventory for period; FP = finished product inventory; WIP = work-in-progress inventory.

It is useful to determine a standard unit cost (cost per unit produced) for each of the project's products and services, which in turn are based upon standard unit costs for the items they comprise. Analysis of profit, cash flow, breakeven, and other financial indicators are dependent upon the estimation and structure of production costs and cost of product sold. Production cost for each project period can be derived on the basis of either fixed and variable costs or direct and indirect costs.

Breaking down costs into their fixed and variable components is useful primarily for breakeven analysis, an important indicator of project risk (see Chapter 7).[30]

Fixed costs are, by definition, constant for all activity levels of production for a period of time. Examples are salaries paid to administrative staff, depreciation, and rent, which remain relatively unchanged over a significant time, perhaps to the planning horizon, although they may be constant only within a limited range of production increases or decreases. If there are planned increases in production scale within the project life there will almost certainly be changes in fixed costs.

Variable costs are directly related to the level of production. The word *variable* implies linearity—that is, the cost increases proportionally to the level of production. When there is zero production, ideally a variable cost is zero. Raw material, packing material, and labor costs (in some situations) are essentially variable. Some varying cost elements may be nonlinear (semivariable) with respect to level of activity—in other words, consumption efficiency varies according to level of operations. An example is fuel used to fire a gas turbine—consumption per kilowatt output varies according to load level, reaching its maximum efficiency near full-load conditions. A fixed number of workers may be retained regardless of production level and additional workers taken on as production increases. Cost of communications is typically constant (fixed) up to a certain level but varies for higher levels of service. Identifying costs as fixed and variable is useful in profit projections and sensitivity analysis.

Marginal cost (the cost of producing one additional unit of output) is a factor in decisions concerning optimal production plans. *Contribution,* the difference between sales price and variable cost (available to cover fixed costs), is employed in breakeven analysis (see Chapter 7). For cash flow analysis it is sufficient to determine total production cost for each period. Information about unit cost for each product—fixed and variable—is useful for product line decisions (product contribution and profitability).

One way to develop variable cost per unit of production (unit variable cost) for a single product is shown in Table 2.11. The unit variable cost is the sum of the values for each item. The following equation is used to

TABLE 2.11   Unit Variable Cost

Item	Quantity per Unit Produced	Variable Cost per Item	Variable Cost
Raw materials			
Components			
Subsystems			
Skilled labor			
Semiskilled labor			
Unskilled labor			
Packaging			
Other			
Unit variable cost			

determine unit variable cost for each operating period (assuming constant prices):

$$v_j = \sum_{k=1}^{k=m} p_k q_{kj}$$

where v_j = unit variable cost, product j
p_k = price (cost) of input item k
q_{kj} = quantity of input item k required per unit of product j

It is possible that, even under the constant pricing assumption, unit variable cost varies over the project life as a result of price escalation (see the earlier subsection "Pricing Project Inputs and Outputs"), in which case the current value is applied to determine variable cost for each period. Elements of factory costs, general and administrative overheads, and marketing and sales costs may be completely or partially variable. Total variable cost per period is the sum of variable costs for each resource consumed in production. For a single product the relationship is as follows:

$$V_j = v_j Q_j$$

where V_j = total variable costs, period j
Q_j = production quantity, period j

For multiple products, variable cost per period is the sum of variable costs for each product (determined from unit variable cost and quantities for each).

Fixed costs can be estimated similarly. The values of the fixed portion of each resource consumed in production are summed (resources and their fixed component may vary by period):

$$F_j = \sum_{k=1}^{k=n} f_{kj}$$

where F_j = fixed cost, period j
f_{kj} = fixed cost, resource k, period j

If quantity or price is expected to vary over the project life (i.e., semifixed or semivariable), fixed expenditures are adjusted accordingly. For multiple products, fixed costs can usually be determined for the entire project, without allocation. If product profitability is an issue, fixed costs associated with a particular product are identified and charged to each, although there is rarely a clear and objective means of allocation. Total fixed cost is the aggregate cost for all products. Production cost is the sum of variable costs and fixed costs for each period:

$$PC_j = F_j + V_j$$

where PC_j = production cost, period j

Direct and Indirect Costs

The breakdown of production costs into direct and indirect costs is useful primarily if the project plan includes multiple products. Direct cost margin is an indicator of product profitability and is useful for product pricing.

Direct costs are those that are readily attributable to a particular product or service. Production materials and labor are usually direct costs because they are clearly attributable. *Indirect costs* are not directly attributable and can only be apportioned to a product. Some examples are management and supervision, communications, depreciation, and finance charges. Direct and indirect costs can have both fixed and variable components.

For project planning purposes (if product profitability and pricing are issues of concern), a system of apportionment must be selected for *indirect costs* or *overheads*. Some possibilities are direct labor cost, direct labor hours, and machine time per unit. For new investment projects, similar projects or technical experts familiar with the production processes are possible sources to guide selection of an appropriate apportionment scheme. In an ongoing enterprise, a cost accounting surcharge or *burden* is usually

TABLE 2.12 Example of Allocation of Indirect Costs

Product	Direct Cost	Direct Labor Hours	Percentage of Direct Labor Hours	Allocation of Indirect Cost	Total Cost
A	120	60	30	300	420
B	150	100	50	500	650
C	200	40	20	200	400
Totals	470	200		1,000	1,470

applied to determine product profitability, which varies by industry and country; burden rates are computed by means of cost-center accounting.

An example of allocation by direct labor hours of indirect costs with a value of 1,000 to each of three products is shown in Table 2.12.

Direct cost margin is the most useful indicator of product profitability (difference between revenue and direct cost). Any scheme for allocating indirect costs is uncertain at best; so direct cost margin offers the most reliable means of determining the contribution of each product to profitability as a means of optimizing the product mix. Direct cost margin can also be determined at various production or enterprise levels—for example, production line (first level), plant unit composed of more than one production line (second level), the complete factory (third level), or the entire enterprise, which may operate more than one production plant. Direct cost margins of all products in combination are available to cover indirect costs.

For *pricing decisions* (if pricing flexibility is possible), the total of direct costs and allocated indirect costs can be used as the basis for determining profit margins for each product in the line. The profit margin for product *j* is the difference between projected revenue (at the selected price) and the sum of related direct and indirect costs.

$$PM_j = \left(\frac{R_j - (DC_j + IC_j)}{R_j} \right)(100)$$

where PM_j = profit margin %, product *j*
   R_j = revenue, product *j*
   DC_j = direct cost, product *j*
   IC_j = indirect cost, product *j*

Direct cost margin and pricing decisions can be based on unit values. For a single product, unit cost can be calculated by dividing total production costs by the number of units produced (unit costs usually vary with capacity utilization). For multiple products, *direct cost* for each product is divided by quantity produced to determine the unit direct cost. The *unit direct cost margin* (sales price minus unit direct cost) is available to cover indirect costs or *overheads*, costs that are not attributable directly to a product.

OPERATING COST, FACTORY COST, AND COST OF PRODUCT SOLD

Typically, operating cost in each period is the total of *factory cost, general and administrative overheads* (G&A), and *marketing and sales costs* (plus costs from other operating divisions), and is a determinant of operating profit (EBITDA).[31] The relationship between *production cost, factory cost,* and *cost of product sold* is described in the "Accounting System" section earlier in this chapter (see Figure 2.2).

Operating Cost Estimates—CYP

For the Cambria Yarns Project (see our web site), estimates of factory costs, general and administrative overheads, and marketing and distribution costs for years 3 through 10 (the years of planned production) are shown in Table 2.13. For the sake of simplicity, the total quantities of inputs for both products (Ne 30/1 and Ne 40/1) are used to generate costs for each item. Values for each year are divided into foreign exchange and domestic currency (used later in analysis of economic impacts); fixed and variable costs are differentiated for the combined production.

Factory Cost and Production Cost

For accounting consistency, *factory cost* in Table 2.13 represents only those costs for producing finished product that is *sold* and for increases (or decreases) in finished product and work-in-process inventories in each period (see the earlier "Accounting System" section). Changes in material inventories *are not included. Production cost* is factory cost adjusted for material inventory changes for each period. The relationship between factory cost and production cost is shown at the bottom of Table 2.13.

Depreciation is normally charged to operating functions that employ depreciable assets. For a manufacturing enterprise, where machinery and equipment represent a large part of the investment, a part of depreciation is charged to factory cost. In other types of enterprises (e.g., service industries), depreciation might be charged mainly to administration. In the Cambria Yarns case, to simplify the presentation and for better cash flow simulation

Year

	3	4	5	6–10
Production level, Ne 30/1, MT	2,809.7	3,167.6	3,136.0	3,136.0
Production level, Ne 40/1, MT	1,204.3	1,357.5	1,344.0	1,344.0
Total production	4,014.1	4,525.2	4,480.0	4,480.0
Percentage of nominal production of 4,480 MT	89.6%	101.0%	100.0%	100.0%

	Base cost, 4,480 MT				3		4		5		6–10	
	F	L	%FX	Type	F	L	F	L	F	L	F	L
Materials												
Raw materials[1]		3,788.7	0.000	V		3,394.6		3,826.9		3,788.7		3,788.7
Auxiliary materials	745.9	67.8	0.917	V	668.3	60.7	753.4	68.5	745.9	67.8	745.9	67.8
Labor[2]												
Skilled[3]		77.8	0.000	VF		77.0		85.9		85.1		85.1
Unskilled[4]		202.2	0.000	VF		186.3		209.4		207.3		207.3
Factory supplies		64.8	0.000	F		64.8		64.8		64.8		64.8
Spare parts consumed	373.2		1.000	F	373.2		373.2		373.2		373.2	
Repair, maintenance[5]		183.0	0.000	F		183.0		183.0		183.0		183.0
Energy[6]		444.4	0.000	VF		401.4		448.6		444.4		444.4
Total Factory Cost					1,041.5	4,367.9	1,126.6	4,887.0	1,119.1	4,841.1	1,119.1	4,841.1
General and administrative overheads												
Skilled labor	0.0	10.6	0.000	F		10.6		10.6		10.6		10.6
Unskilled labor	0.0	7.6	0.000	F		7.6		7.6		7.6		7.6
Expatriate staff[7]	290.0		1.000	F	290.0		290.0		100.0			
Local management staff	0.0	72.8	0.000	F		72.8		72.8		72.8		72.8
Materials, services, insurance, etc.	36.0	13.0	0.735	F	36.0	16.0	36.0	16.0	36.0	16.0	36.0	16.0
Land lease[8]		20.3	0.000	F		20.3		20.3		20.3		20.3

(Continued)

TABLE 2.13 (Continued)

	F	L	%FX	Type	F	L	F	L	F	L	F	L
Total G&A Overheads					326.0	127.3	326.0	127.3	136.0	127.3	36.0	127.3
Marketing and sales costs												
Skilled labor		5.3	0.000	F		5.3		5.3		5.3		5.3
Unskilled labor		1.3	0.000	F		1.3		1.3		1.3		1.3
Materials, services, etc.	58.0	35.6	0.620	V	58.0	35.6	58.0	35.6	58.0	35.6	58.0	35.6
Distribution[9]					578.3	421.1	1,156.7	572.8	1,156.7	572.8	1,156.7	572.8
Total Marketing and Sales Cost					636.3	463.3	1,214.7	615.0	1,214.7	615.0	1,201.7	531.2
Factory cost (incl. FP and WIP inventory)[10]					1,041.5	4,367.9	1,126.6	4,887.0	1,119.1	4,841.1	1,119.1	4,841.1
+ Change in material inventories					(1.2)	1206.3	21.0	235.0	(1.9)	(20.7)	0.0	0.0
Total foreign, local production cost					1,040.3	5,574.3	1,147.6	5,121.9	1,117.2	4,820.4	1,119.1	4,841.1
Production Cost						6,614.6		6,269.5		5,937.7		5,960.2

[1] Quantity per MT finished product; 1,266 MT raw cotton, price US$668.
[2] Costs for labor include surcharges such as holidays, leave, social security.
[3] This item is 91.4 percent variable; fixed = 7.3, variable = 77.8; total cost in year 3 = 7.3 + 0.896 × 77.8.
[4] This item is 97.5 percent variable; fixed = 5.1, variable = 202.2.
[5] Estimated at 0.58 percent of initial fixed asset cost; personnel costs included in factory skilled labor.
[6] This item is 93 percent variable; fixed cost = 31.3, variable cost = 413.3; total cost in year 3 = 31.3 + 0.883 × 413.1.
[7] Administrative expatriate staff to be repatriated; expenditure in year 5 is one-time cost.
[8] Paid to government for use of land in industrial estate.
[9] Costs based upon sales program; see transport costs.
[10] FP = finished product; WIP = work in progress.

(related to inventory buildup for which depreciation is not an outlay), all depreciation has been charged as a general expense and not to factory cost (see the "Accounting System" section earlier in this chapter).

Cost of Product Sold

The relationship between *production cost* and *cost of product sold* for each planning period involves the *change* in inventories (product and materials), which is determined from the estimates of working capital items in each period. Production cost is determined by adding (subtracting) increases (decreases) in material inventories to (from) factory cost, as shown at the bottom of Table 2.13. In this way, when production cost is adjusted for changes in both product and material inventories, the result will be the cost of product sold.

In this accounting system, an *increase* in inventories, that is, product and material costs that are not applicable to sales, has the effect of *reducing* the cost of product sold. A *decrease* of product and/or material inventories has the effect of *increasing* cost of product sold, accounting for the portion of sales that are all or in part from inventories. The cost of product sold is relevant for determining profit and corporate income taxes, so the foreign and local components are converted to the accounting currency and aggregated. For this purpose, estimates of cost of product sold for each period are inserted into the income statement.[32]

Production Cost, Factory Cost, and Cost of Product Sold

Production cost was derived from *factory cost* by adding the change in material inventories. *Cost of product sold* is derived from production cost by subtracting the change in both material and product inventories. Why add material inventories and then subtract? In the project planning process it is necessary to estimate material inventories rather than relying on actual operating data; in this way analysis can conform reasonably closely to standard accounting. In shorthand notation, these relationships can be described as follows:

$$PC = FC + \Delta Mat$$
$$CPS = (FC + \Delta Mat) - \Delta\,(FP + WIP) - \Delta Mat$$
$$= FC - \Delta(FP + WIP)$$
$$EBITDA = R - CPS$$
$$= R - FC + \Delta(FP + WIP)$$

$$CFO = \text{EBITDA} - \Delta(FP + WIP) - \Delta\text{Mat}$$
$$= R - FC + \Delta(FP + WIP) - \Delta(FP + WIP) - \Delta\text{Mat}$$
$$= R - FC - \Delta\text{Mat}$$

where
$PC = $ production cost
$FC = $ factory cost
$Mat = $ material cost
$FP = $ finished product
$WIP = $ work in progress
$R = $ revenue
$CFO = $ cash flow from operations
$\Delta = $ amount of increase or decrease
EBITDA $= $ earnings before interest, taxes, depreciation, and amortization

The CFO result is further adjusted for accounts receivable (A/R) and accounts payable (A/P).

Cost of Product Sold—CYP

The cost of product sold for each operating year for the Cambria Yarns Project is shown in Table 2.14.

TABLE 2.14 Cost of Product Sold—CYP, US$(000)

	Year			
	3	4	5	6–10
Total production cost[1]	6,614.6	6,269.5	5,937.7	5,960.2
Less: Change in product inventory	340.9	38.1	(3.4)	(0.0)
Less: Change in material inventory	1,205.2	255.9	(22.5)	0.0
Cost of product sold (COPS)	5,068.6	5,975.5	5,963.6	5,960.2
Sales	12,663.9	16,260.2	16,260.2	16,260.2
COPS/Sales	0.40	0.37	0.37	0.37
Factory cost	5,409.4	6,013.6	5,960.2	5,960.2
Less: Change in product inventories	340.9	38.1	(3.4)	(0.0)
Cost of product sold	5,068.6	5,975.5	5,963.6	5,960.2

[1]Production costs are not completely variable; some fixed costs affect per-unit COPS in year 4.

FINANCIAL STATEMENTS

Information concerning resource and financial flows is organized in the form of financial statements. These are compilations of estimates on the status and flow of funds and resources committed to and generated by the project. They describe the relationships of assets, liabilities, ownership, income, and outlays. Indicators of financial performance are derived from these statements, which form an important part of the basis for the decision on whether to go ahead with the project.

Typically an income statement, a balance sheet, and several types of cash flow statements are utilized, with data conforming to the accounting system employed so that all statements are mutually consistent.

Pro-forma financial statements are developed to derive financial indicators for analysis and appraisal of the project. Figure 2.11 illustrates the process, which begins with the compilation of information from estimates of *investment costs, production costs, sales revenue* (and other sources), and *project financing*. Financial statements are prepared that cover the entire life of the project to the planning horizon or any number of years based on the requirements of financial institutions, built around estimates of values of financial and resource flows. Uncertainty exists in all of the elements

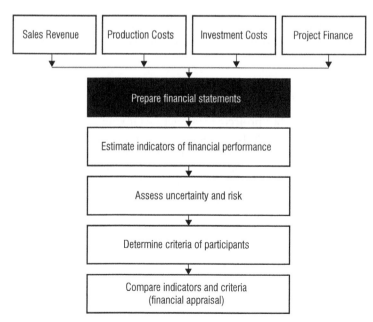

FIGURE 2.11 Financial Statements and Project Appraisal

of analysis, so that any decision based on a comparison of indicators and criteria of stakeholders should be appropriately risk-adjusted.

To deal with a critical liquidity issue (e.g., where seasonal flows of inputs and/or outputs restrict cash availability), it may be necessary to plan in time increments shorter than one year—monthly, quarterly, or semiannually. Short-term planning periods for part of the project (e.g., the start-up phase) can be combined with annual flows for the remaining years to the planning horizon. Adjustments may be necessary for compatibility of short-period parameters: For example, turnover ratios must be modified if they are to be used in working capital or other calculations. The annual COT has to be divided by 12/length of planning period (in months); for example, if annual COT is 16, for quarterly planning COT is $16/(12/3) = 4$.

Aside from the features discussed in the earlier "Accounting System" section, another issue is the method of accounting used in preparing financial statements—cash or accrual. In the cash method, statements reflect all cash inflows and outflows for the period. The accrual method includes any income and expenses incurred but not necessarily transacted financially during the period. Which method is better for a particular project? Certainly the accrual method reflects a more accurate picture of transactions and flows. In all of the examples herein the accrual method of accounting is employed.

Expected values (most easily interpreted as long-term averages or mean values) of financial variables and parameters are best used in developing financial statements, with a bias toward conservatism. Factors of uncertainty, as a measure of potential risk, are generally applied to indicators extracted from these statements (see caveat on double-counting risk in the introduction to this chapter).

Cash Flow Plan and Income Statement

The *cash flow plan* describes projected transactions involving cash and resources attributable to the project. This statement comprises, in essence, the financial plan for the project and is the underpinning of financial analysis. The plan is built up from all sources (inflows) and uses (outflows) of funds, fund equivalents, and other resources planned for each project period (planning, construction, operation, decommissioning if applicable) from inception to the planning horizon, expressed in a common monetary unit. It provides a dynamic overview of the project that is most useful for assessment purposes.

Sources include equity, proceeds from loans, possibly grants and subsidies, revenues from sales of products, income from any investments that are considered part of the project, and decreases in working capital.

Nonmonetary inflows, such as in-kind contributions of investors, have to be counted if they have alternative uses or markets that define their values. Uses of funds include investments in fixed assets, preoperational expenditures, increases in working capital, debt service, operating expenditures including taxes, and decommissioning costs.

The value of assets at the planning horizon is an element of the cash flow plan that can have a significant impact on project assessment, particularly when the time to the planning horizon is short compared with the economic life of major assets. Several terms have been used variously to describe their value: residual, salvage, and terminal value.

Residual value is best applied in situations where the planning horizon is a convenient end point for purposes of project appraisal, but where the enterprise is anticipated to continue operations beyond that time—although a finite planning horizon is selected, project operations may continue indefinitely. As a simulation of the continuing functionality of assets beyond the planning horizon (i.e., to account for resources not consumed or otherwise depleted over time), the value at the planning horizon is taken into account in project assessment. Some assets may be fully depreciated that have not reached the end of their useful life; current assets may have a liquidity value; debt and other obligations may remain to be paid.

A direct method is to apply book value (undepreciated balance of the original investment), which may be a reasonable indicator of both liquidation value and the potential for the resource to generate additional benefits, although there may be good reasons for altering the value considering either liquidation or continuing operation as the likely scenario. Alternatives for valuation include an estimate of replacement or market value at the planning horizon; the value in its best alternative use; or its net productivity from the planning horizon to the end of its economic life. Unless there are reasons for modifying these estimates, residual current assets can be liquidated, and residual current liabilities cleared, at their book values.

Salvage value is best applied at a point in time when the asset reaches the end of its economic life, when it is expected that the asset will be taken out of service. The value, in this case, would be its scrap value.

Terminal value has quite a different meaning. This term refers to wealth accumulated by the project at the planning horizon. In the cash flow plan, a major part of terminal value is usually in the form of uncommitted accumulated surpluses. The residual (or salvage) value of the original assets is part of terminal value. If there are plans in the project scope to retain accumulated surpluses in the enterprise and apply these funds for expansion or for other purposes, the terminal value might be better reflected in the expected value of shares at the planning horizon.

A viability test for the plan is sufficient liquidity, maintained so that funds available are adequate to meet all financial obligations during each project period to the planning horizon.

The cash flow plan is structured to segregate cash flow from operations, investing, and financing activities, which provides a clear description of the basis for flows in each period. This structure is consistent with conventional financial reporting standards.

The income statement and cash flow plan are developed simultaneously because they are interlinked. Interest payments and taxes are determinants of income and elements of the cash flow plan. As a practical matter, *it is best to determine cash flows period by period, maintaining consistency between the income statement and cash flow plan, commencing with the first and progressing through all periods to the planning horizon.*

The *income (profit and loss) statement* provides a periodic (usually annual) view of revenues from operations and other sources versus production costs, and is the basis for determining taxes on income. As the income statement includes some nonflow items (depreciation and amortization) and does not include some flow items (principal repayments), its principle utility for project analysis lies in estimating taxable profit, tax liability, and potential dividend payments. Consequently, the income statement is essential for an accurate estimate of cash flow. For a new investment project the income statement presents the projected results of operations based upon estimated revenues and expenses during a particular period. For an expansion or rehabilitation project the income statement includes differential (with-project minus without-project) sources of revenue and expenditures.

The flow of funds and resources (financial values) is the primary means of assessing viability of the project from the financial point of view, although information from the three statements—income, balance, and cash flow plan—enters into determination of *static* and *dynamic indicators*. However, income and its associated financial indicators are widely accepted as measures of performance. In this respect the income statement provides useful information for prospective investors and other stakeholders for comparison against benchmarks for the industry. Both depreciation and interest are normally deducted before income tax is determined. In the CYP accounting, all operating costs are deducted to determine *operating profit* (EBITDA). The cost of finance (interest on debt plus fees) for the period plus depreciation of project assets is then deducted from operating profit to determine net profit or loss before taxes. Taxes are then estimated at this level and deducted for net income.

In some countries, payment of dividends is restricted by net income in each period; elsewhere, availability of funds and discretion of directors determine dividend policy. There have been instances where enterprises have borrowed funds to pay dividends when earnings and cash are insufficient, mainly to placate shareholders, but this is not advisable for the project plan. Income that is not distributed as dividends is added to reserves.

A distinction is maintained between earnings (profit) and cash flow, which is sometimes estimated for a particular operating period by adding depreciation and amortization to net profit. With accrual accounting this may be an oversimplification, and certainly when financial and investment flows are involved. Free cash flow is a further refinement, with provisions for investment deducted.

Income Statement and Cash Flow Plan—CYP Table 2.15a is the income statement for the Cambria Yarns Project, designed to conform as closely as practicable to internationally acceptable accounting standards. The cash flow plan is shown in Table 2.15b. These tables are generated by inserting appropriate values year by year so that they are mutually consistent. Operating profit, for example, is transferred from the income statement to the cash flow plan in year 3 and then interest is deducted, so that depreciation is not included as a cash flow. As part of this process the amount of debt, equity, and other capital sources is determined in accordance with cash requirements, along with flows necessary to service the debt.

The *cash flow plan* (Table 2.15b) is developed commencing with the first year of the project and proceeding through all other project periods (years). The local partner, Cambria Investors, Ltd. (CIL) is to provide the local portion of investment cost in year 1 in the local currency equivalent of US$1,642.4 (all amounts are given in $US000). Year 1 fixed investment (fixed assets plus preoperational expenditures) is covered with foreign exchange equity from the foreign partner, Namborn Trading Company (NTC) in the amount of US$9,819.8.

In year 2 the foreign exchange portion of fixed assets, preoperational expenditures, and initial working capital is covered with an International Finance Corporation (IFC) loan of US$23,089.9 and the local portion with CIL local currency equity of US$1,020.5. The actual loan balance is increased by interest capitalized during construction of US$1,154.5. In year 3 there is a disbursement of US$1,260.9 by IFC to cover the foreign exchange portion of working capital increments.

The cash flow plan is completed for all other years by calculating interest, taxes, and dividends paid from the income statement and transferring those values to the cash flow plan. Simulation of liquidation of the residual value of fixed assets (at book value) of US$7,457.2 and working capital of US$4,433.8 (total of $11,891.1) are included in year 10 (the planning horizon) under cash flow from investing activities ("Sale—other").

TABLE 2.15a Income Statement—CYP, US$(000)

					Year			
	1	2	3	4	...	9	10
Net revenue (sales)			12,663.9	16,260.2		16,260.2	16,260.2
Other operating revenue			0.0	0.0		0.0	0.0
Total revenue			12,663.9	16,260.2		16,260.2	16,260.2
− Cost of product sold			5,068.6	5,975.5		5,960.2	5,960.2
Gross profit			7,595.3	10,284.7		10,300.0	10,300.0
− Marketing and distribution cost			1,099.6	1,829.6		1,829.6	1,829.6
− General and administrative expense			453.3	453.3		163.3	163.3
Operating profit (EBITDA)[1]			6,042.4	8,001.7		8,307.1	8,307.1
− Depreciation			4,458.9	4,458.9		3,043.3	3,043.3
− Interest expense/ + income[2]			2,487.5	2,550.5		850.2	425.1
− Extraordinary charges/ + credits[3]							(10.7)
Net profit (loss) before tax			(904.1)	992.3		4,413.7	4,849.4
− Corporate tax[4]						1,324.1	1,454.8
Net profit (loss)			(904.1)	992.3		3,089.6	3,394.6

[1] Earnings before interest, taxes, depreciation, amortization.
[2] Year 3 interest is calculated on previous balance plus interest on average balance of disbursement during the year (see the "Debt Service" subsection in this chapter); otherwise interest is calculated on the balance at the end of the previous period.
[3] Sale of fully depreciated office equipment in year 8 and transportation equipment in year 10 at 25 percent of initial value.
[4] Five-year tax holiday from commencement of operations, corporate tax 30 percent of profit.

TABLE 2.10B Cash Flow Plan—C11, US$(000)

					Year		
	1	2	3	4	...	9	10
Cash Flow from Operations							
Operations profit (EBITDA)[1]			6,042.4	8,001.7		8,307.1	8,307.1
− Interest and other finance charges—long-term loan[2]			(2,487.5)	(2,550.5)		(850.2)	(425.1)
− Interest and other finance charges—short-term loan[3]							
− Extraordinary charges/+ credits							10.7
− Corporate tax			0.0	0.0		(1,324.1)	(1,454.8)
Changes in working capital							
+ Decrease (increase) in accounts receivable			(2,255.2)	(640.4)		0.0	0.0
+ Decrease (increase) in product inventories			(340.9)	(38.1)		0.0	0.0
+ Decrease (increase) in material inventories[4]			(1,205.2)	(255.9)		0.0	0.0
+ Decrease (increase) in working capital cash			(47.2)	(20.9)		0.0	0.0
+ Increase (decrease) in accounts payable			1,034.2	214.1		0.0	0.0
Total cash flow from operations			740.6	4,709.9		6,132.8	6,437.9
Cash Flow from Investing Activities							
Sale of (investment in) property, plant and equipment							
Fixed assets—F[5]	(9,373.3)	(20,447.5)				(42.8)	
Fixed assets—L[6]	(1,612.2)	(157.7)					
+ Preproduction expenditures—F	(446.5)	(2,384.4)					
+ Preproduction expenditures—L	(30.2)	(231.4)					
+ Capitalized interest[7]		(1,154.5)					
+ Initial working capital—F		(258.0)					
+ Initial working capital—L		(646.0)					
+ Sale (investment)—other[8]							11,891.1

(Continued)

TABLE 2.15b (Continued)

	Year						
	1	2	3	4	...	9	10
Total cash flow from investment	(11,462.1)	(25,279.5)	0.0	0.0		(42.8)	11,891.1
Cash Flow from Financing Activities							
Proceeds from long-term loans		23,089.9	1,260.9				
+ Capitalized interest		1,154.5					
− Repayment of funds borrowed						(4,250.9)	(4,250.9)
Proceeds from short-term loans[9]							
+ Sales (purchase) of marketable securities							
+ Increase (decrease) in share capital							
Equity CIL	1,642.4						
Equity NTC	9,819.8	1,035.1					
− Dividends paid				(496.1)		(1,544.8)	(1,697.3)
Total cash flow from financing activities	11,462.1	25,279.5	1,260.9	(496.1)		(5,795.7)	(5,948.2)
Total cash flow	0.0	0.0	2,001.5	4,213.8		294.4	12,380.8
Cumulative cash flow	0.0	0.0	2,001.5	6,215.3		8,309.5	20,690.3

[1] Earnings before interest, taxes, depreciation, and amortization.

[2] In year 3, interest is calculated on previous balance plus half of the interest on disbursement during the year ($0.1 \times 23,089.9 + 0.5 \times 0.1 \times 1,295.6$); otherwise interest is calculated on the balance at the end of the previous period.

[3] An 8 percent interest rate on short-term credit is assumed for entire year.

[4] Increase in material inventory is covered as "Initial working capital—F, L".

[5] Transportation equipment replaced in year 9; used equipment sold in year 10 at 25 percent of initial cost.

[6] Office equipment replaced in year 7; used equipment sold in year 8 at 25 percent of initial cost.

[7] Capitalized interest is calculated on the average balance during the period, assuming essentially uniform disbursement throughout the period.

[8] Long-term capital investments (e.g., patents, trademarks, licenses); includes simulated liquidation of residual fixed assets and working capital in year 10 at book value.

[9] Revolving short-term credit used to cover deficit in year 3; assumed repaid at beginning of following year.

Data are obtained from the following sources:

■ Revenue estimates: sales program, Cambria Yarns Project (see our web site, Tables A1.6 and A1.7).
■ Marketing and distribution costs, general and administrative expense (Table 2.13).
■ Cost of product sold (Table 2.14).
■ Depreciation (Table 2.1).
■ Interest payments (Table 2.16).
■ Extraordinary charges and credits represent income from sale of replaced assets, at 25 percent of original cost (Table 2.15b).
■ Income tax is calculated on the basis of 30 percent of *net profit before tax*, in accordance with the prevailing tax code in the host county.

Debt Service

Debt service consists of payments of principal, interest, and fees to cover loans made by institutions or individuals to cover part of the capital investment. The debt service schedule identifies the amount of principal and interest to be paid in each project period. The amount of debt to be incurred is best determined period-by-period in the cash flow plan (Table 2.15b), starting from first period to last.

Debt Service Schedule—CYP   For the Cambria Yarns Project, the debt service schedule is developed in accordance with finance specifications (see our web site) and financing requirements as determined in the cash flow plan. The long-term loan from the IFC is disbursed as shown in Table 2.16. The balance at the end of each period includes interest capitalized during the construction phase (year 2). Disbursement of the loan commences in year 2 as all of the first-year capital expenditures are covered by equity contributions of the partners. Most of the loan, about 95 percent, is disbursed in year 2 (second year of construction). The balance of the loan is disbursed in year 3, to cover increases in working capital. Repayments commence at the end of year 5, in 6 equal installments of principal. During the construction phase (years 1 and 2) interest is calculated on average balance, assuming uniform disbursement over the year. For the operating years, interest is calculated on the balance at the end of the previous period, with the exception of year 3 when it is assumed that the disbursement will occur uniformly during the year.

In developing the debt service schedule, the loan principal at the end of each year is determined from the disbursements indicated in the cash flow plan—US$23,089.9 in year 2, augmented by the capitalized interest in year 2

TABLE 2.16 Debt Service Plan—CYP, US$(000)

	Year									
	1	2	3	4	5	6	7	8	9	10
Long-term Loan										
Disbursements	0.0	23,089.9	1,260.9							
Balance, end of period	0.0	24,244.4	25,505.3	25,505.3	21,254.4	17,003.5	12,752.6	8,501.8	4,250.9	0.0
Repayment					4,250.9	4,250.9	4,250.9	4,250.9	4,250.9	4,250.9
Capitalized interest[1]		1,154.5								
Interest[2]			2,487.5	2,550.5	2,550.5	2,125.4	1,700.4	1,275.3	850.2	425.1
Total debt service			2,487.5	2,550.5	6,801.4	6,376.3	5,951.2	5,526.1	5,101.1	4,676.0
Percentage disbursement		95.1%	4.9%							

[1]Capitalized interest is calculated on the average balance during the period, assuming essentially uniform disbursement throughout the period.

[2]In year 3, interest is calculated on previous balance plus half of interest on disbursement during the year (0.1 × 24,244.4 + 0.5 × 0.1 × 1,260.9/2); otherwise interest is calculated on the balance at the end of the previous period.

of US$1,154.5 in year 1 and another disbursement of US$1,260.9 in year 3 (amounts are in US$000 throughout).

Investment during construction year 1 is covered with NTC (foreign partner) *equity*. The local partner, CIL, provides the local portion of investment cost in years 1 and 2 and the local currency portion of increase in working capital in year 3. All other financing requirements in years 1 to 3 are to be covered with the IFC foreign currency loan (including capitalized interest), under the following terms:

- The loan is to be drawn as required to finance the foreign currency portion of the investment, including the working capital portion in year 3.
- The first repayment is due at the end of year 5, with subsequent payments of equal installments in each of five years thereafter (six payments in total).
- Interest is paid at a rate of 10 percent on the unpaid balance at the end of the previous year.
- Interest can be capitalized during the construction phase.

Real and Financial Flows—CYP   Tables 2.17a and 2.17b,[33] depicting *real* and *financial* flows,[34] demonstrate an alternative structure of the cash flow plan, which is primarily relevant for economic analysis (Chapter 5). Items included in real flows are goods and services produced and consumed by the project. Financial flows include essentially takedown of loans, debt service, and nonmaterial working capital items—receivables, payables, and cash. In this context, the term *cash flow plan* is a misnomer in the sense that the emphasis is on consumption and generation of real resources. Table 2.17a (real flows) and Table 2.17b (financial flows and totals)[35] are a rearrangement of the information in Tables 2.15a and b, so net flow per period and cumulative flows correspond.

Product Profitability   A separate statement can be developed for each product of a multiple product line. It has a form similar to the income statement of Table 2.15a but includes only revenues associated with the product and direct cost items. Direct costs might include materials and labor costs and perhaps some factory overheads that could be directly attributed to the product. Depending on the organization structure adopted, it might also be possible to attribute some administrative and marketing overheads.

Direct cost margin is the difference between product revenues and direct costs. Products can be compared and the product line adjusted to those products indicating the highest margins, unless other business factors demand their inclusion in the product line. A full production year would

TABLE 2.17a Real Flows—CYP, US$(000)

	% FX	1	2	3	...	8	9	10
					Year			
Net Cash Flow—Real		(11,462.1)	(25,279.5)	4,496.3		8,349.6	8,264.3	18,493.0
Inflows				12,663.9		16,260.2	16,260.2	16,260.2
Total net sales				12,663.9		16,260.2	16,260.2	16,260.2
Export	100.0			6,711.8		13,423.2	13,423.2	13,423.2
Domestic	0.0			5,952.1		2,837.0	2,837.0	2,837.0
Outflows		11,462.1	25,279.5	8,167.5		7,910.6	7,995.8	(2,232.8)
Factory cost				5,409.4		5,960.2	5,960.2	5,960.2
Materials								
Raw materials[1]	91.7			3,394.6		3,788.7	3,788.7	3,788.7
Auxiliary materials				729.1		813.7	813.7	813.7
Labor								
Skilled	0.0		0.0	77.0		85.1	85.1	85.1
Unskilled	0.0			186.3		207.3	207.3	207.3
Factory supplies	0.0		0.0	64.8		64.8	64.8	64.8
Spare parts consumed	100.0			373.2		373.2	373.2	373.2
Repair, maintenance	0.0		0.0	183.0		183.0	183.0	183.0
Energy	0.0			401.4		444.4	444.4	444.4
General and administrative overheads				453.3		163.3	163.3	163.3
Skilled labor	0.0		0.0	10.6		10.6	10.6	10.6
Unskilled labor	0.0			7.6		7.6	7.6	7.6
Expatriate staff	100.0			290.0				
Local management staff	0.0		0.0	72.8		72.8	72.8	72.8
Materials, services, insurance, etc.	73.5			52.0		52.0	52.0	52.0
Land lease[2]	0.0			20.3		20.3	20.3	20.3

Marketing and sales costs			0.0	1,099.6	1,829.6	1,829.6	1,829.6
Skilled labor	0.0			5.3	5.3	5.3	5.3
Unskilled labor	0.0			1.3	1.3	1.3	1.3
Materials, services, etc.	62.0	.		93.6	93.6	93.6	93.6
Distribution—export	100.0			578.3	1,156.7	1,156.7	1,156.7
Distribution—domestic	0.0	0.0		421.1	572.8	572.8	572.8
Change in current assets³		0.0	0.0	1,205.2	0.0	0.0	0.0
Material inventories (increase)	0.0			1,205.2	0.0	0.0	0.0
Fixed investment	100.0	11,462.1	25,279.5	0.0	(42.5)	42.8	(10,185.9)
Fixed assets—F	0.0	9,373.3	20,447.5			42.8	
Fixed assets—L	0.0	1,612.2	157.7				
Preproduction expenditures—F	100.0	446.5	2,384.4				
Preproduction expenditures—L	0.0	30.2	231.4				
Capitalized interest	100.0	0.0	1,154.5				
Initial working capital—F	100.0		258.0				
Initial working capital—L	0.0		646.0				
Sale (investment)—other⁴	0.0				(42.5)		(10,175.3)
Extraordinary charges (credits)	0.0						(10.7)

¹Raw cotton is purchased domestically but has import content (see Tables 3-4 and 3-5 on the web site).

²Lease payments intended to compensate government for site development costs—opportunity cost of land plus basic infrastructure.

³Change in product inventories is included in "Factory cost."

⁴Includes simulated liquidation of fixed assets and working capital at book value at end of year 10.

Note: Italic items as shown on our web site are non-shadow-priced and combined as "Other Real Flows (RF)" in Table 3.1.

139

TABLE 2.17b Financial Flows—CYP, US$(000)

					Year			
	% FX	1	2	3	...	8	9	10
Net cash flow—financial		11,462.1	25,279.5	(2,494.9)		(8,146.4)	(7,969.9)	(7,828.1)
Inflows		11,462.1	25,279.5	1,260.9		0.0	0.0	0.0
Proceeds from long-term loans	100.0	0.0	23,089.9					
Capitalized interest	100.0		1,154.5	1,260.9				
Proceeds from short-term loans								
Sales (purchase) of marketable securities								
Increase (decrease) in share capital								
Equity CIL	0.0	1,642.4	1,035.1	0.0				
Equity NTC	100.0	9,819.8						
Outflows		0.0	0.0	3,755.7		8,146.4	7,969.9	7,828.1
Principal repayment, long-term loan	100.0					4,250.9	4,250.9	4,250.9
Dividends paid[1]	80.0					1,410.9	1,544.8	1,697.3
Interest and other finance charges—long-term loan	100.0			2,487.5		1,275.3	850.2	425.1
Interest and other finance charges—short-term loan								
Corporate tax	0.0	0.0		2,255.2		1,209.3	1,324.1	1,454.8
Increase (decrease) in accounts receivable[2]	0.0	0.0		47.2		0.0	0.0	0.0
Increase (decrease) in working capital cash[3]	0.0	0.0				0.0	0.0	0.0
Decrease (increase) in accounts payable	0.0	0.0		(1,034.2)		0.0	0.0	0.0
Total cash flow		0.0	2,001.5	2,001.5		203.3	294.4	12,380.7
Cumulative cash flow		0.0	2,001.5	2,001.5		8,015.0	8,309.4	20,690.1
Total cash flow (see Table 2.15a)		0.0	2,001.5	2,001.5		203.3	294.4	12,380.8

[1] In proportion to shares of foreign and local partners.
[2] Year 3—71.6% F; Year 4: 125.1% F (decrease in local receivables in year 4—see Table 2.8 WC).
[3] No additional financing appears to be required for this item.
Note: Italic lines as shown in our web site are components of working capital changes that are effectively financial flows.

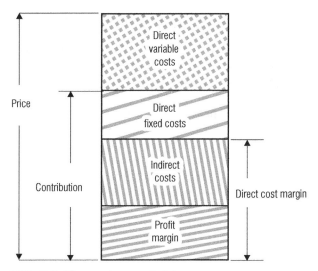

FIGURE 2.12 Product Profitability

probably best serve for comparing direct cost margins in connection with product line decisions, so that the combination of fixed and variable direct costs is representative. Performing this analysis at aggregated production levels planned for the full production year, rather than on the basis of unit revenues and costs, has the advantage of averaging variations. The direct cost margin (see Figure 2.12) is the best basis for selecting the most favorable products to include in the line. Any scheme for allocating indirect costs to each product does not enhance the contrast between product profitability of each product considered for inclusion in the project.

Balance Sheet

The projected balance sheet provides a snapshot or static picture of the project at given points in time. It describes the financial status at the end of each fiscal year (or at other times) for all project phases—construction, operations, and decommissioning (if applicable). It includes an estimate of fixed and current assets and how they are to be financed with debt and equity. In each year assets and liabilities are assigned their estimated values. Assets are valued at initial cost less any accumulated depreciation (unless they are revalued periodically to compensate for inflation).

The balance sheet normally is structured with one side for assets and the other for a combination of liabilities and shareholders' equity, explaining how the assets are financed; *balance* refers to equality between the two sides.

Net asset value (total assets less accumulated depreciation) is covered by a combination of liabilities (short-, medium-, and long-term) and shareholders' equity. The type of financing covering assets is a measure of stability: Fixed assets covered with short-term borrowing is a sure sign of distress, and not a good idea when planning the project.

Information is obtained on value created by the project for equity holders, that is, shareholders' equity or net worth,[36] which is the value of ownership as measured by the difference between estimated values of assets and liabilities. The equity position can comprise capital stock (original value of shares as paid by the shareholders, both common and preferred,[37] and other paid-in capital), retained earnings (undistributed profits), and reserves (e.g., sinking funds and reserves for depreciation). In some countries depreciation expense must be matched by a corresponding amount (or some derivative thereof) converted to depreciation reserve. Aside from the capital stock, the designation and amounts of equity components are for bookkeeping purposes; no funds change hands ordinarily when retained earnings are converted to reserves. Book value, or shareholders' equity per common share, is of interest for sponsors when contemplating disposal of shares. Often the market price of shares is linked to this indicator.

Balance Sheet—CYP The projected balance sheet for the Cambria Yarns Project is shown in Tables 2.18a and b. Entries for each period are drawn from the income statement and cash flow plan. Fixed investment values (fixed assets and preoperational expenditures) are cumulative; cumulative depreciation is obtained from the depreciation schedule indicated earlier. Working capital values in each period are obtained from Table 2.8. As the balance sheet is the description of financial state rather than flow, the *value* of a working capital element, rather than *increments* (as in the cash flow plan) are included.

APPENDIX 2.1: DEPRECIATION METHODS

Straight-Line to Zero

The original cost of the machine is charged to depreciation at equal rates over the depreciation period of the asset. The value at the end of its depreciation is assumed to be zero (no scrap value). Depreciation expense per year is determined by dividing the initial cost of an asset by its useful (economic) life, which is the reciprocal of the depreciation rate. Accumulated depreciation (sum of depreciation from first period of use to the current period) is the provision for loss of asset value. This method assumes that the value of the asset is fully consumed so that there is zero salvage value at the end of its

TABLE 2.18a Balance Sheet, Assets—CYP, US$(000)

	Year										
	1	2	3	4	5	6	7	8	9	10[7]	
Long-term assets											**RES FA**
Fixed assets[1]	10,985.4	31,590.6	31,590.6	31,590.6	31,590.6	31,590.6	31,760.7	31,760.7	31,803.4	31,803.4	7,457.2
Preproduction expenditures[2]	476.7	4,247.0	4,247.0	4,247.0	4,247.0	4,247.0	4,247.0	4,247.0	4,247.0	4,247.0	
− Accumulated depreciation[3]			4,458.9	8,917.9	13,376.8	16,420.1	19,463.4	22,506.7	25,549.9	28,593.2	
+ Long-term financial investments											
+ Goodwill (patents, trademarks, licenses, other)											
Total long-term assets	11,462.1	35,837.6	31,378.7	26,919.7	22,460.8	19,417.5	16,544.3	13,501.0	10,500.5	7,457.2	
Current assets											
Cash and cash equivalents[4]	0.0	0.0	2,001.5	6,215.3	6,839.6	7,407.7	7,811.8	8,015.1	8,309.5	20,690.3	
+ Marketable securities											
+ Short-term cash			47.2	68.1	62.8	60.1	60.1	60.1	60.1	60.1	
+ Accounts receivable[5]			2,255.2	2,895.7	2,895.7	2,895.7	2,895.7	2,895.7	2,895.7	2,895.7	
+ Product inventories[6]			340.9	378.9	375.6	375.6	375.6	375.6	375.6	375.6	
+ Material inventories[7]		904.0	2,109.1	2,365.1	2,342.5	2,342.5	2,342.5	2,342.5	2,342.5	2,342.5	**NWC**
Total current assets	0.0	904.0	6,753.9	11,923.1	12,516.1	13,081.5	13,485.6	13,688.8	13,983.5	14,473.0	4,433.8
Total assets	11,462.1	36,741.6	38,132.6	38,842.8	34,977.0	32,499.0	30,029.9	27,189.9	24,483.8	21,930.3	

[1]Cumulative value of fixed assets including replacements.
[2]Cumulative value of preproduction expenditures, including capitalized interest during two years of construction.
[3]Accumulated depreciation, or the total depreciation up to the period, from depreciation schedule; residual value at planning horizon 7,457.2.
[4]Cumulative cash balance from cash plan statement including working capital cash.
[5]Balance of accounts receivable from working capital statement.
[6]Value of product inventories from working capital statement.
[7]Value of material inventories from working capital statement.

TABLE 2.18b Balance Sheet, Liabilities and Equity—CYP, US$(000)

	Year									
Long-term liabilities	1	2	3	4	5	6	7	8	9	10^7
Long-term loans[1]	0.0	24,244.4	25,505.3	25,505.3	21,254.4	17,003.5	12,752.6	8,501.8	4,250.9	0.0
Other long-term obligations										
Total long-term liabilities	0.0	24,244.4	25,505.3	25,505.3	21,254.4	17,003.5	12,752.6	8,501.8	4,250.9	0.0
Current liabilities										
Bank loans (overdrafts)[2]	0.0	0.0	0.0	0.0						
+ Accounts payable[3]			1,034.2	1,248.2	1,036.2	1,239.9	1,239.9	1,239.9	1,239.9	1,239.9
+ Corporate tax payable										
+ Other short-term obligations										
Total current liabilities	0.0	0.0	1,034.2	1,248.2	1,036.2	1,239.9	1,239.9	1,239.9	1,239.9	1,239.9
Shareholders' equity										
Share capital[4]	11,462.1	12,497.2	12,497.2	12,497.2	12,497.2	12,497.2	12,497.2	12,497.2	12,497.2	12,497.2
+ Current earnings retained[5]			(904.1)	496.1	597.1	1,569.2	1,781.7	1,410.9	1,544.8	1,697.3
+ Retained earnings (–accumulated losses)[6]				–904.1	–407.9	189.2	1,758.4	3,540.2	4,951.0	6,495.8
+ Reserves										
Total shareholders' equity	11,462.1	12,497.2	11,593.2	12,089.3	12,686.4	14,255.6	16,037.4	17,448.3	18,993.0	20,690.3
Total liabilities and equity	11,462.1	36,741.6	38,132.6	38,842.8	34,977.0	32,499.0	30,029.9	27,189.9	24,483.8	21,930.3

[1] Balance of long-term loan at end of period—from debt service schedule.
[2] Balance of short-term loan (overdraft) at end of period—from debt service schedule.
[3] Value of payables from working capital statement.
[4] Paid in equity capital—from cash plan.
[5] Net profit after tax for each period.
[6] Cumulative profits retained: net profit for period plus retained earnings from previous period.
[7] The balance sheet for year 10 does not reflect liquidation of fixed assets and working capital at book value. However, the liquidation is simulated in the cash plan as an inflow of funds. If the assets are actually liquidated the ending balance in year 10 should be adjusted to reflect a zero value for these assets.

TABLE 2.19 Straight-Line Depreciation

Year	Annual Depreciation Expense	Book Value at End of Year	Accumulated Depreciation, End of Year
0	0	1,000	0
1	200	800	200
2	200	600	400
3	200	400	600
4	200	200	800
5	200	0	1,000

$$\text{Depreciation per period} = \frac{\text{Asset value}}{\text{Number of depreciation periods}}$$

economic life. In the example shown in Table 2.19, the original value of the asset is \$1,000 and the useful life is five years. The accumulated depreciation is the sum of depreciation up to and including the particular year.

Straight-Line to Salvage Value

The difference between the initial asset value and the salvage value at the end of economic life is charged to depreciation at equal rates over the depreciation period. Depreciation per period is calculated by dividing the difference by the number of years of depreciation. The depreciable amount is equal to the initial value of the asset minus its salvage value. In the example shown in Table 2.20, the initial value of the asset is \$1,000, the economic life is five years, and the expected salvage value is \$200.

$$\begin{aligned} \text{Annual depreciation} &= \frac{\text{Initial asset value} - \text{salvage value}}{\text{Depreciation periods}} \\ &= \frac{\$1000 - \$200}{5} = \$160 \end{aligned}$$

Declining Balance

In the *declining balance* method,[38] the annual depreciation is determined from some multiple of the straight-line rate, usually set by taxing authorities, multiplied by the undepreciated balance (net book value of asset). The amount of depreciation declines with time as book value diminishes, as shown in the example of Table 2.21 for a fixed rate 1.5 times the straight-line (SL) rate. This is an accelerated form of depreciation, with the advantage

TABLE 2.20 Straight-Line to Salvage Depreciation

Year	Annual Depreciation Expense	Book Value at End of Year	Accumulated Depreciation, End of Year
0	0	1,000	0
1	160	840	160
2	160	680	320
3	160	520	480
4	160	360	640
5	160	200	800

$$\text{Depreciation per period} = \frac{\text{Asset value} - \text{salvage value}}{\text{Number of depreciation periods}}$$

of positive effect on cash flow (lower taxable profit in the early years). The project is more likely not to generate sufficient profits to cover the higher level of depreciation reserves (as compared with straight-line), if required, in the early years. The method is justified by the fact that usually technological depreciation of assets is greater in the early years.

$$\text{Annual depreciation, \%} = (1.5) \left(\frac{1}{\text{Depreciation periods}} \right) (100)$$

$$= (1.5) \left(\frac{1}{10} \right) (100) = 15\%$$

TABLE 2.21 Declining Balance Depreciation

Year	Book Value End of Year	Annual Depreciation	Cumulative Depreciation	Cumulative SL Depreciation	Net Depreciation
0	1,200.0	0.0	0.0	0.0	0.0
1	1,200.0	180.0	180.0	120.0	180.0
2	1,020.0	153.0	333.0	240.0	333.0
3	867.0	130.1	463.1	360.0	463.1
4	737.0	110.5	573.6	480.0	573.6
5	626.4	94.0	667.6	600.0	667.6
6	532.4	79.9	747.4	720.0	747.4
7	452.6	67.9	815.3	840.0	935.3
8	384.7	57.7	873.0	960.0	993.0
9	327.0	49.0	922.1	1,080.0	1,042.1
10	277.9	41.7	963.8	1,200.0	1,083.8

The book value, according to this formula, theoretically never reduces to zero, but the system is set up so that when the straight-line accumulated depreciation exceeds the accumulated depreciation calculated by the declining balance method, the depreciation for that period is, as a maximum, the straight-line depreciation. In the example shown, in year 7 the straight-line accumulated depreciation exceeds the corresponding value for the declining balance method; therefore, the straight-line depreciation (120 as a maximum) is applied. In each year thereafter, the straight-line depreciation is applied until book value is reduced to zero.

Sum of Years' Digits

This is another form of accelerated depreciation. In each year the allowed depreciation is determined on the basis of the remaining life of the asset as a proportion of the total of the digits representing the years during the depreciation period. In the following formula, n is the number of years and j the particular year. The depreciation amount reduces each year, as in the double-declining method. In this method the value of the asset does reach zero at the end of useful life. An example is shown in Table 2.22.

$$\text{Annual depreciation rate, year j, \%} = \left(\frac{(n-j)+1}{\sum j} \right)(100)$$

$$\text{Annual depreciation} = \left(\frac{\text{Annual depreciation rate}}{100} \right)(\text{Original value})$$

Year 2 depreciation is calculated as follows:

$$\% = \left(\frac{(5-2)+1}{15} \right)(100) = \left(\frac{4}{15} \right)(100) = 26.7\%$$
$$= (1000)(0.267) = 267$$

TABLE 2.22 Sum of the Years' Digits Depreciation

Year	Annual Depreciation Expense	Book Value at End of Year	Accumulated Depreciation, End of Year
0	0	1,000.00	0
1	333.33	666.67	333.33
2	266.67	400.00	600.00
3	200.00	200.00	800.00
4	133.33	66.67	933.33
5	66.67	0.00	1,000.00

APPENDIX 2.2: STARTING INVENTORY BALANCE

The procedure for dealing with a situation where there is a starting inventory balance with valuation different from those of the operating periods involves two steps, the first to consume initial inventory (FIFO) and the second for the current inventory resulting from normal production. A suggested model is as follows:

Stage 1

$$EQs_j \geq \left[EQs_{j-1} - \left(Q_j + \frac{Q_j}{COT} \right) \right], N_j$$

$$\Delta EQs_j = \left(EQs_j - EQs_{j-1} \right)$$

$$\Delta EVs_j = \left(EQs_j - EQs_{j-1} \right) bs_j$$

Stage 2

$$EQ_0 = 0, EQ_j \geq 0$$

$$EQ_j \geq \left[\frac{Q_j}{COT}, EQ_{j-1} - Q_j, N_j \right] - EQs_j$$

$$\Delta EQ_j = \left(EQ_j - EQ_{j-1} \right)$$

$$\Delta EV_j = \left(EQ_j - EQ_{j-1} \right) b_J$$

$$\Delta EVt_j = \Delta EVs_j + \Delta EV_j$$

where EQs_j = ending quantity of starting balance, period j
$\quad QI_j$ = quantity consumed in sales or production program; for materials $(P_j \times u_j)$, period j
$\quad SV_j$ = specified value of ending inventory
$\quad EVs_j$ = ending value of starting inventory, period j
$\quad bs_j$ = unit basis for starting balance, period j
$\quad P_j$ = production level, period j
$\quad u_j$ = units of material required per unit of production, period j
$\quad \Delta$ = change in value
$\quad EQ_j$ = ending quantity, period j
$\quad EV_j$ = ending value, period j
$\quad EVt_j$ = total ending value (starting plus current inventory, period j)
$\quad b_j$ = unit basis, period j

The following example is an illustration of the use of this model applied to starting inventory of finished product, where $bs_j = 3$, $b_j = 2$ (constant).

	Period			
	0	1	2	3
EQs_0	100			
N_j		50	0	0
Q_j		30	30	30
Q_j/COT		10	10	10
EV_j	300	180	60	20

Period 1, stage 1:

$$EV_{S_0} = 100*3 = 300$$
$$EQs_1 \geq [100 - (30 + 10)], 50 = 60$$
$$\Delta EQs_1 = (60 - 100) = -40$$
$$\Delta EVs_1 = (-40)\, 3 = -120$$
$$EVs_1 = 300 + (-120) = 180$$

Period 1, stage 2:

$$EQ_1 \geq [10, (0 - 30), 50] - 60 = 0$$
$$\Delta EQ_1 = (0 - 0) = 0$$
$$\Delta EV_1 = (0)\, 2 = 0$$
$$\Delta EVt_1 = -120 + 0 = -120$$

Period 2, stage 1:

$$EQs_2 \geq [60 - (30 + 10)], 0 = 20$$
$$\Delta EQs_2 = (20 - 60) = -40$$
$$\Delta EVs_2 = (-40)\, 3 = -120$$
$$EVs_2 = 180 + (-120) = 60$$

Period 2, stage 2:

$$EQ_2 \geq \left[10, (0-30)_j, 0\right] - 20 = 0$$
$$\Delta EQ_2 = (0-0) = 0$$
$$\Delta EV_j = (0)2 = 0$$
$$\Delta EVt_2 = -120 + 0 = -120$$

Period 3, stage 1:

$$EQs_3 \geq [20 - (30 + 10)], 0 = 0$$
$$\Delta EQs_3 = (0 - 20) = -20$$
$$\Delta EVs_3 = (-20)3 = -60$$
$$EVs_3 = 60 + (-60) = 0$$

Period 3, stage 2:

$$EQ_3 \geq [10, (0 - 30), 0] - 0 = 10$$
$$\Delta EQ_3 = (10 - 0) = 10$$
$$\Delta EV_3 = (10)2 = 20$$
$$\Delta EVt_3 = -60 + 20 = -40$$

In accordance with this model, the reduction in inventory value from the starting balance to the end of period 3 is –280 (i.e., –120, –120, –40). This results from the exhaustion of the original inventory (–300) and the increase of inventory from production in period 3 of 10 units at a value of 2 (i.e., +20).

If the starting balance is zero ($EQs_j = 0$ for all periods), the stage 2 model can be employed directly.

NOTES

1. Analysis (financial *or* economic) refers to the process of first identifying project variables, with particular attention to those that are likely to determine success or failure (or socioeconomic acceptability); and estimating their states or values to the planning horizon; assessing the investment package and capital structure. *Financial analysis* in this context also includes the process of determining

(1) flow of funds related to project inputs and outputs at market values for each project period from inception to planning horizon; (2) calculating quantitative performance indicators and associated risks (uncertainties); and (3) determining appropriate criteria for stakeholders. *Appraisal* (financial or economic) is comparison of criteria with performance indicators.

2. In the light of the global economic meltdown that started in 2007, and experiments in bailing out enterprises that were considered too big to fail, it is likely that such enterprises in future will either be allowed to go into bankruptcy or broken up into smaller, more manageable units.

3. In regard to prospects for building a sustainable economy, which is in the interest of investors as well as other segments of society, committing scarce resources to a failed enterprise narrows the range of economic opportunity.

4. *Parameter* in this context refers to a design feature that can take on multiple values—for example, the yield of ore used in refining metal. Once the plant is constructed, its output is a function of the capacity of the processing equipment, but also the yield in tons of refined metal per ton of raw material.

5. Standard operating costs provide a guide for an operating enterprise for budgeting material costs, wages and salaries, and other expenses involved in production and marketing. They can be used for production planning and to predict the relationship between fixed and variable costs and profit as a function of the level of business activity. Actual operating costs in a production unit may be recorded either chronologically, by job order, or by process, and then compared with standards as a measure of efficiency.

6. For an existing enterprise it is useful to consider scenarios with and without the project and the incremental impact.

7. To provide a more realistic simulation of cash flow, all depreciation in the Cambria Yarns case study is charged as a general expense and not to *factory cost*. In an operating enterprise depreciation would normally be charged to the operating unit utilizing a depreciable asset.

8. Operating divisions for an enterprise may differ from this structure; *operating cost* is the aggregate amount attributable to all operating divisions.

9. Working capital margin represents the amount of current assets to be financed as part of the initial investment with long-term capital, rather than short-term or revolving credit lines.

10. Operating leverage is the percentage of fixed costs in the cost structure (fixed plus variable costs). Higher operating leverage indicates that income is more affected by changes in sales volume. With low variable costs, contribution is high, so that an increase in sales volume results in a profit increment greater than would be the case with relatively high variable cost.

11. *Financial leverage* is measured as the ratio of debt to equity, or debt to total assets; *operating leverage*, the ratio of variable margin (contribution)/operating profit, is a measure of how margin is to be translated into profit; *variable margin* is the difference between revenues and variable costs during an operating period.

12. Risk adjustments should be applied either to criteria or to project parameters but usually not to both, to avoid, in a sense, double-counting.

13. Analysis of alternatives can be applied to nonrevenue projects, with a cost minimization objective.

14. Comparisons of performance indicators with risk-adjusted criteria and decision making are more properly appraisal functions rather than analysis but are included here for purposes of continuity.

15. Depreciation is a cost that does not involve actual outflow of funds but which is taken into account for determining profit and, consequently, tax on income—see the subsection "Depreciation."

16. The hurdle rate is the barrier that has to be equaled or surpassed to satisfy investors.

17. In this context, *marginal* refers to benefits and costs of the preceding time period.

18. The relationship depends upon the price basis. A relative price based on weights of oil and coal, for example, will generally differ from one based on calorific values.

19. The decision affects the applicability of financial criteria; an inflation-adjusted criterion is consistent with constant price analysis, whereas a nominal (market) criterion is better applied when current prices are employed in the analysis (see Chapter 3).

20. See Jason Van Bergen, "Forces Behind Exchange Rates," *Investopedia/Forbes*, 2010, www.investopedia.com/articles/basics/04/050704.asp. Van Bergen cites the following factors as affecting exchange rates between the currencies of two countries: relative inflation, relative interest rates, current accounts deficits, public debt, terms of trade, political stability, and economic performance.

21. The first four methods are described in detail in Appendix 2.1.

22. If assets are periodically revalued in the plan according to regulation (e.g., proportional to anticipated inflation), this relationship is not necessarily true.

23. In the accounting method employed herein, receivables are valued at price rather than factory cost, even though the latter is the amount actually invested. Product inventory is valued at factory cost, so the investment in its typical early buildup is accurately reflected in the cash flow. Since revenue is registered at the time of sale, credit sales require that the revenue be offset with an equal value of receivables so that the net cash flow is correctly zero. This procedure is consistent with accounting practices in most parts of the world.

24. The COT can be calculated for periods other than a year. For monthly planning, the basis should be consistent with the planning period (e.g., 30 days). For example, if the annual cost (basis) for an item is 3,600, the basis for monthly planning is 3,600/12 = 300. For annual planning, with a COT (rotations per year) of 24, the working capital requirement is 3,600/24 = 150. The COT for monthly planning is two rotations per month (i.e., 24/12) and the working capital requirement is 300/2 = 150 (same value). For investment projects extending over several years, except for early periods when detailed planning might be appropriate, annual planning for WCap is recommended.

25. A change in receivables affects the revenue stream and not production cost. Valuing receivables at the sales price provides an accurate reflection of the effect of credit sales on the revenue stream. When receivables are liquidated the revenue stream is enhanced, presumably at the sales price. Any receivables in the starting balance sheet should be valued at their liquidation price.

26. To maintain consistency with respect to discounted cash flow analysis, which is the fundamental basis for financial appraisal, ending values of inventory are

used in the calculations (flows are typically assumed to occur at the end of each period). During a given period, the actual inventory level will vary between minimum and maximum, with the average providing a better indication of the cost of financing working capital. The COT is ideally based on the optimal order cycle. A longer cycle involves more capital tie-up, as shown in Figure 2.6.

27. Additional financing required will be about half the difference between the maximum and base level, or $(5198.5 - 945.2)/2 \times$ US$668—about US$1.42 million. Either internally generated funds or short-term financing can be applied to cover this inventory.

28. Techniques of management science and operations research provide optimization models that can be applied to virtually all project design features; see, for example David Anderson, Thomas Williams, and Dennis Sweeney, *An Introduction to Management Science: Quantitative Approaches to Decision Making* (South-Western College, 2004); and F. Hillier, G. Lieberman, and M. Hillier, *Management Science* (McGraw-Hill, 1999).

29. When market conditions allow little flexibility in pricing decisions, cost reduction is a way to improve profitability.

30. It is important also for competitive analysis. The relative magnitudes of fixed and variable costs decisively influence the structure of industry. Sectors with a higher percentage of fixed costs tend to be more stable.

31. Earnings before interest, taxes, depreciation, and amortization.

32. Internationally acceptable accounting standards are used throughout. However, standards vary among countries, so the systems of accounting employed and resulting taxation should be in accordance with the standards of the host country.

33. All values except prices and unit costs are in US$(000).

34. *Real* flows involve resources generated (units of production) and consumed (factors of production), and not financial flows (e.g., debt, equity, taxes)—in other words, resources employed in creating goods and services. The fundamental resources are land, labor, and capital, which are embedded in intermediate goods and services in many forms that serve as inputs and outputs of the project.

35. For purposes of economic analysis, information in Table 2.17 is transferred to Table 6.1 *Real and financial flows at market prices*. However, the two tables are not identical; some data in Table 2.17 is aggregated in Table 6.1. In addition, agricultural impacts are included to complete the economic analysis and economic cost of assets procured with foreign exchange differs from the financial cost.

36. A distinction can be drawn between *shareholders' equity*, essentially the book value of shareholders' ownership, and *net worth*, more likely a current or realistic valuation based on the actual values of assets and liabilities. Book value often does not reflect replacement or market value. This distinction is not universally adopted.

37. Preferred shares usually have a fixed rate of return. They are similar to debt and have a higher standing than common shares.

38. Multipliers are applied as allowed by tax authorities.

Financial Indicators and Criteria

One of the primary instruments normally employed for appraising the project is a set of concise quantitative measures of projected financial performance. These indicators are classified in two broad categories: static and dynamic. Static indicators are essentially financial snapshots, or measures of the predicted state of the project at discrete points in time. Dynamic indicators are temporally panoramic, taking into account in a single measure the predicted performance over the entire span of the project's life to the planning horizon.

The indicators described here are those that are relevant to project appraisal. They derive from features selected in the process of project design and directly from the financial statements developed in Chapter 2. The range of indicators employed for managing an enterprise is much broader, but many of them do not apply in the context of project development. Ratios and other indicators are compared with benchmarks or standards of the project's industry or sector, to assess projected performance.

As part of the project appraisal process, performance indicators and other project features are compared with criteria of stakeholders, each of which may have specific interests and benchmarks of acceptability.

STATIC INDICATORS

Static indicators are more familiar to most investors as they are utilized widely in capital markets for appraising the value of financial instruments, both debt and equity; they can be categorized as financial ratios and risk indicators. Indicators of existing enterprises are not always appropriate benchmarks for a new project. Markets have a way of swinging between extremes of pessimism and optimism, so that the ratios and other indicators can easily lose their significance. If such benchmarks are to be used, they should be averaged over an extended period (e.g., moving average) to remove cyclical extremes. In the context of project analysis, indicator values are directly dependent on design parameters (i.e., value reflects the decision of the designer); for this reason some simple indicators are of limited relevance for appraisal (e.g., current ratios) as they merely confirm design decisions.

There are *no general standards for static indicators*, no acceptable maxima or minima. Acceptable levels depend on factors that are related to the type of project, cyclical norms (e.g., orders and payments), and risk in the host environment. For example, what is acceptable in country A for a mining company will differ considerably from what is acceptable for a food processing enterprise in country B. The best way to set standards is to use data from existing operations of similar enterprises in the area.

Stakeholder preference is perhaps the most significant constraint on values of these indicators. For example, for purposes of risk avoidance, lenders will invariably limit the amount of debt they are willing to provide to some proportion of the total investment.

TYPES OF STATIC INDICATORS

Most static indicators of interest for project design and appraisal are ratios, which provide snapshots of projected performance and risk. Only a limited number of the many ratios utilized for performance monitoring in commerce and industry are applicable. For the project, the intent is to assess the viability of the investment proposal. Ratios selected for assessment need benchmarks from the industry, or from closely related industries in the host country, for comparison.

Static indicators, or ratios, have the advantage of simplicity but the disadvantage of limited applicability for a new investment; one of the problems is selecting the most representative point in time (or period). Types of static indicators include:

- Financial ratios—profitability, liquidity, turnover, leverage (solvency).
- Payback period,[1] indicating the length of time necessary to recover the investment—a measure of risk.
- Breakeven, an indicator of the degree of safety at the planned operating level in regard to operating loss (discussed in Chapter 7 in the section titled "Quantitative Risk Assessment)."

Financial Ratios

Financial ratios facilitate comparison of alternative configurations and of the project with other similar enterprises. Values are derived from data in financial statements (income and cash flow statements, balance sheet). They can be calculated for each year (or planning period) to the planning horizon. As they vary considerably over time, the most meaningful information is derived from a representative year or period, when production has reached normal planned capacity. As the value of some ratios depends on how profit and capital are defined, knowledge of formulations employed is required to fully comprehend their significance.

For illustrative purposes, in the following examples, values are shown with each formula for the Cambria Yarns Project, year 5, a representative operating period. Values for each component can be found in the financial statements. Tables 3.1a and b are a summary of values for years 3, 5, and 7 and also show values of the variables used in calculating the ratios.[2]

Profitability ratios are indicators of the relationship between profits and sales. They are used to assess the effectiveness of planned operations, particularly useful when compared with data from other enterprises in the same or similar businesses as profit margins vary among industries. Data can be found in the income statement, balance sheet, and cash flow plan.

Depreciation is charged as a general expense after operating profit has been calculated (see Table 2.15a), and not allocated to *factory cost* and other operating functions, as would normally be the case. Accurate simulation of cash flow in the early periods is considered more important than profitability indicators in this context, since discounted cash flow is the major instrument of financial appraisal (see the later section "Dynamic Indicators"). Resources actually invested in finished product inventory, as it is accumulated in the early periods, do not include depreciation, so cash flow estimates will be closer to what will actually be experienced in the operating enterprise created by the project. This is a trade-off engendered by the need to maintain consistent accounting throughout the process of financial analysis.

Gross profit margin (GPM) is the ratio of gross profit, the balance of revenue after deducting cost of product sold, to net revenue. It is generally indicative of the effectiveness of production operations and represents the amount available to cover overhead costs (general and administrative or G&A, marketing, and fixed costs such as depreciation and finance charges) and taxes and to provide profits.

$$GPM\,(\%) = 100\left(\frac{\text{Gross profit}}{\text{Revenue}}\right)$$
$$= 100\left(\frac{10{,}296.9}{16{,}260.2}\right) = 63.3\%$$

Net profit margin (NPM) is the ratio of net profit to net sales, an indicator of the portion of revenues that accrues to the owners as profits, or the amount that is available to draw from the enterprise as dividends or additional investments. This indicator deals with after-tax profit so all costs are included. It is a good indicator of profitability if a representative planning period is selected to compare with a benchmark. It does not have a consistent relationship with the cost of capital for assessment purposes. Typical margins among industries vary widely. High-quality, low-volume products generally have higher margins while high-volume products such as consumer staples generally work on smaller margins.

$$NPM\,(\%) = 100 \left(\frac{\text{Net profit margin}}{\text{Revenue}} \right)$$

$$= 100 \left(\frac{1,194.3}{16,260.2} \right) = 7.3\%$$

Operating profit margin (OPM) is the ratio of profit from operations (gross profit less G&A and marketing costs, or EBITDA) to net revenues. It is an indicator of profitability on primary operations, independent of investment or finance costs.

$$OPM\,(\%) = 100 \left(\frac{\text{Operating profit}}{\text{Revenue}} \right)$$

$$= 100 \left(\frac{8,203.7}{16,260.2} \right) = 50.5\%$$

Return on investment (RoI) is defined as the ratio of annual net profit to total investment and may also be calculated for various degrees of capacity utilization (sensitivity analysis). The total capital invested should include fixed assets, preoperational expenditures, and initial working capital (i.e., what is financed with permanent capital). RoI is an indicator of return from the commitment of capital resources to the enterprise, so in its most useful form the denominator is initial value rather than current value of investment. The ratio is determined by dividing net profit after tax, plus interest[3] (from the income statement), by the total invested capital (from the balance sheet).[4] The rationale for adding back the interest is that the indicator is intended to be independent of financing considerations. RoI can be used in comparing mutually exclusive projects competing for the same investment. For independent appraisal, RoI provides an indication of the project's capability to provide returns sufficient to meet the cost of capital invested in the project.[5]

$$RoI\ (\%) = 100 \left(\frac{\text{Net profit} + \text{interest}}{\text{Total investment}} \right)$$

$$= 100 \left(\frac{1,194.3 + 2,550.5}{38,002.7} \right) = 9.9\%$$

Return on equity (RoE) measures net profit (income statement) against equity contributed (balance sheet). Equity can be defined as *paid-in equity* (equity capital) or *shareholders' equity*, which includes retained profits and reserves. For project analysis, RoE is an indicator of return for investors from the commitment of their own capital resources, so *paid-in equity capital* is the most appropriate denominator rather than the current value of shareholders' equity. This indicator can be determined for periods in which retained earnings and reserves are accumulated but is more appropriate when calculating efficiency of an investor's shares in an operating enterprise.

$$RoE\ (\%) = 100 \left(\frac{\text{Net profit}}{\text{Equity capital}} \right)$$

$$= 100 \left(\frac{1,194.3}{12,497.4} \right) = 9.6\%$$

There is little ambiguity regarding definition of *net profit* in this case, which refers to after-tax profits available to shareholders. In equity markets some investors, particularly preferred shareholders, compare annual (average) dividend net of tax with capital investment.

Limitations of RoI and RoE for Project Analysis   The difficulty of using static indicators RoI or RoE for project appraisal is evident from the values provided in Table 3.1b for the Cambria Yarns Project. Year 3 is start-up, years 5 and 7 are full-production years. Which period is representative of project performance? An additional shortcoming is the fact that these indicators do not take into account the time value of investment and equity contributions. Static rate-of-return is more meaningful if profitability on total investment is fairly constant throughout the project life and can be applied for preliminary evaluation of competing projects and for screening out those that are clearly unacceptable.[6]

Return on assets (RoA) is similar to RoI, relating net profit after tax (income statement) to assets committed to the project (balance sheet). During the start-up phase RoI and RoA should be virtually identical. Differences may appear during the operations phase as total assets are affected by depreciation, working capital changes, and replacement investments. This ratio can be considered as the (mathematical) product of two other ratios—net profit margin (net profit to sales) and asset turnover (sales to total assets):

$$RoA\ (\%) = 100 \left(\frac{\text{Net profit}}{\text{Total assets}} \right)$$

$$= 100 \left(\frac{1,194.3}{36,277.4} \right) = 3.3\%$$

Liquidity Ratios

These ratios are indicative of the ability of the enterprise to generate cash and to meet obligations. During the planning stage, ratios should reflect planned turnover of short-term assets and liabilities. They indicate the ability of the enterprise to meet day-to-day obligations in the short run. Normal values are a function of the type of business. Comparisons with enterprises in the same industry are sometimes difficult. For example, an enterprise relying on imported inputs tends to maintain higher current ratios than one using only domestic inputs. Risk is reduced when short-term assets at least cover short-term liabilities. The standard for the current ratio, which includes more risky asset components, tends to be higher than for the quick ratio.

Current Ratios   Current ratios measure the relationship between current assets and current liabilities (both found in the balance sheet), indicating the ability of an enterprise to cover its short-term obligations. A higher current ratio indicates greater short-term liquidity. Components of current assets are an important consideration—a higher proportion of inventories connotes higher risk, as inventories are generally not as liquid as receivables. Current assets tie up cash, so high levels may indicate that the resources of the enterprise are not well employed.[7] There are no specific standards, but certainly the ratio should be somewhat greater than unity—for most industrial enterprises a ratio of 1.5 is acceptable.

$$\text{Current Ratio} = \frac{\text{Current assets}}{\text{Curent liabilities}} = \frac{5,676.5}{1,036.2} = 5.5$$

$$\text{Quick Ratio} = \frac{\text{Cash} + \text{Marketable securities} + \text{Receivables}}{\text{Current liabilities}}$$

$$= \frac{62.8 + 2,895.7}{1,036.2} = 2.9$$

The *quick ratio*, or acid test, is a more conservative view of short-term liquidity (covering short-term liabilities). Only highly liquid assets, easily converted to cash, are considered as available to cover current liabilities, such as cash, marketable securities, and receivables (balance sheet). If the quick assets are maintained at a level in excess of current liabilities (say 20 percent or more in general, a ratio of 1.2), risk should be acceptable.

Turnover Ratios

Turnover ratios are indicators of how efficiently the project plans to employ its assets. Ratios of greatest interest at the design stage are inventory, asset, and receivables turnover.

Inventory Turnover Rotation of product inventories (balance sheet) in relation to cost of product sold (income statement) is measured in number of days. The ratio is a pure number because both the inventory and the cost of product sold are valued at factory cost. Using *factory cost* as the denominator, rather than *sales revenue* as the basis for the calculation, gives a clearer picture of the number of inventory rotations per year. This ratio (or, alternatively, the stock turnover ratio) measures the rate of converting inventory into sales. *Average inventory* is the average of opening and closing values for the period. A low ratio may indicate a need to look again at the inventory policy adopted in the project plan.

For an operating enterprise, inventory turnover reflects the efficiency of inventory management and velocity of working capital cycles. High inventory turnover may be a reflection of management efficiency but is not always desirable as the possibility of stock-outs and attendant loss of sales and goodwill are increased. Of the activity ratios, this is particularly significant as it can influence many policy decisions, such as purchase, sales, and credit policies, and investment in storage facilities. The calculated inventory turnover should reflect the weighted average of product inventory coefficients of turnover (COTs).

$$\text{Inventory turnover (days)} = 365 \left(\frac{\text{Product inventory}}{\text{Factory cost}} \right) = 365 \left(\frac{375.6}{5,960.2} \right)$$

$$= 23.0 \text{ days}$$

$$COT = \left(\frac{\text{Factory cost}}{\text{Product inventory}} \right) = \frac{365}{\text{Inventory turnover (days)}} = \frac{365}{23.0}$$

$$= 15.9 \text{ rotations per year}$$

Receivables Turnover   This indicator is useful for designing the project's credit policy and also to estimate cash flows from receivables. It should reflect or confirm the policy or assumptions on receivables included in the project plan. It measures the number of days for accounts receivable rotation (debtors) and is related to the COT. A meaningful indicator for project analysis is calculated by dividing average receivables (balance sheet) by credit sales[8] revenue at full capacity (income statement) and multiplying by the number of days per year. A high turnover in receivables is desirable as it reflects a short collection period and reduced need for short-term financing.

$$\text{AR turnover (days)} = 365 \left(\frac{\text{Receivables}}{\text{Credit sales}} \right) = \frac{2,895.7}{16,260.2} = 65.0 \text{ days}$$

$$COT = \left(\frac{\text{Credit sales}}{\text{Receivables}} \right) = \frac{365}{\text{A/R turnover (days)}} = \frac{365}{65.0} = 5.6$$

Leverage Ratios

These ratios are measures of risk associated with the financial plan, the ability of the enterprise to meet its financial obligations. They provide information concerning resilience of the project—that is, its ability to withstand financial shocks that would threaten its existence.

Leverage (or solvency) ratios explain the project's capacity to meet longer-term financial obligations. Financial *leverage* refers to the proportion of debt in the capital structure. Greater debt usually decreases the weighted cost of capital—it is ordinarily cheaper than equity and its cost is tax deductible, thereby increasing returns for equity holders. However, debt increases project risk, so it is advisable to control its use in project financing—in any case, a lender usually demands a proportion of equity for risk avoidance. Leverage ratios basically indicate the relationship of debt to equity or total assets.

Debt/Equity The debt to equity (DE) ratio indicates the relative participation in the investment package of creditors and owners. The ratio is calculated by dividing long-term liabilities by common equity plus preference capital (percent debt/percent equity), all of which are balance sheet items. Financial institutions generally set limits on the ratio to minimize risk: Typically, debt would be permitted up to perhaps 1.5 times equity (60/40); a ratio higher than 2 (67/33) is generally considered risky. If a project generates returns greater than the cost of debt, the equity owners benefit from more debt (trading on equity or positive leverage).

For project analysis the most meaningful value is the relationship of debt and equity in the initial capital structure. In the Cambria Yarns case, debt includes loan disbursements in years 2 and 3 plus capitalized interest. The denominator comprises the contribution of CIL and NTC in years 1, 2, and 3 (see Table 2.15b). In calculating the indicators, the standard values shown in Table 3.1b for year 5 are applied.

$$DE = \frac{\text{Long-term debt}}{\text{Shareholders' equity}}$$

$$\text{Initial capital structure} = \frac{25,505.3}{12,497.2} = 2.0$$

$$\text{Year } 5 = \frac{21,254.4}{12,686.4} = 1.7$$

Fixed Assets Coverage (FAC) This ratio measures coverage of long-term debt provided by fixed assets (plant, machinery, and equipment), both balance sheet items. It also provides information on the amount of fixed assets financed with long-term debt. Lenders favor a high ratio, perhaps 2 or 3 depending upon their assessment of the liquidation value of the assets. The most meaningful indicator compares initial fixed assets to long-term debt in the initial capital structure.

$$FAC = \frac{\text{Fixed assets}}{\text{Long-term debt}}$$

$$\text{Initial capital structure} = \frac{31,590.6}{25,505.3} = 1.2$$

$$\text{Year } 5 = \frac{22,460.8}{21,254.4} = 1.1$$

Debt Service Coverage (DSC)   This is not a leverage ratio in the pure sense but is included here as it indicates the ability of cash generated to cover debt service (interest plus principal repayments). This is one of the major indicators for lenders as it measures the amount of risk in the project related to servicing the debt. The debt service coverage ratio can be defined as the ratio of *cash generated* to *debt service* in any period. Cash generated per period can be defined as *cash flow from operations* plus interest (from the cash flow plan), equivalent to adding interest and depreciation to net profit (from the income statement). An alternative for project assessment purposes is DSC based upon free cash flow, which includes funds provided by equity or liability increases less funds consumed by new investments (e.g., increase in working capital or fixed assets), as shown in the second calculation below. Debt service is the sum of principal repayments and finance charges (interest and fees).

A ratio above 1.5 should normally be acceptable. Financial institutions seek a short repayment period with the lower limit of DSC as a constraint.

$$DSC = \frac{\text{Cash flow from operations} + \text{interest}}{\text{Principal repayment} + \text{interest}}$$

$$= \frac{5,472.3 + 2,550.5}{4,250.9 + 2,550.5} = 1.2$$

$$DSC = \frac{\text{Net profit} + \text{interest} + \text{depreciation} + \Delta\text{liabilities} - \Delta\text{investment}}{\text{Principal repayment} + \text{interest}}$$

$$= \frac{1,194.3 + 2,550.5 + 4,458.9 + 0 - (180.9)}{4,250.9 + 2,550.5} = 1.2$$

Summary of Financial Ratios—CYP

Tables 3.1a and 3.1b provide a summary of financial ratios for the Cambria Yarns Project for years 3, 5, and 7, which are utilized in project appraisal (compared with stakeholder criteria). Table 3.1a is the list of base values from which the indicators are calculated. Table 3.1b is the list of indicators for years 3, 5, and 7. Profitability indicators are in percent and other indicators as ratios.

Payback Period

Payback period is the time required to recover the original investment outlay through annual cash flows. It is a measure of project risk and is usually

TABLE 3.1a Financial Ratios, Base Values—CYP, US$(000)

	Year			
	3	5	7	Initial
Gross profit	7,595.3	10,296.6	10,300.0	
Revenue	12,663.9	16,260.2	16,260.2	
Net profit	(904.1)	1,194.3	3,563.5	
Operating profit	6,042.4	8,203.7	8,307.1	
Total assets	38,132.6	34,977.0	30,029.9	
Dividends	0.0	597.1	1,781.7	
Current assets	4,752.4	5,676.5	5,673.8	
Current liabilities	1,034.2	1,036.2	1,239.9	
Product inventory	340.9	375.6	375.6	
Factory cost	5,409.4	5,960.2	5,960.2	
Long-term debt	25,505.3	21,254.4	12,752.6	
Shareholders' equity	11,593.2	12,686.4	16,037.4	12,497.2
Current liabilities	1,034.2	1,036.2	1,239.9	
Fixed assets	28,547.4	22,460.8	16,544.3	31,590.6
Cash flow from operations	740.6	5,472.3	6,606.8	
Interest	2,487.5	2,550.5	1,700.4	
Principal repayments	0.0	4,250.9	4,250.9	
Depreciation	4,458.9	4,458.9	3,043.3	
Increase in working capital	2,767.1	180.9	0.0	
Increase in inventories	1,546.0	(25.9)	0.0	
Receivables	2,255.2	2,895.7	2,895.7	
Total investment	38,002.5	38,002.5	38,002.5	
Initial equity capital	12,497.2	12,497.2	12,497.2	
Short-term liabilities	1,034.2	1,036.2	1,239.9	
Working capital cash	47.2	62.8	60.1	

calculated from project inception. As the more distant future increases uncertainty, some investors (particularly foreign direct investment) seek to recover their investment in a relatively short period of time. Payback is easily understood: It is calculated by accumulating annual cash flows in each period until the full original investment outlay is recovered. Although a measure widely employed, it does have a few shortcomings. While value is time-dependent, timing of cash flows is not considered. Cash flows generated after payback are not taken into account, which can obscure a clear superiority of one project over another based on performance after the payback period.

Payback Period, Investment The payback period for total investment is essentially the point in time at which the investment (fixed investment plus

TABLE 3.1b Financial Ratios, Indicators—CYP

	Year			
	3	5	7	Initial
Profitability ratios				
Gross profit margin	60.0%	63.3%	63.3%	
Net profit margin	(7.1%)	7.3%	21.9%	
Operating profit margin	47.7%	50.5%	51.1%	
Return on investment	4.2%	9.9%	13.9%	
Return on equity	(7.2%)	9.6%	28.5%	
Return on assets	(2.4%)	3.4%	11.9%	
Liquidity ratios				
Current ratio	4.6	5.5	4.6	
Quick ratio	2.2	2.9	2.4	
Efficiency ratios				
Inventory turnover, days	23.0	23.0	23.0	
Receivables turnover	65.0	65.0	65.0	
Solvency ratios				
Debt/equity	2.3	1.8	0.9	2.0
Fixed asset coverage	1.1	1.1	1.3	(1.2)
Debt service coverage I	1.3	1.2	1.4	
Debt service coverage II	1.3	1.2	1.4	
Coefficient of turnover, inventory	15.9			
Coefficient of turnover, receivables	5.6			

increases in working capital) is recovered from benefits generated during the operations phase. The first formula is developed from profits after tax for each period with interest[9] and depreciation added. The sum is taken to the year in which the cumulative flow changes from negative to positive. The second formula provides identical results.

$$\sum_{j=0}^{n} (-I_j - \Delta WC_j + NP_j + Int_j + Dep_j + Res V_j) \geq 0$$

$$\sum_{j=0}^{n} (-I_j + NCF_j + Res V_j) \geq 0$$

where
I_j = fixed investment outlay, period j
ΔWC_j = increase in working capital, period j
NP_j = net profit after tax, period j

Int_j = interest paid, period j
Dep_j = depreciation, period j
NCF_j = net cash flow from operations j (see Table 2.15b depreciation excluded [added back])
$ResV_j$ = residual value, period j
N = period in which value of formula = 0

Payback Period, Investment—CYP NCF_j includes changes in working capital (increase in inventories and receivables less increase in payables). Illustration is provided in Table 3.2a, based upon data from the Cambria Yarns Project. The crossover from negative to positive in the cumulative flow occurs in year 8. The payback period is then seven years or more.

A short payback corresponds to a high average annual net cash flow. The reciprocal of the payback period can be used as an approximate measure of the profitability of an investment.[10] Payback period is, in a sense, a dynamic indicator as it is dependent upon time-related flows, but is included here because it doesn't adjust for time value as do other dynamic indicators. *Dynamic payback* (see the "Dynamic Indicators" section of this chapter) is determined in a similar manner but applies discounted rather than nominal values.

Payback Period, Equity   Payback period can be determined on the basis of equity. Relevant flows are determined from the cash flow plan, adjusted to reflect the point of view of equity investors. Payback period is the point in time when equity investment is covered by benefits generated during the operation phase, when the cumulative cash flows equal or exceed the equity outlays.

$$\sum_{j=0}^{n} \left(-Equity_j + NCF_j + Div_j + ResV_j \right) = 0$$

Equity$_j$ is subtracted in each period in which a contribution is planned. Dividend payouts (Div_j) to equity holders[11] are added back to period flows from the cash flow plan as the project is credited with generating these benefits. If the payback period extends to the planning horizon, the residual value at that point is added back.

Payback, Equity—CYP   Equity payback for the Cambria Yarns Project is in the eighth year (shown in Table 3.3a), in which cumulative net flow changes from negative to positive. The payback period for each partner

TABLE 3.2a Payback Period for Investment—CYP, US$(000)

			Year					
	1	2	...	6	7	8	9	10
Payback—Investment 1								
− (Fixed assets + PP exp)	(11,462.1)	(25,279.5)		0.0	(170.1)	0.0	(42.8)	11,891.1
− Inventory increase		0.0		0.0	0.0	0.0	0.0	0.0
− Increase in receivables		0.0		0.0	0.0	0.0	0.0	0.0
− Increase in working cap cash				2.7	0.0	0.0	0.0	0.0
+ Increase in payables	0.0			203.7	0.0	0.0	0.0	0.0
Total investment	(11,462.1)	(25,279.5)		206.5	(170.1)	0.0	(42.8)	11,891.1
+ Net profit after tax				3,138.4	3,563.5	2,821.8	3,089.6	3,394.6
+ Interest				2,125.4	1,700.4	1,275.3	850.2	425.1
+ Depreciation				3,043.3	3,043.3	3,043.3	3,043.3	3,043.3
Net flow	(11,462.1)	(25,279.5)		8,513.6	8,137.1	7,140.3	6,940.3	18,754.0
Cumulative net flow	(11,462.1)	(36,741.6)		(9,716.6)	(1,579.5)	5,560.8	12,501.1	31,255.1
Payback—Investment 2								
Real flow	(11,462.1)	(25,279.5)		8,307.1	8,137.0	8,349.6	8,264.3	18,493.0
− Increase in receivables								2,895.7
− Increase in working cap cash				2.7	0.0			60.1
+ Increase in payables				203.7	0.0			(1,239.9)
− Taxes						(1,209.3)	(1,324.1)	(1,454.8)
Net flow	(11,462.1)	(25,279.5)		8,513.6	8,137.0	7,140.3	6,940.2	18,754.0
Cumulative net flow	(11,462.1)	(36,741.6)		(9,716.6)	(1,579.6)	5,560.7	12,501.0	31,255.1
Payback—Investment 3								
− (Fixed assets + PP exp)	(11,462.1)	(25,279.5)		0.0	(170.1)	0.0	(42.8)	11,891.1
+ Cash flow from operations				6,388.2	6,606.8	5,865.0	6,132.8	6,437.9
+ Interest	0.0	0.0		2,125.4	1,700.4	1,275.3	850.2	425.1
Net flow	(11,462.1)	(25,279.5)		8,513.6	8,137.1	7,140.3	6,940.3	18,754.0
Cumulative net flow	(11,462.1)	(36,741.6)		(9,716.6)	(1,579.5)	5,560.8	12,501.1	31,255.1

TABLE 3.2b Dynamic Payback on Investment—CYP, US$(000)

Dynamic Payback	Year							
	1	2	...	6	7	8	9	10
Net flow	(11,462.1)	(25,279.5)		8,513.6	8,137.1	7,140.3	6,940.3	18,754.0
Discount factor	0.921	0.848		0.610	0.561	0.517	0.476	0.438
Discounted net flow	(10,550.1)	(21,416.8)		5,176.9	4,554.3	3,678.4	3,290.9	8,185.2
Cumulative net flow	(10,550.1)	(31,966.0)		(13,761.3)	(9,207.0)	(5,528.6)	(2,237.7)	5,947.5
Rate, %/100	0.086							

can be determined similarly, which may differ based upon flows attributed to each.

DYNAMIC INDICATORS

The saying "Time is money" refers to opportunity cost of an individual's time: If employed in an activity alternative to the normal course of business, what would be gained if the opportunity at hand were forgone? The same principle applies to investment. Commitment of financial or real resources to an industrial or commercial purpose is intended to produce rewards, based on the expectation that the bird in the hand is not only better than two in the bush but will eventually produce two or more in the hand.

A fundamental principle is that control of a resource over time is what counts. Its source is of concern only in regard to the obligations related to assuming control, which opens opportunities for its employment for generating future benefits.

The most effective measures of financial performance for investment projects are indicators that take into account the entire span of time from inception of the project to its planning horizon. Although uncertainty in prediction increases with time, simulated snapshots are more prone to error than measures that encompass the entire span of a project's planned life. To alleviate the problem of increasing uncertainty with time the planning horizon can be shortened, but doing so might neglect operations that could play a significant role in the investment decision. Another advantage of dynamic indicators is inherent smoothing or averaging of inaccuracies over time. The fact that they are so widely employed in the investment arena attests to their usefulness.

Several flow patterns, or streams of funds and resources, for all periods from project inception to the planning horizon are employed to determine dynamic performance indicators. One relates to *dynamic payback*, a means of determining the length of time necessary for an investor to recoup the investment, taking into account the time value of income returns. The cash flow plan, which includes all sources and uses of funds and resources, provides a measure of liquidity (sufficiency of financial resources to meet operating and service needs). Other dynamic indicators, each employing a flow pattern appropriate to its purpose, measure temporally panoramic rates of return on total investment resources committed, on investors' equity, and for venture partners. Capital rationing indicators compare the generation of benefits per unit of scarce resource employed in each alternative project.

Time Value: Effect of Time on Value of Resources

Time is of the essence in evaluating resources; when they are put to work, the benefits to be derived depend upon efficacy of their use and time during which they are employed. Most people prefer to enjoy benefits sooner rather than later. Identical amounts of money available today and next year will most likely not have the same value. The passage of time changes value for several reasons: (1) By forgoing today's consumption, resources can be invested so that their value grows with time; (2) individuals prefer the relative certainty of consumption today rather than risky or uncertain future consumption; (3) inflation, which prevails most of the time in most economies, tends to reduce the future purchasing power of funds.

Resources and Time   The concept of time value is applicable to financial and real (tangible and intangible) resources. Time value is relevant in determining dynamic indicators of project performance as well as for investors' expectations.

If resources are applied judiciously, the value of an investment in the future should be greater than its present value, sufficient to cover the original investment and a surplus at least equal to the rental price[12] of the investment.

Combining Flows over Time   Considering variations in value of monetary units and resources over time, the problem is to combine values over the project life so that they are compatible. If 50 units of outflow (investment) at time 0 (now) generate the inflows shown in Figure 3.1 over the next five periods, how are these amounts to be combined to measure the rate of

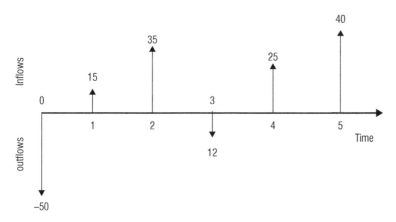

FIGURE 3.1   Combining Flows over Time

return? To express all values in terms of a common time-adjusted unit, discounting and compounding are the basic mathematical principles employed to deal with the relationship between current and future values. Discounting is a method of converting a future value to its present value equivalent; compounding converts a current value to its future value equivalent.

The owner of a unit of money has a choice of spending it now or investing it. If \$1 is spent now, \$1 of consumption benefits is immediately realized. If invested, at some future time the value should increase by earnings on the investment. In this case, if the compounding rate (rate of growth) is i%, \$1 invested at i becomes $\$(1 + i)$ one period into the future. Whether the individual decides to invest really involves two issues: (1) the rate at which the investment will grow, and (2) how the (prospective) investor views future versus present consumption. Generally the owner would not forgo present consumption unless it is advantageous.

A higher growth rate produces a higher amount to be received in the future. The value after one period, when invested at a rate of i, will grow to $(1 + i)$, which is the value at the *beginning* of the second period. If invested for the second period its value will grow to $(1 + i)(1 + i)$ or $(1 + i)^2$. Similarly, at the beginning of the third period the amount $(1 + i)^2$ will be available for investment so that at the end of the third period the original \$1 grows to $(1 + i)^3$. This is the compounding effect. One dollar invested now at a rate of 10 percent per annum grows to $(\$1.10)^3$ or \$1.331 at the end of the third year. The equation for constant growth rate is as follows:

$$FV = PV(1 + i)^n$$

where FV = future value
          PV = present value
          i = rate of growth per period, percent/100
          $(1 + i)^n$ = compounding factor

If $20 is invested for five years at a rate of growth i of 5 percent, its value at the end of the fifth year will be $20 × (1 + 0.05)^5 = $20 × 1.28 = $25.6. Conversely, the present value of a future value is determined by:

$$PV = \frac{FV}{(1 + i)^n} = FV\frac{1}{(1 + i)^n}$$

where $\dfrac{1}{(1 + i)^n}$ = discount factor

If $20 is to be received five years hence with a rate of growth of 10 percent, the discount factor would be $(1/1.1)^5 = 0.062$ and the present value is $20 × 0.062 = $12.4.

Characteristics of Dynamic Performance Indicators   While static financial indicators are essentially snapshots that provide estimates of projected financial performance at a point in time or for a single period of operation, dynamic indicators consider the entire span of the project's life. They are generally considered more reliable in the planning stages as they take a broader view of the project's resource flows.

A uniform characteristic of all dynamic indicators is that transactions (inputs and outputs) in all project periods and at all points in time are adjusted according to the time of occurrence. Only in this way can they be compatibly combined and compared. Discounting and compounding are used to adjust values of transactions from one point in time to another. Normally all values are ultimately converted to the present, taken as the time of project inception. The basis for converting values in various time periods is a discounting or compounding rate related to the cost of capital or investor expectation. Determination of the appropriate rate is discussed in the section "Cost of Capital" in Chapter 4.

Dynamic Payback

As in the calculation of standard (nondiscounted) payback, investment outlays are considered as outflows, and the number of periods is determined for which future net benefits cover outlays. The difference is that while static payback period is based upon accumulation of unadjusted flows over time, for dynamic payback the future flows are discounted. The discount rate is the challenge or hurdle rate for the investor (see "Financial Criteria for Investment Decisions" later in this chapter). The payback period is the number of years, n, it takes for the summation of cash flows to change from negative to positive, indicating that the capital investment plus the expected return has been covered. This method is more conservative than the standard payback as the time required to cover the investment with discounted benefits is greater. Intuitively it is somewhat more meaningful because it accounts for the time value of resources.

$$\sum_{j=0}^{n} \left[-I_j + \left(NCF_j + Res V_j \right) \right] df_j = 0$$

$$df_j = \left(\frac{1}{1+i} \right)^j$$

where df_i is the discount factor. The discount factor depends upon the number of the period j. Discounts are progressively greater over time.

An issue is whether the first period should be numbered 0 or 1. If 0, flows in the period will not be discounted as the discount factor $= 1$ (as is any number raised to the zero power). If it assumed that the flows occur always at the end of the period, then starting the numbering from 1 is appropriate. Another approach is to start the numbering from 0, in which case the first-period flows will not be discounted and all subsequent flows will be discounted to the beginning of period 1. In standard financial calculators the first period *is not* discounted. In spreadsheets such as Microsoft Excel, the first period *is* discounted. This matter is discussed further in the "Financial Criteria" section later in this chapter. In all of the financial calculations related to the case studies, the first period is numbered as 1 (not 0).

Dynamic Payback—CYP Dynamic payback for the Cambria Yarns Project is shown in Tables 3.2a and 3.3b. Net flow for each period is identical to those in Tables 3.2a and 3.3a, respectively. The dynamic payback period for total investment, calculated at the weighted average cost of capital (8.6 percent) is over nine years, the year after which the cumulative net flow changes from negative to positive. For equity, the payback period, discounted at the opportunity cost of equity (12 percent) is slightly shorter than payback on investment, but still more than nine years.

TABLE 3.3a Payback Period for Equity—CYP, US$(000)

	Year							
	1	2	3	...	7	8	9	10
Cash flow	0.0	0.0	2,001.5		404.1	203.3	294.4	12,380.8
+ Dividends					1,781.7	1,410.9	1,544.8	1,697.3
− Equity contribution	(11,462.1)	(1,035.1)	0.0					
Net flow	(11,462.1)	(1,035.1)	2,001.5		2,185.8	1,614.2	1,839.2	14,078.1
Cumulative net flow	(11,462.1)	(12,497.2)	(10,495.7)		(241.2)	1,373.0	3,212.2	17,290.2

Net Present Value

Net present value (NPV) is the fundamental financial measure of value. In virtually every investment arena, financial instruments are valued at NPV, which is the present value of future net benefits to be derived from ownership of assets. This holds in the conventional equity and credit markets as well as in the world of highly speculative finance. As a dynamic indicator, NPV is calculated as the sum of time-adjusted values of outflows (negative) and inflows (positive) for each time period to the planning horizon. Outflows are costs and inflows are benefits. NPV can be determined for total

TABLE 3.3b Dynamic Payback on Equity—CYP, US$(000)

	Rate	0.12						
	Year							
	1	2	3	...	7	8	9	10
Cash flow	0.0	0.0	2,001.5		404.1	203.3	294.4	12,380.8
+ Dividends	0.0	0.0			1,781.7	1,410.9	1,544.8	1,697.3
− Equity contribution	(11,462.1)	(1,035.1)	0.0		0.0	0.0	0.0	0.0
Net flow	(11,462.1)	(1,035.1)	2,001.5		2,185.8	1,614.2	1,839.2	14,078.1
Discount factor	0.893	0.797	0.712		0.452	0.404	0.361	0.322
Discounted net flow	(10,234.0)	(825.2)	1,424.6		988.8	651.9	663.2	4,532.8
Cumulative net flow	(10,234.0)	(11,059.2)	(9,634.6)		(3,876.7)	(3,224.7)	(2,561.5)	1,971.3

investment, for the entire equity, or for a particular investor or class of investors.

Net present value indicates the magnitude of benefits generated by the investment. Capital has a depletion cost and a rental cost (actual or opportunity). The value of NPV at a particular discount rate i represents the surplus generated over and above investment depletion at the selected discount rate (the hurdle rate of return on invested capital)—that is, the value that would be generated by the project in excess of the investment plus rental cost if all goes according to plan. The discount rate i to be applied is logically the expectation of return. The statement NPV = 0 means that the capital is recovered and the rental charge or expectation is realized, with no excess wealth generated. Normally if NPV is zero to positive, the project is acceptable. If the discount rate is the opportunity cost of capital, or its return in the best alternative application, then a nonnegative NPV indicates that there is no alternative project that will yield a better return. If several mutually exclusive projects are under consideration, the NPV ratio (discussed later in this chapter) may indicate the best choice for investment.

Calculating NPV Net present value is based upon funds and/or resource flows during each planning period to the planning horizon. Estimates of flows in each period derive from an engineering study of resources committed to, and generated by, the project. Once the flows in each period have been converted to a standard unit of account, a discount rate can be applied to the flow in each period. The discount factor varies from period to period (see the earlier subsection "Time Value"):

$$NPV(i) = \sum_{j=0}^{n} NCF_j * df_j$$

In the following example, inflows and outflows are shown for each period to the planning horizon. The net flow is the difference between inflows and outflows. A positive (negative) value signifies a net inflow (outflow). Discounting is applied to the net flow in each period at two different discount rates of 10 percent and 15 percent. The assumption is that all flows occur at the beginning of the period (year 0 flow not discounted; this is unlike the case study calculations in Chapters 3 and 6). NPV is determined as the sum of the discounted values in each period. In the example, NPV at a discount rate of 10 percent is 745 and at 15 percent is −573.

Year	Outflow	Inflow	Net Flow	Discount Rate 10%	Present Value	Discount Rate 15%	Present Value
0	10,000	0	(10,000)	1.0000	−10,000	1.0000	−10,000
1	500	4,000	3,500	0.9091	3,181	0.8696	3,044
2	1,000	4,000	3,000	0.8264	2,479	0.7561	2,268
3	5,000	4,000	(1,000)	0.7513	−751	0.6575	−658
4	3,000	7,000	4,000	0.6830	2,732	0.5718	2,287
5	3,000	8,000	5,000	0.6209	3,104	0.4972	2,486
Net present value					745		(573)

Relation between NPV and Discount Rate For most projects NPV decreases with increasing discount rate. At low rates of discount, NPV is relatively high for a favorable project and decreases as the discount rate is increased. Above some discount rate NPV is negative. For some cash flow patterns it is possible that NPV again turns positive as the discount rate is further increased. This can happen when there is more than one negative-positive change in net cash flows from one period to the subsequent period; it is usually not a problem because NPV has a definite value for any discount rate and is normally evaluated at a rate determined by the decision maker. A typical relationship between NPV and discount rate is shown in Figure 3.2.

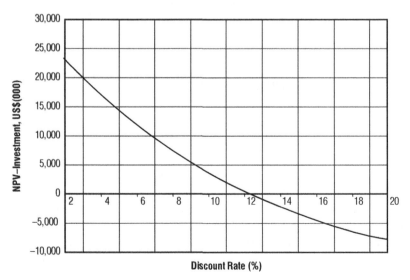

FIGURE 3.2 NPV Investment versus Discount Rate

NPV Investment   NPV investment or NPV(I) is the value of generated benefits in excess of the investment committed to the project. From this perspective, investment and operating costs are considered outflow, with revenues generated from sales as inflow, as illustrated in Figure 3.3—a simplified representation of project flows. In the upper section, investment is covered by a combination of debt and equity (financial inflow). Benefits are generated in the form of revenues that are offset by a combination of operating costs and debt service (financial outflow).

From the perspective of total investment (middle section), flows related to project financing (debt, equity, and debt service) are (essentially) irrelevant.[13] Outflow is the investment; net benefits are the differences between revenue and operating costs. In the lower section, revenue and operating costs are combined into net benefits. NPV(I) indicates the excess generated by the project over and above the depletion of capital invested (there may be some residual value at the planning horizon) and rental cost or expected rate of return. For the calculation the relevant flows are derived from a combination of *cash flow from operations* (CFO) and *cash flow from investment* (CFI), obtained from the cash flow plan (Table 2.15b). By convention, corporate taxes are included in the outflow because after-tax criteria are typically applied to NPV for appraisal purposes. No adjustment is necessary as taxes are deducted in CFO (see the following formula). It

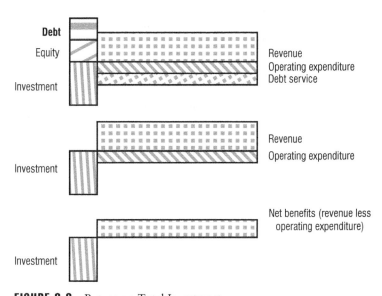

FIGURE 3.3   Return on Total Investment

is necessary to add back interest payments that are deducted in CFO as financial flows are not relevant to the calculation of this indicator.

$$NPV(I) = \sum_{j=0}^{n} \left(CFO_j + CFI_j + \text{Interest}_j\right)df_j$$

where $NPV(I) =$ net present value, total investment
   $CFI =$ cash flow from investments
   $CFO =$ cash flow from operations

NPV(I)—CYP   Calculation of NPV(I) for the Cambria Yarns Project is shown in Table 3.4. The value is US$5,947.4, signifying that this amount of surplus is generated. NPV is calculated mathematically by multiplying each period flow by the appropriate discount factor (for the period) and summing the result, as shown at the bottom of Table 3.4. As the project is financed from both equity and debt, the weighted cost of capital is the discount rate, in this case 8.6 percent (see the subsection "Weighted Average Cost of Capital" in Chapter 4).[14]

Inflows and outflows can be discounted to the beginning or end of the first period—the choice will have some effect on NPV. Discounting to the very beginning of the project is usually more realistic if flow of funds commences at that point. Some consideration may be given to the time within each period that the flows actually occur. A typical assumption is that all flows occur at the end of the period. In some cases, more accurate estimates of timing may have significance.[15]

NPV Equity   Net present value for the equity portion of invested capital, or NPV(E), is developed from the cash flow plan. Each period net flow is discounted at a rate appropriate for the equity investor.

$$NPV(E) = \sum_{j=1}^{j=n} \left(-E_j + NCF_j + Div_j\right)df_j$$

where $E_j =$ equity contribution
   $Div_j =$ dividends paid

The discount rate for total investment and for equity stakeholders will not be the same if some of the investment is financed with debt. Expectation of return differs in credit versus equity markets. Equity investment is usually structurally riskier than debt, requiring a higher rate of return. The

TABLE 3.4 Net Present Value, Investment—CYP, US$(000)

Cash Flow Plan					Year					
	1	2	3	4	5	6	7	8	9	10
Cash flow from Operations			740.6	4,709.9	5,472.3	6,388.2	6,606.8	5,865.0	6,132.8	6,437.9
Cash flow from Investment										
Investment	(11,462.1)	(25,279.5)	0.0	0.0	0.0	0.0	(170.1)	0.0	(42.8)	11,891.1
+ Interest	0.0	0.0	2,487.5	2,550.5	2,550.5	2,125.4	1,700.4	1,275.3	850.2	425.1
Net flow, investment	(11,462.1)	(25,279.5)	3,228.1	7,260.5	8,022.9	8,513.6	8,137.1	7,140.3	6,940.3	18,754.0
Real Flows (post income tax)										
Real flows	(11,462.1)	(25,279.5)	4,496.3	7,707.7	8,229.6	8,307.1	8,137.0	8,349.6	8,264.3	18,493.0
− Increase in A/R			(2,255.2)	(640.4)	0.0	0.0	0.0	0.0	0.0	2,895.7
− Increase in working cap cash			(47.2)	(20.9)	5.3	2.7				60.1
+ Increase in A/P			1,034.2	214.1	(212.0)	203.7	0.0	0.0	0.0	(1,239.9)
− Corporate tax								(1,209.3)	(1,324.1)	(1,454.8)
Net flow, investment	(11,462.1)	(25,279.5)	3,228.1	7,260.5	8,022.9	8,513.6	8,137.0	7,140.3	6,940.2	18,754.0
Discount factor	0.920	0.847	0.780	0.718	0.661	0.608	0.560	0.515	0.474	0.436
Discounted values[1]	(10,550.1)	(21,416.8)	2,517.2	5,211.2	5,300.2	5,176.9	4,554.3	3,678.4	3,290.9	8,185.2
									Sum	5,947.5

Discount (hurdle) rate	8.6%
Net present value (NPV)	5,947.5
Internal rate of return (IRR)	12.4%

[1] Annual *Net Flow, investment* discounted by weighted cost of capital (8.6%); assumes all flows at end of period.

hurdle rate (expected rate of return) for the equity stakeholder is usually based on the stakeholder's cost of equity capital, either the actual cost (see Appendix 3.1) or the opportunity cost (expected rate of return in the most favorable alternative investment). Rather than apply the weighted *cost of capital* for the equity portion of investment, the *cost of equity* (expected or *hurdle* rate of return on equity) is applied.

NPV(E) indicates whether a project is acceptable for the investor (NPV $\geq$ 0) and provides other important information. It explains the project's effect on wealth creation—that is, the amount of surplus generated and accruing to owners (shareholders) over and above equity contributed plus its expected rate of return (*rental* cost), assuming the project proceeds according to plan. Accumulation of surpluses might be reflected in increased value of ownership (shares), which could either be liquidated or dedicated to continuing operations at the planning horizon.

Another approach to NPV(E) is to consider only the outflow (from the investor's perspective) of equity and inflows of dividends and residual value. This viewpoint may be relevant for minority equity holders who have only a tentative interest in the project and who plan to divest their shares at some point. It would certainly be appropriate for preferred shareholders, who do not actually own the enterprise but are more akin to lenders. Investors who purchase stocks in securities markets usually take this point of view, but it is not particularly relevant for investment projects. The cash flow plan in such cases is limited to inflow of equity, expected payment of dividends in each period to the planning horizon, and divestiture at the planning horizon, when the market value is to be collected.

The value of common shares (price at point of sale) reflects the accumulation and reinvestment of surpluses and also the proportion of earnings previously paid out as dividends; if dividend payouts are low or nonexistent in what is normally considered a growth enterprise, the residual value will tend to be greater at the end. For enterprises that pay out large dividends, the reverse is generally true. Market forces also enter the picture, for common and, usually to a lesser extent, preferred shares with a fixed rate of return. Although the return on preferred shares is nominally independent of earnings, preferred dividends can generally be paid only when funds from earnings are available, and prevailing credit market rates at the time of sale will have an effect on price.

NPV(E)—CYP   NPV(E) for the Cambria Yarns Project is shown in Table 3.5; the value is $1,971.3 at a hurdle rate of 12 percent. This means that equity stakeholders expect to recover their capital, earn their expected rate of return, and also realize a surplus in excess of the 12 percent return.

TABLE 3.5 Net Present Value, Equity—CYP, US$(000)

					Year					
	1	2	3	4	5	6	7	8	9	10
Cash flow plan	0.0	0.0	2,001.5	4,213.8	624.3	568.1	404.1	203.3	294.4	12,380.8
− Equity contribution	(11,462.1)	(1,035.1)	0.0	0.0	0.0	0.0	0.0	0.0	0.0	0.0
+ dividends	0.0	0.0	0.0	496.1	597.1	1,569.2	1,781.7	1,410.9	1,544.8	1,697.3
Net flow, equity	(11,462.1)	(1,035.1)	2,001.5	4,709.9	1,221.5	2,137.3	2,185.8	1,614.2	1,839.2	14,078.1
Discount factor (12%)	0.893	0.797	0.712	0.6436	0.567	0.507	0.452	0.403	0.360	0.322
Discounted values	(10,234.0)	(825.2)	1,424.6	2,993.3	693.1	1,082.8	988.8	651.9	663.2	4,532.8
Discount (hurdle) rate	12.0%									
Net present value (NPV)	1,971.3									
Internal rate of return (IRR)	15.3%									

Internal Rate of Return (IRR)

Internal rate of return (IRR) is a dynamic indicator that measures the generation of net benefits arising from investment, from project inception to the planning horizon. It is compared with criteria for project appraisal. Generally IRR should be higher than the cost of capital (see the later "Financial Criteria" section). The IRR can be determined in relation to total investment, for equity only, or from the perspective of a particular equity stakeholder or class. IRR can be explained in several ways:

- *A discount rate at which NPV = 0.* When NPV equals zero, the investment consumed plus the investments' rental cost is just covered by future benefits.
- *A discount rate at which the present value of outflows equals the present value of inflows.* Inflows and outflows discounted at the IRR net to zero. Outflows and inflows can be discounted separately, then summed and combined algebraically; or the net of inflows and outflows can be discounted and summed. The results will be identical.
- *A rate at which the project generates net benefits for the investor to the planning horizon.* This is the most useful and descriptive interpretation of IRR.

Calculation of IRR involves precisely the same flow pattern as used for NPV. The discount rate is the variable. A search routine is used to scan through the NPVs for each discount rate[16] to find the particular value $i^* =$ IRR for which the sum of net flows for all project periods is zero.

IRR Investment   Calculating IRR(I) uses the same pattern of period flows as NPV(I). The relationship is as follows:

$$NPV(I) = \sum_{j=1}^{j=n} \left(CFO_j + CFI_j + \text{Interest}_j\right)\frac{1}{(1+i^*)^j} = 0$$

where $i^* =$ Discount rate that nets summation to zero IRR. The i^* for which NPV(I) equals zero is an IRR(I).

IRR Investment—CYP   For the Cambria Yarns Project, the flows of Table 3.4, NPV(I), make up the basis for the calculation. The IRR is calculated as 12.4 percent (see Table 3.4). The relationship between NPV(I) and discount rate is illustrated in Figure 3.2. The discount rate at which the curve crosses the zero axis is the IRR(I), about 12.4 percent.

IRR Equity The IRR for the portion of the project financed with equity, IRR(E), is calculated using the same flow pattern as developed for NPV(E) in Table 3.5. The basis for this calculation derives from the cash flow plan (Table 2.15b), net cash flow in each period accruing to the project's owners, from which planned dividends are deducted to assess project liquidity. For NPV(E) and IRR(E) calculations, the equity contribution in each period is deducted, and dividends added back (to account for generation of funds from which they are paid by the project) to the net cash flow for each period.

$$NPV(E) = \sum_{j=0}^{n} \left(-E_j + NCF_j + Div_j\right) \frac{1}{(1+i*)^j} = 0$$

where IRR(E) is the value of $i*$ that sets the present value of the net flows to zero, the rate at which the equity generates net benefits for shareholders.

IRR Equity—CYP For the Cambria Yarns Project the IRR(E) calculation is shown in Table 3.5 (15.3 percent.) This compares with the IRR(I) of 12.4 percent in Table 3.4 and indicates positive leverage arising from favorable borrowing at 10 percent (see the "Financial Criteria" section later in this chapter and the "Cost of Capital" section in Chapter 4).

Limitations of IRR Relying on IRR for appraisal can be problematic under some circumstances. An irregular pattern of cash flow may lead to multiple IRR's[17]—for example, if a major expansion or decommissioning involving large capital flows is planned during the project life. If there is more than one credible IRR, the challenge is to decide which one to use, although the hurdle or cutoff rate (expected rate of return for the investor) can be compared with the minimum IRR as a measure of acceptability. Furthermore, the method of calculating IRR leads some to conclude that inordinately high IRRs are unrealistic.

Reinvestment of Surpluses For NPV and IRR calculations, the net flow in each period is discounted; these discounted values are then summed. An IRR occurs when the sum of the present values for all project periods equals zero. A precise mathematical equivalent is to compound the positive periodic values at a reinvestment rate to the planning horizon and sum them (terminal value of positive flows); discount the negative values at the same rate and sum them (present value of negative flows); discount the terminal value of positive flows at the same rate to the present; and add the result to the present value of negative flows. The result is NPV. If NPV = 0 then the discount rate applied is an IRR. This illustrates the mathematical equivalence of the assumption of reinvestment at the discount rate with the standard method of calculating IRR. The concern is that it may not be possible to find such reinvestment opportunities for surpluses over the project's life. This also applies to NPV; however, in calculating NPV the discount rate is selected by the decision maker (usually cost of capital) and represents the expectation of return on present and future capital resources.

Modified IRR (MIRR) *Modified internal rate of return* (MIRR) is a form of IRR that takes into account assumptions concerning opportunities for reinvesting generated project surpluses and the return on capital reserves to be applied to future investment. The intent is to circumvent problems associated with IRR. One simple solution is to ignore IRR entirely as a measure of project worth. Net present value is a much more fundamental way to assess an investment project as it provides a definitive result: Either NPV *is* nonnegative at the cost of capital or it *is not*.

MIRR is not without its detractors. An objection is that an investment decision should not be dependent on other opportunities for reinvestment of generated surpluses.[18] In this method the assumption that the surpluses generated by the project are reinvested at the IRR is avoided by simulating the reinvestment of surpluses at a more realistic rate of return to the planning horizon. The terminal value of surpluses (FV) is matched with the present value (PV) of deficits (mainly the initial investment) to determine an equivalent rate of return for the project. Reinvestment of surpluses and coverage of deficits at more realistic rates can be simulated as follows:[19]

$$FV = \sum_{j=0}^{n} NCF(\text{positive})_j \left(1 + i_{\text{reinvestment}}\right)^{n-j}$$

$$PV = \sum_{j=0}^{n} |NCF(\text{negative})_j| \left(\frac{1}{1 + i_{\text{borrowing}}}\right)^{j}$$

$$MIRR = \left(\frac{FV}{PV}\right)^{\frac{1}{n}} - 1$$

A single discount rate MIRR equates the terminal value of positive flows (FV) with the present value of negative flows (PV). MIRR is positive (a condition of acceptability) if FV is greater than PV. PV is calculated with absolute values of the NCF(negative)$_j$. If $i_{\text{reinvestment}} = i_{\text{borrowing}}$ then MIRR is also an IRR.

The subscript *borrowing* in the equation is a bit misleading. This is better viewed as a secure credit market rate (highly rated debt instrument), generally with low interest rates as compared with return on more risky debt or equity. *PV* simulates the commitment of resources to the project to cover outflows, mainly the investment—resources that are conceptually, if not actually, set aside in secure instruments to cover investment costs as required.

The MIRR is more applicable to equity analysis than to return on investment. The reason is that the former deals with funds that are available for reinvestment, whereas the latter is concerned essentially with resources. MIRR is, if anything, more a financial technique than one that can deal with other types of resources.

Net Present Value Ratio

Net present value ratio (NPVR) is used in capital rationing—that is, it is intended to find the best use of available capital, the biggest bang for the buck. Any projects with positive NPV can be pooled and selected in whole or in part (if separable) to yield the best return from a limited amount of capital for investment, with priority based upon the value of NPVR for each project possibility. It is a measure of net benefits generated per unit of capital investment. The ratio is *net present value* (NPV) to *present value of investment*, PV(I), determined by discounting values of all investments in each period, including increments of working capital, to present value at the selected discount rate. The ratio can be interpreted as the amount of surplus value generated per unit of investment. It can be used to compare alternative investments (projects)—those with higher NPVRs are more desirable from this perspective.

$$NPVR = \frac{NPV}{PV(I)}$$

NPVR can be determined with respect to total investment or equity only.

NPVR and PV(I)—CYP   The method of calculating the present value of investment PV(I) and NPVR for total investment for the Cambria Yarns Project is shown in Table 3.6. PV(I) is the sum of investment (fixed assets, preoperational expenditures, and capitalized interest) in all periods to the planning horizon, discounted at the same rate used to determine NPV (8.6 percent in this case).

TABLE 3.6 Net Present Value Ratio—CYP, US$(000)

	Year									
	1	2	3	4	5	6	7	8	9	10
FI + POI + CI	11,462.1	24,375.5	0.0	0.0	0.0	0.0	170.1	0.0	42.8	0.0
Increase in WC		904.0	2,814.3	741.3	180.8	(206.5)	0.0	0.0	0.0	0.0
Total investment	11,462.1	25,279.5	2,814.3	741.3	180.8	(206.5)	170.1	0.0	42.8	0.0
Discount factor (8.6%)[1]	0.920	0.847	0.780	0.718	0.661	0.608	0.560	0.515	0.474	0.436
Present value	10,550.1	21,416.8	2,194.6	532.0	119.4	(125.6)	95.2	0.0	20.3	0.0
PV[1]	34,802.9	NPV		5,947.5		NPVR	0.17			
Discount rate	0.086									

[1]Weighted cost of capital, tax adjusted.

FI = fixed investment; POI = preoperational expenditures; CI = capitalized interest.

186

The NPVR is 0.17. This means that the project generates 0.17 units per unit of investment—that is, 17 percent of the total investment—as surplus value. The value is meaningful only when comparing investment alternatives.

Liquidity

An essential feature of project design is maintenance of financial liquidity—in other words, a nonnegative cash balance for all periods to the planning horizon. This condition indicates that the plan is financially viable—that is, there will be sufficient funds throughout the project life to cover all cash requirements. The "Cumulative cash flow" line of the cash flow plan of Table 2.15b provides an indication of whether sufficient funds are available to avoid a cash shortfall at any time from project inception to the planning horizon. The plan is developed to ensure that there is no period with a cumulative deficit. If in any planning period a cumulative deficit appears, this means that up to that point the design lacks sufficient sources of funds to maintain liquidity.[20] Either the revenue and cost structure has to be modified or other sources of funds have to be identified. A deficit in any particular period is not necessarily a problem, as long as there is a sufficient buildup of cash in prior periods to cover it.

Stakeholder Views on Indicators

Static and dynamic indicators have differing levels of relevance to the interests of stakeholders; the significance of each indicator to investors, lenders, guarantors, or licensors depends on their particular aspirations and criteria. Investors are primarily concerned with indicators that reflect return on their investment. Lenders focus on those that affect the ability of the project to service debt. Guarantors are concerned with the possibility of default and its consequences. Licensing agencies seek to approve viable enterprises but also those projects with positive effects on economic development goals. Indicator relevance has particular importance in presenting information about the project.

As an example, Table 3.7 uses a scale of 1 (most interested) to 3 (low interest to no level of interest) to rate the level of interest for each type of stakeholder, but the ratings may vary by country, region, or even specific stakeholders involved. These ratings also vary according to circumstances surrounding any particular project, such as investor experience and background, sector, and general business climate.

TABLE 3.7 Indicator Relevance for Stakeholders

Static Indicators	Investor	Lender	Guarantor	Regulator
Profitability ratios				
Gross profit margin	2	2	3	3
Net profit margin	1	2	2	3
Operating profit margin	2	2	2	3
Return on investment	1	2	2	2
Return on equity	1	2	3	3
Return on assets	2	2	2	3
Liquidity ratios				
Current ratio	1	2	2	3
Quick ratio	1	2	2	3
Efficiency ratios				
Inventory turnover, days	2	3	3	3
Receivables turnover	1	3	3	3
Solvency ratios				
Debt/equity	1	1	1	2
Fixed asset coverage	2	1	1	3
Debt service coverage	1	1	1	3
Breakeven	1	2	2	2
Dynamic Indicators				
NPV	1	2	2	2
IRR	2	2	3	3
NPVR	1	3	3	3
Payback	1	2	2	3
Dynamic payback	2	3	3	3

Relevance scale: 1 = highest, 2 = moderate, 3 = little to none.

FINANCIAL CRITERIA FOR INVESTMENT DECISIONS

The primary financial (commercial) issue is whether projected returns meet minimum requirements and expectations. Investors seek an adequate return on their capital; financiers want assurance that debt will be adequately serviced. The question is, how do stakeholders decide if they are satisfied with what they learn from analysis? Each of them—investors, financiers, guarantors, and licensors—has particular criteria, or benchmarks, for measuring project acceptability. The goals and objectives of each individual or partner in a joint venture, corporate entity, or other party to the project usually differ. Performance indicators are to be compared with criteria. If criteria are met or exceeded, presumably the project will be regarded favorably; if not, it will either be rejected or perhaps be recycled in some way.

Another problem in defining financial criteria is inflation and currency exchange rates. The effect on selection of appropriate criteria in an operating environment with high inflation has to be considered. If the project involves foreign exchange requirements or earnings, exchange rate fluctuations have to be anticipated in determining criteria. Financial criteria should not simply be referenced to debt and equity markets. How market rates of return relate to appropriate criteria depends upon on how benchmarks are selected.

Determination of criteria is a crucial exercise; if they are not properly defined, the decision process goes awry. An issue that confronts investors and other participants is how multiple criteria can be regarded in composite when only some are satisfied. Criteria may have to be adjusted for risk associated with the business environment and the reliability of information (see Chapter 7).

Static Criteria

During the project development phase, static indicators that are usually most significant for participants are debt/equity ratio, debt service coverage, profit margins, payback period, and breakeven. The project's capital structure must comply with debt/equity requirements fixed by lenders based upon their assessment of risk. If multiple sources of debt are to be employed, seniority and risk associated with each type of debt will invariably have to be taken into account.

Another criterion applicable for some projects, particularly infrastructure, is the *first-year return*. This criterion is not particularly relevant to most industrial projects, in which losses during the start-up phase are a normal outcome of the learning curve (early inefficiencies in labor productivity, material consumption, etc.), and where demand must be developed through marketing and distribution programs. It is not strictly a static criterion as it involves information over a number of project periods. The idea is to find the optimal time to begin the project—in other words, the earliest year when the first-year return exceeds the cost of capital. Postponing project implementation makes sense only if the potential stream of benefits or costs increases independently of the timing of project commencement, a situation that prevails mainly in infrastructure services such as roads, where traffic grows independently of the project. The method uses a sliding time scale for analysis, assuming increasing demand for the product or service. The project is simulated as commencing in a series of periods (years), under conditions that are expected to prevail from inception to the planning horizon. For each alternative, net cash flow in the first positive year is divided by the total net cash flow in the negative years. The result is the first-year return. The logic is that the sum of the string of negative flows is essentially the initial investment. The optimal time to begin the project is the earliest year in which the first-year return exceeds the opportunity cost of capital. An earlier start will result in a return that is less than the cost of capital, and a later start in a missed opportunity to earn the cost of capital.

Typically, lenders are not likely to approve projects financed with greater than 65 percent or so of debt. The debt service coverage ratio should be significantly greater than unity (1.0) to minimize lender risk. A consistent ratio above 1.5 is preferred. A lower ratio may be tolerable to lenders if careful sensitivity analysis reveals a low probability of a liquidity crisis.

Profitability ratios are meaningful primarily in relation to standards for the project's industrial sector. Indicators such as variable margin (surplus of revenue over variable cost), factory margin (surplus of revenue over factory cost), after-tax profit margin (after-tax profit as a percentage of revenue), return on investment (RoI), and return on equity (RoE) vary by industry. These indicators should be developed for representative years or periods, at or near full plant capacity. Standards can be derived from secondary sources. Most publicly traded companies publish periodic financial reports from which representative indicators can be determined. Financial service companies and international trade organizations are potential sources of information regarding standard values of indicators. Project indicators that are significantly different from sector standards may be cause for concern regarding project costs, financial structure, or projected revenue stream.

Breakeven should be developed for one or more periods during the start-up phase, for typical operating periods during the debt retirement phase, and for the postdebt phase of operations. The standard varies by industrial sector. Low-margin products typically have higher breakeven ratios. In general, a lower value is better, but the standard should be consistent with industry norms for the project's scale; large deviations call for further investigation.

To assess project risk, sensitivity analysis on project parameters most subject to uncertainty can reveal project vulnerability as reflected in static indicators, if applied through the range of parameter variability supported by historical information and opinions of experts in the field. The methods explained in Chapter 7 can then be applied to assess risk.

Dynamic Criteria

The basis for setting dynamic financial criteria—the hurdle rate for NPV and cutoff rate for IRR—typically is the cost of capital, or expectation of return,[21] which varies for stakeholders. The *opportunity cost of capital* (the potential return on the most favorable alternative investment) or the actual cost of capital to finance the project can be applied (these are fundamentally the same). For an existing enterprise planning to finance the project internally, the criterion is essentially the weighted cost of its capital structure; the challenge for the new investment project is the internal cost of capital if it is to be financed internally. If this criterion is satisfied, the new investment provides a return that equals the existing cost of capital—in other words, investors recover their investment plus a specified rental cost. This assumes that the enterprise invests in certain types of projects related to its business, so factors that could affect the rate, such as inflation and risk, are probably already taken into account. When multiple sources are used for project finance, the relevant criterion is the weighted average cost of capital (see Appendix 3.1 "Example of Cost of Capital Calculations" for an explanation of how it is derived); if part of the project is to be financed with new debt, then the internal and external capital costs have to be weighted to find the composite opportunity cost. Market returns on equity and debt may enter into its calculation.

The hurdle rate may be further affected by risk and inflation (see the subsection "Criteria and Capital Markets" for a discussion on how these factors affect market rates of return and criteria). Aside from the expected base rate of return derived from the opportunity cost of capital, subjective factors may cause a prospective stakeholder to adjust the barrier depending on the risk/reward characteristics of the project. Risk-averse investors generally seek fairly secure returns with moderate expectations of return; risk takers are more inclined to seek high-risk investments with high returns. Other subjective factors involve personal preferences (e.g., geographic, demographic, climatic, product applications).

Net present value is the primary financial indicator, applied across the entire spectrum of investment activities as the measure of value and acceptability, with the advantage that the method produces a definitive result, which is not always the case for internal rate of return (IRR). Setting the *challenge rate* or *hurdle rate* (discount rate) to determine NPV for the project is fundamental to financial appraisal. An acceptable NPV must be nonnegative; if the project is *challenged* with the *hurdle* of a particular discount rate, a negative NPV is grounds for rejection. For IRR the criterion is the *cutoff rate*; a projected IRR below the cutoff rate is usually considered unacceptable.

NPV is a more effective tool than IRR for assessing financial viability of investment projects. IRR is more applicable in credit markets, where flow patterns are more regular, moderate, and definitive. In applying NPV in project assessment, a *definitive signal* is obtained—that is, NPV is either negative or nonnegative.

Mutually Exclusive Projects   When deciding between two mutually exclusive projects—for example, capital constraints allow investment in one

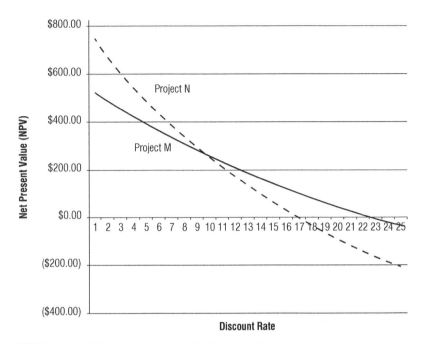

FIGURE 3.4   NPV for Two Mutually Exclusive Projects

or the other—NPV and IRR can provide conflicting signals. Differences in cash (or resource) flow patterns and project life can produce relationships of NPV versus discount rate as shown in Figure 3.4.[22] NPV of Project N is *higher* than NPV of Project M at discount rates below the crossover rate of about 10 percent, but *lower* than that of Project M above the crossover rate At a cutoff rate of 15 percent both projects appear acceptable, with Project M apparently more favorable on the basis of its higher NPV. The example illustrates the superiority of NPV as an assessment tool. A definitive hurdle rate will clearly show one project to be more favorable than the other (except at the rate for which NPVs are equal). The advantage is even more fundamental. The hurdle rate represents the criterion for returns expected to be generated by the project considering the likely application of surpluses. Internal rate of return is not particularly meaningful at levels much higher than the cost of capital.[23]

Financial Leverage and Cutoff Rate   One way of conceptually viewing the effect of leveraging, the benefit to equity investors of financing part of the project with debt, is to compare return on total investment in which *project* *financing is excluded,* versus the situation with the financing package in place. It is assumed that the amount of equity to be provided by sponsors is constrained, and that the balance of the financing package must be covered with debt. If the project generates returns greater (less) than the cost of debt, leverage will be positive or favorable (negative or unfavorable) for equity investors.

Figure 3.5 is a graphic illustration of financial leverage and its relation to the cutoff rate as the cost of capital (there are a few simplifications here, particularly with respect to the tax shield effect of interest in most environments—see Table 3.8 for an example). Debt service is a function of cost of debt: As cost increases (decreases), net flow in each period with respect to equity decreases (increases), affecting the rate of return (IRR equity). In fact, if the cost of debt is just equal to the rate of return on investment, the effect of covering part of the investment with debt would be essentially nil, were tax consequences not considered.

In the upper area, a simple cash flow pattern for a project is shown. There is an initial outflow representing assets committed to the project, with a constant level of net benefits generated for a number of years. Project

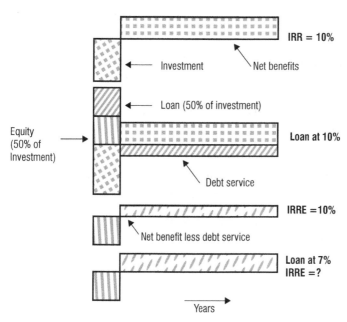

FIGURE 3.5 Financial Leverage and Cutoff Rate

financing is not considered at this point. The return on total investment is 10 percent.

The project is financed (second illustration from the top) with equal amounts of equity and debt. The interest rate is 10 percent, such that the amount of debt service (assuming a constant, annuity-type repayment plan) is equal to one-half the net benefits.

The next illustration shows the position of the equity owners. Equity finances one-half of the project but receives only one-half of net benefits (the other half is used for debt service). What is the NPV for equity holders? It must be 10 percent.

In the last illustration the cost of debt is assumed at 7 percent, lower than the 10 percent return on total assets committed to the project. From the point of view of equity, accrual of surplus generated from the half of the project financed with debt raises its rate of return. If the cost of debt were higher than 10 percent, the effect would be to reduce return on equity. It is clear from this illustration that lowering the cost of debt and, consequently, the cost of capital for a particular capital structure, is beneficial for the project. The cutoff rate should be at least equal to the cost of capital; otherwise, a project could be approved but would not generate satisfactory returns to investors.

The effect of financial leverage can be seen in comparing the project's return on equity with return on investment (value of assets committed to the project). In the Cambria Yarns Project the returns on equity and investment are 15.3 percent and 12.4 percent respectively, reflecting the effect of cost of debt (10 percent) below the return on investment (see the "Dynamic Indicators" section).

To consider a flexible debt/equity structure, a more appropriate comparison is between the project financed completely with equity, at one extreme, and with some limiting ratio of debt to equity at the other. The return on equity, IRR(E), for each scenario is calculated on an after-tax basis. Here the outcome is not so clear, as the relationship between the two situations depends upon (a) the proportion of debt and equity, (b) the rate of interest on the debt, and (c) the tax rate on earnings.[24]

An example is shown in Table 3.8, where the tax shield provided by the interest deduction more than offsets the effect of an interest rate higher than the return for the project financed completely with equity, with IRR(E) = 15.3 percent. When the project is financed with 50 percent equity and 50 percent debt at an interest rate of 16.0 percent, higher than the return for all-equity financing, IRR(E) increases to 17.2 percent, the result of *shielding* of the interest on the debt from taxation, at a rate of 20 percent in this example.

TABLE 3.8 Leverage Effect on IRR—Equity

Project Financed Completely with Equity

Tax Rate	20.0%			
Year	0	1	2	3
Cash flow from operations		40.0	40.0	40.0
+ Depreciation		10.0	10.0	10.0
Cash flow from financing				
+ Equity	100.0			
Taxable profit		30.0	30.0	30.0
− Corporate tax		6.0	6.0	6.0
Cash flow from investment				
− Investment	100.0			
Net cash flow	0.0	44.0	44.0	44.0
− Equity	100			
Net cash flow from equity	(100.0)	44.0	44.0	44.0
IRR(E), 100% equity	15.3%			

Project Financed 50% with Equity and 50% with Debt, $r >$ IRR(E) 100% equity

Interest Rate	16.0%			
Year	0	1	2	3
Cash flow from operations		40.0	40.0	40.0
+ Depreciation		10.0	10.0	10.0
Cash flow from financing				
+ Equity	50.0			
+ Loan principal	50.0			
Outstanding loan		50.0	30.0	10.0
− Repayment		20.0	20.0	10.0
− Interest		8.0	4.8	1.6
Taxable profit		22.0	25.2	28.4
− Corporate tax		4.4	5.0	5.7
Cash flow from investment				
− Investment	100.0			
Net cash flow	0.0	17.6	20.2	32.7
− Equity	50.0			
Net cash flow from equity	(50.0)	17.6	20.2	32.7
IRR, 50% equity, r > IRR(E)	17.2%			

Inflation and Dynamic Criteria   Projects are normally appraised at constant prices. When inflation is general and uniform (i.e., all inputs and outputs are similarly affected), there is usually no need to adjust prices for financial analysis—price relationships of inputs and outputs are relatively unaffected. Analysis can be performed using the assumption of constant (non-inflation-adjusted) prices, either those prevailing at present (recommended) or at some future point in time.

If cost elements are expected to change *relative* to general inflation, then *escalations* should be included, even when performed at constant prices. Scarcities of certain commodities may force their particular prices higher, but if there is not a general impact on prices, only relative changes should be included.

The currency in which debt is designated can affect nominal debt service requirements and their constant price equivalents. The real, or inflation-adjusted, cost of fixed-rate debt denominated in domestic currency actually reduces under inflation. The effects of relative inflation and possible exchange rate fluctuation on foreign currency inflows or outflows are factors to take into account when analyzing the rate of return at constant prices. Debt denominated in a stable foreign currency becomes nominally more expensive with domestic inflation if exchange rates adjust—the effect in real terms depends on the relationship between inflation and currency exchange rates.

General inflation is part of the nominal (market) cost of capital as markets reflect diminishing value of domestic currency over time. The relationship between the nominal, real (at constant prices), and inflation rates (aside from the element of risk) is expressed approximately by:

$$i_{nom} = i_{real} + i_{\text{inf } l}$$

or, more correctly:

$$i_{nom} = (1 + i_{real})(1 + i_{\text{inf } l}) - 1$$

where i_{nom} = nominal rate of return
i_{real} = real rate of return
$i_{\text{inf } l}$ = inflation rate

The relationship is explained in Figure 3.6, in which patterns of inflows and outflows are shown for a project at nominal (current) prices and at constant prices. For simplicity, investment occurs at the start and the benefits and costs are uniform for each period to the planning horizon. Suppose

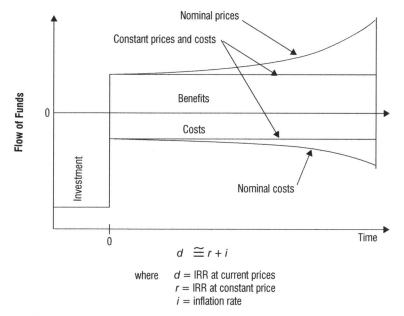

FIGURE 3.6 Effect of Inflation on IRR

the IRR is first determined for the project using constant prices—for an acceptable project, benefits must *exceed* costs. When both benefits and costs are inflated, benefits will show greater increase, because their base values are higher. Consequently, under conditions of inflation, the nominal (inflated) differences between benefits and costs during each period will be greater than the corresponding differences under constant pricing.

If net benefits are higher in each period for the inflation case, the IRR should also increase. By what amount? Usually close to the inflation rate. In other words the nominal or inflation-based IRR will exceed the constant price IRR by approximately the rate of inflation included in current pricing estimates. The following example illustrates the relationship between the rates of return (IRR) calculated for the same project under current and constant price assumptions. For years 1 through 5, net cash flows are shown for the constant price case and the inflation case. Net flows in each period for the constant price case are inflated at a 10 percent rate. The total inflationary effect depends upon the number of years of inflation. For example, the constant price value of 5,000 in the second year is inflated by the factor $(1.1)^2$ or 1.21; the value of 6,000 in the third year is inflated by $(1.1)^3$ or 1.331.

Year	Constant Price Flow	Current Price Flow
0	−15,000	−15,000
1	4,000	4,400
2	5,000	6,050
3	6,000	7,986
4	6,000	8,785
5	6,000	9,663
IRR	r = 21.6%	d = 33.8%

The IRR at constant price, $IRR_{real} = 21.6$ percent and at current (inflated) price, $IRR_{nom} = 33.8$ percent. When prices are inflated to expected current levels, the IRR so determined is higher than the nominal rate of return by approximately the rate of inflation. The real rate of return, linked to actual purchasing or economic power of net benefits, may not change.

$$IRR_{nom} = IRR_{real} + i_{infl} + (IRR_{real})i_{infl}$$

$$IRR_{nom} = 0.216 + 0.100 + (0.216)(0.100) \text{ or } 33.8\%$$

Constant or Current Prices?   Should analysis be performed at constant or current prices, and what should be the decision criterion in either case? Even under hyperinflationary conditions, it is usually better to perform rate-of-return analysis at constant prices, expressed in a stable foreign currency. Special accounting methods may be necessary to simulate project flows that conform to regulations in the host country—for example, revaluation of book values of fixed and current assets (including adjustments to corresponding annual depreciation charges) and liabilities.

As general inflation normally affects prices of both inputs and outputs, nominal returns will be affected by inflation, but if costs and benefits are appropriately deflated or constant prices are applied, application of inflation-adjusted criteria as benchmarks will provide appropriate investment signals. Suggested guidelines for analysis at constant or current prices are summarized in Table 3.9.

■ Zero inflation or all inputs and outputs similarly affected: Prices should be at a constant level but include relative price changes anticipated (escalations and reductions); it is appropriate to use the real cost of capital as the criterion (hurdle or cutoff rate), the nominal market rate adjusted for inflation, but including any risk premium. If using the weighted average approach (Appendix 3.1), components of the cost of

TABLE 3.9 Current versus Constant Prices

	Constant Prices	Current Prices
Conditions	Zero inflation or all inputs and outputs affected equally; relative increase in prices included (escalations)	Price inflation and its effect on liquidity, particularly in case of foreign exchange exposure
Hurdle rate and cut-off rate	Real cost of capital—nominal cost adjusted for inflation; real return on most favorable alternative project	Nominal cost of capital (market price); nominal return on most favorable alternative project

capital have to be adjusted for inflation effects, which may be reflected in market indicators such as price/earnings ratios for equity or interest rates on debt instruments.

- Price inflation with concerns about liquidity: It is better in this case to do the analysis at current (or nominal) prices with the nominal (market) cost of capital or nominal opportunity cost (based upon the expected return on the most favorable alternative investment) as the criterion. One significant application of current price analysis is to confirm liquidity during the early periods when the level of debt service for foreign currency–denominated loans may escalate from inflation-induced domestic currency devaluation. Possible liquidity problems may arise related to high cost of loans denominated in domestic currency. Constant price analysis is usually a more accurate way to determine rate of return.

Investor versus Lender Criteria under Inflationary Conditions Investors and their creditors may have differing views concerning the question of analysis at constant or current prices; nevertheless, primary concerns of one are at least secondary concerns for the other. Differing viewpoints are summarized in Table 3.10.

For investors seeking a satisfactory rate of return, analysis is more appropriately performed using constant prices. The combination of constant prices and real cost of capital reflects constant purchasing or economic power of future costs and benefits. At current prices it is more appropriate to apply the nominal cost of capital as the criterion.

The lender is interested primarily in recovering principal and receiving interest and other charges; liquidity is the main criterion. The ability of the project to service its debt may be affected by inflation, particularly in the case of high interest rates scaled to the level of inflation by the market,

TABLE 3.10   Investor versus Lender Criteria under Inflation

	Perspective	
	Investor	Lender
Participant	Satisfactory rate of return	Recovery of loan principal and interest
Analysis	Constant prices, real[1] cost of capital	Current prices, nominal cost of capital
Criteria	Real opportunity cost of capital	Nominal opportunity cost of capital; flow of fund sufficient to cover debt service

[1]Nominal market rate adjusted for inflation but including any risk premium.

or where there is foreign currency exposure. In either case, at least for the early periods, analysis under current prices should be performed with the intention of investigating whether the project can maintain adequate liquid reserves to service the debt. The rate of return under conditions of inflation is ordinarily only of secondary interest.

Criteria and Capital Markets   In the absence of cost-of-capital data, criteria can be referenced to credit and equity capital markets. The market reflects a combination of a base rate of return, inflation, and risk factors. The base return is a fundamental risk-free and inflation-adjusted rate. A good benchmark is the most secure investment (e.g., Eurobonds or U.S. Treasury issues).

If capital markets are used as the benchmark for the discount rate (opportunity cost of capital), the relationship of market price components should be taken into account. An *inflation-adjusted standard* should be applied as the criterion—the nominal market rate *reduced by the rate of inflation* (if any), with any risk premium included. In other words, only inflation should be stripped from capital market rates in determining the benchmark. *It is inconsistent to apply a criterion that is highly affected by inflation as a benchmark or hurdle for a project analyzed at constant prices.*

If the environment entails high economic or political risk, investors seek higher rates of return as a hedge against calamity. The market adds a risk premium onto the nominal rate depending on the nature of the investment. Investments can be classified essentially as aggressive, growth, or income, with decreasing expectations of return, respectively. In credit markets the nominal expectation is lower, mainly because risk is usually lower than in equity markets. Ratings of credit instruments by respected risk analysts are a factor in market rates of return (although widespread inaccuracies in ratings of these agencies leading up to the financial crisis that erupted in 2007 brings this into question). Expected rates of return in capital equity markets are also affected by inflation, which tends to erode the purchasing (or economic) power of future earnings, with an inflation premium added to the real rate to compensate for the decrease. The relationship of nominal market cost of capital to its elements is approximately:[25]

$$\eta = \beta^* + \rho + \iota$$

where η = nominal market rate
β^* = base rate of return
ρ = risk premium
ι = inflation rate

The difference between the *base rate of return* and the *real rate* discussed earlier is that the base rate is inflation- and risk-adjusted market rate, while the real rate is only inflation-adjusted. A *base rate* benchmark relevant for investment project appraisal purposes is secure, inflation-adjusted government bonds, or a rate such as LIBOR (the interest rate that London banks charge each other for one-month, three-month, six-month, and one-year loans and considered to be virtually risk-free) adjusted for the yield curve with respect to loan duration. For debt instruments, the risk premium is not necessarily the spread between the bond rate and the risk-free rate; other factors involve credit worthiness, i.e., risk of default.

For the portion of the project financed with debt, in setting their rates lenders may reference medium-term government bonds or other traded financial instruments as the basis for the low-risk or risk-free rate, which would be adjusted for the risk associated with the project. For an existing company financing the project internally, its cost is determined in accordance with the weighted average cost for the capital structure of the enterprise (debt plus equity), which may be partially or completely referenced to capital markets.

Price/earnings ratios in equity markets can be used as the basis for expected rates of return on equity for the sector, although in volatile markets these ratios can vary considerably. The inverse of the price/earnings ratio is an indicator of the currently expected rate of return on equity. This can be compared with the reported return on shareholders' equity from corporate balance sheets and income statements for the industrial sector. Rates of return on investment can also be obtained from financial reports of publicly traded companies (or reports of other enterprises that may be available through personal contacts), adjusted for the current level of inflation and differential risk for the type of enterprise. If an existing company plans to finance the project partially or completely from internal sources, the benchmark is the cost of capital in accordance with its financial structure. Estimating the cost of preferred equity is relatively straightforward as it is based on a dividend fixed at the time of issue. For ordinary (common) equity, and for debt, cost can be determined in several ways (see example in Appendix 3.1) with an average of the results used as the estimate (a weighted average may be more appropriate depending on the reliability of each method of calculation).

Financial Criteria—CYP   Although the domestic currency appears to be overvalued by about 15 percent, the government has insured the company against a major portion of exchange rate risk, agreeing to an exchange rate determined by an index of domestic prices relative to international markets. This alleviates the problem of having to take into account possible devaluation of the local currency that would make imports of machinery and materials and foreign debt exposure more expensive and that would negatively impact on repatriation of profits.

In the absence of exchange rate guarantees, it would be prudent to evaluate the project assuming estimated devaluation. In fact, prudence might dictate such an assessment in any case, considering the risk that the government would be unable to fulfill its commitments.

Each partner considers components of the price of equity capital, as shown in Table 3.11. The benchmark rate is higher for CIL because there is an inherently higher premium demanded on equity capital as a result of the relatively low level of industrial experience in the country, and also a reflection of the relatively high inflation rate in the country. The inflation rate for each is dependent essentially on the rates in each of their countries. For NTC, aside from government guarantees, it is assumed that absolute returns will match exchange rate adjustments and that it will consequently be insulated from local inflation in regard to repatriating its earnings. CIL has no such protection, but it is assumed that the current inflation will continue to affect both inputs and outputs in the same way. The higher

TABLE 3.11   Equity Capital Criteria—CYP (Percent)

	Nominal Benchmark Rate of Return, %	Risk Premium	Risk-adjusted Benchmark	Relevant Inflation Rate, %	Hurdle Rate, Adjusted for Inflation, %
NTC	10	4	14	2	12
CIL	18	2	20	8	12

business risk premium for NTC results from its assessment of possibilities for change in the government's attitude toward foreign direct investment.

Both partners arrive at a hurdle rate of 12 percent. Their reasoning is predicated on capital markets and their particular variables. As the partners have decided that it is appropriate to perform the primary financial analysis at constant prices, each partner reduces the benchmark return for its equity by the anticipated inflation rate (NTC: 14 −2 = 12 percent, CIL: 20 − 8 = 12 percent). These criteria are applied in financial appraisal of the project as described in Chapter 8.

ANALYSIS OF JOINT VENTURES

Partners in a joint venture have their own financial perspectives: Each regards the situation differently, regarding values assigned to assets, sales, and costs; expectations of return and other criteria; disposition of assets; assessment of risk. For these reasons, financial indicators are developed to provide a clear understanding of project implications from each partner's perspective.

A joint venture agreement specifies the financial terms of partnership—the type, timing, and contribution of equity; degree of responsibility for debt incurred by the project; proportion of ownership; dividend distribution; and other costs and benefits. Dynamic indicators derived from the cash flow plan are the most effective means of evaluating the project in regard to their respective criteria.

NPV and IRR—Joint Venture Partner

An approach similar to NPV_{Equity} and IRR_{Equity} can be applied to determine a joint venture partner's financial perspective. Elements that enter into the determination of NPV and IRR for a partner (NPV_{JVP} and IRR_{JVP}) are as follows:

− Equity contributions of partner ($Equity_{j(\text{partner})}$)
   Equity contributions of the partner in each period are outflows.
+ Share of surplus/deficit per period ($NCF_{j(\%\text{partner})}$)
   A share or percentage of the net surplus/deficit from the integrated cash flow plan, including the residual value of assets at the planning horizon, for each period is attributed in proportion to common share ownership or agreement of the partners. The residual value represents liquidation or the functional value of the assets available at the planning horizon that would generate future benefits for the partner.

+ Partner's dividends $(Div_{j(\%partner)})$

Distributions of earnings to the partner, payable on common and/or preferred shares, represent inflows from the point of view of the partner.

$$NPV_{JVP} = \sum_{j=1}^{n} (-Equity_{j(\%partner)} + NCF_{j(\%partner)} + Div_{j(\%partner)}) df_j$$

Joint Venture Partner NPV and IRR—CYP

An example from the Cambria Yarns Project is shown in Table 3.12 for the CIL partner. Period net cash flow from the cash flow plan (Table 2.15b) is adjusted by the proportion attributed to the partner. The nominal proportion of equity provided by CIL is 21.4 percent; however, apportionment of surplus and dividend payout is reduced to 20.0 percent by agreement (whether this apportionment of benefits is justifiable is an issue for the partners). (See CYP *Project Finance* on our web site). The partner's equity contribution is deducted and dividends added.[26] NPV_{CIL} is positive at the discount rate applied (12 percent): US$314.5(000).

The IRR for a joint venture partner is determined from the same pattern of resource and funds flow as for NPV.

$$NPV_{JVP} = \sum_{j=1}^{n} (-Equity_{j(\%\%partner)} + NCF_{j(\%\%partner)} + Div_{j(\%\%partner)})$$

$$\times \left[\frac{1}{1 + i_{(discount)}} \right]^{j} = 0$$

The IRR for CIL is the discount rate $i_{(discount)}$ for which NPV = 0. For a partner with both common and preferred ownership, it is best to determine IRR independently for each. The share of surplus/deficit and the share of residual value are not really applicable in the case of preferred ownership, which is closer to the position of lender than that of equity holder. For preferred shares, inflows are fixed income per period, and outflows are the preferred equity in the periods of contribution.[27]

If each partner in a joint venture receives benefits in proportion to equity contributed, the returns (e.g., IRR) for each should be identical to the return for the integrated investment; if not, returns will differ. This can occur if partners agree to a distribution of ownership that differs from the proportions of their equity contributions, justified by special benefits

TABLE 3.12 NPV and IRR—CIL Partner, US$(000)

	% Equity	20.0%								
Year	1	2	3	4	5	6	7	8	9	10
Cash Flow Plan	0.0	0.0	2,001.5	4,213.8	624.3	568.1	404.1	203.3	294.4	12,380.8
Cash flow plan, CIL (20.0 %)	0.0	0.0	400.3	842.8	124.9	113.6	80.8	40.7	58.9	2,476.2
− Equity CIL	(1,642.4)	(1,035.1)	0.0							
+ Dividends, CIL	0.0	0.0	0.0	99.2	119.4	313.8	356.3	282.2	309.0	339.5
Net flow, CIL	(1,642.4)	(1,035.1)	400.3	942.0	244.3	427.5	437.2	322.8	367.8	2,815.6
Discount factor (12%)	0.893	0.797	0.712	0.636	0.567	0.507	0.452	0.404	0.361	0.322
Discounted values	(1,466.4)	(825.2)	284.9	598.7	138.6	216.6	197.8	130.4	132.6	906.6
Discount (hurdle) rate	12.0%									
Net present value, 12%	314.5									
Internal rate of return	14.7%									

provided by a partner to the project that are not directly monetary (e.g., access to markets).

The IRR for the CIL partner in the Cambria Yarns Project is shown in Table 3.12. The value is 14.7 percent, a bit less than that for total equity (Table 3.5), the result of allocation to the CIL partner of a share of benefits lower than its proportion of the nominal equity contribution (see Table 4.1).

NPV and IRR for the NTC partner are shown in Table 3.13. The IRR here is slightly higher than IRR for total equity because NTC receives a share of the benefits higher than the proportion of its equity contribution.

Joint Venture Financial Negotiations

To determine the distribution of ownership and benefits to be derived by joint venture partners, agreement must be reached concerning the value of monetary or in-kind assets contributed by each. If each partner is to contribute an amount of equity funds over time, the question is more directly resolved, although contributions in different currencies may present problems of current and future exchange rates.

Other potentially contentious factors relate to intangible assets brought to the venture by each partner or the value of in-kind assets: By what method are they to be valued so that the partners can agree on the distribution of ownership? One of the methods suggested in the "Valuation" subsection later in this chapter might be employed for in-kind assets. Perhaps the most accurate method for an ongoing productive entity is the present value of future generated benefits. The Victoria Coke Project (see our web site) is an example of the financial outlook for partners in a modernization project. In this case, book valuation of assets of the existing company (one of the partners) apparently overstates their actual value.

PROJECT OF AN ONGOING ENTERPRISE

For a currently operating enterprise, at any point in time decision makers have the choice of essentially standing pat—taking no action that affects the tenor or composition of the business—or undertaking a project to materially alter its state and future prospects (e.g., restructuring or turnaround). A third alternative is liquidation or sale. In the face of competition, or the need to provide improved products or services, enterprises eventually undertake expansion, modernization projects, or another form of revitalization. Existing companies, rather than individuals or groups launching new enterprises, are responsible for a large proportion of investment—to expand, rehabilitate,

TABLE 3.13 NPV and IRR—NTC Partner, US$(000)

	% Equity	80.0%								
Year	1	2	3	4	5	6	7	8	9	10
Cash Flow Plan	0.0	0.0	2,001.5	4,213.8	624.3	568.1	404.1	203.3	294.4	12,380.8
Cash flow plan, NTC (800%)	0.0	0.0	1,601.2	3,371.0	499.5	454.5	323.3	162.6	235.5	9,904.6
− Equity NTC	(9,819.8)									
+ Dividends, NTC	0.0	0.0	0.0	396.9	477.7	1,255.4	1,425.4	1,128.7	1,235.8	1,357.8
Net flow, NTC	(9,819.8)	0.0	1,601.2	3,768.0	977.2	1,709.8	1,748.7	1,291.3	1,471.4	11,262.4
Discount factor (12%)	0.893	0.797	0.712	0.636	0.567	0.507	0.452	0.404	0.361	0.322
Discounted values	(8,767.7)	0.0	1,139.7	2,394.6	554.5	866.2	791.0	521.5	530.6	3,626.2
Discount (hurdle) rate	12.0%									
Net present value, 12%	1,656.7									
Internal rate of return	15.4%									

or otherwise modify the structure or perhaps to merge operations of two or more enterprises.

The stimulus for embarking on an expansion or modernization project can arise from negative or positive signals—either deteriorating operating conditions or perceived prospects for increased benefits to shareholders. Negative signals indicating need for expansion, modernization, or rehabilitation may include the following:

- Loss of market share to competitors.
- Increasing sector competition, with new entrants implicitly indicating confidence in their ability to successfully compete with existing producers.
- Obsolescence arising from competitive advantages of emerging technologies, which may become apparent to management.
- Declining technical efficiency, with increasing consumption of resources in production or other enterprise functions, resulting from deteriorating facilities or management lapses.
- Decline in top or bottom line (revenue, profitability).
- Decline in shareholder value, as markets perceive looming problems for the enterprise, which may be the first indication of the need for a revitalization project.

Some positive signals suggest emergence of market opportunities: advancing technology, new international trade agreements, improving domestic and/or international business climate. Positive or negative signals give rise to the following questions:

- What are the consequences of doing nothing? How will the enterprise fare if it continues in its present mode of operations? Does the current configuration of the company represent the best use of committed resources?
- What will be the effect of the project? Will the expanded, modernized, or rehabilitated configuration have a positive impact on profitability and other performance indicators?
- Is the project justified as an investment? Is it sufficiently attractive to warrant commitment of additional resources? Would it be attractive to a new investor?

Revitalization Themes

The enterprise revitalization plan can include one or more measures to bring about operating improvements: increases in quality, yield, volume of output;

lower costs; ability to serve new markets; diminished risk. Projects may be undertaken for:

- *Expansion*—increased capacity of existing lines or additional lines to serve new or a larger proportion of existing markets with economies of scale and increased market reach (wider geographical penetration).
- *Modernization*—installation of improved technology or upgraded monitoring and control functions.
- *Diversification* through product differentiation (increasing the degree of uniqueness in products offered), expanding an existing product line or adding new ones, or backward or forward integration.
- *Rehabilitation* of production facilities and other operational elements of the enterprise that have deteriorated from use or neglect and require new investment.
- *Restructuring or turnaround*—realignment and reassignment of enterprise functions to achieve greater efficiencies.
- *Disposal of unproductive or underperforming assets*, permitting reallocation of capital to better uses.
- *Merger or acquisition* to provide synergies, resulting in greater operational efficiency and profitability.

Some potential benefits to the enterprise:

- Enhanced position in the market, increasing share, or even creating new markets resulting from product or promotional innovations.
- More reliable performance and greater efficiencies resulting from adoption of advanced technology.
- Smoother and more effective operations as functions are restructured and personnel are assigned new responsibilities and moved vertically and horizontally, with some added and others sent abroad to new and different challenges.
- Improved financial performance.
- Greater value in the revitalized enterprise as perceived by securities markets, if the project is viewed as a beneficial conception.

Some potential technological implications of revitalization projects:

- *Economies of scale:* at higher output levels, production factors at lower cost from price breaks or quantity discounts; reduced unit cost by spreading fixed costs (e.g., production supervisors) over higher levels of production.

- *Changes in technological coefficients* (existing and added facilities): lower quantities of resources per unit of output; improvement in extraction rates from raw materials; lower maintenance costs for the new production system as a consequence of improved design.
- *Extended life of the enterprise:* operations extended beyond what would have been the anticipated shutdown if the project had not been implemented.
- *Improved environmental compatibility:* mitigation or elimination of adverse environmental impacts on the region or workers' health and welfare; labor cost savings from improved health of workers; additional revenues from recovered waste; savings in material consumption; reduced potential for damage claims from the host community.

Mergers and acquisitions present an additional set of challenges; what looks plausible in theory is not always achievable. Many high-profile acquisitions and mergers falter as market dynamics, or the clash of corporate cultures, create unforeseen difficulties. Integrating operating entities can be mutually beneficial, but the pieces have to fit together so that overall operating efficiency is improved.

Financial Analysis of Revitalization Projects

The method of analyzing a revitalization project differs significantly from a start-up, particularly in regard to its incremental impact—the difference in scenarios with and without project implementation (i.e., how the infusion of new capital alters future conditions for the enterprise)—expanded operations, improved efficiencies, and their effects on future benefit and cost streams.

For an existing enterprise undertaking revitalization, it is not always clear what constitutes the project or its impacts. Existing assets to be committed may have multiple uses; opportunity costs of assets assigned to the project have to be taken into account; efficiencies—economies of scale or technological improvements attributable to the project—may feed into operations that appear superficially unrelated.

Starting Balance   In an operating enterprise, for the sake of simplicity it might be tempting to consider the project as a new entity, under the enterprise umbrella but completely autonomous. For a small project of a large enterprise this might be close to reality, but rarely does it occur in practice. There are inevitably links between the project and the existing organization, although in some cases small to negligible. In most cases the project is an appendage, something like a new organ that has to function in harmony and synchronization with the rest of the enterprise.

To begin financial analysis of such a project, the *starting balance* (SB) for the existing enterprise—the compilation of assets, liabilities, and equity at *time zero* ($t = 0$), the time immediately preceding the start of the project—is a point of departure and an essential feature. The starting balance sheet is a snapshot of the status of the enterprise at commencement of the project.

A realistic assessment of the amount of capital invested in the existing enterprise is required, which is not necessarily reflected in book value of assets and liabilities as they appear in the company's accounts (see the "Valuation" subsection later in this chapter). If discounted present value is to be the method of analysis, values taken from the accounts of the company usually *will not serve* to construct the starting balance, which should accurately reflect the impact of assets and liabilities on future financial flows.

With the exception of enterprise liquidation, analysis of a rehabilitation project is essentially future-oriented. The original value of existing assets is of minor interest. Of importance are associated future costs and benefits to be generated. Only those aspects of the past upon which future financial events may be predicated are relevant. Proper development of financial scenarios requires (1) determination of net worth based on realistic assessments of the values of assets and liabilities assigned to the project (the actual commitment of investors), and (2) simulating the effect of balance sheet elements on future cash flows.

The following types of adjustments should be considered:

- Assets to reflect actual values at project inception (e.g., liquidation price, opportunity cost, or value in the best alternative application).
- Depreciation rates to reflect their future impact on earnings and taxation.
- Inventories, receivables, and payables valued, and their liquidation timed, to reflect realistic assessments of their financial consequences; receivables, for example, may have to be written down to reflect uncollectable accounts.
- Debt service—outlays of principal, interest, and financial fees—to reflect anticipated payments.

Scenarios of Interest   Figure 3.7 represents scenarios and their relationships, to develop a complete picture of the revitalization project. The without-project scenario (I) describes the future in the absence of change (i.e., the enterprise does nothing). The future is predicated on the assumption that there will be no significant changes to the product line or modus operandi, except perhaps what steps are necessary to maintain current

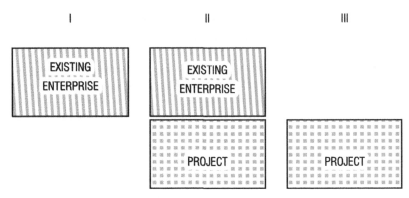

FIGURE 3.7 Scenarios for Revitalization Projects

market share and profitability. How markets react will be a function of the entrenchment of the product and marketing strategy and actions of competitors and substitutes.

The "enterprise plus project" scenario (II) is a projection of future performance of the company with the project implemented, a prediction of financial consequences of future events related to both existing operations and any additions or modifications resulting from the project, taking into account new production facilities and changes in performance of existing facilities (e.g., application of more advanced technologies in some areas, modifications in the product line or process, or termination of existing lines and facilities).

Another interesting viewpoint is the "project in isolation" scenario (III). This is the incremental effect of the project, which can be regarded in some respects as a separate entity, particularly if it is to be financed with new money from external sources. It is the difference in anticipated performance *with* and *without* the project (not before and after), taking into account synergies (e.g., upgrading old facilities with technology provided by the new partner in a merger) and efficiencies resulting from the project (e.g., economies of scale).

Method of Analysis   The financial analysis for each of these scenarios follows normal analytical procedures after setting up the starting balance (assets, liabilities, and net worth or shareholders' equity). In addition to financial capital and operating flows, account is taken of physical and other resources that flow into (e.g., existing finished product and material inventories) or out of the project (e.g., an asset committed to external purposes). In any case, future flows of capital and operating funds and resources for each period starting from project inception and ending at the planning horizon are included in the analysis.

For a relatively small enterprise with a project that has a large impact, an effective way to perform the analysis is to project the future without and with the project, as in Figure 3.7. This may not be practical for a large enterprise. If the project is small relative to the company's integrated operations it may be necessary to sort out incremental impacts directly. If the large company has separate profit centers—divisions or subsidiaries that function more or less autonomously—the incremental method may be suitable.

Cash flow from $t = 0$ (project inception) onward to the planning horizon is developed for each scenario and for each planning period. The financial incremental impact is the difference in cash flows between the *without* and *with* scenarios in each period. At the planning horizon, the *residual value* of assets and liabilities is included as inflow.

What value of assets should be assumed to exist at that point in time? The pricing system used in the analysis is one determinant. If constant pricing is employed, the values of assets ordinarily are not inflated to estimate their anticipated value. If assets are truly expected to change in value relative to general inflation, then this could legitimately be reflected in the estimated future value at the planning horizon. Ordinarily the analysis would not include an assumed terminal value of shares reflecting appreciation over time.[28]

It may be necessary to identify synergistic effects on existing operations of operational features of the project. For example, efficiencies in existing lines attributable to the project should appear in project flows, even though these lines are part of the existing enterprise and not directly related to the project; price breaks on project inputs also utilized in existing operations is another example. An advantage of identifying synergistic effects is that it helps in deciding what is really the scope of the project. Neglecting this factor increases the likelihood that revenues more accurately attributable to other activities might be inadvertently included in the project, and costs that should be included are ignored (e.g., complete or partial employment of existing facilities are assumed to be sunk costs when they either have alternative uses or can be sold).

If the project is financed wholly or in part with new equity from external sources, the issue of proportions of ownership by old and new investors inevitably arises, and how benefits from synergies or economies financed by new investors are to be apportioned. These types of issues, and suggestions about how they might be resolved, are discussed in the earlier section titled "Joint Ventures."

NPV and Present Value of Future Benefits   NPV for each of the scenarios (Figure 3.7) and *present value of future net benefits*, from $t = 0$ (i.e., the beginning of the project) to the planning horizon, can be determined and compared by discounting at the opportunity cost of capital for the enterprise. If the project is to be financed by new investors or with other external sources of capital, the discount rate for the project and for existing operations may differ.

Applying the same discount rate and planning interval to each scenario in Figure 3.7 results in the following relationships:

$$NPV_{EP} = NPV_E + NPV_P$$

$$NPV_P = NPV_{EP} - NPV_E$$

where NPV_{EP} = project implemented (existing enterprise plus project)
NPV_E = existing enterprise without project
NPV_P = project only

Net present value with respect to equity (NPV_E) is the present value of flows from $t = 0$ to the planning horizon, with equity (net worth from the initial balance and any future equity contributions) considered as outflow. The following relationship is applicable to both with-project and without-project scenarios:

$$NPV_E = -Equity_{SB} + \sum_{j=1}^{n} (-Equity_j + NCF_j + Div_j)df_j$$

where $Equity_{SB}$ = equity (shareholders' equity or net worth) in the starting balance

Equity in the starting balance should reflect the actual net worth—that is, assets minus liabilities, as they exist at project inception. Methods for determining value are discussed in the later subsection "Valuation." For the project-only scenario, $Equity_{SB}$ is not relevant—NPV can be determined either directly from relevant flows or indirectly as the difference between the without-project and with-project scenarios.

Internal Rate of Return   The internal rate of return for the enterprise, enterprise plus project, and project alone can be compared as an indication of the project's financial acceptability. IRR can be determined for the equity contributions and total investment (the former usually of greater significance in terms of the investment decision) by finding the discount rate that sets NPV to zero:

$$NPV_E = -Equity_{SB} + \sum_{j=1}^{n} (-Equity_j + NCF_j + Div_j) \left(\frac{1}{1 + i_{disc}} \right)^j = 0$$

where $i_{disc} = IRR$

As a general rule, if the project results in improved overall profitability, IRR for the enterprise with the project implemented will be higher than for the enterprise without the project. IRR for the project as a separate investment would usually be higher still. If IRR for the enterprise with the project is lower than for the *status quo*, the project investment is too high relative to additional benefits to be derived and the project should probably be rejected.

Case Study: Victoria Coke Project

An example of a modernization-rehabilitation project is presented on our web site as the Victoria Coke Project. Cash flows and dynamic indicators are developed for each of the three suggested scenarios and the financial implications of the project for stakeholders assessed.

Valuation   Project sponsors may be faced with the need to determine what an ongoing business is worth. The issue of valuation arises if the project involves merger or acquisition of an existing external operation. Owners or shareholders of the acquired entity will have to be compensated sufficiently to satisfy their criteria, although the manner of integrating the existing and acquired entities determines the value to the project.

A determination of value is necessary when assets are either traded or applied in-kind, as the basis for negotiation between buyer and seller or between partners in a joint venture, in which case the relative values of assets committed to the project are an issue.

If the acquired operating unit is to continue to function in its current mode without significant alteration, the methods described in this section are applicable. Otherwise, synergistic impacts can be taken into account using discounted cash flow methods described in earlier sections, "Analysis of Joint Ventures" and "Projects of an Ongoing Enterprise."

The appropriate valuation method depends to a large extent on the intentions of the owners of an enterprise: (1) The business can continue operating (perhaps with expansion or some other project in mind); (2) it can be sold as a going concern; (3) the assets can be dedicated to an alternative purpose; or (4) it can be dismantled and the assets liquidated.

Continuing Enterprise   If the enterprise is to continue operations in the current mode, its balance sheet may not be a good gauge of value. The prices or values of assets and liabilities may not be relevant; what is important is how these assets can be utilized to generate future benefits. The value of the enterprise can be determined as the present value of future net benefits discounted at the opportunity cost of capital. Only assets necessary for the operational entity should be included in the package. If some level of current assets (inventories and receivables) is essential to continue operations, they should be included in the package against which future benefits are credited, although they may have terminal residual value that at least partially offsets the investment. Assets that are nonperforming in this sense can be valued (and perhaps liquidated) separately.

Selling a Going Concern   Project sponsors might have ideas concerning the best employment of existing assets that differ from those of the existing owners. Some assets might best be liquidated, others modified or expanded, or applied to the same or different uses. In any case, the project sponsor's perspective comes into play. The process of valuation is similar to that for an existing enterprise, but the framework is the sponsor's vision for employment of the assets, expectation of return, and risk assessment. The fundamental mechanism in this case is also the present value of estimated future benefits, discounted at the *sponsor's* risk-adjusted opportunity cost of capital. For a potential investor, whether seeking acquisition or merger, the past is only relevant in terms of its future impacts.

In evaluating investment options, historical information is best used to simulate future performance from the point of view of the owner or prospective acquirer. Values and liquidation schedules for current assets and liabilities should constitute the best estimates that accurately reflect their future financial impacts. Under these conditions, net worth, or shareholders' equity, as reflected in the balance sheet may not be meaningful. Current balances should reflect values of assets and liabilities linked to future funds and resource flows, while depreciation rates, for example, should be set to simulate anticipated future depreciation and its influence on earnings and cash flow.

Alternative Application   The owners of an asset can set a value by considering its use in the next most favorable application. This is its opportunity cost, which can be determined on the basis of future benefits that would be derived by the owners if the asset were deployed in the alternative use.

Liquidation   If the enterprise is to cease operations and its assets are to be liquidated, their value to alternative users (buyers) will depend upon whether they will be scrapped or used in other applications, as is, or after rehabilitation by the new owner. To assess liquidation value for the enterprise, the balance sheet is important as long as it reflects actual market values of assets and liabilities. The book value of an asset may or may not represent its liquidation value. Financial analysis would consist of establishing a current balance sheet for the proprietors that reflects the liquidation value of all assets, the settling value of all outstanding liabilities, and the net worth or residual monetary value that would accrue to the owners upon liquidation.

Valuation Parameters   For an existing entity, the present value of future benefits can be determined by applying a discount rate to projected net flows in each period to the planning horizon, which may be short if the investors plan to acquire and dispose of the assets quickly, or extended if the intent is to operate some or all of the facilities. The discount rate is the risk-adjusted cost (or opportunity cost) of capital. A summary of the parameters is as follows:

Option	Valuation Base	Criterion
Continue operations	Present value of future benefits for owner	Owner's hurdle rate
Sell as going concern	Present value of future benefits for buyer	Buyer's hurdle rate
Alternative application	Present value of benefits	Owner's hurdle rate
Liquidate assets	Market value of assets	Replacement cost

From the perspective of the asset owner or buyer, optimization of returns may involve a combination of the options shown (e.g., some assets continuing operations, others sold as an operating entity, and still others liquidated).

In case of liquidation, the market may or may not reflect value. An appropriate criterion might be replacement cost, which if higher than the market could be indicative of market failure. Conversely, the asset could be a white elephant: impressive in size and power but not of much practical use.

Valuation based upon discounted flow (benefits and costs) principles can be determined either directly by discounted flows for each period from project inception to the planning horizon, or indirectly by adding back the present value of equity to NPV_{equity}. The latter relationship is based on the fact that the present value of equity (PV_{equity})—that is, the sum of equity contributions in each period discounted to the present (project inception) at the cost of capital—is subtracted from the flow of benefits and costs to determine NPV_{equity}.

$$V_{enterprise} = NPV_{equity} + PV_{equity}$$

where $V_{enterprise}$ = value of enterprise
PV_{equity} = present value of equity at time of valuation

In any case, valuation should be based upon a realistic construction of the balance sheet (assets and liabilities valued on replacement cost, market value, or some other supportable basis) and estimates of future benefits and costs. Either benefits (inflows) and costs (outflows) in each period can be separately discounted, each at the cost of capital, and then summed, or alternatively, the difference between benefits and costs for each period can be discounted.

Another useful relationship concerning valuation in case of an expansion or modernization project deals with flows after and not including $t = 0$: ignoring all infusions of equity capital and net worth in the starting balance, with the same discount rate and time frame applied to all three scenarios.

$$PV_{EP} = PV_E + PV_P$$
$$PV_P = PV_{EP} - PV_E$$

where PV_{EP} = present value, project implemented (existing enterprise plus project)
PV_E = present value, existing enterprise without project
PV_P = present value, project only

PV is the present value of net future flows, and is a measure of *value of the enterprise*.[29] One method for its calculation is to add the present value of equity contributions in each period (including $t = 0$) to the corresponding NPV. Alternatively, the appropriate discount rate can be applied to cash flows in each period from the first (not including $t = 0$, that is, the starting balance) to the planning horizon, ignoring equity inflows and adding back dividend payouts. This is a way of establishing relative values for the existing and expanded or rehabilitated enterprise with the project implemented.

It is also useful for negotiations when new investors provide equity for the project.

Valuation Based upon Market Capitalization   Enterprise value (EV) for an ongoing enterprise whose shares trade in the market is defined as market capitalization plus preferred stock plus debt minus cash and equivalents.[30] Market capitalization is the number of common shares multiplied by the per-share price. Cash is subtracted because it is considered a nonoperating asset. This measure is essentially the market's assessment of the value of ongoing operations, somewhat equivalent to NPV(I), except that the *present value of investment* would have to be added back (recall that NPV = 0 indicates that the original investment is recovered *and* the yield is equal to the hurdle rate). An indicator similar to payback is enterprise value divided by EBITDA (EV/EBITDA)—that is, the number of years required to recover the enterprise value from operating profits.

Valuation Example   A valuation example is presented on our web site, "Victoria Coke Project, Rates of Return and Valuation." In this case the book value of company assets, estimated by a certified public accountant, is considerably greater than indicated by the present value of future benefits that can be generated. Valuations of the existing assets, the revitalized company (with the project), and the project in isolation form the basis for negotiations between the existing owner and a partner who is to provide equity to finance the project.

APPENDIX 3.1: EXAMPLE OF COST OF CAPITAL CALCULATIONS

The hurdle rate (or challenge rate) for an investment is the discount rate used in assessing future costs and benefits, as explained in Chapter 2. As a general rule, if the net present value (NPV) for the project is nonnegative when benefits and costs are discounted at the hurdle rate, the project is considered acceptable for investment on the basis of this financial criterion.

The opportunity cost of capital is frequently applied as the benchmark for deciding on viability of a project. *Opportunity* in this case refers to the best alternative use of resources. For an existing enterprise utilizing its own capital resources for the project, its opportunity cost is considered to be its actual cost of capital, as the expectation of return on capital is ordinarily at least equal to its cost.[31] It is not absolutely necessary that a project generate sufficient returns to cover capital depletion and specified rental cost (return on capital) to be viable; however, to generate surplus wealth, an excess of benefits over costs is essential. The benefits, in this case, must include returns at least equal to the benchmark rate (in addition to covering capital depletion), as any alternative use has to be regarded relative to this expectation.

Projects are usually financed either with new capital consisting of a combination of debt and equity, or, for an existing enterprise, partially or totally with capital from its own reserves. The overall cost is typically taken as the weighted average (weightings based on value) of debt and equity composing its existing capital structure. The following example explains how an existing enterprise determines its cost of capital for a new investment project to be financed internally. If new sources of financing are required, the cost of capital is determined on the basis of the proportions of internal and external capital to be employed.

Consider a company with the following balance sheet items (liabilities and equity only), all values in US$(000), with the corporate tax rate assumed to be 20 percent of profits.

Current liabilities	
Accounts payable	100
Bank overdraft 6%	50
Total	150
Long-term Liabilities	
Bank loan, 6.0%, 2xx5	150
Debentures, 5%, 2xx3	75
Convertible bond, 3% coupon, 50 shares common	
equity, 2xx3	300
Note, 7%, 2xx4	90
Total	615
Equity	
Preferred shares, 10 thousand, 8%, market value $25	250
Other shareholders' equity, current market value of	
common shares $22 per share[1]	360
Total	610

[1] Other than preferred stock, shareholders' equity consists of the following items: common stock, $0.05 par value, 800,000 shares authorized; additional paid-in capital, 120; retained earnings, 60; reserves, 140.

Cost of Capital for Debt and Equity

Current Liabilities

- *Accounts payable.* There are late payment charges, but the company usually complies with payment terms so the cost of accounts payable is essentially zero.
- *Bank overdraft.* The 6 percent interest on balances is the only charge; the cost of this capital is therefore equal to the interest rate of 6 percent.

Long-Term Liabilities[32]

- *Bank loan, 6.0 percent 2xx5.* Interest on the amount of principal is the only cost (i.e., 6 percent).
- *Debentures, 5 percent coupon, 2xx3.* Current market value is $900. The cost per period is considered as the sum of the coupon rate and the excess of market value over par (issue) value for per each remaining year to maturity (three, in this case). This is divided by the average of par and market value to determine the rate.[33]

$$\frac{\text{Bond coupon} + [(\text{par value} - \text{market value})/\text{average remaining life}]}{(\text{par value} + \text{market value})/2}$$

$$= \frac{50 + (1000 - 900)/3}{(1000 + 900)/2} = 0.088$$

- *Convertible bond, 4 percent coupon, convertible to 50 shares common equity, redemption 2xx3.* The issue price for bonds was $950, with par value of $1,000. Each bond converts into 50 common shares, with an average expected market price per share of $22. The coupon value of 4 percent requires a payment of $40 per bond per annum. As only the interest part of the return on the bond is tax deductible, the calculation is after-tax. With a corporate tax rate of 20 percent, the cost is $32 per bond (40 × 0.8).

  It is assumed that the bonds were issued at the beginning of the current year (2xx0). Inflow from the sale of the bond was the issue price of $950. The redemption value per bond is 50 (common shares per bond) times the conversion price of $22 (expected value at conversion), or $1,100. The rate is determined from internal rate of return based upon cash flow per bond:

Year	2xx0[1]	2xx0	2xx1	2xx2	2xx3
Inflow	950				
Outflow coupon		32	32	32	32
Redemption[2]					1,100
Total outflow		32	32	32	1,130
Net flow	950	−32	−32	−32	−1,132

[1]This simulates inflow of funds at beginning of 2xx0; all other flows are assumed at end of period.
[2]Conversion.

Assuming that the inflow (sale of convertible) was at the beginning of 2xx0 and discounting to the beginning of the same year, the internal rate of return, or applicable discount rate, is 6.9 percent.

■ *Note, 7 percent. 2xx4.* As this is a marketable security, the cost is determined in a manner similar to the 5 percent debenture.

$$\frac{\text{Note coupon} + [(\text{par value} - \text{market value})/\text{average remaining life}]}{(\text{par value} + \text{market value})/2}$$

$$= \frac{70 + (1,000 - 840)/4}{(1,000 + 840)/2} = 0.1195 \text{ or } 0.12$$

	Value $(000)	Pretax Cost	After-tax Cost	Weight[1]	Weighted Cost
Accounts payable	100	0.000	0.000	0.131	0.000
Bank overdraft	50	0.060	0.048	0.065	0.003
Bank loan, 6%	150	0.060	0.048	0.196	0.009
Debentures, 5%	75	0.088	0.070	0.098	0.007
Convertible bond, 3%	300	—	0.069	0.392	0.027
Promissory note, 7%	90	0.12	0.096	0.118	0.011
Total value	765			1.0000	0.058

[1]Weight is the ratio of value of item to total.
Note: Weighted cost of debt, C_{dt}.

The weighted, after-tax cost of debt is 0.058 or 5.8 percent

Equity

■ *Common shares.* The cost of common equity can be estimated as the average value of the several methods employed in its calculation. The bases for calculation in this example are dividend payout per share, earnings/ price ratio, earnings plus growth rate, the (price/earnings)/growth (PEG) ratio, and the capital asset pricing model (CAPM). With the exception of preferred shares, the following alternative methods are applied to all shareholders' equity, as they are estimates of the current opportunity cost of shareholder investment.

- *Dividend/market price.* Current dividend level is $1.10/share, market price $22/share, so cost is $1.10/22.00 = 0.05$.
- *Earnings/market price.* Current earnings are $1.50 per share; $1.50/22.00 = 0.068$.
- *Earnings plus estimated growth rate.* Markets typically price in a consistent growth rate to the prevailing earnings/market price ratio, predicated on the assumption that the market does not fully recognize the value of the shares. In this case, the growth rate of 12 percent per annum in earnings is added to the earnings/price ratio: $0.068 + 0.12 = 0.188$.
- *Price/earnings to growth (PEG) ratio.* This index is widely employed as an indicator of relative value. A PEG of 1 indicates fair value: $(P/E)/G = 1$ or $P/E = G$. According to this criterion (assuming stability in the growth pattern), the fair market value of shares is the product of earnings and growth rate, in this case 1.50×12 or $18, with a cost of capital of $1.50/$18.00 or 0.083. This can also be calculated as 1/growth rate $(1/12 = 0.083)$.
- *Capital asset pricing model.* The market rate of return in the equity market is 10 percent (i.e., 0.10) and the risk-free rate (e.g., medium-term government bonds) is 4 percent (i.e., 0.04). Common shares in this industry typically have a volatility index (β) of 1.4. The estimate is developed as follows:

$$C = RF + \beta(MKT - RF) = 0.04 + 1.4(0.1 - 0.04) = 0.124$$

where $\quad \beta =$ risk index—that is, measure of volatility of the shares compared to general market movements, or β
$\quad RF =$ risk-free rate (secure credit market)
$\quad MKT =$ rate of return in equity market, averaged over five years

- *Preferred shares, 8 percent, noncumulative.* The cost is based upon the ratio of the current dividend to the average market price of the shares. The market values have ranged from a high of $125 to a low of $89.

$$\frac{\text{Current dividend}}{\text{Average market price per share}} = \frac{8.00}{(125 + 89)/2} = 0.077$$

The *weighted cost of equity, C_{eq}, at market cost* is calculated according to the proportions of common and preferred equity: 59 percent and 41 percent, respectively.

	Value $(000)	Cost of Element	Percent Value Weight	Weighted Cost	Total Cost of Equity, Common and Preferred
Common shares	360				
Dividends/market price		0.050	0.590	0.030	0.062
Earnings/market price		0.068	0.590	0.040	0.072
Earnings plus growth rate		0.188	0.590	0.111	0.143
PEG ratio		0.083	0.590	0.049	0.081
CAPM		0.124	0.590	0.073	0.105
Average cost of equity (common plus preferred)					0.092
Preferred shares, 8% noncumulative	250	0.077	0.410	0.032	
Total value	610				

The average weighted cost of shareholders' equity is the sum of the weighted preferred and common equity cost for each method. The average is 0.092 or 9.2 percent as the estimated cost of equity. A weighed average might be more accurate depending on the confidence in each method of equity cost assessment.

The total cost of capital is estimated as the weighted values of the cost of debt ($\approx$5.8 percent) and equity ($\approx$9.2 percent), or about 7.3 percent. The total value of debt is 765 (160 current plus 615 long-term) and of equity is 610 (250 preferred and 360 common).

$$C_{capital} = w_{dt}c_{dt} + w_{eq}c_{eq}$$

$$= \left(\frac{765}{1,375}\right) 5.8 + \left(\frac{610}{1,375}\right) 9.2 \cong 7.3$$

A variable for the project designer is the target debt/equity ratio. From this analysis, the cost of debt is found to be below the cost of equity. It appears to be advantageous for the company to leverage the project; the extent will be determined by constraints on the availability of debt financing and the actual cost of debt and equity allocated specifically to the project.

NOTES

1. Payback period, as a measure of the recovery of investment over time, is inherently a dynamic indicator. Another type of payback measurement is *dynamic payback*, in which discounted flows cover the initial investment (see the "Dynamic Indicators" section in this chapter).
2. Some of the ratios for the Cambria Yarns Project are not within generally accepted standards, but the lender has taken on the additional risk in conformance with its mission to promote investment in the country.
3. In some formulations both interest and depreciation are added back to net profit after tax. Another, more consistent formulation applies income generated by investment before interest, taxes, and depreciation (EBITDA) as the profit indicator. Net profit in the formula shown is after-tax profit, which takes into account the effect of interest charges on tax. In some formulations, interest added back is adjusted by the factor $(1 - T)$, where T is the tax rate, as a matter of preference, which accounts for the reduction in taxes resulting from deductible interest expense. In the dynamic equivalent, internal rate of return (IRR) and net present value (NPV) for investment, the full amount of interest is added back to cash flow.
4. Total initial investment includes fixed assets and preoperational expenditures in years 1 and 2, capitalized interest in year 2, and working capital financed with proceeds from the long-term loan in years 2 and 3.
5. The simple rate of return calculation is based on accounting conventions that differ from country to country depending on legislation or regulation, and that may or may not reflect real profitability. If the legislative or regulatory framework differs significantly from the approaches described, the calculations should be adjusted to local conditions. For example, depletion and depreciation allowances can significantly affect taxable income and profitability.
6. Rate of return can be used to compare alternative technologies considering total annual production costs at full capacity utilization. The margin between sales revenue and cost of product sold (gross profit) is related to respective investment costs; rate of return could be used to assign priority.
7. For the examples in the Cambria Yarns Project, the current and quick ratios are higher than would normally be the case. The values are completely dependent upon assumptions included in the project design, as reflected by the items included in each, and the days of coverage assigned. Assigning higher

values for current and quick ratios is conservative, as more capital is needed for short-term financing. In the examples, current assets include receivables, material and product inventories, and short-term liquid assets (only cash included in working capital in this case). Current liabilities are based on operating costs excluding labor and leasing at the specified turnover. For the quick ratio, the numerator includes only receivables and short-term liquid assets (marketable securities have not been included in the financial analysis). Cash accumulated from operations is not included in either ratio, as these funds are normally destined for other purposes.

8. In the example all sales are considered to be credit sales.

9. In some formulations interest is adjusted by the tax rate T to reflect the actual outflow (interest is usually a tax-deductible expense). Whether this adjustment $(1 - T)$ should be included is a matter of choice. However, the principle is to simulate the accumulated cash return on investment, which excludes financial flows; interest and depreciation were deducted to determine net profit, so are added back; the net profit calculation takes into account the effect of interest on taxes.

10. The approximation is relatively close if the investment phase is short, the annual net cash flows are fairly constant, and the project life exceeds 10 to 15 years. For a constant net cash flow with infinite planning horizon, the reciprocal of the payback exactly equals the IRR.

11. In this formulation only one class of common shares is assumed. Dividends paid on preferred shares should not be added back to cash flow as they do not accrue to common shareholders.

12. The rental price is the expected return on the investment.

13. For after-tax NPV(I), finance costs are relevant only as a determinant of tax.

14. Discount factors, and all other calculated financial and economic values, were calculated using internal spreadsheet functions, such as those in Microsoft Excel. Some numbers (e.g., discount factors) are shown rounded to the lowest decimal point indicated. For this reason there may be small discrepancies between many of the calculated values and their counterparts calculated with numbers of lower precision (few decimal points).

15. Discount factors are calculated from year 1 to year 10, which means that first-year flows are discounted. This is equivalent to discounting all flows back to the *beginning of the first year* or the start of the project, as if the flows actually occurred at the end of each year. This matter is further discussed in *Dynamic payback* (see Dynamic Indicators in this chapter).

16. Most commercial spreadsheet programs and financial calculators have built-in search routines that calculate IRR based on array values associated with a sequence of periods. These instruments usually contain programs that perform many of the standard financial calculations (e.g., IRR, NPV, schedules of depreciation, debt service). Alternatively, the simplest search routine is to calculate NPV for discount rates starting at zero and increasing until NPV changes from positive to negative; then a more accurate value at which NPV = 0 can be found with interpolation.

17. Changes in period flows from negative to positive, or vice versa, generate mathematical roots of the polynomial equation describing the relation between discounted values of period flows, each of which is an IRR.
18. The reinvestment assumption is equally applicable to ordinary calculation of NPV, which calls the objection into question. If surpluses were to be used for some other purpose (e.g., consumption), the discount rate would not likely be the cost of capital but rather the rate at which future consumption is discounted.
19. Normally for a growing enterprise, funds will be absorbed internally in expansions of the enterprise beyond the project. In other situations these funds will be employed in other enterprises or subsidiaries. Opportunities to reinvest surpluses in projects with inordinately high rates of return are available but usually carry high risk. There are also high-risk instruments available in equity and credit markets (e.g., the junk bond market).
20. Cumulative cash flow for any period in the analysis usually represents the ending value. *During* the period, liquid portions of working capital would be available to cushion variations in the balance.
21. Although the cost of capital is the usual benchmark (actual cost or opportunity cost), a particular investor may wish to make adjustments according to perceptions, preferences, and tolerance of risk associated with project features.
22. At low discount rates, NPV of capital-intensive projects tend to be lower and labor-intensive projects higher. The reverse is true at high discount rates.
23. This is true if the assumption that the method of calculation of IRR inherently involves reinvestment of surpluses is accepted (an assumption not universally shared). It is unlikely that a firm will invest in projects with returns much different from their cost of capital.
24. The level of debt affects profit and taxes, which in turn affects return on equity.
25. The mathematically correct nominal market rate would also include the products of β, ρ, and ι, but these products are usually small and can be ignored. In credit markets rates are often set by adjusting a relatively secure rate such as the London InterBank Offered Rate (LIBOR)—for example, LIBOR plus 2— to account for risk and duration.
26. NCF_i is *postdividends*. This is then allocated, according to agreement on share distribution, to each partner. Then the specific partner's equity contributions are deducted and dividends are credited.
27. The value of preferred shares at the planning horizon should be taken into account in evaluating the return on preferred equity. It would not be reasonable to assume full recovery of the initial value unless the business plan is predicated on the assumption of ongoing activities for a considerable time after the project's planning horizon (a possible subject of negotiation for the preferred shareholder). Otherwise residual assets available to generate income may be small or nil, unless the plan includes replacements to maintain plant capacity. One way to estimate the residual value of preferred equity is to use the percentage of residual asset value to the original value of the assets. This accounts for reinvestment intended to maintain the level of operations beyond the planning horizon.

28. Recovery of an estimated share value would be applicable if the scenario included planned disposal of shares at some point in time. The planning horizon would be from project inception to the time of sale. Accruals to the shareholder would include only dividend and other payouts and the estimated value of shares at the time of sale. The future value of shareholdings should take into account any surpluses generated and retained during each operational period, compounded at the expected rate of return on capital.

29. The fundamental mechanism of market valuation of traded shares in an enterprise is present value (PV) of future net benefits. The intrinsic discount factor is adjusted for risk and inflation, as discussed in the subsection "Criteria and Capital Markets." The valuation system is far from perfect, as illustrated by periodic outbreaks of seemingly irrational exuberance or despair, and directed toward a particular security, segments, or the entire market.

30. Why is debt added and cash subtracted? A potential buyer is interested in the value of assets, which are covered by a combination of equity and debt (preferred shares are quasi-debt). A buyer would not pay or otherwise finance acquisition of cash, and for that reason cash and equivalents are excluded. From another viewpoint, cash is a nonperforming asset.

31. This concept is somewhat related to the issue of corporate culture. An ongoing enterprise considering a new investment is most likely to opt for projects with production, market, and financial characteristics similar to those of the existing operational framework, not necessarily true for a conglomerate as an entity, but applicable for its operating units or enterprises.

32. In all calculations the number of years is based on the current year as 2xx0.

33. A more accurate way to determine actual rate of return for financial instruments is to find the internal rate of return (IRR) for the inflows and outflows. As an example, for the 5 percent debenture of 2xx3, the flows would be as follows for the three periods (the initial value is determined at time $t = 0$):

Year			
0	1	2	3
(900)	50	50	1,050

The corresponding IRR is about 9 percent rather than 8.8 percent by the approximation method.

REFERENCES

Anderson, D. R., T. A. Williams, and D. J. Sweeney. 2010. *An introduction to management science: Quantitative approaches to decision making*, 13th ed. Cincinnati: South-Western College Publishers.

Biermann, H., Jr., and Seymour Smidt. 1992. *The capital budgeting decision: Economic analysis and financing of investment projects*, 8th ed. New York: Macmillan.

Cohen, J. B., S. M. Robbins, and A. E. Young. 1986. *The financial manager*. Columbus, OH: Publishing Horizons (NIP).

Derkinderen, F. G. J., and R. L. Crum. 2009. *Risk, capital costs and project financing decisions*. Boston: Springer-Verlag.

Haugen, R. A. 2000. *Modern investment theory*, 5th ed. Englewood Cliffs, NJ: Prentice-Hall.

Hillier, F., G. Lieberman, and M. Hillier. 1999. *Management science*. Columbus, OH: McGraw-Hill.

Terry, Brian. 1996. *International finance and investment*, 2nd ed. London: Chartered Institute of Bankers.

United Nations Conference on Trade and Development (UNCTAD). 2003. *How to prepare your business plan*. New York and Geneva: UNCTAD.

Van Bergen, Jason. 2010. Forces behind exchange rates. *Investopedia/Forbes*. www.investopedia.com/articles/basics/04/050704.asp.

CHAPTER 4

Financing the Project

Financing to cover investment—fixed and current assets committed to the project—is obtained from equity funds or in-kind contributions, credits, and in some cases grants and subsidies provided by government entities for projects that conform to social objectives.

A primary challenge for project sponsors is accumulating funds in the amount and at the time required. The main issues are (1) identifying sources of debt and equity capital (and subsidies if applicable), (2) methods and timing of acquisition, (3) the capital structure or share of investment capital to be covered from each source, (4) the cost of capital, and (5) sharing and alleviating risk for lenders and other participants.

Sources of capital have to be identified—lenders, investors, grantors, suppliers, and other institutions and individuals providing financial or in-kind resources to cover capital expenditures. The sources of finance (whether funds, securities, or in-kind) can generally be classified as debt or equity. Debt involves borrowing and equity connotes ownership. The project incurs debt by borrowing from lenders who are willing to finance part of the project in exchange for promise of future payments consisting of a rental price (interest); fees,[1] commissions, and discounts that may add to the rental price; and repayment of principal. Equity participants expect to gain from accumulation of operating surpluses, some or all of which may be distributed in the form of dividends.

How financial resources are allocated to the project is an essential question in preinvestment analysis regarding coverage of capital requirements and financing costs. It also has a bearing on the cost of capital for investors and creditors—the principle basis for financial criteria. Preliminary assessment of project financing possibilities is usefully undertaken in the very early stages of project development to indicate the order of magnitude of the required capital outlay.

Financial resource constraints could define project parameters well before the investment decision, and at various stages of project formulation.

The availability of capital could constrain project size or configuration down to minimum economic level,[2] beyond which even large deposits of accessible raw materials do not justify investment.

Engineering design describing the physical configuration of the project and its operating parameters is necessary to assess financial requirements: Capital outlay can be estimated only after plant capacity and location have been decided (at least tentatively), and costs estimated for project implementation (e.g., site development, buildings and civil works, technology and equipment). Operational information is required to estimate revenue and cost streams and current accounts, so that working capital (finance required for operations)—too often underestimated or even neglected—can be estimated. There may also be a need to cover operating deficits in the early stages of operations.

CAPITAL STRUCTURE

Capital for the initial investment is normally covered by a combination of equity and debt in the form of long-term loans and other credits, including a base level of working capital. Additional working capital requirements are typically covered with additional short- and medium-term loans, usually from domestic commercial banks. To avoid excessive administrative and other costs, at least the minimum requirement for working capital permanently tied up in inventories (raw materials, work-in-progress, finished goods, and spare parts) and receivables should be covered with long-term funds (equity capital and long-term loans).

The decision on proportions of capital sources to cover project assets—the capital mix—hinges on the relative cost of debt and equity in capital markets; proportions are usually constrained by lenders, who seek to reduce risk by limiting the proportion of debt in the finance package. Other factors are the type of project to be financed; for example, low-profit-margin industries tend to require greater leverage. Credit markets are affected by monetary and fiscal policy, so the cost of debt can fluctuate widely. Leverage is advantageous for sponsors as long as the project generates returns greater than the cost of debt, but it increases risk.

A higher proportion of equity reduces debt service obligations and increases pretax profit (greater leverage even at relatively high rates can increase profit, depending on tax rates—see example in Table 3.8); it is favorable when the real, inflation-adjusted cost of borrowing is high and when the opportunity cost of equity capital is low (limited opportunities for investment).

The implications of alternative patterns and forms of financing can be assessed to determine the optimal structure in regard to availability of resources and financial returns.[3] Some of the factors to be taken into account in setting debt-to-equity proportions are as follows:

- *Capital service rate.* Debt frequently carries a fixed rate (floating rates and other risk transfer or sharing devices are sometimes applied—see the later subsection "Innovative Financing"); equity usually does not have a fixed rate of return, generally depending on profits and management policies.
- *Service preference.* Creditors usually have legal claims to debt service before payment of dividends to equity holders.
- *Claim on profits.* Creditors have no claim on profits, which accrue only to shareholders (equity).
- *Redemption/repayment.* Creditors expect to have principal repaid; equity usually has no such claim to redemption, but can be liquidated in securities markets (which usually requires registration in a securities exchange) or private (over-the-counter) sales.
- *Liquidation preference.* In case of liquidation, creditors usually have preference before equity holders for repayment of loan balances and interest due; claims of preferred shareholders (e.g., dividends) are satisfied before those of ordinary shareholders.
- *Claim on net worth.* Equity has claim to accumulated wealth, or net worth, of the enterprise; creditors have no claim to ownership.

The financial structure of the project is defined at a point in time (e.g., the commencement of the project) with a balance sheet (see Chapter 2). Assets and their values are listed on one side: fixed assets (plant and facilities), pre-operational expenditures (organization and start-up expenditures, including any interests accumulated and capitalized during the construction phase), and current assets (inventories, receivables, short-term instruments, cash).

The financial structure is described by the right side of the balance sheet ("Balance of assets and liabilities") in Figure 4.1. Assets are covered with liabilities—long-, short-, and medium-term debt, accounts payable (and other short-term liabilities), and shareholders' equity (paid in equity, retained earnings, and other reserves).

Financial Structure—CYP

For the Cambria Yarns Project, the financial structure is shown in Table 4.1. Proportions of debt and equity are 67.1:32.9 or a ratio of about 2.0. The foreign partner is to provide 78.6 percent of the equity in foreign exchange

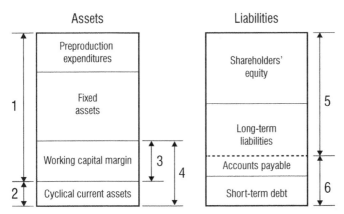

FIGURE 4.1 Financial Structure—Balance of Assets and Liabilities
Code: 1 = fixed investment; 2 = cyclical components of current assets; 3 = working capital margin; 4 = total current assets; 5 = permanent capital; 6 = current liabilities.

and the local partner 21.4 percent in local currency. Because the local currency is overvalued, the partners have agreed to 80.0 percent NTC, 20.0 percent CIL distribution of shares that takes into account a 20 percent premium on foreign exchange (see CYP on our web site, "Financing the Project").

In addition to the financial sources indicated, there may be a short-term need to cover raw cotton purchases. The maximum amount could be

TABLE 4.1 Capital Structure—CYP, US$(000)

Investment	Percent	Amount
Debt (IFC loan)	67.1	25,505.3
Equity	32.9	12,497.2
Total		38,002.5
D/E ratio	2.0	

Equity Breakdown		
Namborn Trading Company (NTC)	78.6	9,819.8
Cambria Investors, Ltd. (CIL)	21.4	2,677.4
Total		12,497.2

Adjusted Equity Breakdown		
Adjustment for 20% FX premium		
Namborn Trading Company (NTC)	81.5	11,783.7
Cambria Investors, Ltd. (CIL)	18.5	2,677.4

as high as US$1.44 million. As the average amount of investment in raw cotton inventory is taken into account in working capital estimates, short-term finance would have to cover only the difference between the average and the peak (see the section "Estimating Working Capital" in Chapter 2).[4]

Risk

Commitment of financial resources to the project is almost never without risk, which arises from uncertainties in information, error, and the vicissitudes of nature. Expectations of project financiers, whether lenders or owners, are strongly influenced by their level of participation (what is at risk), the degree of risk, and their particular tolerance for risk. Available methods of risk immunization can help to alleviate what might otherwise prove to be insurmountable barriers (see Chapter 7). An example of quantitative risk analysis related to fluctuations in yarn export prices for the Cambria Yarns Project is provided in CYP (see our web site) "Project Risk."

Equity Finance

Equity capital provided by sponsors and other investors confers ownership of the enterprise. Equity shares can be traded in an established market when accepted by its governing board or at mutually agreed prices between buyer and seller. Unlike debt, there is usually *no assurance of redemption* of investment, unless by prior agreement between the owners.

In countries with developed capital markets, equity funds can be raised through public issue of shares, usually underwritten by investment banks and other financial institutions. Institutions specializing in industrial financing participate to varying extents, usually as minority shareholders.

To promote investment in some countries, public agencies acquire equity holdings initially and release them gradually to domestic entrepreneurs or to the equity market. Whether offered in public markets or through private placement, an issue for project sponsors is how to apportion their own equity and equity raised through sale of shares. The decision depends upon availability, and actual or opportunity cost of sponsors' financial resources versus the cost of securing external equity finance (the issue is whether the price that external investors are willing to pay is consistent with expected returns).

Ordinary Shares   *Ordinary* (*common*) shares confer ownership of assets (other than those that are leased) and rights to financial surpluses and profits, but usually the last right over assets in case of bankruptcy (i.e., the residual value after paying off creditors). Ordinary shares can be offered through private placements or capital markets.

Sponsors normally provide the equity capital, or issue shares through private placement or equity markets. There may be more than one class of ordinary shares within an enterprise, with rights to profit distributions, options and warrants, voting privileges, and other benefits and conditions incorporated into the capital structure as defined in articles of incorporation or in a partnership agreement.

In most regulatory environments, distributions (dividends) from funds generated by the project are usually limited to the amount of profit for a given period or retained in previous periods; ordinary dividends are paid only if sufficient funds are available. In some business environments, dividend policy is the prerogative of a corporate board of directors, or, in the case of partnerships, by common agreement of the parties, without a mandatory link between profits and distributions. Some portion of profit is usually retained as reserves for future investment or for other purposes, increasing shareholders' equity and wealth.

Preferred Shares   *Preferred* shares provide a relatively secure return for conservative investors, more akin to debt than equity. Generally dividend payouts are a fixed amount per share set at the time of issue. Dividends on preferred shares are at least partly independent of profit, usually without, or with limited, voting rights. The shares can be cumulative or noncumulative in regard to dividends.[5] Project sponsors can issue preferred shares to attract needed capital that might not be available otherwise. Preferred equity has a claim to dividends in the event of liquidation of assets before ordinary common equity holders can exercise their rights. In case of bankruptcy, preferred shareholders are usually first in line (after creditors) for redemption of the share value at the time of issue.

Debt Finance

Equity can be leveraged with borrowed capital to cover asset and operating costs. Loans from investment and development banks are generally secured to cover *permanent* capital—fixed assets and minimum level of working capital. Merchant banks are a potential source of short-term operating finance. Leveraging capital with debt, or *trading on equity,* has its advantages as long as the project can earn more than its cost, but excessive use of debt financing increases risk.

Lenders may agree to swap debt for equity, either as an investment promotion measure or because it seems to make good business sense (also to alleviate liquidity crises in ailing but promising enterprises). Investment bankers may also participate as equity participants, possibly combining long-term financing with an equity stake. Development institutions sometimes provide equity with the proviso that their stake will be retired at a future date.

Alternative debt coverage and sequences can be examined to find the optimal cash flow plan. For example, less expensive forms of debt can be utilized early in the project, when liquidity is an issue. Debt of various durations (short, medium, long) and types (bank loans, debentures, suppliers' credit) can be alternatively sequenced in regard to disbursement and repayment.

Debt service for a project period includes repayment of principal, interest, and other charges such as placement and commitment fees and commissions levied by the lender or agent. Interest is the major cost for rental of capital, usually at a percentage rate applied to the unpaid balance at the end of the prior period. Typically an annual rate is specified, with charges based on the equivalent monthly or quarterly rate. For example, if the nominal annual rate is 12 percent the monthly rate is 1 percent. A premium may be required for early redemption. When other charges are imposed the actual percentage rate (APR) is higher than the nominal interest rate.

The real, or inflation-adjusted, cost of debt is discussed in the subsections "Inflation and Dynamic Criteria" and "Criteria and Capital Markets" in Chapter 3. An approximate relationship between the real and nominal cost that does not account for fees and other charges is to reduce the nominal interest by the average rate of inflation in the denominated currency (see "Inflation and Dynamic Criteria" in Chapter 3).[6]

Disbursement Schedule   Term loans are disbursed according to a negotiated schedule. The lender may be willing to allow the project to take down the loan as needed, as long as interest is paid on the outstanding balance, but may levy a commitment fee on principal that has not been disbursed. The disbursement schedule is often predicated on conditions—for example, the requirement that all equity be committed to the project before loan disbursements are made. Disbursements may be phased according to percentage of work to be completed. In another type of arrangement, invoices are paid directly by the bank or other financing institution.

Amortization Methods   The lender usually prescribes the timing and amounts of principal and interest payments. Standard schemes are (1) constant principal per period, (2) annuity type with fixed payment amounts, and (3) a negotiated plan based upon the capacity of the borrower to repay. Constant principal amortization requires larger debt service during start-up.

$$P = \frac{B_0}{n}$$

where P = principal payment

B_0 = initial loan balance

n = number of repayment periods

Example: $B_0 = 1,000, N = 10, r = 10\%$

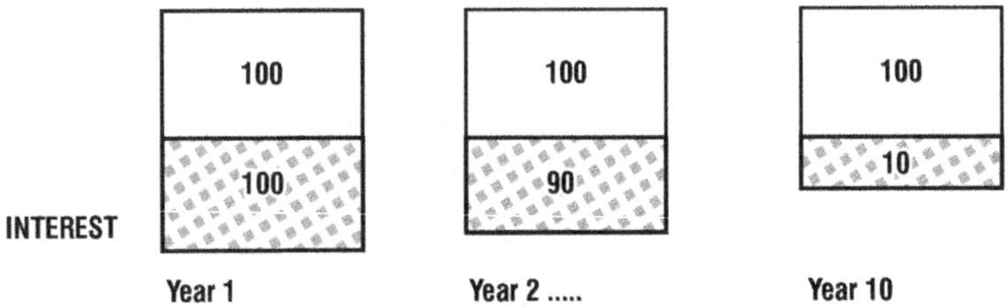

INTEREST

Year 1   Year 2 .....   Year 10

FIGURE 4.2   Constant Principal Amortization

The annuity type, through a gradual buildup of principal repayments, is preferable for a new enterprise because the debt-service burden in early periods when liquidity may be an issue is lower. Regardless of how the debt is repaid, the present value of payments at the specified borrowing rate is the same; only the pattern of principal and interest payments differs.

Constant Principal   To determine the periodic payment, the loan principal is divided by the number of installments. Interest is paid on the outstanding balance at the end of the period preceding the payment (see Figure 4.2). The repayment profile covers only principal repayments. For example, a loan amount of $1,000 with repayment in 10 annual installments requires a repayment of principal of $100 in each of the ensuing 10 years (unless a grace period is granted). By agreement with the lender, unpaid interest may be added to the principal; interest would then accrue on the principal balance plus capitalized interest.

Annuity   The total debt and interest is repaid in equal installments. The formula is developed for a finite number of periods based upon the initial balance, the interest rate, and the number of periods, as shown in Figure 4.3. The proportions of principal and interest within each installment vary. In the early periods the amount of amortization is relatively small, while interest amount (share) is high. The principal payments increase as the outstanding balance diminishes and the interest portion declines.

$$P = B_0 \frac{i(1+i)^n}{(1+i)^n - 1}$$

where P = principal payment
        B_0 = initial balance
        i = interest rate
        n = number of repayment

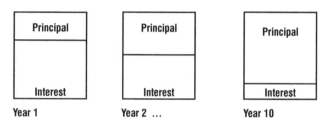

FIGURE 4.3   Annuity Amortization

Negotiated Repayments   The repayment schedule is negotiated with the lender according to the capacity of the borrower to repay. Projected free cash flow accruals over the project life can be used in negotiations. Repayments may or may not include interest; however, interest accrues and, if not paid, is added to the principal balance. This form of amortization of debt is more aligned with the needs of the project.

One type of negotiated loan repayment profile is the *lump-sum* payment or *balloon payment,* which may or may not include capitalized interest accumulated during the term of the loan. In this scheme there is a single repayment of principal at the end of a designated interval. The agreement can call for small periodic principal and interest repayments during early periods with the major repayment at the end of the loan term. The advantage to the project is relief from heavy debt servicing requirements in the early stages when cash constraints are usually problematic. The disadvantage is higher finance charges.

Grace Period   To relieve the pressure on project sponsors in the early going, as cash flow is limited by production inefficiencies and the rate of market penetration, lenders may grant a period of grace, a moratorium on repayments for a defined length of time. The start of principal payments is postponed for a designated number of periods. Usually the grace period defines time from the first disbursement to the first repayment of principal. For example, for a project with a one-year construction phase, if the loan is disbursed initially at the start of the construction phase with a two-year grace period, the first repayment is due at the end of the first production year or the beginning of the second. The length of postponement of principal payments is based upon the ability of the project to generate sufficient cash to service the debt. Without a moratorium on repayments, the project leadership might be required to expend scarce resources and energy seeking short-term financing to cover cash needs. Although principal repayments are postponed, interest on the unpaid balance after commencement of production is usually payable.

Capitalized Interest During construction or start-up phases, when the project expects to generate losses with little or no cash flow, lenders may be willing to capitalize interest due, adding the amounts of interest to the principal. Interest payments are compounded, but this is often the only way to cover these costs. Capitalized interest can usually be amortized for tax purposes after the commencement of production.

Long-Term Loans Long-term loans usually have a term of several years—the amount and duration is constrained by security concerns of the lender, such as capital structure requirements (particularly the ratio of debt to equity), convertibility of preferred shares, or a dividend payout plan. In developing countries long-term loans are available from national development banks, often financed through bilateral aid programs with industrialized countries. They normally cover procurement of fixed assets, preoperational expenditures, and perhaps a base level of working capital.

Bonds and Debentures Guarantees are usually required for the issuance of bonds or debentures (unsecured debt instruments backed only by the credit of the issuer) through private placement or credit markets. These instruments carry fixed or floating rates. The cost of capital includes underwriting or placement costs. The market for bonds and debentures tends to be fairly limited for new projects, but is usually employed to finance expansion projects of well-established, existing enterprises. In some cases large lending institutions issue bonds and debentures for the sole purpose of financing a project. These bonds carry reasonable rates as they are supported by the faith and credit of the lending institution. There is a market for high-risk *junk* bonds, but assistance from an experienced institution should be sought for this type of financing. Rates on these instruments are usually considerably higher than for other types of financing, and therefore they are not applicable to most projects.

Short- and Medium-Term Loans Commercial banks and other local financial institutions provide short- and medium-term loans, with durations from months to a few years, to cover working capital needs (e.g., materials and product inventories), which serve as collateral, or to cover short-lived assets (e.g., vehicles). Trade credits and deferrals (e.g., taxes, wages) are other sources of short-term finance, often without cost if payment schedules are met.

Commercial or merchant banks cover short-term or cyclical requirements for *working* capital (e.g., export credits) in the form of short-term notes, credit lines, overdrafts, or revolving credits. Overdrafts provide essentially credit on demand. Normally the credit line is limited to a balance specified by the lender and depends on the creditworthiness of the borrower. Revolving credits are similar, but are normally used for more cyclical requirements. A typical example would be export credit, in which the bank finances production of the order, and which is repaid upon delivery. Commercial bank overdrafts permit withdrawals by account holders that exceed credit balances so long as the maximum designated deficit is not exceeded; the account holder is required to pay interest on any outstanding debit (deficit) balance.

Other Institutional Financing of Projects Development banks and industrial finance corporations operating at state and national levels in many countries in the process of industrialization provide foreign currency loans financed by international institutions such as World Bank Group affiliates, the International Development Association, and the International Finance Corporation (IFC). They offer low-cost loans for preferred industries and rely primarily on financial planning rather than collateral as security, but tend to be more involved in project monitoring.

The IFC provides loans directly to enterprises in developing countries. Its criteria for acceptability of an applicant are as follows: location in a member developing country; private sector; technical soundness and good profitability prospects; benefit to the local economy; environmentally and socially sound. Smaller projects can be financed indirectly through financial intermediaries who are clients of the IFC. Regional development banks, such as Asian Development Bank, African Development Bank, Inter-American Development Bank, and the European Bank for Reconstruction and Development, are organizations set up by a group of regional governments in cooperation with industrialized countries to provide loans for investment projects in private and public sectors. Some governments have set up bilateral agencies to finance investment projects. Some examples are Germany—Kreditanstalt für Wiederaufbau (KfW); Japan—Japan Bank for International Cooperation (JBIC); Denmark—Industrialisation Fund for Developing Countries (IFU); and France—Agence Française de Développement (AFD). Bilateral loans are sometimes in the form of tied aid, in which the credit is conditional on purchase of equipment or supplies from a particular source—usually in the lending country.

Special funds have been set up by organizations interested in infrastructure development to promote industrialization, either on an international or national level—for example, the OPEC Fund for International Development, the Aga Khan Fund for Economic Development, IGI Investment Bank of Pakistan, and the Kuwait Fund for Arab Economic Development. These types of organizations typically finance projects at the regional or national level. Although their primary focus is on infrastructure, their investments provide the foundation for industrial and commercial development.

Pension funds and *life insurance companies* control large pools of financial resources that are invested to cover benefits to retirees and policyholders. They may invest directly, but generally seek secure opportunities with well-established enterprises. They are generally not interested in fledgling projects and demand guarantees or insurance against risk.

Mutual funds are pools of capital that generally invest in securities, equities, and fixed income. These funds issue shares to raise financial resources that are then invested. Most funds have a particular investment style: aggressive, growth, growth and income, or conservative.

Venture capital funds seek promising high-risk, high-return projects for investment, collecting funds from general partners (investment banks and wealthy individuals), the major contributors, and from limited partners who provide smaller contributions. For an enterprise with little history it is often difficult to raise capital in public equity and debt markets or traditional lending agencies. Venture capitalists often take significant ownership and control of the enterprises that they finance. Funds of this type operate in most parts of the world.

Social security funds in some countries may be available for relatively secure equity positions in investment projects. These funds are generally not available to risky projects, and particularly not to highly leveraged ones. A typical investment would be a revenue-generating infrastructure project.

Innovative Financing   Some debt structures offer attractions of risk alleviation and higher yield to lenders, going beyond conventional financing when the project's access to credit is otherwise restricted or closed. Financial institutions may agree to these mechanisms to spread or shed risk; they are primarily available to fairly large, low-risk infrastructure projects, or to investments in major industrial enterprises. Some are derivatives, with market prices depending on values of underlying assets. Many such instruments are now employed—only some of the more conservative ones are described here. Ironically, in recent years some of these mechanisms have been used to leverage enterprises excessively or to add to the revenue stream, with an attendant *increase* in risk, with unfortunate consequences.[7]

Floating-Rate Notes   Issuance of these notes is possible mainly for well-established enterprises, usually underwritten by brokerages or other large financial institutions. They are debt instruments issued by the borrower (i.e., the project). They carry a current coupon payment that is periodically adjusted to some standard such as the London Interbank Offered Rate (LIBOR). Rate risk (usually tied to inflation) falls to the borrower so that lenders are inclined to accept lower rates.

Shared Equity Loan   The lender provides funds at below-market rates in return for an equity share (profit sharing) in the enterprise (sometimes called an "equity kicker"). An additional inducement for the lender is direct participation in project management and the benefits of profit distribution. Foreign lenders might demand protection against the possibility of nationalization that would preclude repatriation of profits or capital. Development banks provide equity for some projects to facilitate the launching of new ventures or the privatization of state-owned enterprises, or when a sector is opened for private investment. Funds are sometimes channeled through intermediaries when the fund cannot directly provide the necessary expertise. These institutions do not usually take on a controlling interest in the project, and plan to divest their holdings as soon as their development objective is realized.

Flexible Maturity Loan   The absolute level of debt service payment remains constant (similar to an ordinary annuity type loan), with periodic adjustments in proportions of principal and interest covered by each payment as conditions change in credit markets. When rates rise, amortization (principal) is reduced and debt maturity increases accordingly. At very high rates the fixed payment may not cover interest on the outstanding balance, so the excess is added to the principal. These types of loan are primarily offered by development banks.

Graduated Payment Loan   Debt service payments vary according to a formula linked to the revenue stream, which is normally expected to increase over time. In some versions graduations occur on a predetermined schedule. It is possible to have negative amortization during early phases of revenue buildup. If debt service payments do not cover both interest charges and principal, the principal balance is commensurately increased. In this way, the largest proportion of debt service occurs when the project is fully operational with normal revenues.

Price Level Adjusted Loan As a means of protecting against the risk of inflation, the lender seeks to maintain the real value of outstanding principal by linking the repayment schedule to a price index. The principal is adjusted periodically according to the index, with periodic payments adjusted accordingly. The borrower prefers to index on sales revenue or prices of project output (this will tend to maintain the real level of profit), the lender on *consumer price index* (CPI) to maintain the real rate of return. An obvious advantage to the lender in adopting the borrower's point of view is that the borrower is more likely to maintain the servicing schedule.

Transferable Loan Instrument (TLI) Transferable loan instruments (TLIs) standardize the system of transferring lending commitments from primary to secondary markets. They provide an option to international lending institutions to convert loan commitments to one or more transferable instruments, thus extending the range of their portfolio and spreading risk.

The TLI has a single repayment date, usually aligned with one of the scheduled repayment dates. In Figure 4.4 the arrows represent the flow of funds. The solid arrows represent the sale of TLIs to secondary banks and the takedown of the loan by the project. The dashed arrows represent repayment of the loan and maturity of the TLIs (essentially, the lender cancels the TLIs with loan repayments). Creditors have great flexibility in managing their assets; buyers of TLIs (particularly second- and third-tier banks) are attracted by the short-term, small-denomination, tradable paper.

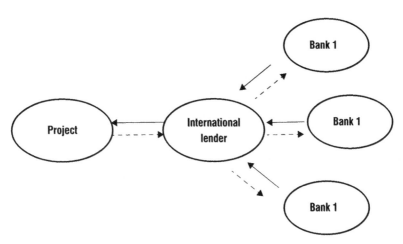

FIGURE 4.4 Transferable Loan Instrument (TLI)

Syndicated Loan Large industrial and infrastructure investment projects may be financed by a syndicate comprising a temporary association of banks that provides credit or that underwrites debt instruments to finance the project. By combining their resources, the syndicate can provide larger amounts of capital than would be possible for any one of them. One or more banks act as lead manager of the syndicate, which generally proposes terms and conditions of the loan or other debt instruments, the basis for negotiations between the parties. Risk management is a central feature of the agreement, intended to reduce risk of default by project sponsors. Risk is spread among syndicate members; the agreement may contain provisions to cover, for example, currency risk, political risk, devaluation, credit insurance, and/or performance guarantees. In some cases a portion of the credit facility is financed with equity to strengthen investor and lender confidence.

Revolving Underwriting Facility The lender, usually a syndicate comprising a number of lending institutions, commits a fixed amount of funding for the duration of the facility. The borrower (project) draws down funds by selling short-term notes (e.g., three or six months). The syndicate markets the notes, retaining the unsold portion. The borrower essentially has access to long-term financing, but at short-term rates (normally lower than the rate on long-term instruments). Possible elements of cost to the project are the note discount, the spread on the note (the difference between the note rate and a slightly higher rate paid by the borrower), plus underwriting fees.

Internally Generated Funds In addition to share capital and loan finance, an important financial source from operations is funds generated and retained by the project as accumulated reserves (retained profits and depreciation) in the form of cash and other liquid assets. These resources can be used for financing working capital increments that may be required as production increases from start-up levels to full production, or for fixed investments (e.g., replacements or expansion).

Funds can be raised through sale of assets—the main issue is whether revenue from the sale, to be invested in the project, yields more than the old operation. Assets may be underperforming or command a high price in abnormal market conditions. The basis for deciding whether to exercise this option is the difference between the without-project and with-project situations—the yield on the assets without the sale compared with their yield when invested in the project and with the previous use of the assets terminated. The difference between these scenarios represents the net effect of the sale.

Subsidies and Grants   Governments and other institutions interested in economic growth of a particular country or region may provide grants or subsidies to finance industrial or agricultural investments or operations. Grants ordinarily cover some portion of fixed-asset investment; subsidies are usually applied to production costs, particularly to widen distribution of basic goods. Acceptance by the project of subsidies and grants may confer a degree of ownership (equity) to grantors; in some cases support is provided without compensation of any kind. As they often involve complicated bureaucratic clearances with attendant delays, some form of short-term credit may be required to cover the interval before the actual receipt of funds, planned well in advance to avoid project overruns resulting from postponement or cancellation of this type of support.

Other Sources of Finance   If sufficient financial resources are not available from conventional sources, sponsors may have to become creative and look toward unconventional ways of funding the project. A number of financing options are available that reduce the amount of capital to be mobilized in the early stages, when there is high demand for capital and limited supply.

Trade Credits   Suppliers of capital goods and operating materials may be willing to supply credit on deferred-payment terms. The repayment schedule can spread out over a number of years, the length depending on the supplier's capacity to finance the sale. In some industrialized countries, exporters are financed by investment promotion agencies such as export/import banks and other types of export credit agencies, which provide incentives such as low-interest loans, insurance against nonpayment by overseas customers, guarantees for buyers' loans to facilitate import of products from supplier enterprises, and political risk insurance in overseas markets.[8] These organizations also may provide other services, such as marketing, trade, and technical assistance.

Advanced Payments   Consumers or marketers of project output, or third parties (e.g., importers, distributors, or downstream producers), might be willing to advance payment in exchange for assignment of rights to purchase a specified part of production, either to fix their purchase price or to secure the output if scarcity is foreseen.

Leasing   Leasing is a way of acquiring control of plant machinery and equipment without the need for large capital investment. This may be a viable option for acquiring at least some of the plant and equipment when financial resources are scarce. Leasing essentially represents a form of off-balance-sheet financing, which may be an option when there are debt/equity ratio constraints or the project is not otherwise in a position to further increase its indebtedness. The assets are contained in the balance sheet of the lessor (grantor of lease) and not in the balance sheet of the project.

If leasing is an option, which alternative is more advantageous—leasing or purchase of capital assets—has to be decided: that is, which of them would result in the lowest present value of costs, also taking into account liquidity impacts and risks. Tax implications for leasing versus purchase are to be included in the respective cash flows. If the same tax regulations are applicable to lessor and lessee, they are both able to purchase equipment under the same terms and conditions, and have similar access to finance, the cumulative leasing cost should not differ significantly from purchase cost. Buying power and/or credit rating of the lessor may lower the leasing cost compared with total cost of purchase if part of the lessor's cost advantages are passed on to the lessee.

The lease usually requires an initial nonrefundable payment, periodic leasing fees (rents), and additional payments under the agreement.[9] The duration of leasing contracts is generally shorter than the economic life of an asset; the lessee may have the option to purchase the equipment from the lessor at market, book, or some other value. The contract may specify sale at lease termination, with the lessee receiving the sale price net of lessor's selling cost.[10]

Funds to finance leases may be obtained from independent leasing companies (service organizations, lease financing companies, lease brokers), banks, insurance companies, pension funds, and industrial development agencies. International financial institutions, such as the International Finance Corporation (IFC), have financed leases for investment projects.

Some benefits for the lessee:

- Leasing requires no initial capital outlay.
- Fees ordinarily do not change with inflation or price escalation.
- The lessor retains title to the asset, along with risk of obsolescence.
- If leasing on favorable terms, there may be an improvement in profitability.

Some disadvantages for the lessee:

- Residual value of the asset at the end of the lease period usually reverts to the lessor, unless otherwise specified in the agreement.
- Maintenance as specified in the contract may be inconsistent with the production program.
- As a senior fixed obligation, the lease may affect the ability of the project to borrow.

- Leased assets cannot serve as collateral for the project.
- The present value of lease payments may be higher than the purchase price.

Factoring and Invoice Discounting   Sale of present or future receivables to a financial institution is a way of raising funds. The agreement usually covers a fixed amount of receivables up to a specified date, with the bank assuming the credit risk. Other services may be provided: credit administration, accounting, client selection (to avoid risky sales). Normally receivables are discounted and adjusted for the risk of bad debt, to make it an attractive proposition from the bank's point of view.

BOT Financing

Large infrastructure or major industrial projects at the national or international level are financed with a range of schemes involving combinations of government financing, syndicated debt, and private equity. Build-operate-transfer (BOT)[11] (and its variants) employs private investment for infrastructure projects that have traditionally been in the public domain.

The BOT concept is applied in revenue-generating projects in the transportation or utilities sectors, such as toll roads, bridges, rail lines, power plants, and water impoundment. The project is undertaken by a private enterprise or a consortium for a specified duration, after which ownership is usually returned to the host government. The period of concession is determined primarily by the length of time necessary to provide an acceptable rate of return to private investors. Variants involve design, leasing, management, construction, and financing options—for example, BOO (build, own, and operate, without obligation to transfer) and BTO (build, transfer, and operate, with installment payments in lieu of the purchase price).

Arrangements are usually fairly complex. Parties to the agreement may include a government agency; a sponsor (usually a consortium typically including a construction group, an operator, a financing institution, and others) that proposes to construct, operate, and finance the project; a construction contractor (who may be a member of the consortium); an operations and maintenance contractor; as well as lenders, equity participants, and perhaps some others (e.g. equipment suppliers, insurers, consultants).

Assets of infrastructure projects generally have limited market value and provide little security for lenders (it is a bit difficult to repossess a dam); financing is secured primarily through agreement on how the revenue stream will be applied to service equity and debt and other supporting provisions or guarantees. Host governments are attracted by the BOT scheme for infrastructure projects for the following reasons, among others:

- Capital is mobilized by the private sector, reducing public spending with attendant improvement in host country credit rating.
- Financing does not appear in the national accounts, which is politically attractive.
- Presumably efficient management, discipline, and initiative associated with the private sector are applied in construction and operation.
- The infrastructure facilities are returned to public control after a period of operation by private investors.

Private investors can be attracted to these types of projects if the environment is propitious. Aspiring governments can offer inducements with legislative action or guarantees regarding repatriation of profits or special exemptions (e.g., taxation, labor regulations, immigration).

These projects are usually set up as special purpose entities so that the debt does not appear on the books of the sponsor (any member of the consortium). Financing often involves limited-recourse senior debt, with limited access to sponsors' assets in case of default; or sponsors may be granted the right to abandon the project after construction, in which case the lender may take control.

Risk management is the most important dimension of financial management. Project finance is more concerned with how risk is allocated rather than shared: Once identified, the sponsor has to either absorb risk elements or spread them among participants (e.g., contractors and lenders) or to third parties (e.g., insurers, guarantors). Each risk element is ideally assigned to the party best able to control or otherwise manage it. Lenders usually demand a higher proportion of equity than for conventional projects since there is no security provided by the sponsor's (i.e., borrower's) balance sheet.

COST OF CAPITAL

Capital has a *rental cost* and a *consumption cost*.[12] Capital consumption is normally accounted as depreciation or depletion allowances, as assets diminish in value from deterioration, obsolescence, or exhaustion. The rental cost is a charge by owners for the use of capital, who would otherwise profit by its employment in alternative uses. An investment project should generate a return (rental cost) that is at least equal to the cost of capital employed, which may differ for investor classes and for the total investment capital. An example of detailed computation of costs of capital is provided in Appendix 3.1.

The project employs capital resources in the form of buildings, machinery and equipment, transportation and communications facilities, and intangible assets. Most are physical entities that must follow the laws of nature—

with use they tend to deteriorate.[13] Eventually the buildings, machinery, and equipment lose their effectiveness to provide the function for which they were originally intended—they have to be retired, dismantled, or discarded. This is the justification for economic depreciation. The employment of capital, therefore, has a built-in cost of *depletion*, consumption, or reduction in value, as the related assets depreciate or degrade technologically.

Capital transfers are usually executed through monetary exchanges. Sometimes an investor provides in-kind capital in the form of goods or services. Normally funds are provided in the form of equity or debt and converted to capital resources by the project.

Providers of equity and debt expect to be compensated for their capital contributions—return of their capital plus the rental price or rate of return. Each investor (or class) has a particular rate of return based upon the investor's *opportunity cost* (the return that could be realized and that would have to be forgone) if the capital is invested in the project—ordinarily the best alternative opportunity or the actual cost of capital to be invested. For each source the project should yield a rate of return at least equal to the provider's expectation.

Cost of Equity

Equity holders expect to be compensated by the portion of profits that they receive and the stake that they retain in the enterprise. As in any other commitment of capital, the equity contributor expects full compensation for the original contribution plus a reasonable rate of return, either based upon what is available in the best alternative investment or according to expectation based on personal preference or other criteria. The opportunity cost differs for each investor or institution because the available *alternative opportunities* and *risk tolerances* differ. Alternatives and risk tolerance are not necessarily independent—each investment alternative has its particular types and levels of risk. Risk-averse investors forgo opportunities for aggressive but risk-laden projects, or in some cases insist on a higher risk premium than a more aggressive investor; however, in general their expectations are more modest than for aggressive investors.

The return, or benefit, for the project's equity capital investor is the accruing portion of dividends, claim to generated surpluses, and residuals (perhaps reflected in the market value of equity shares). The equity participant expects that these accruals cover the initial investment and also provide a return equal to, or in excess of, the actual or opportunity cost of capital. For an existing enterprise financing the project internally, the cost is the weighted value of equity sources, which can be determined in several ways (e.g., dividend/market price, earnings/market price, earnings/market price plus growth rate). Preferred equity generally has a defined cost; the amount of dividend per share per time period is usually specified when shares are issued.

Cost of Debt

A cost is incurred by the project on borrowing or issuing debt instruments to raise capital. The actual cost of debt is not necessarily the interest rate payable at regular intervals to creditors. Cost for the project as borrower can best be determined via discounting methods, using the discount rate that equates the present value of financing outlays—principal repayments, interest (tax adjusted), and fees, less redemption—with net proceeds to the project on issue of the debt. Borrower and lender rates are not necessarily the same if there are third parties involved (commissions and fees) or tax effects.

Debt Parameters

- *Interest* is the rental charge for the funds placed at the disposal of the borrower. The charge is paid usually at a defined time interval, by month, quarter, year, or other time increment. It is usually expressed as a percentage of the outstanding debt balance at the end of the previous period; normally payments are due at the end of the period.
- *Commissions* are one-time payments to the lender or to brokers or agents for services, usually for arranging the loan agreement or for underwriting a debt issue.
- *Fees*, or special charges to the borrower, can be based upon commitment (portion of the loan dedicated to borrower's account but not disbursed) or for placement of the loan; fees can be expressed as *points* (one percent) of the total loan amount.
- *Discounts* are reductions in disbursements of principal. Rather than receive the full amount of principal, the lender discounts the loan by a percentage so that the borrower receives less than the principal. At maturity the full amount of the loan or note must be repaid. U.S. Treasury bills, for example, are discounted to bill purchasers (lenders to government) who receive the full face value of the bill at the maturity date.
- *Redemption premium* is the difference between the amount of the loan or note and the total payment at the time of maturity of the loan or note. The amount can be positive or negative. If positive, it represents an additional cost to the borrower. To enhance the attractiveness of publicly issued debt instruments, particularly callable instruments, the issuer may increase the reward to lenders (purchasers) by offering discounts and /or redemption premiums over the par (issue) value.

■ *Maturity period.* Except for revolving credit lines, most debt instruments have maturity dates, a point in time when the principal must be redeemed or repaid to the lender.

Weighted Average Cost of Capital

An *approximate* formula for calculating the cost of debt in terms of a rate per annum is:

$$C_d = \frac{I(1 - T) + \dfrac{FV - PR}{n}}{\dfrac{FV + PR}{2}}$$

where C_d = cost of debt, percent per annum
         I = interest payable per annum
         T = tax rate (percent)
        PR = net amount from debt issue
        FV = redemption amount
         n = number of periods from issue to redemption

In this simplified model, the total cost for the project consists of interest and principal. $I(1 - T)$ is the tax-adjusted interest payable. Interest is normally deductible as an expense and thus the post-tax interest is relevant. PR is the value of proceeds realized by the project from the debt issue, FV the amount payable on debt redemption, and n the number of periods or years before the issue matures. The redemption price for a bond issue normally equals the issue price. On a callable bond, the redemption may have a premium to compensate bondholders for the shorter (forced) maturity. The term in the denominator is the average debt outstanding.

As the redemption price is reduced, the cost of capital also diminishes. If the issue and redemption price are the same, typical of bonds that are held to maturity (the original term of the issue), $PR = FV$ and the formula shows that the post-tax interest rate $[I(1 - T)]/PR$ is the cost of capital.

The exact actual cost of debt (including fees) would take into account timing of all the flows related to the particular source of debt. It would be the discount rate $i_{discount}$, which sets the following relationship to zero:

$$PR - \sum_{j=1}^{n} \left[(\text{interest}_j + \text{fees}_j)(1 - T) + \text{repayment}_j \right] df_j = 0$$

where

$$df_j = \frac{1}{(1 + i_{\text{discount}})^j}$$

If there is more than one source of capital employed in financing the project, the costs of individual sources can be combined into a composite *weighted cost of capital* (see Chapter 3, Appendix 3.1). The cost of elements in the capital structure of the enterprise might be considerably different from the current market. If, for example, credit market rates are currently considerably different from the cost of instruments in the capital structure of the enterprise, it might be prudent to use current marginal cost in lieu of historical cost.

For an ongoing enterprise contemplating a new investment, the balance sheet provides the breakdown of the existing permanent capital structure, forms of debt, and the components of *shareholders' equity* or *net worth*. The cost of equity is derived from the breakdown of shareholders' equity in the balance sheet, which may consist of capital stock, preferred shares, retained earnings, and reserves.[14] Either the actual cost for each individual source (say, for preferred shares) or the opportunity cost can be determined. A typical equity structure is shown in Figure 4.5 (also see Figure 4.1). For a project financed with new equity, the opportunity cost for investors is based upon their alternative investment opportunities. The cost of each source of debt (e.g., accounts payable, overdraft, loans, notes, bonds, debentures) has to be ascertained and inserted into the calculation.

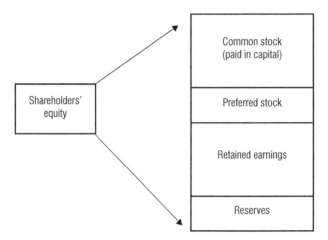

FIGURE 4.5 Breakdown of Shareholders' Equity

Another factor to be considered is the assumption on weights, typically based on book value (balance sheet amounts), but market value of the capital or the financing plan weights may also be considered. For example, par (or book) value of common shares is often much different from market value. In fact, in securities markets, capitalization of an enterprise is usually calculated on the basis of market value of common shares outstanding (see the subsection "Valuation Based upon Market Capitalization" in Chapter 3).

For a single source of debt and equity, or if the composite cost of each multiple source is known, calculation of weighted average cost of capital can be determined in the following manner:

$$WACC = Cost_{debt}(1 - T)w_{debt} + Cost_{equity}w_{equity}$$

$$w_{debt} + w_{equity} = 1$$

where $WACC$ = weighted average cost of capital (percent)
w_{debt} = weight of debt (debt/investment)
w_{equity} = weight of equity (equity/investment)

The cost of debt is adjusted by the factor $(1 - T)$ (if not previously included in the calculation) because interest on debt is usually a tax-deductible expense.[15]

Cost of Capital—CYP   In the Cambria Yarns Project the weighted average cost of capital is based upon the relative proportions and costs of debt and equity, as shown in Table 4.2.

Debt is adjusted by the tax rate of 30 percent. The applicable discount rates are 8.6 percent for the total investment and 12 percent for the equity portion of capital.

TABLE 4.2   Weighted Average Cost of Capital—CYP, Amounts in US$(000)

Source	Amount	Percent	Cost (%)	Tax Adjusted Cost (%)[1]	Weighted Cost
Debt	25,505.3	67.1	10	7	4.7%
Equity	12,497.2	32.9	12	12	3.9%
Total	38,002.5	100			8.6%

[1]Tax rate on net profit is 30 percent.

Significance of Cost of Capital

The cost of capital often serves as a benchmark (discount rate) for the hurdle or challenge rate of return for financial appraisal of the project, which is considered acceptable for investment only if it can generate a return at least equal to the weighted cost of capital. (See Chapter 3.)

The cost for each source of available capital can provide guidance on the most favorable capital structure for the project, the proportions and types of equity and debt to be included in the total investment package. Considering the relative cost of sources can help to refine capital structure decisions. Deciding between leveraging—employing high proportions of favorably priced debt to finance investments, considering its tax advantages—or reducing risk with higher proportions of equity capital, is an issue for investors, lenders, guarantors, and other stakeholders.

NOTES

1. Lenders and their agents may also demand fees—origination, commitment, and others.
2. *Minimum economic size* refers to the level of production below which the project is noncompetitive either in local or export markets as a result of diminishing economies of scale.
3. A rule of thumb applied by some consultants is that total equity capital should be able to cover possible losses over a five-year period (assuming the worst-case scenario).
4. For standard production of 4,480 metric tons (MT) of yarn, the maximum and minimum investment in raw cotton inventories is 5,198.2 MT and 945.2 MT, respectively. The difference between maximum and average is one-half the difference between maximum and minimum. Multiplying this value by the cost per ton (US$668) and by the percent of normal capacity (101.1 percent in year 4), the maximum cyclical requirement for additional short-term finance could be about US$1.44 million.
5. Unpaid dividends accumulate as a liability to the enterprise and must be paid before dividends are paid on common shares. Preferred shares may be redeemable or nonredeemable, with the redemption period varying between 5 and 15 years. They can be set up for conversion to common shares, in which case the dilution effect of conversion would be of interest to the project's common shareholders.
6. The actual percentage rate (APR) is equivalent to the internal rate of return on debt, and includes adjustments for discounts, fees, commissions, and other charges.
7. For a more thorough discussion see Charles Woelfel and Charles J. Woelfel, eds., *Encyclopedia of Banking and Finance,* 10th ed. (Columbus, OH: McGraw-Hill, 1994).

8. Some examples: The Export Credits Guarantee Department (ECGD) of the United Kingdom promotes exports by providing guarantees, insurance, and reinsurance against loss through default in payment by importers. The U.S. Commodity Credit Corporation (CCC) guarantees a portion (up to 65 percent) of export sales for up to 180 days of credit extended to importers, with the proviso that dollar-denominated notes signed by importers secure the credit. Similar guarantees and insurance are available from Export-Import banks and other export promotion agencies in most industrialized countries.

9. The leasing contract specifies the breakdown of responsibility for maintenance, repair, and insurance.

10. If the market value is greater than the book value, usually the margin is split between the lessor and the lessee, at a rate determined in the contract.

11. *Guidelines for Infrastructure Development through Build-Operate-Transfer (BOT) Projects* (Vienna: UNIDO, 1996) is a thorough treatise on the nature and organization of BOT and similar infrastructure projects. These projects are generally public-private partnerships (PPP). A good summary of project structure in Australia is "Build Own Operate Transfer (BOOT) Projects" at www.mcmullan.net/eclj/BOT.html.

12. Conventionally the *cost of capital* is understood to be the rental cost.

13. Other forms of capital resources, such as intellectual and human, also tend to deteriorate over time.

14. The *shareholders' equity* section of the balance sheet provides quantities of common and preferred shares, but in determining cost of capital, values are related to current market conditions, as explained in Appendix 3.1. Shareholders' equity items such as retained earnings and reserves, which do not relate to markets, can be priced as common equity shares.

15. The cost of debt in this context should include only the rental or interest charge, and not the return of principal.

REFERENCES

McMullan, John, ed. Build own operate transfer (BOOT) projects. *Electronic Construction Law Journal.* http://www.mcmullan.net/eclj/BOT.html.

Merrett, A. J., and A. Sykes. 1974. *The finance and analysis of capital projects.* 2nd ed. London: Longman.

Seitz, N., and M. Ellison. 1999. *Capital budgeting and long-term financing decisions.* 3rd ed. San Diego: Harcourt Brace Jovanovich.

Skully, M. T. *ASEAN financial co-operation: Developments in banking, finance and insurance.* London: Macmillan, 1985.

United Nations Industrial Development Organization. *Guidelines for infrastructure development through build-operate-transfer (BOT) projects.* Vienna: UNIDO, 1996.

Woelfel, Charles, and Charles J. Woelfel, eds. *Encyclopedia of banking and finance,* 10th ed. Columbus, OH: McGraw-Hill, 1994.

CHAPTER 5

The Economic Perspective

S takeholders most directly involved in the project—investors and lenders—might feel confident about an investment decision based on market-related, risk-adjusted indicators derived from financial analysis as described in Chapters 3 and 4. However, there is an inevitable dependency of these indicators on the macro environment—the economic, social, and political milieu. Prices of inputs and outputs, for example, could be tied to the economic cycle; a high rate of economic growth might change the demand/supply relationship for some goods and services with prices commensurately affected. The designer is well advised to take into account external factors that could significantly affect project performance. In fact, there is increasing likelihood of severe resource constraints, particularly fossil fuels, but also other commodities, within the next few decades.

The project's host economy is composed of producers applying resources (e.g., land, labor, capital) to generate and distribute goods and services to consumers. Management of the economy—that is, attempts to allocate resources according to national goals—is generally the province of government institutions, such as the central bank, the treasury, or the council of economic advisers. In the context of an investment project, economic analysis[1] is an attempt to determine how employment of resources consumed and benefits generated by the project respond to private and public aspirations in the host community or the national economy as a whole.

Determining the project's impact on the macro environment is useful for reasons beyond those related to financial impacts of the economic cycle. Knowledge of the state and trends in the host economy is a window to potential developments that can affect project viability. The project is more likely to be supported if its design is compatible with regional and national goals and aspirations.

For the enterprise created by the investment project, economic analysis is, in reality, too restrictive a description of what is demanded. In a world straining at the edges of its finite physical capacities, the viewpoint has to be expanded to the social and ecological domains, and it is in this sense that the term is used hereinafter. So the *economy*, in its broader sense, is composed of producing and consuming units and the wider social and ecological milieu in which they function. To ensure the success of the enterprise, it is advantageous for investors to look beyond financial considerations as a means of anticipating and adjusting to the complex of economic, social, and ecological forces in the operating environment. Although economic concerns can be overridden by other decision criteria, knowledge of economic consequences is a useful, if not necessary, feature of any framework for investment decision making.

The degree of economic analysis should be commensurate with the project's impacts. As Albert Einstein said, "Not everything that counts can be counted, and not everything that can be counted counts." This applies as well to the analysis of projects as it does to the domain of science. E. F. Schumacher, in his 1973 treatise on industrial development, *Small is Beautiful, Economics as if People Mattered*, dismissed cost/benefit analysis as an attempt to "undertake to measure the immeasurable." What is advocated here for purposes of appraisal is to take into account project impacts within the broader range of interactions with the host community, the 'wider domain.' Cost/benefit analysis is a quantitative method of assigning values to resources consumed and generated by the project to measure its contribution to one or more socio-economic objectives. These values have to be consistent with the objectives for which the optimal investment program is sought, for example, in terms of value-added if maximization of national income is the criterion. However, any other unit of measurement consistent with the objectives can be employed, for example an index of self-reliance if that is the primary concern of the government. It is also to be recognized that some resources are difficult or impossible to convert to a unit of quantitative measurement. In assessing the project, these resources have to be treated differently. All environmental issues, as one example, are not subject to monetary valuation. While pollution of a favorite body of water used for recreational purposes by the community may have quantifiable economic consequences, the loss of such a resource for the enjoyment of the public is essentially unquantifiable. In other words, assessment of the project does not end with the quantification of impacts, which may be only a component of the overall assessment of the state in affected communities with the project implemented as compared with conditions in its absence. Environmental Impact Assessment (EIA), when properly performed to cover all relevant aspects of the wider domain, complements ECBA and can usually be considered a necessary adjunct.

For small enterprises, concern may be limited to the host community, possibly only in qualitative terms. The full scope of analysis described primarily in Chapter 6 is applicable only to projects (industry or infrastructure) that have a regional or national impact. For any project between these extremes, the approach should be adjusted so that the costs of investigation do not significantly consume the benefits to be derived from the project. This is not only good policy, but it also becomes good business practice.

Economic analysis is applicable to the private and public sector, both to revenue and nonrevenue projects. All require allocation of resources for the generation of benefits. Knowledge of the impact of resource allocations has relevance regardless of sector. For private-sector projects, analysis checks compatibility of private objectives with government goals. In the public sector, where benefits are often difficult to measure, it helps in the selection of projects for implementation within budget constraints.

A project in the private or public sector, although its production of goods and services apparently serves the needs of investors and consumers, might have positive and, more often, negative impacts upon both its immediate and more distant surroundings. Deterioration of the living conditions of host area populations is a cost that is usually not internalized (i.e., included in project costs). If included, these costs would reduce the project's profitability and perhaps convince the investor to abandon the project idea. For both revenue and nonrevenue projects, it is in the best interests of investors and other project stakeholders to take into account costs and benefits that are not directly related to project inputs and outputs (negative and/or positive externalities).[2]

This chapter and the next contains details of economic cost/benefit analysis for the Cambria Yarns Project (CYP), with quantitative information presented in a series of tables.

PRIVATE SECTOR

For private investors, economic analysis is intended to provide an understanding of consequences beyond the purely commercial domain, in which financial benefits are the fundamental measure of acceptability. Such an investigation can reveal tensions or distortions in the environment that may eventually realign, with consequences for the enterprise. It is also a means of anticipating and adjusting to forces, external and internal, with which the project inevitably interacts. Scarcity is an important factor in valuing resources, and such an evaluation may well indicate future market adjustments to prices—for example, to an over- or undervalued local currency that affects import and export transactions.

There are other good reasons for including assessment of external factors, even if investors have little instinctive interest in this type of evaluation. Corporate objectives and investment policies may not be in harmony with socioeconomic policies of the host country, region, or area. This can lead to conflicts and adverse consequences for the project. The state and trends in the economy, involving policies on income distribution, environmental protection, or international trade, may have significant impacts upon financial feasibility. Economic benefits generated by the project may leverage appeals for favorable public policies and actions, such as protection from imports at dumping prices, granting permission or licenses for the acquisition of foreign technology, approval of foreign equity participation, and government guarantees.[3]

PUBLIC SECTOR

In the public sector, the purpose is to examine effects on the wider domain of projects intended to provide a specific good or (more often) service to a target population, the direct recipients of benefits. Resource flows directly engendered by the project, and the indirect or external effects that arise from existence of the enterprise created, are valued differently in this context, as the view is extended to the local, regional, national, or international socioeconomic environment.[4]

Investment projects are undertaken to attain the goals of their promoters. In public-sector revenue projects, the usual intent is to cover the costs of providing a public service through sales revenues or user fees. Nonrevenue projects, mostly financed and implemented by the public sector, might have multiple objectives, depending on the service to be provided (roads, education, health services, etc.), but also on specific local conditions and problems addressed.

While it is relatively easy to apply objective measures that allow comparisons between alternative revenue projects, such comparisons are much more difficult for projects in nonrevenue sectors. Public-sector projects are intended to serve the need for improved public services. Particularly in less-developed countries, demands for service improvements exceed the resources available for their implementation. The problem is to allocate scarce resources to obtain maximum benefits from their application. What seemed an easy choice of goals for revenue projects (i.e., covering the cost of public services) now becomes quite complicated. The question for the decision maker is this: Is it better to build a stretch of the road, or a local school, or perhaps improve water supply to a group of villages? All the projects are needed, but the funds available might suffice to implement only one of them.

In real life, the choice for the public-sector decision is much more complicated. There are more projects, and several regions in the country with different ethnic, professional (trade unions), and business pressure groups. Donors and financial institutions each have their own priorities, not necessarily coinciding with the priorities of decision makers at the government or investor level.

The needs are subjective. The public official charged with the responsibility for resource allocation might feel that the city needs a new indoor swimming pool. However, the mayor would like the city to finance a road that bypasses the city center to reduce traffic and related number of accidents. The city counselors would gladly vote for building a new school (three of them are teachers). Under such conditions an objective method is needed to allow comparison between projects that would make the best use of the limited budget.

GENERAL RATIONALE FOR ECONOMIC EVALUATION—WHO NEEDS IT?

Economies vary in the degree of economic planning, from more centralized to widely decentralized decision making. In centrally planned economies, or where there is some degree of government planning, industrial investment decisions are likely to require approval of national authorities with multiple objectives and corresponding criteria for investment resources. For economic planners, economic assessment of investment decisions is a practical means of directing the economy at the project level. Where decisions are decentralized, criteria are left largely either to investors or local authorities. In almost any circumstance, economic net benefit—the excess of benefits over costs—is a rational criterion for investment decision making at the project level.

Although commercially oriented stakeholders are most directly concerned with markets, technical aspects, and financial returns that determine project viability, their interests are best served by taking into account the wider domain that encompasses both commercial and socioeconomic environments, particularly where industrial planning is weak or nonexistent.

As resource constraints are encountered in an increasingly crowded world, the importance of considering how a project will fare in the broader context of the economy takes on greater significance. The price of a scarce resource may not presently reflect its true economic value, perhaps a temporary phenomenon resulting from lack of sufficient information about availability and consequences of its use or generation. Economic analysis is relevant for stakeholders if only to have a preview of the situation that will eventually prevail when information concerning resources that the project produces or on which it depends becomes more widely available.

Need for economic analysis of investment projects arises from market imperfections that vary only in degree among countries and economic transnational unions. Although the market is widely considered to ensure the best allocation, market prices are not as free as the ideal free market would require. Under the best of circumstances the market mechanism alone cannot ensure optimal allocation of resources from the regional, national, or global point of view. Maximization of financial surplus at the enterprise level does not fully reflect all the government development objectives. Competition may be inadequate, allowing for monopolistic control of markets. Government intervention (e.g., taxes, subsidies, customs duties, interest rates, price controls, import quotas) often distorts local market prices of internationally traded goods and services, so that prices, in which a project's costs and revenues are calculated, do not reflect true economic value.

Economic analysis generally responds to either or both of two objectives of each government: growth and equity. Achieving economic efficiency is consistent with a resource allocation that tends to maximize growth of the economy. The equity objective aims to alter income inequities among identified population groups and to attain a reasonable distribution of growth benefits, which is not necessarily consistent with the growth objective. A government decision maker can select for project parameters that reflect a position with respect to these objectives, which the project sponsors are well advised to take into account if approval by authorities is necessary.

In a developing country, capital is generally in short supply. As current savings flow into investment, the government may assign a relatively higher value to future consumption than investors do, depending upon its temporal outlook. The government may choose a discount rate for project ranking that is lower than the market rate of interest, indicating a higher value assigned to future benefits than the value indicated by the choices of private enterprise,[5] or place greater weight on economic development in depressed regions of the country. A national objective may be to restructure the labor market by promoting projects that would develop valuable technical skills for workers or address a problem of unemployment or underemployment in a region.

The most fundamental reason for stakeholders to be interested in economic analysis is that the project must *live* in the environment in which it is to be created—it must be able to prosper and grow. A project's compatibility with its wider domain is conducive to project success. This has relevance for all investment projects, both large and small.

MACROECONOMIC VIEW—IMPACT ON THE NATIONAL ECONOMY

An investment project becomes part of the economy at the local, regional, national, or international level. For larger projects, economic analysis is intended to discover to what degree the economy is affected, most commonly at the national level.

Economic cost/benefit analysis (alternatively, *national cost/benefit analysis*) examines the relationship between the macroeconomic view and the project (microeconomic view). The macroeconomic environment is a major component of the project's environment, its *wider domain*, as designated herein and described at length in Chapter 1.

Projects are appraised and implemented by their promoters (investors) at the micro scale. However, the larger the project, the greater its impact on its immediate and wider environment. Some large-scale projects create impacts in the host region and within other regions in the country, as well as across borders. Some examples include cases of air or water pollution carried over borders by winds or rivers. To fully understand the merits and demerits of projects to be implemented, it is necessary to study such impacts, even though investors are not normally inclined to be interested in them. Public licensing authorities are usually obliged to consider wider impacts beyond investors' concerns, justified by their responsibility to promote the public welfare by improving the economy and protecting it from harmful pollutants.

Although each project, large or small, has an impact upon and, to some extent, modifies its wider domain, it is impractical for public authorities to study all of these impacts prior to licensing. Larger-size projects[6] justify such studies and possible imposition of design features and implementation modalities. In such case, the microeconomic perspective of investors is measured against the macroeconomic point of view of the government. While an investor seeks the best use of his capital (return or net revenues), the government's goal is to maximize the national product, increasing consumption and investment to foster long-term growth and development of the country. The government is primarily concerned with effects within the country (while usually respecting relevant international cooperation commitments) and in incomes that accrue to nationals. The synthetic indicator used to measure growth of the national economy is related to gross domestic product (GDP) or gross national product (GNP), both reported in statistics of the national accounts. However, these indicators almost universally relate to market valuations of goods and services, and miss or obscure many elements of the economic system.

Methods of estimating the project impacts on the wider domain, and more precisely on the national economy (in the broader economic, social and ecological sense), normally reflect the project's contribution to GDP/GNP, but need adjustment for the aforementioned reasons. National accounts are presented schematically in Figure 5.1 and elaborated in more detail in Figure 5.2.

The synthetic macroeconomic goal expressed by the authorities' policies typically is long-term growth of the national product, which ostensibly serves to satisfy various needs of the population. The immediate target sought in each project is its contribution to GDP or its equivalent, *value-added*. The two approaches to economic analysis of the project presented in Chapter 6

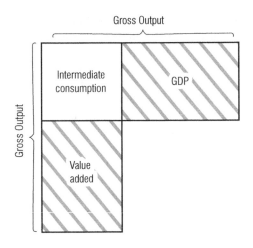

Gross output = Intermediate consumption + GDP
Gross output = Intermediate consumption + Value added

FIGURE 5.1   Gross Domestic Product

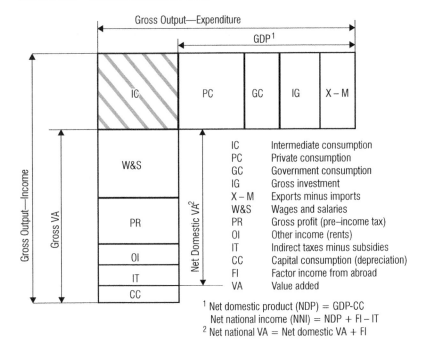

IC	Intermediate consumption
PC	Private consumption
GC	Government consumption
IG	Gross investment
X – M	Exports minus imports
W&S	Wages and salaries
PR	Gross profit (pre–income tax)
OI	Other income (rents)
IT	Indirect taxes minus subsidies
CC	Capital consumption (depreciation)
FI	Factor income from abroad
VA	Value added

[1] Net domestic product (NDP) = GDP-CC
Net national income (NNI) = NDP + FI – IT
[2] Net national VA = Net domestic VA + FI

FIGURE 5.2   Relation of National Accounts to Project Analysis

refer to methodologies that attempt to measure the project's contribution to national objectives expressed in terms of GDP or value added. However, they are further refined by considering scarcity of resources and external effects.

The composition of each of these macroeconomic indicators (see Figure 5.2) provides some information about the focus of analysis in each case, both of them concerned with distribution of income and consumption. In the value-added approach the primary distribution of income derives directly from the project design. In the approach described there is no attempt to deal with resource scarcities, although it is possible to include effects of external, but linked economic activity.

The second group of methodologies concentrates on estimation of appropriate prices[7] (see the sections "Price Distortions" and "Economic Pricing Principles" in this chapter) for the project's costs and benefits that do account for scarcity. Differences between prices of the project's inputs and outputs in the financial analysis (actually paid or received in the market) and *economic prices* calculated according to recommended methods constitute additional benefits (or costs) attributable to different identified groups of beneficiaries. In other words, distortions in market prices attributable to scarcity or market intervention are treated as a zero sum game, with a gainer and loser.

Of the approaches to determining shadow prices, those most widely applied have been designed by international organizations and donor organizations in industrialized countries. Consequently, they have been applied universally to projects financed by the donor (financing) institutions, regardless of the country in which the project was implemented, allowing donors to compare profitability of projects implemented by those organizations. Similarly, some governments concerned with the use of scarce resources adapted the methodology to local conditions, which differ in details and procedures for reaching conclusions. However, they share common elements—ingredients out of which the methodology is prepared. As in the culinary arts, the same ingredients might serve to create different meals—in this case, different methodologies.

The discussion on shadow pricing and value-added method in this and the next chapter is intended to describe common elements necessary to estimate economic profitability without entering into procedures and intricacies of the many alternative approaches. Although numerical results of calculations for the two methods would differ,[8] ranking projects (in order to select the "best " ones to be implemented) by either method should provide the same results, which is one of the primary objectives of analysis from the government's point of view.

How can these more formal methods be applied in a practical way? And for what purpose? For cost-benefit analysis, national or regional parameters are required. These have to be standardized to have any meaning, particularly as some are subjective. Only a central authority, or major development institution, such as a development bank, could be the repository of this kind of information that would be applied universally to all projects. An individual project sponsor could independently develop these parameters, and then use them to influence industrial lenders and regulators, but the results would be necessarily suspect. Only when the parameters, and even the specific methodology, are spelled out in detail by some central authority will such results have respectability.

On the other hand, the value-added approach described, even though it is less attuned to the nuances of economic valuation involving scarcity and ecological impacts, does have the merit of being an objective measure, depending as it does on market values of the resources consumed and generated. In either case, since this level of analysis relates primarily to projects of larger scale, it should be supplemented with Environmental Impact Analysis (EIA) and an Environmental Impact Statement (EIS).

PRICE DISTORTIONS

The starting point of the shadow pricing approach is the assumption that the market mechanism, and more precisely free competition, directs the economy toward the optimal allocation of resources. However, as previously discussed, markets are not as free as the term *free market* is defined in classical economics. Consequently, economic values of resources consumed and generated by the project are usually not reflected in their market prices. Market distortions cause economic value and market price to diverge. In a perfect market with free information flow, ubiquitous potential suppliers, and lack of constraints, there would be no deviation between market and economic price. In the real world nothing is perfect, including markets, resulting in price distortions that derive from a variety of causes, as seen in the next subsections.

Market Imperfections

In a perfect capital market, the expected rate of return by capital subscribers should be equal for projects with equal risk. However, rates vary widely for credit, which constitutes a substantial portion of total capital invested, largely attributable to credit market distortions. In countries where capital markets are usually not well developed, price distortions in capital markets are exacerbated by imperfections in other markets.

Smaller national markets are often dominated by one or a few suppliers (monopoly or oligopoly) with the ability to set prices in the absence of competition. A consumer monopoly (*monopsony*), domination and control by one or more buyers, exists in some markets, such as industrial inputs.

Wide price fluctuations result from producers competing for a limited export market with low elasticity of demand (i.e., demand does not change significantly with regard to change in price).

In a free labor market, wages paid should be equal to marginal product. For many reasons, actual earnings of labor (mainly unskilled) do not reflect equilibrium of supply and demand for labor. Unskilled workers in growing sectors earn more than casual labor in conventional sectors such as agriculture. Underemployment creates situations where individuals consume more than their marginal product. If the government tries to adjust by increasing compensation to meet the consumption requirement, marginal production tends to remain constant and a gap is created between market prices and social costs.

Perfect markets require free flow of information, but in many environments knowledge of availability and consequences of resource use is incomplete or misleading. Most consumers, in such cases, are not aware of alternative uses of a resource, of substitutes, or of the implications of product choices for individual or collective welfare.

Market Interventions

Governments, in some cases, impose constraints on trade (e.g., quotas and import duties) to protect a particular industry. In the absence of foreign competition, industries are able to raise prices beyond international levels without fear of having them undercut by alternative suppliers. Quotas on imports create a supply gap that further distorts the price of the goods on local markets. Tariffs and duties represent transfers from consumer to taxing authorities that may not reflect product value.

From the commercial perspective, taxes are costs and subsidies receipts. Economically, taxes and subsidies are transfer payments (moving costs and benefits from one social segment to another); they are factors of distribution of benefits. Taxes and subsidies alter the normal resource allocation pattern and consequently affect the structure of prices. Fiscal and monetary policy moves, such as creating large budget deficits or too rapid expansion of the money supply, may result in too much money (demand) chasing too few goods (supply), creating inflation as a result. A gap in supply in sectors such as agriculture, which is relatively inelastic, results in rapid price increases (inflation). Price controls inevitably result in distortions between market price and economic value. The usual result is restricted supply, as marginally profitable producers withdraw from the market, exacerbating the inflation problem. The government may favor some domestic consumers and producers for local markets by maintaining an overvalued national currency, which may be accompanied by selective import controls and exports subsidies. Prices are then distorted in regard to world markets. Imports become relatively cheap and exports not profitable (smaller export revenues don't cover domestic manufacturing costs). Demand for foreign exchange exceeds supply, often resulting in the emergence of a parallel market in the currency, in which the exchange rate reflects a premium over what would otherwise be the free exchange rate. The result is distortion in prices at the border (imports and exports), and usually in domestic prices also.

Resource Constraints

Resources not freely available to the market cause price distortions. If the use of a scarce resource involves its diversion from another productive use, the productivity loss in its alternative application may not be fully taken into account by the market. The way that resources are distributed can distort prices, with regional differences arising from transportation or other bottlenecks (see the subsection "Resource Constraints" in Chapter 1).

Externalities

Externalities are project impacts that do not affect financial inflows and outflows, and represent project impacts other than costs and benefits of resources valued by the market and in the economy. The cost-benefit approach to analysis takes into account beneficial external effects not considered in commercial analysis—for example, creation of infrastructure service facilities by public and private entities that are linked to the existence of the project (but not part of it) such as communications, energy, railways, or upgrading worker skills that confer future public benefit.

As an example of externalities in the petroleum industry, consumers in the United States and many other countries pay for gasoline in accordance with the commercial needs of producers. However, often these producing companies enjoy many subsidies at government (and ultimately consumer) expense that are not reflected in the price. In addition, petroleum deposits exist in politically unstable countries that demand military alertness, if not intervention, for securing supplies, which is also not reflected in the price at the pump. The cost for these externalities is collected through taxation (often postponed with heavy government borrowing). The alternative would be to pay more for gasoline, which would presumably decrease both demand and the necessity for securing supplies.

Some externalities may be negative. Product life-cycle benefits and costs are rarely, if ever, taken into account by the market, such as the environmental impact and cost (normally borne by the government and paid with taxation) of product disposal, environmental degradation or displacement of

© The Rocky Mountain News / Dist. by United Feature Syndicate, Inc.

populations. Others are costs or benefits of social and cultural perturbations or health impacts possibly arising from project operations.

Economic analysis takes into account these impacts on elements of the wider domain that are linked economically or technologically and that have *quantifiable social benefits or costs* (in terms of the accounting unit). *Non-market impacts* that are not actually bought and sold but that can sometimes be converted to monetary equivalents are considered, such as the effect on property values resulting from environmental degradation. Impacts that cannot be expressed in monetary terms are evaluated qualitatively, often as part of an EIA.

As information concerning the consequences of consumption and generation of resources becomes more widely available, markets increasingly reflect impacts that may not currently affect the bottom line (profit). A thorough analysis of the project anticipates these factors and constructively addresses them in the interests of direct stakeholders and the broader community. To provide a framework for identifying effects to be considered, it is useful to classify the types of impacts that might be of concern.

Economic Impacts

- *Contribution to economic development.* The project's quantifiable contribution to economic development of the region may engender a positive image that can be helpful in promotion.

- *Upstream and downstream linkages.* Upstream linkages, such as increased production of an input directly attributable to the project, can either be included as part of net benefits or internalized for purposes of economic analysis. Linkages permitting more or better downstream production can be taken into account; the net effect could be negative if linked activities are displaced or otherwise eliminated.
- *Infrastructure effects.* The project may require investment in new infrastructure with cost borne by the government; if the improvement serves only the needs of the project it can be considered economic cost, with some or all of it offset if there are benefits for other economic activities. Infrastructure developed and paid by the project provides economic benefits.
- *Life-cycle impacts.* A product has a life cycle—it is manufactured, used, then either recycled or discarded. Some consequences of manufacturing, use, and disposition may be external to the project: manufacture—costs of public safety; use—cost of compliance with public regulation; disposal—use of publicly supported facilities. Any or all of these, if significant, are included in economic analysis.

Social Impacts

- *Displacements.* The project may displace or require relocation of populations, with quantifiable benefits and costs; social impacts exist regardless of whether affected populations are compensated.
- *Culture.* Products, production methods, and distribution may perturb local cultural patterns for the betterment or degradation of existing cultural norms, with attendant quantifiable benefits or costs. For example, the product introduction may induce a publicly supported information program, which has a more general public benefit, explaining and circumscribing limitations of use.

Technological Impacts

- *Environment and habitats.* Licensing authorities considering a project for approval may require an environmental impact study covering consequences for physical, social, and economic environments, which is complementary to economic analysis. Some impacts in each area may be subject to quantification or otherwise compatible with the economic accounting unit (AU). Impacts may be covered in the environmental impact assessment (EIA), if warranted, and/or the economic analysis (e.g., at accounting prices) depending on the degree of quantification possible. All significant impacts covered in the EIA can be cross-referenced if included quantifiably in economic analysis. How impacts can be

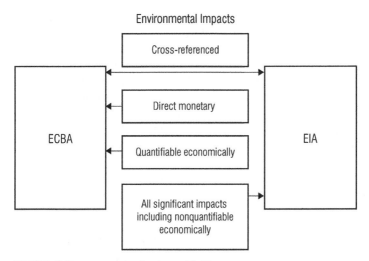

FIGURE 5.3 Economically Quantifiable Impacts

integrated into the analysis as a function of economic quantification is illustrated in Figure 5.3.

- *Status of technology.* Transfer of technology that it is sustainable in the domestic environment is a benefit that should be considered, particularly if it can be replicated and applied in other economic activities. Benefits of training project personnel in generally applicable skills and not of a proprietary nature—skills that can be replicated elsewhere in the economy with the project as a nucleus—may be quantifiable in terms of the economic AU.

Merit Goods

The concept of a merit good is based on the idea of values that are held in common by society—values that are different from those expressed in individual demands. For example, an education program might be considered to have positive social merit whereas tobacco and alcohol are viewed as having negative social merit. Private firms tend to disregard the effects of merit or demerit goods and concentrate on actual profits, but governments (presumably as representatives of the people) consider them as additional social benefits or costs.

Political Constraints

Governments often attempt to achieve distribution of wealth at the micro or project level that they would be reluctant to do at the macro level.[9,10]

Economic inertia impedes intentions of governments to remove price distortions through economic policy changes. Powerful forces resist change in the status quo. Inertia developed over long periods of drift in the political economy is like a huge ship in the ocean, difficult to turn in the short distance. Structural Adjustment Programs promoted by the World Bank and International Monetary Fund and implemented in a number of developing countries in the 1990s were an attempt to remove the distortions. Although the price mechanisms work better, social problems still remain. Resistance to change in the pattern of inequitable distribution of incomes arises from opposition of the potentially injured side of the political spectrum. Redistribution through corrections in pricing mechanisms is generally favored on one side and opposed on the other. Incumbent governments are reluctant to overtly antagonize constituents and can possibly achieve their goals through selection of projects, goals that would otherwise be politically unpalatable. Projects allow for distribution of incremental benefits without overtly affecting the macro relationships, which governments are often reluctant to modify.

There is a natural reluctance of project sponsors (and their clients) to include externalities in the pricing system. Even when there is consciousness of beneficial or harmful external impacts, individual enterprises or consumers resist either pricing in or paying for them. They either choose to ignore them or prefer to let the society at large deal with such matters, as if it were someone else's problem.

APPLICABILITY AND SCOPE

Economic appraisal, as any study, has its cost. Is it worth the effort? The *Guide to Project Appraisal* published by the UN Industrial Development Organization says, "Those who evaluate projects by [economic] analysis should evaluate their own work by the same criteria. It is easy to become so involved in the theoretical niceties of economic project appraisal that it is carried to the point where it produces only superfluous information instead of better investment decisions."[11]

An investment project becomes part of the larger economy, precipitating changes by generating and consuming resources. A producer interacts with suppliers, clients, and financial institutions, and with society. A manufacturing company becomes part of the community, sustained by its presence and contributing to its welfare. In the larger view, it is of considerable interest to understand these interactions, but to what extent is it practical and useful?

The scope of economic analysis depends, to some extent, on the size of the project. Public officials scrutinize large project proposals to a greater extent than small ones, because their impacts are greater. Investors in large projects, as a result of impositions by authorities and internal security reasons, might extend the analysis to a wide range of issues.

Sponsors of small projects might well limit their analysis to potential regulatory changes that could affect operations and to the concerns of inhabitants of the locale. In some cases local planning and zoning boards function to control industrial and commercial enterprise, often imposing constraints on emissions and other impacts. Even where such constraints do not exist, a proactive stance has the advantage of clearing the air and forestalling potential opposition from local citizens, whose reactions may be heightened as a consequence of impacts of which they were unaware.

The scope of analysis described herein encompasses the broader range of issues that should be selectively addressed depending upon the circumstances of the project.

Economic pricing is limited to costs and benefits of resources whose values are significantly distorted and/or consumed in significant quantities (including externalities) and with significant social impacts for which only qualitative assessment is possible. For a small project, the price of a resource may be highly distorted, but its economic impact is bound to be small to insignificant due to small quantities involved. However, even for micro and small enterprises, consciousness of economic and social forces is useful if only to understand better the future course of markets and public policy.

If economic analysis is warranted, its depth may vary with project stage, increasing as the project nears the investment decision point. To what depth ripples in the economy created by the project are to be studied depends on significance; at the later stages, study of more than one round of impacts is often warranted. For example, a dam project has the direct impact of providing energy and irrigation. It creates secondary impacts of inundated areas and attendant loss of existing land use, displacement of populations, and disruption of habitats. Tertiary effects might include disruption of nutrient distribution patterns in river deltas, increased salinity, and waterlogging of irrigated farmland.

When resources are scarce, prudence suggests that they be applied in the manner that will do the most good. By adopting the economic perspective, investors supplement their own concerns with those of the host community. As project sponsors are greatly motivated to make good decisions, public decision makers are thereby more inclined to respect their ideas. However, even the wise and sharp-eyed owl occasionally misses a tasty morsel, its range of observation limited by the vagaries of its environment. The question of whether a project investment is an appropriate use of resources appears to be answerable from at least these two perspectives, but they tend to merge in the longer term as resource information becomes more widely available, and to the extent that a holistic view of the enterprise is adopted.

Economic analysis can provide important information even if project revenues cover all project costs (private and public sectors). If the investment is to be covered only partially by income in the form of tariffs or fees (e.g., a transportation system with rider fees covering only operating rather than investment costs), economic analysis is warranted to determine whether the project is an acceptable use of public resources. If a project requires the allocation of public resources with no attendant revenues, the justification for economic analysis is clear, as the most accurate way of determining value for the project's output. The output of nonrevenue projects can be monetized in most circumstances.[12]

Characteristics of Analysis

Although financial analysis can serve as an underpinning, the characteristics of economic analysis differ considerably from the financial point of view:

- Project outputs (benefits) and inputs (costs) are valued at shadow prices[13] that reflect their economic values. Commercial benefits are measured in regard to revenues or profits, economic benefits in terms of the value of resources consumed and made available to society. Commercial costs are measured in market prices of production factors. Economic prices of outputs reflect their contribution to economic objectives; inputs reflect the opportunity forgone when a resource is applied to the project. Economic prices are applied to inputs and outputs to determine the net benefit of the project. In the approach described in Chapter 6, a distinction is made between real and financial flows, the latter included only for estimating distribution effects.
- Rather than focus on the top or bottom line, direct economic impacts and effects on trade, markets, employment, income distribution, and foreign exchange flows arising from the project's production and consumption of goods and services are considered in economic analysis.
- Externalities, values assigned to impacts beyond those of the project's output of goods and services and consumption of resources in their production, are included in the analysis. *Economic impacts* are upstream and downstream linkages (affecting performances in related productive activities, such as improved utilization of installed capacities, or new investment initiatives), infrastructure effects (improvements or degradations attributable to the project), and changes in trade balance and foreign exchange flow. *Social impacts* involve cultural factors (e.g., changes in lifestyles), displacements of surrounding populations, and changes in income distribution. *Technological impacts* relate to changes in the state of technology employed in the region or country; product life-cycle

impacts (e.g., disposal, reuse, recycling); and how project technology affects surrounding environment and habitats.

- Social time preference[14] rather than cost of capital is the primary basis for the hurdle rate to be applied to calculate present worth of economic costs and benefits.

Methods of Analysis

For projects involving a small city or town, it may be sufficient to conduct a survey of the affected population to ascertain issues of concern and their possible resolutions, particularly if the impacts affect lifestyle rather than health or other environmental factors.

More formal methods for assessing the project's economic impact would be applied to larger commercial and nonrevenue projects. *Economic cost/benefit analysis* (ECBA) measures economic and social values of benefits and costs of resources generated and consumed by the project during each period and integrates them into a single measure of value. Some of the methodologies use shadow prices; others measure benefits in terms of value added (VA), the project's contribution to national income. In both approaches, net benefits for each project period are aggregated to a net present value using a social discount rate. Value-added analysis (VAA) is usually not applied beyond the level of economic efficiency,[15] with supplementary indicators providing information about distribution of benefits.[16]

Although it is possible to target different objectives, the usual criterion in both approaches is optimization with respect GNP/GDP (aggregated VA is essentially GNP). This means that, in principle, it should be possible to derive similar, if not identical results with either method. However, in the VA method described, as previously mentioned, there is inherently no attempt to deal with scarcity of resources (shadow prices) or externalities other than linked economic activity. Some items excluded as costs in the shadow pricing approach are benefits in VAA.[17] Whether the methods provide similar results in regard to ranking alternative projects for implementation depends on the amount of distortion in related markets and the degree of a wider range of externalities; in most cases, these methods should lead to equivalent results.

Analytical Framework

Economic analysis is undertaken to understand the project's economic context—policies reflected in local, regional, or national economic plans; distortions in the economy that may affect the future of the enterprise; and compatibility with concerns of the surrounding community or those of regional or national planning authorities.[18] In the more formal approach (the

TABLE 5.1   Economic Analysis Framework

	Commercial	Economic
Applicability	All projects	Public- and private-sector projects—scope depending on range of impacts
Objectives	Maximize return on invested capital and/or wealth accumulation	Improve standard of living
Constraints	Existing infrastructure, legal regulations, risk tolerance	Government priorities on development, income distribution, savings rates of income groups, balance of payments situation
Parameters	Market prices	Economic prices reflecting scarcity of resources, national parameters
Resources	Investor's financial strength	National resources (labor, land, capital, mineral deposits, etc.)
Criteria	Returns on equity and investment, yield curve on debt instruments	Maximize benefits from use of national resources, equitable income distribution among contemporaries and generations

subject of much of the following discussion), the issue is how the project contributes net economic benefits and satisfies distribution criteria with the use of available resources—for example, to what extent allocating resources to the project provides increased GNP and more equitable demographic and temporal distribution of benefits in the country.[19]

Table 5.1 provides a comparison of characteristics of commercial and economic analysis within this framework:

- *Applicability.* A similar approach to commercial analysis is applicable to all investment projects, whereas the type of economic analysis is a function of the size and scope of impacts, ranging from an assessment of expressed concerns of affected citizens to formal cost/benefit for projects with significant consequences.
- *Objectives.* Investors seek to maximize return on invested capital, to accumulate wealth while minimizing risk; the economic perspective is related to national goals, such as improved standard of living or national security, to maximize benefits from use of national resources, or to achieve more equitable wealth distribution.
- *Constraints.* The commercial view is constrained by formal and informal (e.g., political) regulation of industry, and by infrastructure capacities

and resource availability; the economic view is constrained by development priorities of governing bodies (e.g., a particular region) or how income is to be distributed and by government regulation.

- *Parameters.* Whereas market prices and rates of return on equity and debt instruments are the basis for commercial (financial) analysis, the economic viewpoint requires a different type of *price* based upon scarcity of the resource (i.e., the effect on national objectives from their use or generation) and application of national parameters such as savings rates, weightings for income distribution among income groups, balance of payments, valuations of resources reflecting their scarcity (e.g., shadow price of labor, foreign exchange), and social discount rate.
- *Resources.* Business acumen and financial strength are principal resources from the commercial viewpoint; economic analysis is predicated on the application of natural resources, land, labor, and capital in relation to economic goals.
- *Criteria.* Investors seek to maximize return on investment, at least equal to their cost of capital; economic criteria are a reflection of priorities of affected populations, embodied in political platforms, statutes, and regulations, and in the economic discount rate (EDR) as a benchmark for ECBA.

For ECBA, commercial objectives (profit maximization), resources consumed and generated at market prices, and criteria (cost of capital) *may* serve as points of departure.

Acceptability is usually based upon multiple criteria—for example, impact on GNP or public income; distribution of income among social groups; infrastructure improvements; growth in targeted industrial sectors; effects on employment, education, and health; economic independence; technological progress; balance of payments and foreign exchange earnings; regional development; and national security. In the ECBA method described in Chapter 6, only the first two items are considered.

Differing perspectives of regional or national authorities versus sponsors on project evaluation are summarized in Table 5.2 with respect to objectives and characteristics.

ECONOMIC PRICING PRINCIPLES

Economic prices—also called *shadow prices* or *accounting prices*—are ideally derived from a classical general equilibrium economic optimization model.[20] This type of model is formulated with an objective function describing the effects of the use and generation of resources on the measure of economic value (e.g., GNP, national income) within constraints on the

TABLE 5.2 National versus Project Perspectives

Element	National	Project
Development	Public benefits (e.g., national income)	Investor benefits (e.g., financial surplus)
Capital investment	Mobilize for social welfare	Invest for rate of return
Prices	Shadow prices	Market prices
Range	Direct	Direct and indirect
Discount rate	Social discount rate	Cost of capital
Foreign exchange	Balance of payments	Project requirements
Employment	Creation	Exploitation
Technology	Public benefit	Improved market share
Natural resources	Conserve, preserve environment	Resource requirements
Location	Economic stimulation, strategic value	Minimize operating costs

use of resources (technological coefficients for each economic activity and a limit for the resource as a whole). The shadow price of a resource is the increment of the value of the objective function resulting from increased availability of the resource by one unit.

An example of a linear optimization model (see Figure 5.4) illustrates the formal definition of a shadow price.[21] An objective function relates the overall criterion to the impact of constrained variables and their coefficients. The value of the objective function can be considered as economic benefit, the variables as economic resources, and the coefficients as the benefit per unit of resource.

$$\text{Objective function: } z = 4x + 3y$$

Production of a unit of x contributes 4 units and y contributes 3 units of economic benefit (expressed in terms of the AU). There are constraints on the two resources required, labor and capital, which are available only up to 10 and 12 units, respectively. These constraints can be expressed as follows:

$$5x + 2y \leq 10 \quad \text{(labor constraint)}$$

$$3x + 4y \leq 12 \quad \text{(capital constraint)}$$

Products x and y consume 5 and 2 units of labor respectively, and 3 units and 4 units of capital. The optimal solution is the point where (in this case) the constraints intersect and the objective function is at its maximum

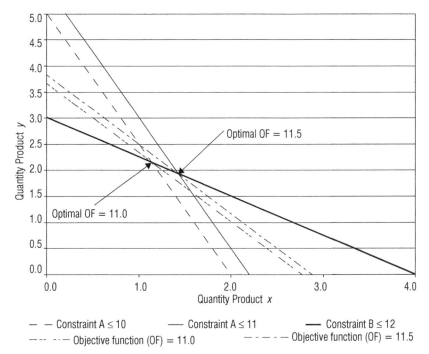

FIGURE 5.4 Shadow Prices—Linear Optimization Model

without violating the constraints:

$$\text{Constraint A: } 5x + 2y = 10$$

$$\text{Constraint B: } 3x + 4y = 12$$

$$\text{Unique solution: } x = \frac{8}{7}, y = \frac{15}{7}$$

$$z = 4\left(\frac{8}{7}\right) + 3\left(\frac{15}{7}\right) = 11$$

At this point the value of the objective function is 11. What is the marginal effect of relaxing (or tightening) the constraint on resource A by one unit?

$$\text{Constraint A: } 5x + 2y = 11$$

$$\text{Constraint B: } 3x + 4y = 12$$

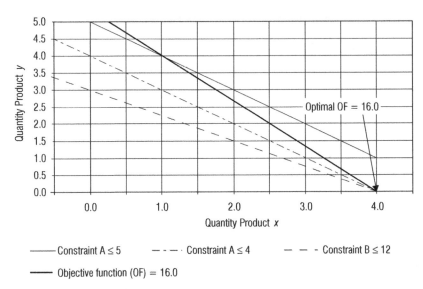

FIGURE 5.5 Shadow Prices of Nonscarce Resource

$$\text{Unique solution: } x = \frac{10}{7}, y = \frac{27}{14}$$

$$z = 4\left(\frac{10}{7}\right) + 3\left(\frac{27}{14}\right) = 11.5$$

The new value of the objective function is 11.5. In terms of the accounting unit used in the objective function, the value of a unit of resource A, or its shadow price, is 0.5 units ($11.5 - 11.0 = 0.5$).

More generally, the confluence of constraints defines the feasible region of possible combinations of variable values. The optimization process seeks to maximize the objective function while not violating any constraints.

Scarce resources have nonzero shadow prices. In this type of theoretical model, the shadow price of a resource that is not scarce (not fully committed elsewhere) is zero. For example, if the relationship of constraints A and B were as shown in Figure 5.5, resource A (say labor) would have zero shadow price because it is not a constraint on increase in the objective function. In this case the consumption of resources as related to production of x and y is as follows:

$$\text{Resource A: } x + y \leq 5$$

$$\text{Resource B: } 3x + 4y \leq 12$$

$$\text{Objective function: } z = 4x + 3y$$

The objective function seeks the optimal solution, in this case its maximum value, constrained only by the nonnegativity requirement for resources on product y, so the optimal objective function value is 16 ($x = 4$, $y = 0$).

The complexity of building and maintaining a classical economic model and other constraints[22] leads to a second-best approach to estimation, in which *accounting prices* are employed in lieu of shadow prices. The term *second-best* designates a situation in which the best solution, for whatever reasons, cannot be applied. In this case the comprehensive model of the whole national economy allowing calculation of shadow prices is not available. Alternative ways of estimating prices are required. With due diligence they would be second-best to a solution of the model. In applying this approach, according to the UNIDO *Guide to Practical Project Appraisal* mentioned earlier, "there is considerable empirical evidence that governments can do good by stealth through decisions on individual projects even when, at the same time, they find it impossible ... to 'get the prices right.' "[23] Input/output analysis is an alternate approach to shadow pricing, based upon decomposition of project inputs and outputs, and relating prices to a few primary factors such as the shadow prices of labor, foreign exchange, and taxes/subsidies.[24]

The terms *shadow price* and *accounting price* are used interchangeably, but the reference is invariably to accounting prices. In the methods described they are prices derived from a second-best, or direct, approach to estimating their values. The accounting price of an input can be defined as its economic opportunity cost—that is, the cost to the economy of utilizing one (marginal) unit of the resource in the project, which is the opportunity forgone in its best alternative use. For an output, the accounting price is the contribution of one more (marginal) unit to the economic objective(s). *Marginal* refers to incremental unit.

For the economy as a whole, an investment project is an increment in itself. In other words, the *incremental impact* of the project is to be examined. Analysis takes into account the differential between the with-project and without-project scenarios (i.e., with *minus* without). As a simple example, consider a case of a project consisting of a technology investment that results in a reduction in the consumption of a material input.

	Without Project	With Project	Differential
Technology cost	0	200	200
Material cost	800	500	−300
Totals	800	700	−100

The net effect of the project is the differential cost of technology (+200) and the negative cost (or benefit) of the change in material cost (−300). The total differential is (+200) + (−300) = −100, or a benefit of 100.

Applicability of Accounting Prices

It is unnecessary and unduly complicated to shadow price all project inputs and outputs. Resources should be shadow priced selectively based upon simultaneous application of two criteria: (1) resources having a prominent effect on the analysis (costs or benefits), meaning those constituting a significant portion of the flows; and (2) resources for which the market price is far out of line with the real value to society (as an indicative rule, not less than about 5 percent). Especially to be considered are main products, imported and importable materials, and main domestic inputs with significant cost implications. Of particular interest are primary factors—labor (unskilled labor is often highly distorted from the market price due to minimum wage government regulations), capital, and foreign exchange transactions.

Economic Accounting Unit

An accounting unit (AU) is required to express value in economic terms—in some treatises on the subject, it is called the *numeraire*. The unit selected for valuing inputs and outputs should be consistent with units of the policy objective. For example, if government policy seeks increased income, economic values could alternatively be expressed in terms of consumption or investment, or some other measure consistent with the primary objective. If there are multiple quantifiable objectives, the project is evaluated in regard to each, with a weighting system used to combine the results into a single measure of value.

An accounting unit used to quantify economic impact should describe the following components:

- *Currency*. Domestic or foreign currency is selected.[25] Values expressed in other currencies are converted to the selected currency at the official exchange rate. The currency used in the accounting unit determines the numerical value of costs and benefits. The selection of domestic or foreign currency to express value is inconsequential—values will differ, but the outcome will be identical for project ranking purposes.
- *Prices*. Either border (international trade) or domestic prices are applicable; an exchange may be directly related to a transaction, or induced as a consequence of the use or generation of the underlying item.[26]
- *Current or constant prices*. Generally, constant prices are assumed to be those at project startup. Current prices can be derived from constant

prices by applying an appropriate inflator. Constant prices, as in financial analysis, are most frequently employed for estimating future costs and benefits, as inflation forecasting is highly uncertain.

- *Time dimension.* Economic values are compared and aggregated at a point in time (usually project commencement) by discounting and/or compounding.
- *Level.* Values can be expressed in terms of income, or in consumption or savings/investment to which the income stream can be applied. All are mutually convertible.
- *Class of recipients of project benefits.* If distribution is a factor in the economic value of inputs and outputs, the base recipient class is specified. Distributions to other classes of recipients can be converted to values equivalent to distributions to the base recipient class.

For the Cambria Yarns Project, the AU has the following specifications: currency—foreign (US$); prices—border; constant; discounted to present (project inception); level—consumption; base economic class—neither taxed nor subsidized.

Economic Parameters

Planning authorities may specify, either subjectively or objectively, national or regional parameters that either are shadow prices or are applicable to the calculation of other national or regional parameters. For economic analysis to be a meaningful instrument for resource allocation, a level playing field requires that all projects be treated equally. A constant set of parameters, derived for the region, the country, or an individual enterprise, should similarly apply to all projects under consideration.

Subjective parameters include the *cutoff discount rate* (economic discount rate below which the project is unacceptable) and the *income weight by economic class or region* (the degree of preference assigned by authorities to each).

Objective parameters derive from statistics. Examples include *marginal propensity to save* for benefit recipient classes, *marginal return on capital* (rate of return on invested capital at the margin), *balance of payments,* and *income distribution.* The *shadow price of labor* may be specified by planning authorities, derived from a combination of objective and subjective factors, possibly varying by region, in particular for larger size countries. The planning authority typically sets the *shadow exchange rate* as a means of improving a trade imbalance (this parameter is objective in the sense that the export/import relationship on which it is based is measurable).

Pricing Levels

Economic prices can be determined at several stages in the analysis. *Economic efficiency prices* are valuations of resources that reflect the impact of the use or generation of the good or service on uncommitted income—that is, without regard to distribution and responsive to the criterion of income growth. *Social prices* take into account the distribution of income and other measures of social welfare. In the method described herein,[27] distribution of benefits among contemporaries and among generations is addressed; social prices are not determined per se. Distortions between efficiency and market prices are adjusted by weighting factors to determine distribution-induced consumption increments for classifications of stakeholders. The intent is ultimately to provide a method for appraising the project on the basis of a system of accounting prices with adjustments for distribution effects.

Pricing Bases

Economic prices are intended to reflect the impact on the economic objective of a marginal unit generated or consumed by the project, as the case may be—that is, to provide an indication of the real benefits and costs to the economy of the country or region of the use and generation of project resources.

Border prices (depending upon how "the economy" is delimited for purposes of optimization) are applicable for goods that are either internationally traded or that have impacts on trade—cost, insurance, and freight (CIF) for imports and free on board (FOB)[28] for exports, both adjusted appropriately for inland transport and handling costs. The border price is the world market (competitive) price brought to the project's gate (see the subsection "Traded Goods" later in this chapter for a more thorough explanation).

For nontraded goods, consumer *willingness to pay* (WTP) reflects the marginal utility for consumers and is applicable when the effect of generating or consuming the resource is on demand. As the accounting price for each unit of output is the *marginal* WTP, consumer surplus[29] should ideally be included in the estimation of value.

Production cost is the best estimate of value when the effect is on supply. Components of production cost are priced at their respective economic values, best accomplished by decomposing the item into traded, domestic intermediates and nontraded components in two or three rounds, which should provide sufficient precision. Ultimately, decomposition can lead to the disappearance of domestic intermediates so that only traded and nontraded components remain, which simplifies the job of determining the economic price.

The frame of reference for pricing decisions by central authorities, or by project personnel in the absence of guidance from central authorities, varies according to the degree to which global markets or local economic autonomy are assumed to predominate. In practice, one or a combination of the following perspectives can be employed:

- *Global markets.* A global perspective places emphasis on international markets as the most accurate gauge of value, reflecting the most efficient allocation of resources on this most competitive market of reference. With a truly global pricing framework national borders essentially disappear: Optimization with respect to allocation of resources is sought on a global level; virtually all goods and services, except those that are clearly nontraded (the domestic price is above export price but below import price), are valued at the global trade price, adjusted for transportation and handling.

- *Society's goals.* The rationale of the system of accounting prices "is that of estimating those prices that would prevail in the economy if it were to operate so as to maximize society's ends. This maximization is constrained by the available resources, and by the possibilities of the tax system."[30] This begs the question, what is *society*? Is it the human population of the world, the country, the region?[31] Assignment of value would depend to some extent on the dimension of society. Trade associations of nations, for example, erect barriers that restrict external trade, even though trade restrictions among member states are prohibited. Even major industrialized countries erect trade barriers when it appears to be in their interest. Currently, cost benefit analysis is most commonly applied at the national level[32] (in some cases regional), using estimates of costs paid by, and benefits accruing to, citizens of the host economy. In either case, traded items are priced at the border of the economic union or country, as the case may be, and may differ in some cases from global prices.

- *Development policies.* Trade restrictions are a reflection of government development policy. Goods and services precluded or restricted from trade should be priced at the domestic accounting price (consumer willingness to pay or the cost of production, as applicable). "The price in the home market ... applies in cases where government policy isolates commodities from foreign markets through import or export prohibitions or quotas."[33]

Whether pricing rules are predicated primarily on the international market framework or respect national or regional priorities, as expressed by interventions of governments,[34] is an issue for decision makers. Global mobility of production factors and free trade tend to favor adoption of international markets as the gauge of value.

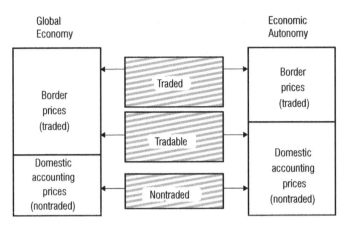

FIGURE 5.6   Economic Pricing Assignment

System of Accounting Prices

To determine economic and social value, goods and services are classified according to the degree of tradability. Items that have an effect on trade are priced at the border; those that are sold in the domestic market are essentially priced at the value of nontraded domestic resources consumed in production or WTP.[35] The assignment of a resource to one of these groups, and the accounting price decision, depends to some extent on the pricing framework adopted by the analyst, or by planning authorities if applicable.

In the final analysis, either the border price[36] or the domestic accounting price (WTP or production cost) has to be applied to each input and output. A scheme for assigning items to one category or the other is shown in Figure 5.6. If the perspective is global investment optimization, there will be a greater tendency to assign items to the *traded* category.[37] If economic autonomy, as reflected in trade restrictions, is accepted as the framework for decision making, items in the *tradable* category will more likely be assigned to the *nontraded* category.

A global viewpoint leads to greater emphasis on international markets as the frame of reference for value. Border prices are applied in most cases on the premise that trade barriers will eventually fall during future project operations.

If there is a greater inclination to accept national or regional development policy and goals as expressed by constraints on trade, items for which trade constraints exist will more likely be placed in the nontraded category and domestic prices (consumer or producer prices as applicable, with content shadow priced) will be applied to a greater extent. For these items, the likelihood of trade policy changes that would affect pricing decisions should be considered.

Traded Goods   *Traded* goods are those that are actually traded (either imported or exported) or that affect trade. In this case, increased production causes an increase in exports or a decrease in imports of project outputs (import substitution). Similarly, consumption by the project results in more imports or fewer exports of project inputs (export diversion). The basic measure of value is FOB (free-on-board) for exports and CIF for imports,[38] each converted to *border prices* by adjusting for inland charges (e.g., transport to or from the project site, agents' fees and commissions). Inland charges are deducted from the FOB price for goods priced as exports. There may be offsetting savings attributable to the without-project scenario.

Export diversion of an input—that is, a good that would otherwise be exported in the absence of the project—is priced at FOB, representing the export earnings forgone (opportunity cost) when a unit of the input is consumed rather than exported. Without the project, the item, say a ton of iron ore, would be exported by first moving it from the mine to the port. With the project, the ton of iron ore will be shipped from the mine to the steel mill instead. The forgone FOB earnings would be reduced by the inland costs from mine to port,[39] but there is an additional cost of moving the coal from mine to steel mill if the project is implemented. In other words, the adjusted border price, or accounting price, is FOB minus transport from mine to port (equivalent of the border price), plus transport[40] from mine to steel mill.

Another possibility is import substitution. The starting point to determine border price is CIF, the avoided cost of the previously imported item, say a tractor that would now be produced by the project. Without the project, the tractor arrives at the port and is then moved to the market. Its price (assuming a competitive market) would include CIF plus inland transportation cost to the market. With the project implemented, the tractor is shipped from plant to market. Both CIF and the cost of transport and handling from port to market are avoided, but there is a cost for moving the tractor from plant to market. The border price, or accounting price, is CIF plus transport from port to market, minus transport from plant to market. This would approximate the price received by the tractor factory under competitive market conditions.

Domestic costs are shadow priced according to the rules for nontraded goods. If the use of transportation facilities precludes their use in other productive activities, *willingness to pay* is the appropriate benchmark. If the project develops its own facilities that do not have an impact on demand by other users, the production cost is relevant.

Tradable Goods Some goods are not traded, but *would be traded* in the absence of trade barriers such as tariffs, quotas, and other trade restrictions. Progressive integration of the world economy and liberalization of trade and other economic policies during the past few decades has reduced the incidence of tradables, so that in all but a few remaining command economies goods can be considered either traded or nontraded. Discussion of this category is included here for completeness.

In these situations, rather than simply accept the trade status of a good under prevailing conditions, a greater depth of analysis is undertaken to determine the appropriate price. These goods have to be assigned either border or domestic prices, depending on the specific circumstances (see Appendix 5.2). The following are some of the considerations that may apply for tradable goods:

- *Tradable outputs.* If the import price of a *tradable output* (i.e., it would have been imported were it not for the project) is lower than the domestic price (both measured in economic terms), the accounting price of the output is the border price rather than the (higher) domestic value. In other words, the opportunity forgone is the lower-priced import of the good rather than domestic manufacture. In terms of distribution effects, consumers lose by paying higher than the import price and the project gains by receiving more than the import price.
- *Tradable inputs.* Goods procured locally by the project that *would have been exported* were it not for use by the project are priced at the border, which is the opportunity forgone. If they could have been exported, but are not as a result of trade policies of the country, the higher of the export price or the domestic price (both measured in economic terms) is assigned. If the export price is higher, the opportunity forgone is the export earnings. A higher domestic price reflects the actual economic cost, either consumer willingness to pay or the domestic resources used in production of the input.[41]

For project inputs that *could be imported*, but are not, the appropriate pricing framework (see earlier section, "Pricing Bases") has to be selected. The global markets perspective suggests that the real social value is the *lower* of domestic or border price.[42] If the border price is lower, it would be preferable for the project to import, and consequently the *lower* border price is to be assigned. "To take the higher price would mean an overestimation of the real value of the input."[43] Applying the lower (import) price tends to increase economic profitability of the project, even though this more favorable import option is not exercised. Does it make intuitive sense to apply a price that provides the project a more favorable outlook than is actually the case? If the goal of the decision maker is to optimize global economic development, such a choice is perfectly logical. The difference between the higher domestic price and the international price has a distribution effect, valued according to the weighting assigned to the gainer and loser. However, if the pricing framework is development policy that precludes import of the input in favor of expanded domestic supply, the item would be considered as nontraded and the relevant accounting price would be the (higher) domestic market or producer price (both measured in economic terms).

Nontradables

Some goods are excluded from trade by the combination of production and international transport costs, which raise the import price above local production cost and the sales price above the international market price. Goods that are not traded as a result of tariffs, quotas, and other barriers to trade erected by regional or national authorities in response to trade policy might be treated as nontraded, depending upon the *pricing framework* adopted and whether the constraints on trade are expected to continue to the planning horizon.

The following rules can be applied if either the good is nontradable or the pricing framework is responsive to government trade policy:

- If an input is diverted from other domestic users, the effect is on demand and the basis for pricing is the *willingness to pay* by other potential users.[44] If the result of the demand by the project for additional input is an increase in local production, the *marginal production cost* is the relevant price.
- If the effect of the project output is to provide *more for local users* (increased consumption), consumers' willingness to pay is the relevant accounting price, under relatively free market conditions. If the project output *replaces existing production* (decreased output of alternate producers), the marginal cost of *replaced production* (decomposed and shadow priced) is the relevant accounting price.[45] The net benefit is the difference between the (presumably) less-efficient existing production and the cost of the new production.

For both outputs and inputs, the supply (producer) price is applicable if marginal supply is perfectly elastic or if marginal demand is perfectly inelastic. The demand (consumer) price is applicable if marginal demand is perfectly elastic or if marginal supply is perfectly inelastic.[46]

For example, if the marginal supply of a project *input* is highly elastic (higher percentage change in supply than percent change in price), the existence of the project stimulates increased production. In this situation the supply (producer) price is applicable. If supply is inelastic, project

	Effect of Project Outputs and Inputs on	
	Demand	Supply
Highly elastic	Demand price	Supply price
Highly inelastic	Supply price	Demand price

consumption tends to reduce availability for other users so the demand (consumer) price is applicable.

If, at the margin, demand for project *output* is highly elastic, more is available for users, so the demand price is relevant. If it is inelastic, the project displaces other production, so the supply price (displaced producer) is relevant.

Infrastructure Services   For domestically produced (nontradable) services such as electricity, water, gas, steam, transport, or communications, the accounting price is the domestic market price or service provider cost, whichever is higher. If the domestic price is lower than production cost, the subsidy represents a distribution effect—consumers gain and the provider of the service or the grantor of the subsidy (government) loses. In some cases infrastructure services (e.g., electricity), are internationally traded, in which case border pricing might be more applicable.

Summary of Pricing Rules   Goods and services produced (outputs) or consumed (inputs) by the project are ultimately priced either as traded or nontraded. Selecting the appropriate pricing basis takes into account the status of local production of these items and effects on trade (exports and imports). Each of these categories might include tradable items, depending upon the pricing framework adopted and views of the analyst concerning future trade policy. Another factor is consumer and producer surplus.[47]

If project output or input affects trade, the accounting price is the border price:

Traded Items	Inputs	Outputs	Accounting Price
Supply	Reduced exports	Increased exports	FOB less inland costs
Demand	Increased imports	Reduced imports[a]	CIF plus inland costs

[a]Import substitution.

For nontraded items, the accounting price is either WTP or production cost (PC):

Nontraded Items	Inputs	Outputs	Accounting Price
Supply	From increased production	Displaces other production[a]	PC
Demand	Less for other users	More available for local consumers	WTP

[a]Cost of displaced production, which is normally less efficient than the new production; the net benefit is the cost of the displaced production less the cost of the new production.

A weighted average of the demand and supply price is appropriate if input is supplied by a combination of reduced availability to other users *and* stimulation of new output; or if the production of an output both increases availability for local users *and* supplants existing production.

Indirect Taxes and Subsidies

Taxes on traded goods are transfer payments and therefore not included in the accounting price.[48] For nontraded goods, if the effect of the project is on *demand for an input or output*—diversion of inputs that are in fixed supply from other producers, or addition to the market of consumer goods—indirect taxes are included in the accounting price as part of consumer willingness to pay (the demand price). If the effect of the project is on *supply of an input or output*—the existence of the project causes additional input to be produced (by others), or the output supplants production by others—indirect taxes should not be included as they are not a part of marginal production cost (the supply price).

Inclusion of a subsidy in the price of an input or output depends on whether it represents a cost to society. If a subsidy is drawn from scarce resources not balanced by a corresponding benefit, the subsidy may be considered a cost. If the subsidy confers other societal benefits, it would not necessarily be considered a cost. If there are no compensating benefits, the subsidy is excluded for an output but included for an input. For example, a subsidy that allows an otherwise internationally uncompetitive producer to export does not necessarily reflect economic value for the country. That portion of export earnings is excluded (or added as a project cost). The subsidy in this case is a transfer from government to the project. However, if government policy is to foment exports for strategic or other reasons, the subsidy could be included in the economic value of the export.

For example, the subsidy permits production of a pharmaceutical that reduces health care costs to the populace that would otherwise be borne by the government (grantor of the subsidy). The corresponding benefits might offset the cost. A subsidy paid by the government to the producer of a

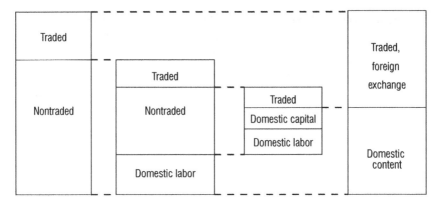

FIGURE 5.7 Decomposition of Production Cost

basic good, equivalent to increasing consumer purchasing power, reflects the government's social distribution policy. It may be considered a societal benefit and included in the accounting price of the product.

Decomposition

Goods for which the (marginal) cost of production is the basis for the accounting price determination can be decomposed to have a more accurate assessment of economic value, as illustrated in Figure 5.7. Tradable (or traded) components of the item can be valued at border prices. Nontraded items can be further decomposed for increased accuracy into their traded and nontraded content (two or three such iterations would normally suffice to have accurate enough result for this analysis). At the end of this procedure all inputs and outputs are classified as either traded or nontraded. Consequently all inputs and outputs can ultimately be expressed in terms of foreign exchange and domestic content. The labor component is priced at the shadow wage rate. Remaining elements can normally be valued at market price. This level of detail is justified for items that meet the criteria for shadow pricing—large impact on the outcome and large distortion from market price.

SHADOW PRICES OF PRIMARY RESOURCES (NATIONAL PARAMETERS)

Shadow prices of labor, capital, and foreign exchange are fundamental to the analysis. As shown in Figure 5.7, with the use of decomposition, economic prices for most items can be determined from the prices of these primary resources.

Shadow Price of Labor

The *shadow wage rate* (SWR) is the economic cost of assigning a worker to the project. It represents forgone benefits[49] that would otherwise be attributable to the worker in the absence of the project. The SWR can be estimated using some (or all) of the elements suggested by several investigators:[50]

- *Forgone marginal production at accounting prices.* For unskilled labor in the developing countries, the forgone marginal production is the value of subsistence activities carried out in the absence of the project. For skilled labor drawn from the market or from abroad, the wage can be a reflection of forgone output. However, if the project trains its own skilled workers, rather than drawing them from the rest of the economy, the cost is essentially that of producing the skilled worker, one part of which would be training costs (discussed shortly).
- *Cost of increased consumption* to compensate additional effort of a previously unemployed person as a consequence of employment in the project. This cost may be considered as a proxy of the SWR. Often the SWR is estimated as the equivalent of daily food supply for the worker's family.
- *Social cost of reduced leisure* that would be enjoyed by the worker in the absence of the project.

In regard to the last item, although a factor in some approaches to SWR, it might be considered inappropriate for poorer countries with fragile or nonexistent social safety nets (e.g., lack of access to unemployment benefits paid by the state). However, availability of these benefits can be a disincentive for undertaking a low-wage job, where unemployment benefits may equal or exceed net wages after accounting for costs of employment (perhaps even forgone leisure). This situation prevails in many transition countries.

If the project employs unskilled workers and trains them so that they acquire skills, the *cost of training* is attributable to the project. Project-specific training costs that have no application outside the project should be included (shadow priced) as part of the cost of labor. General training that provides skills and increased productivity beyond the project time frame can be considered an economic benefit although it is a cost for project. Personnel *infrastructure*, such as housing and facilities for health care and recreation, may be required. If constructed by the project, it is part of the cost of labor attributable to the project, provided that there are no attendant benefits (i.e., if the facilities are to be applied only to the needs of project workers during the project's life). There is also the possibility of a benefit from the upgraded lifestyle of workers attributable to the facilities, or if the facilities will be useful beyond the project life.

Project workers may be recruited from an area that requires them to *migrate*. The cost of moving workers and their families from their homes to the plant site is attributable to the project. In the economic analysis, the SWR would be a recurring cost, while migration and other ancillary items might be one-time costs or benefits.

The SWR differs for categories of labor. Expatriate workers—engineers, technicians, and other skilled workers recruited from abroad—are generally compensated completely or partially in foreign exchange, either directly or through conversion rights. Their cost is the *border* price, the foreign exchange equivalent of CIF converted by the shadow price of foreign exchange (if expressed in local currency). The portion of wages of expatriate personnel transferred abroad is not considered an economic benefit (economic analysis is most often national, as discussed in the earlier section, "Macroeconomic View—Impact on the National Economy").[51] The domestic component, if any, usually needs no shadow pricing.

The SWR for local skilled workers is determined in regard to scarcity and source. Usually the wage is a reflection of production forgone in alternative employment. The rules for pricing previously discussed are applied.

Capacities of semiskilled workers are not generally applicable to other types of employment. The project would usually be required to provide specialized training, which is a part of the SWR, determined on the basis of the cost of producing these semiskilled workers (e.g., recruitment and training).

If unskilled labor is plentiful (nonscarce), its shadow price as determined by a classical optimization model would be zero. However, in most cases the SWR for unskilled labor is estimated between 50 and 100 percent of the official minimum wage set by the authorities to protect the poor. The shadow wage of unskilled labor is sometimes expressed in term of quantities of basic commodities.

Shadow Price of Project's Assets

The rules for pricing assets are similar to those for other inputs. If the asset is fully traded, its economic value is the border price. Nontraded components of assets are shadow priced according to rules similar to those for other inputs: If the project induces increased production of the capital good, the shadow price is the cost of production; if the project diverts the capital good from other potential users, consumer willingness to pay is the appropriate pricing basis. Labor and foreign exchange components involved in production of the asset are valued according to the shadow pricing rules previously described for project inputs.

Shadow Price of Foreign Exchange (Shadow Exchange Rate)

Currency exchange rates may respond to market conditions or may be controlled directly or indirectly by the government. If there is an official exchange rate (number of local currency units per unit of foreign currency), it is applicable for commercial transactions involving exports, imports, and international payments. Import payments in foreign exchange (FX) and export earnings are usually transacted through the central bank at the official rate of exchange.

Import quotas present opportunities for less-efficient local producers protected by the quotas. Consequently the relationship between the border price in FX at the official exchange rate and the domestic price is distorted. When exchange between domestic and foreign currencies is controlled, a price mechanism implicitly follows the distorted market. Inevitably, distortions arise between the values of the two currencies, even when the rate floats according to some indicator. In some cases, tiered exchange rates are administered by the government in an attempt to somewhat regulate FX flows. Import and export duties and subsidies are often employed in an attempt to correct trade or payments deficits—interventions that are bound to distort exchange rates further.

A distorted foreign exchange rate is problematic for the economy as it is difficult to control trade equilibrium. An overvalued local currency (undervalued FX) causes irregularities in FX allocation. It is difficult to attract and retain foreign direct investment (FDI). Mechanisms for controlling the use of scarce foreign exchange must be established and maintained, adding to government operating costs. Exporters find it difficult to compete, and importers, although paying import duties, are subsidized in a hidden form (are allowed to buy FX at a low price). Authorities usually tolerate a parallel currency market to avoid raising tensions. Once FX distortions are in place they are difficult to change, as politicians run the risk of raising the displeasure and opposition of affected parties (usually influential domestic producers and consumers).

When the price of FX is controlled, values of the project's international transactions usually differ from their values at the official exchange rate. Costs and benefits derived on the basis of the official exchange rate do not convey the real impact of the project on the country's economy. The official exchange rate usually underestimates valuation of foreign exchange components and requires adjustment to reflect true economic value. One caveat is that the resultant distortion in the price of foreign exchange is generally not sustainable in the long run. Depending on length of the planning horizon, it may be prudent to anticipate what the exchange rate would be if controls were removed or relaxed, and determine economic prices accordingly.

Even when the exchange rate is determined by the market mechanism (a *floating* exchange rate, which prevails in most market economies), international flows of capital (including FDI) might distort exchange rates and lead to a trade imbalance,[52] which may require significant adjustments including a much different level for the exchange rate. Application of the shadow exchange rate (SER) in economic analysis for the project in this situation would be fully justified. The SER, which anticipates the future shape of the economy and its environment, can be approximated using one of the methods suggested in the next subsection.

The marginal cost of acquiring foreign exchange in relation to domestic resource prices can be estimated from the degree of ownership conferred to providers of foreign exchange flows into the country. The black-market price usually overestimates the value of foreign exchange, as it contains a risk premium and is a price in a narrow market with limited supply and very specific demand. The real value lies between the official and black-market prices. *Purchasing power parity* is determined from the price of a typical basket of goods measured in the domestic currency compared with the price of the same basket of goods measured in the foreign currency. The price in domestic and foreign currency for internationally traded goods can be directly compared.

If central authorities do not provide guidance, one of the following approaches to determining the shadow price of foreign exchange may be applied. All of them reflect only actual trade exchanges; they would have to be corrected if there is considerable foreign debt service to be covered by exports.

Relation of Foreign and Domestic Trading Prices The amount of import duties (T_M) and export subsidies (S_X) necessary to balance trade is the basis for the shadow price. Where quantitative restrictions are important, their tariff equivalents should be included. Any prohibitive quantitative restrictions or tariffs should also be taken into account, if possible.

$$SER = OER\frac{(M + T_M) + (X + S_X)}{M + X}$$

where SER = shadow exchange rate
   OER = official exchange rate
   M = CIF value of imports (at the official exchange rate)
   X = FOB value of imports (at the official exchange rate)
   T_M = import taxes
   S_X = export subsidies (or tax rebates)

Trade Deficit   The trade deficit—excess of imports over exports—is a measure of the distortion in foreign exchange value. The value of exports is the total of visible (essentially merchandise) and invisible (essentially services) receipts. The value of imports is the sum of visible and invisible payments. If trade is in balance ($M = X$) the SER is equal to the OER, meaning that there is no distortion. Taxed goods are valued at market prices as a measure of consumer willingness to pay.

$$SER = OER \left(1 + \frac{M - X}{M} \right)$$

Relation of Import Prices in Domestic and International Markets   The SER is determined from a weighted average of the ratio of domestic to import price for each imported item. The CIF price in foreign currency is expressed in local currency *at the official exchange rate.*

$$SER = \sum_{i=1}^{n} f_i \frac{p_i^D}{p_i^{CIF}}$$

where f_i = fraction of foreign exchange for imported good i
p^D_i = market price of good i in domestic market
p_i^{CIF} = CIF price of good i expressed in local currency

This formulation reflects price distortions of imported products resulting from an overvalued national currency.

CONVERSION AND ADJUSTMENT FACTORS

Market prices are the usual point of departure for converting to economic efficiency prices. If there are exchange rate distortions, the process, depending on the method adopted for estimation, could be completed in two steps. First the market price (MP) is adjusted for distortions other than exchange rate to a value with distortions removed (VDR); then the VDR is adjusted for exchange rate distortions (VEF, or economic efficiency value). Each of these steps is accomplished by converting the original value to the adjusted value using either adjustment factors (AF) or conversion factors (CF).

$$CF = \text{accounting price/market price}$$
$$AF = CF - 1$$

Consequently:

$$AVAL = VAL \times CF$$

$$ADJ = VAL \times AF$$

where $AVAL$ = adjusted value (in accounting prices)
        VAL = original value (in market prices)
        CF = conversion factor
        AF = adjustment factor
        ADJ = adjustment value (difference between AVAL and VAL)

The CF expresses the ratio of adjusted and original values. The AF defines the difference, which could be used for analysis of distribution effects. If economic analysis stops short of estimating distribution effects, conversion factors would be more appropriately used instead of AFs.

Conversion of a market price to its economic efficiency value is illustrated in the following example:

Import price (CIF) of item:	F100 (100 units of FX)
Import duties	10 percent of import price
Official exchange rate:	1F = 5L (five units of local currency per unit of FX)
Shadow exchange rate:	1F = 6L

(F and L refer to denominations of foreign and local currencies, respectively).

Step 1

$$CF_{VDR} = \frac{VDR}{MP} = \left[\frac{100 - (0.1)(100)}{100} \right] = \frac{90}{100} = 0.9$$

$$VDR = (MP)(CF_{VDR}) = (100)(0.9) = 90$$

$$AF_{VDR} = CF_{VDR} - 1 = 0.9 - 1 = -0.1$$

$$ADJ_{VDR} = (100)(-0.1) = -10$$

Step 2

$$CF_{VEF} = \frac{SER}{OER} = \frac{6}{5} = 1.2$$

$$VEF = VDR(CF_{VEF}) = (90)(1.2) = 108$$

$$AF_{VEF} = CF_{VEF} - 1 = 1.2 - 1.0 = 0.2$$

$$ADJ_{VEF} = (VDR)(AF_{VEF}) = (90)(0.2) = 18$$

$$ADJ_{TOT} = ADJ_{VDR} + ADJ_{VEF} = -10 + 18 = +8$$

In the example, all values are expressed in local currency. The preliminary adjusted value VDR is 90 after removal of import duties. The distortion is −10, which indicates that in the absence of government intervention (import duty), the domestic price of the imported product would be 90 instead of 100, just because of this distortion. The conversion factor for VEF is 1.2, so the adjustment factor is 0.2 and the VEF adjustment is 18. The total adjustment is the sum of the VDR and VEF adjustments. Again, this indicates that in a nondistorted market, the price of the imported product would be higher by 8L than at present. The amount of adjustments is used in the income flow analysis for determining distribution effects.

APPENDIX 5.1: COSTS AND BENEFITS OF REVENUE PROJECTS

A project that generates a revenue stream, whether in the private or public sector, is almost invariably appraised by the sponsor (promoter) to ascertain financial viability. This is not, or at least shouldn't be, the last word on the matter, and it is not only the question of externalities. Before going into some of the intricacies of economic analysis of projects, the wider context within which projects are implemented has to be analyzed.

Within a particular country's national boundaries, the sovereign national government often specifies conditions for the project to be approved for implementation in a particular location. The project has to comply with local laws and regulations, pay taxes and customs duties, and is sometimes mandated to procure certain inputs from domestic markets at prevailing prices, including hiring and remunerating labor at the local rates.

The national border[53] separates resources available in the country from resources of the rest of the world (some of them may not be controlled by citizens of the country). How these national resources are employed determines the standard of living of the population, and represents at least a partial constraint on capacity of the country to provide its citizens consumption goods, which is considered the best measure of economic growth and progress, well-being, or welfare by most mainstream economists.

In the historical process of economic development, available resources (labor, capital, and land) have been allocated to different types of activities through the market mechanism and through government interventions. A country's economic structure, which the project inherits, can only be modified, in the long run, through new investments.

Several questions arise, such as: Does the present structure of investment guarantee the best use of scarce resources? Does the existing resource allocation process guarantee their best use in the future? Before attempting to answer this question, what does "the best use of resources" mean?

An enterprise is said to work efficiently if it fully uses its capacities and manufactures products that are sold without accumulating unnecessary stocks. Enterprise efficiency could be improved by getting rid of redundant labor, or by making new investments to improve operations. Efficiency improvement of the national economy is more complex, having three dimensions: static, dynamic, and distributional.[54]

1. *Static efficiency* requires that three simultaneous conditions be fulfilled: full employment of resources within national borders, consumption of the right combination of inputs, and production of the right combination of outputs. *Right* is defined in terms of relative values, measured by society's willingness to pay (WTP).
2. *Dynamic efficiency* is a condition in which the economy is growing at the right rate (defined in terms of society's choice between present and future consumption).
3. *Distributional efficiency* is a condition in which general agreement exists that the output of society is equitably distributed.

Every economy ideally tends in the longer run toward this state of efficiency, the combined result of both market mechanisms and government intervention. In theory, if the market mechanism worked perfectly, the economy should find its state of efficiency. However national markets are not perfect (information flow is incomplete and nonuniform, competition is undermined by monopolistic practices, etc.). Consequently, the market fails in its role of efficient resource allocation. For most countries, small national markets allow large producers (those who apply modern, large-scale production technologies, or those who entered the market early and at low cost, while current high entry costs are a deterrent to later entrants) to gain monopolistic positions. Other reasons for market failure are the projects' external effects (*externalities*) and the existence of public goods that are difficult (if not impossible) to price.

Market failure gives justification for government to intervene in economic activities. Government involvement very often results in failure—the government's interventions are insufficient, excessive, or sometimes unnecessary, often dictated by political pressures of the moment. As a result of these market and government failures, allocation of national resources to their best theoretical use is not guaranteed.

The actual allocation is the best use that entrepreneurs envision under prevailing conditions in this imperfect market, which might be quite different from the theoretical optimum. The imperfect market, with its inefficiencies, could function during extended periods of time, seemingly quite normal to the citizens of the country, protected by customs barriers, taxes, subsidies, and controlled prices of some (or most, in centrally planned economies) products. In free-market economies, and even in some command economies, the inherited allocation, in particular, of capital resources is virtually impossible to alter through government intervention, so deeply entrenched are the forces that created it. What is possible to change, however, is the allocation of *incremental* resources (investment of the incremental capital stock of the country). Investment, in this case, should be guided not by visible signals from the market (local prices of products, resources, and material inputs into production), but rather by virtual prices better reflecting the hypothetical situation of a more competitive economy, including those of externalities engendered by the existence of the project.

A fundamental step in determining the economic value of the project is to convert financial prices to virtual prices of the *hypothetical free market,* where no producer enjoys monopolistic control over prices. The procedures for calculating the economic value of a project vary, depending on the methodology applied, two of which are described in this chapter and the next. There are, however, some common elements for most of the methodologies and the basic principles remain the same: a standard economic accounting unit (EAU) aligned with socioeconomic objectives; the impact of consumption or generation of a unit of resource expressed in the EAU; compilation of the magnitudes of resource flows and calculation of their composite effect expressed in the EAU; and comparison with criteria of acceptability.

Until recent times, economic analysis has been national in the sense that it dealt with everything that happened within borders and resulted in determinations of benefits and/or costs to the citizens of the host country. Globalization of economic activity reduces the importance of national borders; growing concerns for the global environment are changing the perspective on economic analysis of projects.

APPENDIX 5.2: GLOBAL PRICING FRAMEWORK— IMPORTABLE INPUT FORGONE

Figure 5.8 shows the distribution effects, based upon the global pricing framework, of forgoing an importable input in favor of domestic supply (import is precluded by quota). There are different possibilities for selecting the pricing framework in doing ECBA (see the earlier subsection "Pricing Bases"). The global point of view has almost all prices, except those clearly nontraded (or nontradable) at the international trade price. But there are other points of view. A system can be designed based upon national

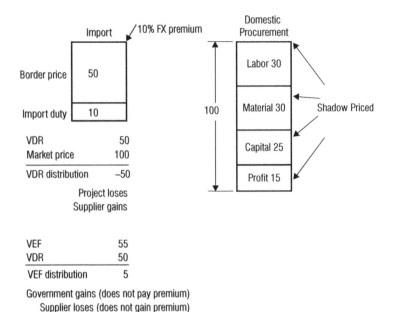

FIGURE 5.8 Global Pricing Framework—Importable Input Forgone

priorities, in which case some items are priced domestically even though they could be imported.

On the left side of Figure 5.8, the global perspective is selected: the difference between the domestic price and the international price is treated as a distortion with distribution effects. Applying the global pricing framework, the international price is 50 (all values expressed in domestic currency at official exchange rate). The premium on foreign exchange is 10 percent as a result of overvalued domestic currency (VEF = 50 × 1.1 = 55). The border (international) price (55) is the accounting price (VEF). The import duty (a transfer) is neither paid nor collected, representing a gain for the project (it pays 100, but would have paid 60 for the import) and a loss for the government. The net distribution effect is as follows:

	Supplier	Project	Government
VDR distribution	+50	−50	
VEF distribution	−5		+5
Import duties		+10	−10
Net distribution effect	+45	−40	−5

On the right side of the figure is the case where national priorities are the basis for pricing; the decision not to import is in accordance with government priorities. The input can be internalized (included as part of the project) because its production is wholly dependent on the existence of the project, priced, in this case, at domestic production cost (addition to supply). Its value of 100 can be decomposed into its constituents—labor 30, materials 30, capital 25, and profit 15—and each element appropriately shadow priced, including distribution effects.

NOTES

1. The concept of economic analysis has been employed in a financial context. *Economic value-added* is intended to measure *economic* profit of an enterprise, defined as *net profit after tax minus the opportunity cost of capital invested*. This estimates the excess (or deficit) of the rate of profit/capital invested relative to the minimum acceptable rate of return for shareholders.
2. Appendix 5.1 is a more thorough discussion of cost and benefits for revenue projects. A similar treatment of externalities applies to nonrevenue projects.
3. The government may offer incentives if the investment is beneficial for the economy but not necessarily attractive from the point of view of investors; or it may create impediments in the form of higher taxes and duties in certain areas for undesirable technologies if the project imposes social costs for the economy.
4. This and the subsequent chapter deal with methods of assessing economic impacts of the project's generation and consumption of real resources, and distribution effects related to real and financial resources. Economic and social impacts that are fiscally quantifiable should be an integral part of this analysis. Impacts that are nonquantifiable can be evaluated as part of environmental impact assessment (EIA), which is complementary to economic analysis.
5. A lower discount rate gives greater weight to future benefits—in other words, the present value of future benefits is greater as the discount rate is decreased.
6. In relation to the size of the economy.
7. Designated as *economic, accounting,* or *shadow* prices to distinguish them from market prices, in which the project's financial costs and benefits were estimated.
8. In the method of value-added analysis (VAA) presented, shadow or accounting prices, which take into account the opportunity cost of resources consumed and the impact on supply or demand for resources generated, are not considered. If shadow pricing were applied in VAA, the quantitative results should be similar, if not identical.
9. The actions of governments toward seeking more equitable distribution of wealth vary widely. Ideally, greater equity would be achieved through Pareto improvements, where changing allocation of resources that improves the condition of one person would not make anyone else worse off.

10. The criteria of government planning authorities in licensing or otherwise approving projects can be oriented to the solution of a particular economic, social, or ecological problem. For example, if there is chronic unemployment, projects that are more labor-intensive might be favored, although technological retardation may be a longer term concern.

11. UN Industrial Development Organization, *Guide to Practical Project Appraisal: Social Benefit-Cost in Developing Countries* (Vienna: UNIDO, 1986), 4.

12. For example, the hedonic pricing method attempts to impute values for environmental change by identifying their effect on the market price and price movements of economic resources. The level of environmental quality may be reflected, for example, in local housing prices or labor markets. Prices at different locations of these resources are assumed to reflect the implicit market value of the environmental variation.

13. Shadow prices are economic values of resources, which would prevail in a hypothetical undistorted market. Ideally, shadow prices are measures of the marginal change in an objective function resulting from change of available resource by one unit. They can usually be reasonably approximated (the so-called second-best approach) without resorting to an economic optimization model from which they theoretically derive. A social price reflects the distribution impacts of generation or consumption of the resource.

14. Social time preferences reflect the weight that society attaches to future as opposed to present consumption. For economic evaluation, time preferences are expressed by the social discount rate, which usually differs from the discount rate applied in financial analysis of projects.

15. M. Chervel and M. Le Gall, *Manual for Economic Evaluation of Projects* (Paris: Publisud, 1989), contains an extensive treatment of the value-added approach to economic analysis of projects based upon the *effects method*; see also M. Chervel, *L'évaluation Économique des Projets: Calculs Économiques Publics et Planification* (Paris: Publisud, 1987).

16. Economic efficiency refers to the growth objective, without accounting for distribution impacts on affected populations.

17. For example, in the cost-benefit approach labor is treated as a cost, whereas in the VAA method it is a benefit (part of the VA attributable to the project). However, the apparent discrepancy is corrected if shadow pricing is applied in each method. In cost-benefit analysis, repatriated payments, for example dividends paid to foreign shareholders, are excluded (treated as real outflow) from calculation of net benefits at efficiency prices (see Table 6.1). These payments (e.g., dividends to foreign investors) might also have distribution effects if the foreign currency value is distorted. In VAA, repatriated payments are deducted from net domestic VA (NDVA) to determine net national VA (NNVA). For this reason, if the project includes repatriated payments, the NNVA result rather than NDVA should more closely approximate the shadow pricing result at efficiency level.

18. *Economic analysis* is sometimes used interchangeably with *socioeconomic analysis*; the former generally refers to valuation at *economic efficiency* prices, while

the latter includes distribution effects and more general consideration of cultural and social factors.

19. The basis for optimization of resource utilization may be the locality (e.g., city), the nation (country), the region (e.g., an economic union), or the global economy.

20. More extensive discussion of economic pricing is found in the UNIDO *Guide* cited earlier, pages 22–27, and in the *Manual for the Evaluation of Industrial Projects*, prepared jointly by UNIDO and the Industrial Development Centre for Arab States (IDCAS) (Vienna: UNIDO, 1993), pages 54–58.

21. Shadow prices for more complex systems are determined with optimization programs. In linear systems, shadow prices are the values of dual variables associated with each resource constraint.

22. I. M. D. Little and J. A. Mirrlees, *Project Appraisal and Planning for Developing Countries* (London: Heinemann, 1974), 368.

23. UNIDO, *Guide to Practical Project Appraisal*, 20.

24. See J. D. Macarthur, "Estimating Efficiency Prices through Semi-Input-Output Methods: A Review of Practice in Available Studies," *Journal of International Development* 6 (1) (1994): 19–43.

25. Most descriptions of economic cost/benefit analysis (ECBA) use U.S. dollar and Indian rupiah in the foreign and local accounting unit, respectively, mainly for historical reasons and to acknowledge the contribution of Indian economists in developing ECBA.

26. If the accounting unit is based upon domestic market prices, any item involving a foreign currency *transaction* is converted by *adding* the foreign exchange premium (regardless of the currency used to express value and assuming an overvalued local currency). The exchange rate distortion is the difference between the value at the official and shadow exchange rates. If the accounting unit is based upon border prices, any item transacted in the domestic market is converted to border prices by *subtracting* the foreign exchange premium.

27. The method is similar to that of the UNIDO *Guide* but with significant differences, particularly regarding effects of income distribution.

28. Applying international market prices for economic value has a solid justification: International markets, due to their size, are more competitive than smaller national markets and therefore less susceptible to market imperfections (but nothing always works perfectly).

29. This is the aggregate amount realized by consumers as a consequence of price decreases resulting from the existence of the project as a supplier.

30. Little and Mirlees, *Project Appraisal*, 72.

31. An environmental impact assessment (EIA), for example, generally applies an ecological perspective of *society*, whereby effects of project operations on other species and habitats are taken into account.

32. This means the national level as defined by the host country's borders.

33. L. Squire and H. G. van der Tak, *Economic Analysis of Projects* (Washington, D.C., and Baltimore, MD: World Bank and Johns Hopkins Univ. Press, 1984), 32.

34. Interventions of governments include trade barriers or preferential treatment of some industries or sectors.
35. Decomposition may reveal traded components that should be priced at the border.
36. The border price means the international market price brought to the project level.
37. It may be prudent to confirm the validity of border prices as a measure of economic value. They should not be predicated on *dumping* practices—prices inconsistent with production factor costs of the exporter applied temporarily to gain market share, or wanton environmental degradation or exploitative labor practices.
38. The international price, FOB or CIF, is the amount of foreign exchange gained or expended.
39. This is the equivalent of the border price at the mine.
40. In this discussion, *transport* means shipping and handling charges, shadow priced as appropriate.
41. For further discussion see UNIDO/IDCAS, *Manual for the Evaluation of Industrial Projects*, 57.
42. If the local currency is overvalued, imports can appear less expensive from the commercial viewpoint while actually more expensive economically.
43. UNIDO/IDCAS, *Manual*, 58.
44. Whether *willingness to pay* is an adequate approximation of the accounting price should be investigated. Conditions for a relatively free market should prevail: (1) The good is freely available; (2) no customer exerts buyer's monopoly power; (3) marginal change in supply (increase or decrease) does not affect the price; (4) no suppliers of inputs that are necessary to produce the good realizes monopoly profits through artificially inflated prices. If these conditions do not apply, attempts should be made to estimate economic value in the absence of the identified distorting constraint(s).
45. Collecting information on the cost of displaced production may present difficulties. Estimates can be obtained from reports or studies of similar operations. If the displaced competitor is a publicly traded company, information may be available from annual reports, or from the reports of similar companies.
46. Squire and van der Tak, *Economic Analysis*, 33.
47. If the supply or demand elasticity is nonzero and if supply and demand relationships are known (this information is often difficult to obtain), consumer and producer surpluses (incremental areas under demand and supply curves) should be considered. If the price of output is reduced with increased production, some consumers will pay less than they would have (and continue to be willing to pay) without the project. If prices of inputs increase with increased consumption, some efficient suppliers will realize prices higher than what they accepted without the project, and would still be willing to accept.
48. By definition, the border (accounting) price is FOB or CIF, corrected for domestic transportation and handling costs.
49. At the level of economic efficiency, units of measure other than income could conceivably be employed. For example, the output could be measured directly

in terms of its contribution to a national security indicator or in net energy units.

50. Including Squire and van der Tak, *Economic Analysis*, 83; and Little and Mirlees, *Project Appraisal.*

51. Wages are included as part of *value-added*, but repatriated wages are deducted because they are expended outside national boundaries.

52. Asian Development Bank, *Guidelines for the Economic Analysis of Projects* (ADB, 1997), 125; inflow of capital is considered a factor distorting the exchange rate.

53. This includes territories over which the national government has dominion.

54. W. A. Ward and B. J. Deren, *The Economics of Project Analysis: A Practitioner's Guide* (Washington, D.C.: World Bank, 1993).

REFERENCES

Dasgupta, Parth, S. Marglin, and Amartya Sen. 1972. *Guidelines for project evaluation.* Vienna: UNIDO.

Hansen, John R. 1986. *Guide to practical project appraisal: Social benefit-cost in developing countries.* Vienna: UNIDO.

Little, I. M. D., and J. A. Mirrlees. 1974. *Project appraisal and planning for developing countries.* London: Heinemann Educational Books.

Londero, E. 2003. *Shadow prices for project appraisal: Theory and practice.* Cheltenham, Glos, UK: Edward Elgar Publishing.

Macarthur, J. D. 1994. Estimating efficiency prices through semi-input-output methods: A review of practice in available studies. *Journal of International Development* 6 (1), 19–43.

Sen, Amartya. 1985. *Resources, values and development.* Reprint, Cambridge: Harvard University Press, 1997.

Souto, G. 2001. *Los precios sombra en España a partir del sistema input-output.* Madrid: Hacienda Pública Española.

Squire, L., and H. G. van der Tak. 1975. *Economic Analysis of Projects.* IBRD staff working paper 194. Washington D.C.: World Bank.

UNIDO and IDCAS. 1993. *Manual for Evaluation of Industrial Projects.* Vienna: UNIDO.

Ward, W. A., and B. J. Deren. 1993. *The economics of project analysis: A practitioner's guide.* Washington D.C.: World Bank.

CHAPTER 6

Economic Cost/Benefit Analysis

I t is axiomatic that when assessing any opportunity, its benefits should exceed its costs. From the commercial perspective the issue is rather straightforward. When considering the project in the context of its wider domain, benefits and costs are not so readily identified or valued. As discussed in the previous chapter, the framework of economic optimization in which the project is to be assessed (e.g., regional, national, global) determines to some extent how resources are to be priced. Other factors enter the picture, such as tradability and additions to, or subtractions from, supply or demand.

Economic cost/benefit analysis (ECBA) is a method of systematically organizing and evaluating resource flows and other project impacts from the economic perspective that measures the project's impact on goals in the economy of interest, such as change in gross national product (GNP), gross consumption, balance of payments, employment, or security. The approach described in this chapter is based upon the project's impact on consumption (GNP, or national income, converted to consumption equivalent) as the accounting unit (AU). As a result of commercial analysis, flows of resources generated and consumed directly by the project are identified and priced at the market, then typically converted from market prices to their economic equivalents—prices that reflect the impact on socioeconomic indicators. Distribution effects and other external consequences are taken into account. The incremental economic impact of the project is measured as the difference with and without project implementation, not necessarily identical with the difference between before and after. All project-induced activities within the bounds of the economic domain of interest (delimited geographically to locality, nation, region, world) are included: resources employed in moving output to a port, upstream and downstream additions or reductions, as well as and social and environmental consequences.

The main elements applicable to ECBA—economic costs and benefits resulting from the project's direct and external generation and consumption of resources, their significance, and justification for inclusion—were presented in the previous chapter. They can be used in different combinations to estimate economic impacts. The problem is now to decide on how to use the ingredients to "cook" a method to be applied to the project, taking into account conditions in the country, region, or other geographically delimited area in which it will produce economic consequences. Methods of analysis designed by international or national development organizations can be applied directly or, more appropriately in most cases, simplified and/or adapted.

In the approach described herein, benefits and costs are first aggregated at economic efficiency prices, in terms of change in uncommitted income. This is a means to evaluate the project's contribution to the *growth* objective (e.g., increase in gross domestic product). An additional effect is distribution of income as it flows into savings, with its impact on future consumption, and into direct consumption. This level of analysis employs essentially subjective weights to value distribution of income flows and consumption among social groups, to measure effects of the project on the *equity* objective. Adjustments may be applied to reflect the degree of the project's conformance with national or regional goals. Production of *merit* goods tends to enhance, and *demerit* goods to diminish, project value. The process is illustrated in Figure 6.1. In the final stages, sensitivity analysis is applied to gauge possible variations in the outcome as a result of uncertainties. Economic appraisal (more precisely socio-economic appraisal in this context) involves comparison of economic net present value (NPV) and internal rate of return (IRR), as well

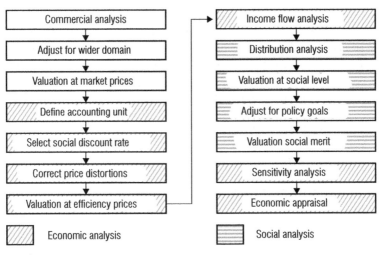

FIGURE 6.1   ECBA Process

as supplementary efficiency indicators (see the section titled "Supplementary Indicators" later in this chapter) with criteria.

ADJUSTMENTS FOR THE WIDER DOMAIN

The range of concerns relevant to economic analysis expands beyond the commercial domain. Impacts of economically linked upstream and downstream activities, as well as environmental and social impacts, are included in the analysis (see Figure 1.1). Those that can only be assessed qualitatively are addressed separately. The real and financial consequences of these external impacts might be added to those of the project and included in all further stages of economic analysis.

In the Cambria Yarns Project, directly related agricultural activity is included in the analysis (i.e., *internalized*). Changing production from sorghum to cotton involves changes in farmer income. Imports are increased, local supply of agricultural inputs decreases, and there are adverse environmental impacts from increased use of pesticides.

VALUATION AT MARKET PRICES

Valuation of the project at market prices (the project's financial cash flow) is a point of reference for economic analysis. The flows of inputs and outputs at market prices are divided into *real* and *financial* flows. Real flows are those concerned with resources—goods and services generated and consumed by the project. Flows related to financing (e.g., equity, grants, debt, and other obligations) are relevant only to the extent that they affect distribution aspects. Both types of flows may involve distortions that are relevant to *social analysis*, but for analysis at the *economic efficiency* level, only real flows are relevant.

Real and Financial Flows—CYP

An example from the Cambria Yarns Project of the separation of project flows into real and financial components *at market prices* is illustrated in Tables 6.1a and 6.1b. Information is drawn from Tables 2.17a and b (real and financial flows) in Chapter 2. Table 6.1a is then modified to identify items with market distortions. All *real* (as opposed to financial) project flows are listed that require adjustment to remove distortions both for price imperfections and for foreign exchange. Real items not requiring adjustments are aggregated as "Other real outflows." Domestic sales are priced economically as "willingness to pay" (WTP), the local demand price. In Table 6.1b only those financial items affecting distribution are included. In our web site version of Tables 6.1a and b the spreadsheet links with Tables 2.17a and b are eliminated; only the values are shown. For working capital items, only the foreign exchange portion of the initial buildup in year 2 (no financial items are included) requires adjustment. A portion of the increase in accounts receivable (a financial flow) in year 3 (about 53 percent of the value is in foreign exchange) is covered with the IFC foreign exchange loan disbursement. Other working capital items are not included in Table 6.1b because they are financial flows that have no impact on the economic evaluation at the level of economic efficiency.

Financial flows—principal, capitalized interest, and equity as inflows, and domestic dividends and income tax as outflows—are included in Table 6.1b only to provide a foundation for shadow pricing with regard to distribution effects. They are not included in the net flow for valuation at efficiency prices because their conversion factors $CF = 0$ (which is the same as the adjustment factor $AF = -100$ percent). Flows in Tables 6.1a and b are the basis for calculation of economic NPV and IRR at market prices.

For the purpose of economic analysis, agricultural impacts in converting farmland from sorghum to cotton production are internalized, even though farms are independent operations (see CYP on our web site for detailed discussion). From the economic perspective it is more appropriate to view integrated agriculture and yarn production as the entity of interest.

Agriculture—CYP

Impacts of conversion to cotton production, per hectare of converted land, are shown in Table 6.2. The incremental effect at market prices is *with-project* minus *without-project*. The incremental value with distortion removed (VDR) and the value adjusted for foreign exchange (VEF), or value at economic efficiency level, are shown for each input and output. Domestic content comprises materials (50 percent), capital (30 percent), and labor (20 percent). The market price of materials and capital fully reflects the VDR; the VDR converstion factor (CF_{VDR}) for labor is 0.5. The overall CF_{VDR} for domestic content is 0.9. Incremental imports are priced at the border (adjusted for foreign exchange premium). Runoff impact is expressed in economic prices. Imports are adjusted to reflect the 25 percent premium for foreign exchange.

The quantity of cotton required is based upon a yield of 79 percent (21 percent cotton waste). To produce 4,480 tons of cotton yarns requires 5,671 tons of raw cotton (4,480/0.79). With an expected average yield of

TABLE 6.1a Real Flows at Market Prices—CYP, US$(000)

Percent of nominal capacity				91.7	101.4	100.0		100.0
					Year			
	%FX	1	2	3	4	5	...	10
Total real flows		(11,462.1)	(24,125.2)	3,220.4	8,442.5	6,360.3		15,743.5
Real flows—project		(11,462.1)	(24,125.2)	4,496.5	9,853.7	7,751.9		17,135.2
Inflows		0.0	0.0	12,663.9	16,260.2	16,260.2		16,260.2
Total net sales				12,663.9	16,260.2	16,260.2		16,260.2
Export	100.0			6,711.8	13,423.2	13,423.2		13,423.2
Domestic	0.0			5,952.1	2,837.0	2,837.0		2,837.0
Outflows		11,462.1	24,125.2	8,167.3	6,406.5	8,508.3		(875.0)
Land development	0.0							
Raw materials	0.0			3,394.6	3,826.9	3,788.7		3,788.7
Auxiliary materials	91.7			729.1	821.9	813.7		813.7
Unskilled labor	0.0			195.1	218.2	216.2		216.2
Spare parts consumed	100.0			373.2	373.2	373.2		373.2
Energy	0.0			401.4	448.6	444.4		444.4
Expatriate staff	100.0			290.0	290.0	100.0		0.0
Materials, services, insurance	73.5			52.0	52.0	52.0		52.0
Materials, services, etc.	62.0			93.6	93.6	93.6		93.6
Distribution—export	100.0			578.3	1,156.7	1,156.7		1,156.7
Fixed assets—F	100.0	9,373.3	20,447.5	0.0	0.0	0.0		0.0
Preoperational expenditures—F	100.0	446.5	2,384.4					
Initial working capital—F	100.0		258.0					
Dividends paid, FX[1]	100.0			0.0	396.9	477.7		1,357.8
Other real outflows[2,3]	0.0	1,642.4	1,035.3	2,059.9	(1,271.4)	992.2		(9,171.2)

(Continued)

313

TABLE 6.1a (*Continued*)

Percent of nominal capacity	%FX	1	2	3	4	5	...	10
					Year			
				91.7	101.4	100.0		100.0
Real flows—agriculture[4]		0.0	0.0	(1,276.2)	(1,411.2)	(1,391.7)		(1,391.7)
Output				2,459.0	2,719.1	2,681.5		2,681.5
Imports	100.0			2,494.6	2,758.4	2,720.3		2,720.3
Domestic content[5]	0.0			(377.0)	(416.9)	(411.1)		(411.1)
Total operating cost				2,117.5	2,341.5	2,309.2		2,309.2
Farmers' surplus[6]	0.0			341.4	377.5	372.3		372.3
Pesticide runoff impact				(1,617.6)	(1,788.7)	(1,764.0)		(1,764.0)

[1] Foreign partner NTC repatriates 80 percent of dividend distributions.

[2] Sum of all real flows for which shadow price equals market price, excluding capitalized interest in year 2 (not a real flow), but including land lease payments that are considered "economic rent."

[3] Value in year 10 includes residual value of fixed assets and real components of working capital (financial components of working capital deducted).

[4] Benefit is incremental (difference with and without project).

[5] Diminished domestic content at financial level is an economic gain, reduces total operating cost.

[6] Incremental farmers' surplus generated as a result of the project, which is internalized (integrated into project).

TABLE 6.1b Financial Flows at Market Prices—CYP, US$(000)

Percent of nominal capacity				91.7	101.4	100.0		100.0
				Year				
	%FX	1	2	3	4	5	...	10
Financial flows[1]								
Inflows								
Proceeds from long-term loans	100.0	0.0	23,089.9	1,260.9				
Capitalized interest	100.0		1,154.5	0.0				
Equity NIC	100.0	9,819.8	0.0	0.0				
Equity CIL	100.0	1,642.4	1,035.3	0.0				
Outflows								
Dividends paid, domestic	100.0			0.0	99.2	119.4		339.5
Corporate tax	100.0			0.0	0.0	0.0		1,454.8
Increase (decrease) in A/R[2]	100.0			1,195.3				
Repayment principal, long-term loan[3]	100.0			0.0	0.0	4,250.9		4,250.9
Interest and other financing, long-term loan[3]	100.0			2,487.5	2,550.5	2,550.5		425.1
NPV market		(1,393.8)						
IRR market		9.2%						

[1]Financial totals not shown as they are not relevant to economic analysis—included only for analysis of distortions.

[2]In year 3, 53 percent of accounts receivable are covered with foreign exchange IFC loan; no additional distribution effect.

[3]Debt service on IFC FX loan applied as cost of assets procured with these funds, including increase in FX receivables of US$1,195.3 in year 3.

0.45 tons per hectare, about 12,600 hectares will have to be converted to cotton production. The price of raw cotton has been estimated from an analysis of historical price movements and trends, in a manner similar to that for finished product. The price, delivered to the factory gate, is estimated at the local equivalent of US$668 per ton. Values related to conversion of the 12,600 hectares required are presented in Table 6.2 (also see the later subsection "Conversion from Market to Efficiency Prices," the discussion concerning raw cotton).

The change in net income of farmers is considered a distribution effect, or a surplus of US$45.5 per hectare with the project compared with US$15.95 for presently grown sorghum, an increment of US$29.55 per hectare.

In Tables 6.1a and b, farmers' revenues (inflow) from cotton sales are balanced by the value of cotton purchased from farmers by the project (outflow). As agricultural activities are internalized, ordinarily these two values would be equal; however, the latter is reduced by the value of forgone sorghum production. The net economic agricultural impacts are summarized in "VDR—CYP" later in this chapter

TABLE 6.2 Agricultural Impacts of Conversion from Sorghum to Cotton Production—CYP, US$ per Hectare

	With Project	Without Project	Incremental Effect	VDR	VEF	FX Premium
Output per hectare	300.60	87.78	212.82	212.82	212.82	0.00
Imports	226.10	10.20	215.90	215.90	269.88	53.98
Domestic content[1]	29.00	61.63	(32.63)	(29.37)	(29.37)	0.00
Total operating cost	255.10	71.83	183.27	186.53	240.51	53.98
Farmers' surplus	45.50	15.95	29.55			
Adverse environmental						0.00
impacts[2]	150.00	10.00	140.00	140.00	140.00	0.00
Net impact	(104.50)	5.95	(110.45)			
Farmers' surplus[3]	45.50	15.95	29.55			

[1] VDR of domestic content: materials (50 percent) and capital (30 percent) at market price; labor (20 percent) – CF = 0.5; overall CF = 0.9.

[2] Includes agricultural runoff and emissions from the plant.

[3] Farmers gain incremental surplus of 29.95; the project is considered beneficiary of the foreign exchange premium.

DEFINE THE ACCOUNTING UNIT

The accounting unit (AU) is selected to express economic value of inputs and outputs in terms of economic objectives (common denominator). If growth alone is the objective, the AU would best be expressed in terms of uncommitted income, adjusted for price distortions (including foreign exchange). When social impacts are of concern to decision makers, the AU is more appropriately expressed in terms of consumption.

Accounting Unit—CYP

In the Cambria Yarns Project (on our web site), the planning agency (Ministry of Planning) is the licensing authority. Approval with concessions is available to the project if it is consistent with national goals, which are oriented toward improving the distribution of wealth in the country. The Ministry insists on a unit of measure that reflects its social objectives, so the corresponding AU is selected for the project analysis. It expresses benefits and costs in terms of present value of consumption at constant domestic market prices, taking into account the distribution effects of the project among social groups (referenced to the base level of consumption) and the savings impact.

Economic Discount Rate

There is, in general, a difference between the financial and the social cost of capital, the discount rate appropriate for economic appraisal of projects. Just as the discount rate for financial analysis is fundamentally the market-based cost of capital, an economic discount rate (EDR) is the cost of deferred benefits—that is, the rate at which future benefits are discounted to their present equivalent. The rate has to be consistent with the selected accounting unit (AU). A common basis is society's willingness to trade present consumption for future consumption.[1]

The EDR is applied to determine economic NPV. As a general rule, the EDR is a parameter that is applied uniformly to all projects in the country for consistent comparisons, although it may comprise a weighted average of several components (e.g., private, public, foreign investment) as specified by the planning authority.[2] The investment program in the country can be fine-tuned in the economic framework, raising or lowering the barrier by adjusting the EDR, perhaps in response to capital or other constraints as determined by the decision-making authority (planning, if it exists).[3] In most cases, *this is the most practical means of determining an appropriate EDR.*

If not specified by the planning authority, selection of the EDR is left to the discretion of the licensing authorities, if applicable, and to stakeholders if no external guidance is available.[4]

For public-sector projects (primarily infrastructure), the EDR might be set at a very low rate, even close to zero, as government backing lowers risk as compared with private sector projects. Lowering the discount is also a means for the government to direct resources toward favored regions or sectors. For some public sector projects, future benefits might be considered as valuable as present consumption. A costly flood prevention project, with benefits expressed in avoided damage at some unknown date in the future, would probably never be implemented if economic indicators (NPV, IRR) were calculated applying a discount anywhere near market rates. Of the three components that normally comprise the discount rate (risk-free rate, inflation, and risk), if the risk component is negligible (for example, in case of a stable investment environment), when applying constant price analysis, only the risk-free rate would remain.

In the ECBA method described, all benefits and costs are converted to consumption equivalents, so the consumption rate of interest (CRI) would ideally be used to discount future net benefits, but it is not easily determined.[5] One way to try to determine the appropriate EDR is to deduce it empirically from the history of project selections. The EDR is the discount rate at which projects become acceptable. The economic rates of return (EIRR) for projects that have been accepted and rejected can be determined and examined for a pattern that would reveal the cutoff rate.

For a public-sector project, financed with public funds, the EDR would be based upon the government's assessment of its opportunity cost with respect to national goals. In other words, if an alternative project has an economic rate of return of X%, this project should be "challenged" with at least that discount rate.

A standard premium (lowering the discount rate) can be applied to the domestic cost of capital as a spur to investment. Perhaps the most practical approach to setting the EDR is to start with the actual cost in capital markets (marginal return on capital) and adjust for the prevailing economic conditions. The basic relationship is:

$$EDR = C_c - pr$$

where C_c = market cost of capital
pr = premium for domestic investment projects

The premium can be set according to the existing and predicted states of the economy. When demand for capital is strong (e.g., a predicted high rate of economic growth), the barrier can be set higher by lowering the premium. When the economy is weak, the rate can be lowered (higher premium). In other words, the *discount rate is adjusted to clear all available investment capital.* By setting the hurdle rate at a certain level, only those projects that meet this criterion are selected, weeding out those that are of lesser importance from the economic perspective. In relating the EDR to capital markets, a consistent approach requires setting a uniform premium and applying it for the project under consideration, taking into account international and domestic components of the capital structure.

In the Cambria Yarns Projects, the Ministry of Planning has set a premium of 5 percent for the domestic portion of capital, reducing the cost of CIL equity from 12 percent to 7 percent. Although the financial cost of capital (weighted average, total investment) is 8.6 percent (see Table 4.2), predicated on the after-tax cost of debt reduced from 10 percent to 7 percent, this reduction does not apply to economic analysis, as the true cost of the foreign loan is the total foreign exchange used to service the debt. The weighted EDR to be applied is 10.2 percent, as illustrated in Table 6.3.

Conversion from Market to Efficiency Prices

Converting from market to economic efficiency prices (revenues and costs) is most conveniently accomplished in a two-step process. First, market prices are converted to value with distortions removed (VDR)—that is, all distortions other than foreign exchange are removed. Second, VDRs are adjusted for foreign exchange content and shadow exchange rate to determine VEF.

Values with Distortion Removed (VDR)   Items are selected for shadow pricing as discussed in the subsection "Applicability of Accounting Prices" in Chapter 5. Those not in need of shadow pricing are included at their market

TABLE 6.3   Weighted EDR—CYP, Percent

	% Total Investment	Capital Amount, US$(000)	Rate, %	Adjusted Rate, %	Weighted Values
Debt (IFC loan)	67.1	25,505	10.0	10.0	6.7
Equity (NTC)	25.8	9,820	12.0	12.0	3.1
Equity (CIL)	7.0	2,678	12.0	7.0	0.5
	100.0	38,003		Weighted EDR	10.3

values. Distortions are determined for real flows and for relevant financial flows, although only real flows are included in the measure of economic efficiency.

Market prices are adjusted for imposed (e.g., taxes, subsidies) or structural (e.g., monopolistic pricing) distortions. Some of the adjusted prices may be national or regional parameters (e.g., shadow price of labor, shadow price of foreign exchange). Border prices are applied for main traded goods and services, adjusted for the shadow price of foreign exchange.[6]

VDR—CYP   In the Cambria Yarns Project, some of the real and financial flows of Tables 6.1a and b are adjusted, considering their significance to the outcome of the analysis. Market prices of all other items are assumed to reflect their economic values ($CF_{VDR} = 1.0$ and no FX adjustment).

- *Land.* The project is to be constructed on a prepared site in an industrial estate. The land used for the project has essentially the following economic cost components: (1) opportunity cost of forgone use when applied to industrial activity, (2) general infrastructure development costs, and (3) project-specific site development costs.

  The government developed the industrial estate and the specific site selected for the express purpose of locating industrial enterprises, in accord with its plans for the region. It intends to recover these costs in the form of *economic rent,* by arranging leases with occupants of the industrial estate that are intended to compensate the government for its investment.[7] According to a lease agreement, the project will pay for 45,000 square meters at US$0.45 per square meter, which is included in operating costs. As economic rent, the lease payment to the government of US$20,300 is treated as a real flow in the economic analysis (included in "Other real flows" in Table 6.1a).

  Project-specific site development cost of US$150,000 (see Table 6.4a), including the installation of infrastructure services, is essentially a subsidy from the government to the project. The VDR distribution is the full value of this subsidy.

- *Export sales.*[8] Export sales are priced at FOB. Inland transfer costs are included as marketing costs so no further adjustment to FOB is necessary to convert to border price.

- *Raw cotton.* In the economic analysis, cost of raw cotton production is internalized as an activity directly related to the existence of, and integral with, the project. Internal impacts from the conversion of the 12,600 hectares of farmland from sorghum to cotton production, as reflected in Table 6.4a are as follows:

  1. Increased cotton production.
  2. Elimination of sorghum production.[9]

3. Decreased consumption of locally available domestic resources (domestic content).
4. Increased imports of machinery and materials.
5. Increase in farmers' revenues—a distribution effect.
6. Adverse external environmental impact on the local area in the form of runoff of agricultural chemicals to the river that flows through the area.

■ *Auxiliary materials.* Auxiliary materials are priced at CIF and adjusted by the shadow exchange rate (SER). Import duties of 25 percent are imposed on the CIF price of imported materials, so the VDR conversion factor is 0.80 (1/1.25 = 0.8).

■ *Energy.* The energy price does not reflect the economic cost of production and distribution of energy, which is 20 percent higher than the price to consumers.

■ *Labor, unskilled.* This is estimated at 50 percent of market wage.

■ *Imported capital items.* Fixed assets, preoperational expenditures, and initial working capital are financed with a foreign currency loan from the IFC in the amount of US$23,089.9 in year 2.[10] This loan is tied directly to the project and would not be available for other investment in Cambria. For this reason, the *economic cost of these investment items is the foreign exchange debt service payments* (principal and interest). A second disbursement in year 3 ($1,260.9) is planned to cover finished product and work-in-progress inventory (US$42.8 and US$22.8 respectively), as well as receivables in the amount of US$1,195.2 (all figures in US$000).

■ *Inventories.* Increments of material inventories are included in "Other real outflows" because no adjustment is required. Increments of product inventories are included in factory cost and its underlying elements and adjusted accordingly.

■ *Imported goods and services.* The project consumes goods and services priced in foreign currency—spare parts, expatriate staff, materials and services, and export distribution services. No VDR adjustment is necessary.

■ *Foreign equity.* The project receives foreign equity from NTC. At the VDR level no adjustment is necessary. However, the project gains the foreign exchange premium on foreign equity, which represents a loss to the equity provider.

■ *Dividends.* Foreign dividends are considered an economic cost, so are treated as real outflows.[11] There is also a distribution effect if the SER is not equal to the official exchange rate (OER). As local currency is overvalued, dividends paid in foreign exchange represent a gain to the project and a loss to the government, which pays the premium.[12] To reflect the distributional effect of dividends paid to nationals, the conversion factor at the VDR level $CF_{VDR} = 0$. The project loses and the external sector gains (effects on the external sector are not included in the distributional analysis—see Tables 6.9 and 6.10).

- *Taxes.* Taxes are treated as a transfer from the project to the government.[13] The conversion factor is zero.
- *Agriculture.* Distribution effects at VDR level are attributable to the elimination of sorghum production, reduced domestic content, and the incremental farmer's revenues.

VDR level calculation results are shown in Tables 6.4a and 6.4b. These are the relevant market values of Tables 6.1a and b (Table 6.2 for incremental agriculture items) adjusted for price distortions. "Net flow—VDR" is the sum of real flows related to the project and to agriculture. The result of removing distortions other than FX is shown in Table 6.4a, where "Real net flow—VDR" is the sum of flows for the project itself and agriculture flows attributed to it. At this level (see Table 6.4b), economic NPV is negative (2,664.5) and the economic IRR (EIRR) is about 5.5 percent.

Value at Efficiency Price (VEF—with Adjustments for SER)

The final step in determining economic efficiency value (VEF) is to convert VDR values by adjusting for foreign exchange content. Only the foreign exchange content of each item is converted by multiplying it by the *conversion factor for foreign exchange* (CF_{VEF}). For items with partial foreign exchange content the conversion is effected as follows:[14]

$$VEF = VDR^*(1 - f) + VDR(f)CF_{VEF}$$

where f = foreign content (percent)
CF_{VEF} = conversion factor for foreign exchange, *SER/OER*

VEF—CYP In the case of the Cambria Yarns Project, the shadow exchange rate is estimated to be 25 percent higher than the official exchange rate (overvalued domestic currency), so foreign exchange flows (value of imports) are adjusted upward by this percentage to convert to VDR to VEF. The adjustment factor AF_{VFX} is 0.25, which represents the distortion related to the shadow rate of foreign exchange.

$$CF_{VEF} = \frac{SER}{OER} = \frac{1.25}{1} = 1.25$$
$$AF_{VEF} = CF_{VEF} - 1 = 1.25 - 1 = 0.25$$

TABLE 6.4a Real Flows—VDR, US$(000)

Percent of full production level					91.7	101.4	100.0		100.0
						Year			
	CF^{TM}	%FX	1	2	3	4	5	...	10
Real net flow—VDR			(11,612.1)	(1,293.3)	858.3	6,108.2	(232.6)		11,276.1
Real project flows—VDR			(11,612.1)	(1,293.3)	2,172.1	7,561.2	1,200.2		12,708.9
Inflows					12,663.9	16,260.2	16,260.2		16,260.2
Export	1.00	100.0			6,711.8	13,423.2	13,423.2		13,423.2
Domestic sales[1]		0.0			5,952.1	2,837.0	2,837.0		2,837.0
Outflows			11,612.1	1,293.3	10,491.7	8,699.0	15,060.0		3,551.3
Land development[2]	1.00	0.0	150.0	1,293.3					
Raw materials[3]	1.00	0.0			3,394.6	3,826.9	3,788.7		3,788.7
Auxiliary materials[4]	0.80	92.0			583.3	583.3	583.3		583.3
Unskilled labor[5]	0.50	0.0			97.6	109.1	108.1		108.1
Spare parts consumed	1.00	100.0			373.2	373.2	373.2		373.2
Energy[6]	1.20	0.0			481.7	538.3	533.3		533.3
Expatriate staff	1.00	100.0			290.0	290.0	100.0		
Materials, services, insurance, etc.	1.00	73.0			52.0	52.0	52.0		52.0
Materials, services, etc.	1.00	62.0			93.6	93.6	93.6		93.6
Distribution—export	1.00	100.0			578.3	1,156.7	1,156.7		1,156.7
Foreign loan principal[7]	—	100.0			0.0	0.0	4,250.9		4,250.9
Foreign loan interest[7]	—	100.0			2,487.5	2,550.5	2,550.5		425.1
Fixed assets—F[8]	1.00	100.0	9,373.3	0.0					
Preproduction expenditures—F[8]	1.00	100.0	446.5	0.0					

(*Continued*)

TABLE 6.4a (Continued)

Percent of full production level	CF[TM]	%FX	1	2	3	4	5	...	10
					91.7	101.4	100.0		100.0
						Year			
Initial working capital—F[8]	1.00	100.0		258.0					1,357.8
Dividends paid FX	0.00	100.0			0.0	396.9	477.7		(9,171.2)
Other real outflows	1.00		1,642.4	1,035.3	2,059.9	(1,271.4)	992.2		(1,432.8)
Real agriculture flows—VDR					(1,319.9)	(1,452.8)	(1,432.8)		(1,432.8)
Output	1.00				2,459.0	2,719.1	2,681.5		2,681.5
Imports[9]	1.00	100.0			2,494.6	2,758.4	2,720.3		2,720.3
Domestic content[10]	0.90	0.0			(339.3)	(375.2)	(370.0)		(370.0)
Farmers' surplus	0.00	0.0			303.7	335.9	331.2		331.2
Pesticide runoff impact	1.00	0.0			(1,617.6)	(1,788.7)	(1,764.0)		(1,764.0)

[1] Although domestic sales could be exported, the VDR accounting price is taken as the domestic price because it accords with national development policy; therefore, there is no distribution effect for consumers.

[2] Land developed by government—subsidy to project.

[3] Cotton price reflects economic value; as farm operations are internalized, the outflow is partially canceled by the output (inflow to agriculture); the difference is the foregone revenues from sorghum production.

[4] Duty on imported materials is 25 percent; CF = 1/1.25 = 0.8.

[5] Total unskilled labor cost.

[6] Energy production cost 20 percent higher than price.

[7] Debt service for IFC foreign exchange loan to cover capital assets in year 2 (FA 20447.5; PPE 2384.4; WC 258.0) and WC increments in year 3 (PRODUCTS 65.6; AR 1195.2).

[8] See note 7 for foreign capital items in year 2.

[9] Imports are incremental values from Table 6.3 adjusted for production levels in years 3 and 4.

[10] VDR of domestic content: materials (50 percent) and capital (30 percent)—market; labor (20 percent)—CF = 0.2; overall CF = 0.9.

TABLE 6.4b Financial Flows—VDR, US$(000)

Percent of full production level						91.7	101.4	100.0		100.0
	CF$_{VDR}$	%FX	1	2	3	4	5	...	10
							Year			
Financial flows—VDR										
Inflows										
Equity NIC	1.00	100.0	9,819.8							
Outflows										
Dividends paid, domestic	0.00	0.0			0.0	0.0	0.0		0.0
Corporate tax[1]	0.00	0.0			0.0	0.0	0.0		0.0
Repayment principal, long-term[2]	1.00	100.0			0.0	0.0	4,250.9		4,250.9
Interst and other finance charges, long-term[2]	1.00	100.0			2,487.5	2,550.5	2,550.5		425.1
NFV VDR	(2,664.5)									
IRR VDR	5.5%									

[1]Tax holiday years 3 through 6.
[2]Debt service on IFC FX loan applied as cost of assets procured with these funds, including increase in FX receivables of US$1195.3 in year 3.

The results for the cotton project are shown in Table 6.5a and Table 6.5b. The foreign exchange content of all items at VDR level is multiplied by the factor $CF_{VFX} = 1.25$. The result is the net flow at economic efficiency prices after adjustments for the foreign exchange premium (VEF). The net flow of Table 6.5a is the sum of real flows adjusted for the foreign exchange effect (real project flows including agriculture—financial flows not included). At this level, when discounted at the EDR of 10.3 percent (see Table 6.3), the economic NPV is negative (i.e., $-2,999.5$) and the IRR_{VEF}, before considering distribution and other effects, is 5.8 percent (see Table 6.5b and Figure 6.2).

Net real flows, valued at the VDR level (Table 6.4a) and with adjustment for the shadow exchange rate (Table 6.5a), are discounted at the EDR to determine economic NPV and IRR. The values represent the total effects of the project, with internalized agriculture and externalities. NPV at market prices, VDR and VEF levels are shown in Figure 6.2. Distribution effects for savings and direct consumption are also shown.

Income Flow Analysis

Distorted prices reflect contribution to distribution objectives of the government when prices are either controlled or the result of monopolistic market structures. These distortions, determined as the difference between project costs (or revenues) expressed in market and efficiency prices, are incremental distribution effects. *Price distortions* (economic benefits or costs over/below market prices) and distortions related to currency exchange rates (shadow price of foreign exchange, or SER) are taken into account in income flow analysis to determine distribution effects related to inputs and outputs attributable to the project.

Providers and consumers of goods and services would be appropriately charged or compensated for their economic cost or contribution at efficiency prices. It would be inappropriate to include the full cost of wages, for example, in the labor distribution adjustment, as the distribution impact of the project is only the difference between the market wage and the shadow price of labor.

Distortions in real and financial flows are included in the income flow analysis. The total distortion in market prices for each relevant flow of resources and funds is the sum of distortions identified in the VDR and VEF adjustment processes:

$$VDR \text{ distortion} = VDR - MV$$

$$VFX \text{ distortion} = VDR(f)AF_{VFX}$$

where MV = market value
AF_{VFX} = adjustment factor for foreign exchange

TABLE 6.5a Real Flows—VEF, US$(000)

	%FX	1	2	3	4	5	...	10
Percent of full capacity				91.7	101.4	100.0		100.0
FX conversion factor, CF$_{VEF}$ = 1.25								
					Year			
Net flow—economic efficiency		(14,067.1)	(1,357.8)	822.6	7,425.0	58.1		11,903.2
Adjusted for SER project		(14,067.1)	(1,357.8)	2,760.1	9,567.4	2,171.0		14,016.0
Inflows				14,341.8	19,616.0	19,616.0		19,616.0
Export	100.0			8,389.7	16,779.0	16,779.0		16,779.0
Domestic sales	0.0		1,357.8	5,952.1	2,837.0	2,837.0		2,837.0
Outflows		14,067.1		11,581.7	10,048.5	17,445.0		5,600.0
Land development	0.0	150.0						
Raw materials	0.0			3,394.6	3,826.9	3,788.7		3,788.7
Auxiliary materials	92.0			716.9	716.9	716.9		716.9
Unskilled labor	0.0			97.6	109.1	108.1		108.1
Spare parts consumed	100.0			466.5	466.5	466.5		466.5
Energy	0.0			481.7	538.3	533.3		533.3
Expatriate staff	100.0			362.6	362.6	125.0		
Materials, services, insurance, etc.	73.0			61.6	61.6	61.6		61.6
Materials, services, etc.	62.0			108.1	108.1	108.1		108.1
Distribution—export	100.0			722.9	1,445.8	1,445.8		1,445.8

(Continued)

TABLE 6.5a (*Continued*)

| | | Percent of full capacity | | | 91.7 | 101.4 | 100.0 | | 100.0 |
| | | FX conversion factor, CF$_{VEF}$ | 1.25 | | | | | | |

	%FX	1	2	3	4	5	...	10
					Year			
Foreign loan principal	100.0				0.0	5,313.6		5,313.6
Foreign loan interest	100.0			3,109.4	3,188.2	3,188.2		531.4
Fixed assets—F	100.0	11,716.6	0.0					
Preproduction expenditures—F	100.0	558.1	0.0					
Initial working capital—F	100.0		322.5					
Dividends paid, FX[1]	100.0			2,059.9	496.1	597.1		1,697.3
Other real outflows[2]	0.0	1,642.4	1,035.3	(1,937.5)	(1,271.4)	992.2		(9,171.2)
Agriculture—adjusted for SER					(2,142.4)	(2,112.9)		(2,112.9)
Output	0.0			2,459.0	2,719.1	2,681.5		2,681.5
Imports	100.0			3,118.2	3,448.0	3,400.4		3,400.4
Domestic content	0.0			(339.3)	(375.2)	(370.0)		(370.0)
Farmers' surplus	0.0			(319.9)	(353.8)	(348.9)		(348.9)
Pesticide runoff impact	0.0			(1,617.6)	(1,788.7)	(1,764.0)		(1,764.0)

[1] Premium on dividends paid to NTC in foreign exchange.
[2] Residual value adjusted for foreign exchange receivables, $2,423.6.

TABLE 6.5b Financial Flows—VEF, US$(000)

	%FX	1	2	3	4	5	...	10
Percent of full capacity				91.7	101.4	100.0		100.0
FX conversion factor, CF_{VEF}	1.25							
					Year			
Financial flows[1]								
Inflows								
Equity NIC	100.0	12,274.7						
Outflows								
Dividends paid, domestic	0.0			0.0	0.0	0.0		0.0
Corporate tax	0.0			0.0	0.0	0.0		0.0
Repayment principal, long-term[2]	100.0			0.0	0.0	5,313.6		5,313.6
Int. and other finance charges, long-term[2]	100.0			3,109.4	3,188.2	3,188.2		531.4
NPV VEF	(2,999.1)							
IRR VEF	5.8							

[1]Financial flows are not included in net flow at economic efficiency prices.
[2]Covered in "Real outflows" representing outflow for capital items.

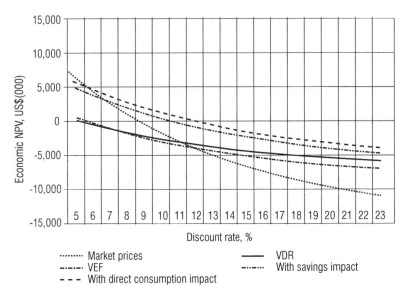

FIGURE 6.2 Economic NPV versus Discount Rate—CYP, US$(000)

Each step is essentially a zero-sum process, with a gainer and a loser.[15] The VDR distortion is the difference between VDR at adjusted prices and at market prices. The foreign exchange distortion is the difference between the VEF (VDR adjusted for foreign exchange distortion) and the VDR.

The sign of the difference indicates whether the project gains or loses. For an inflow, a positive (negative) difference indicates that the economic value is higher (lower) than the market price that the project actually receives—the project loses (gains). For an outflow, a positive (negative) difference indicates that the economic value is higher (lower) than the price paid by the project, so the project gains (loses).

Distribution effects of financial flows do enter into the income flow analysis. Taxes are paid by the project to the government, representing a loss to the project and a gain for the government. Dividends paid by the project to domestic shareholders are treated as financial flows, a loss for the project and gain to shareholders (external sector).[16] A portion of dividends (outflow) is paid in foreign exchange; the premium is taken into account as a gain for the project and loss to the external sector.[17] NTC equity (inflow) is paid to the project in foreign exchange; so the premium is a gain for the project and a loss for the external sector. Lease payments are considered economic rent (see *lease payments*), but land development costs are a subsidy to the project.

Although expatriated dividends are transfer payments, they actually diminish project benefits accruing to local entities. Unlike taxes or domestic dividends, with $CF_{VDR} = 0$, FX distribution effects (distortions) for expatriated dividends are calculated as:

$$VEF_{\text{distortion for transfers}} = Market\ value(f)AF_{VEF}$$

For example, suppose a dividend paid by the project to a foreign investor has a market (financial) value of 100, with 25 percent FX content and FX premium of 30 percent. Foreign transfers (amounts paid to foreign nationals) are considered economic costs.[18] The distortion is calculated as follows:

$$VEF_{\text{distortion-for-transfers}} = 100*0.25*0.30 = 7.5$$

where

$$AF_{VEF} = CF_{VEF} - 1 = \frac{SER}{OER} - 1 = 1.3 - 1 = 0.3$$

As an outflow, the positive sign indicates that the project gains (economic value higher than what the project actually pays). If *SER* is less than *OER*, CF_{VEF} will be negative so that the distortion has a negative sign, representing a loss for the project.

An example of distribution effects of applying the *global pricing framework* in a case of a tradable input precluded from import by trade policy of the country is provided in Appendix 5.2.

VDR and VEF Distribution—CYP

The results of VDR and VEF distribution analysis for the cotton project are shown in Tables 6.6a and 6.6b (VDR) and in Tables 6.7a and 6.7b (VEF). Gainers and losers are indicated in each table (P = project; G = government; W = workers; F = farmers; E = external sector). Only adjusted items are shown. A summary of distribution effects for each group is shown in Tables 6.8a (project) and 6.8b (other).[19] Positive values are gains, and negative values losses, for each group.[20] Groups selected for distribution analysis depend upon the social structure in the project's host environment and with significant distributional impacts as a consequence of the project.

TABLE 6.6a VDR Distribution, Real Flows—CYP

Percent of full capacity	Gain	Loss	1	2	3	4	5	...	10
					91.7	101.4	100.0		100.0
						Year			
Real flows									
Inflows									
Export	P	G			0.0	0.0	0.0		0.0
Domestic sales					0.0	0.0	0.0		0.0
Outflows									
Land development	P		150.0						
Raw materials									
Auxiliary materials	G	P			(145.8)	(238.6)	(230.4)		(230.4)
Unskilled labor	W	P			(97.6)	(109.1)	(108.1)		(108.1)
Spare parts consumed					0.0	0.0	0.0		0.0
Energy	P	G			80.3	89.7	88.9		88.9
Expatriate staff					0.0	0.0	0.0		0.0
Materials, services, insurance, etc.					0.0	0.0	0.0		0.0
Materials, services, etc.					0.0	0.0	0.0		0.0
Distribution—export					0.0	0.0	0.0		0.0
Foreign loan principal									
Foreign loan interest									
Fixed assets—F			0.0						
Preproduction expenditures—F			0.0						
Dividends paid, F					0.0	0.0	0.0		0.0
Initial working capital—F			0.0						
Other real outflows	—	—	0.0	0.0	0.0	0.0	0.0		0.0
Agriculture									
Output					0.0	0.0	0.0		0.0
Imports	P	W			0.0	0.0	0.0		0.0
Domestic content[1]					37.7	41.7	41.1		41.1
Farmers' surplus	F	P			(34.1)	(37.8)	(37.2)		(37.2)

[1] Assume labor-related; project gains (does not pay premium), workers lose premium.

TABLE 6.6b VDR Distribution, Financial Flows—CYP

Percent of full capacity						91.7	101.4	100.0		100.0
								Year		
Financial Flows	Gain	Loss	1	2	3	4	5	...		10
Inflows										
Equity			0.0							
Outflows										
Dividends paid, domestic[1]	E	P				0.0	(99.2)	(119.4)		(339.5)
Corporate tax	G	P				0.0	0.0	0.0		(1,454.8)

[1]Dividends to domestic stockholders could be considered a transfer to a domestic class (e.g., profit earners).

Distribution Analysis

Income distribution effects engendered by the project are weighted to reflect their consumption contributions. The income stream can be viewed as flowing into two streams, as shown in Figure 6.3, either to savings/investment (s) or to consumption (1 − s). The portion applied to savings/investment sets up a stream of future consumption (intergenerational). Direct consumption (contemporaneous) is weighted to reflect the social goals of decision makers.[21]

Savings Impact   According to the model presented, when a unit of income is applied to savings, an infinite series of investments is generated based upon the savings rate (marginal propensity to save) of the group receiving the income. The effect on future consumption varies for each affected group according to its particular savings rate.

The effect of the incremental income stream on future consumption for each group can be determined as

$$P^{inv} = \frac{(1-s)q}{i-sq}$$

where P^{inv} = shadow price of investment
s = marginal propensity to save for group
q = marginal return on capital invested
i = social rate of discount (EDR)

TABLE 6.7a VEF Distribution, Real Flows—CYP, US$(000)

Percent of operating capacity										
				91.7	101.4	100.0	100.0	100.0	100.0	100.0
							Year			
Real Flows	%FX	Gain	Loss	1	2	3	4	5	...	10
Inflows										
Export	100.0	G	P			1,677.9	3,355.8	3,355.8		3,355.8
Domestic sales	0.0					0.0	0.0	0.0		0.0
Outflows										
Land development	0.0			0.0						
Raw materials	0.0									
Auxiliary materials	92.0	P	G			133.7	133.7	133.7		133.7
Unskilled labor	0.0					0.0	0.0	0.0		0.0
Spare parts consumed	1.00	P	G			93.3	93.3	93.3		93.3
Energy	0.0					0.0	0.0	0.0		0.0
Expatriate staff[1]	100.0		E			72.5	72.5	25.0		0.0
Materials, services, insurance, etc.	73.0	P	G			9.6	9.6	9.6		9.6
Materials, services, etc.	62.0	P	G			14.5	14.5	14.5		14.5
Distribution—export	100.0	P	G			144.6	289.2	289.2		289.2
Foreign loan principal[2]	100.0	P	G			0.0	0.0	1,062.7		1,062.7
Foreign loan interest[2]	100.0	P	G			621.9	637.6	637.6		106.3
Fixed assets—F	100.0	P	G	2,343.3						
Preproduction expenditures—F	100.0	P	G	111.6						
Initial working capital—F	100.0			0.0	64.5					
Dividends paid FX[3]	100.0	P	G	0.0	0.0	0.0	99.2	119.4		339.5
Other real outflows[4]		G	P	0.0	0.0	0.0	0.0	0.0		723.9
Agriculture										
Imports[5]	100.0	F	G			623.6	689.6	680.1		680.1

[1]Expatriate staff paid in US$, so collect premium on foreign exchange.
[2]Government pays premium on foreign exchange loan principal and interest.
[3]Premium on dividends paid to NTC.
[4]Distortion related to collection of foreign exchange receivables at end of project.
[5]Government pays exchange premium on agricultural imports.

TABLE 6.7b   VEF Distribution, Financial Flows—CYP, US$(000)

Percent of operating capacity				91.7	101.4	100.0	100.0	100.0		100.0
						Year				
	%FX	Gain	Loss	1	2	3	4	5	...	10
Financial flows										
Inflows										
Equity NIC	100.0	P	E	2,454.9						
Outflows										
Dividends paid, domestic	0.0					0.0	0.0	0.0		0.0

The formula represents the infinite series of deferred consumption benefits generated by marginal investments from savings/investment for each group and for each operating period.[22] The shadow price of investment is the consumption value of a unit of savings for each group. J. Weiss, in UNIDO's *Practical Appraisal of Industrial Projects*, says: "P^{inv} can be thought of as the present value of the stream of consumption directly attributable to the marginal investment $(1 - s)q$, discounted at an artificial rate of discount $(i - sq)$ representing the social rate of discount (EDR) corrected for reinvestment by subtracting the rate of accumulation sq from i."[23] Although s varies by group of project stakeholders, the marginal return on capital is a parameter that can be applied universally. Parameter values (s, q, and i) are assumed constant from project inception to the planning horizon.

Distribution Impact of Savings—CYP   The distribution impact of savings for the Cambria Yarns Project is shown in Table 6.9. The propensity to save for each group is estimated from statistical data. The marginal return on capital is estimated at 10 percent. The EDR is estimated at 10.3 percent, (the weighted cost of capital for the project, adjusted for the premium on domestic investment; see the subsection "Economic Discount Rate" and Table 6.3).

At this stage of analysis, NPV and IRR can be determined from this stream of flows as is shown in Table 6.9. Values labeled as "Economic impact including savings" are the sum of economic values at efficiency level (VEF) in Table 6.5a and the "Total economic value of savings." Including the distribution weighting for savings, the NPV is 399.9, which is the sum of NPV at VEF level (−2,999.1) and the savings impact (3399.0), each

TABLE 6.8a Distribution Summary, Project—CYP

		SUM		Year						
		Gain	Loss	1	2	3	4	5	...	10
Project	PR	C	P	2,604.9	64.5	(123.9)	(1,670.0)	(655.9)		(3,391.0)
Domestic sales	PR	P	G	0.0	0.0	0.0	0.0	0.0		0.0
Land development	PR	G	P	150.0						
Auxiliary materials	PR	W	P			(145.8)	(238.6)	(230.4)		(230.4)
Unskilled labor	PR	P	P			(97.6)	(109.1)	(108.1)		(108.1)
Energy	PR	P	G			80.3	89.7	88.9		88.9
Domestic content (agric.)	PR	P	W			37.7	41.7	41.1		41.1
Farmers' surplus	PR	F	P			(34.1)	(37.8)	(37.2)		(37.2)
Dividends paid, domestic	**PR**	**E**	**P**			0.0	(99.2)	(119.4)		(339.5)
Corporate tax	PR	G	P			0.0	0.0	0.0		(1,454.8)
Dividends paid FX	FX	P	G			0.0	99.2	119.4		339.5
Export sales	FX	G	P			(1,677.9)	(3,355.8)	(3,355.8)		(3,355.8)
Auxiliary materials	FX	P	G			133.7	133.7	133.7		133.7
Spare parts consumed	FX	P	G			93.3	93.3	93.3		93.3
Expatriate staff	FX	P	G			72.5	72.5	25.0		
Materials, services, insurance	FX	P	G			9.6	9.6	9.6		9.6
Materials, services, etc.	FX	P	G			14.5	14.5	14.5		14.5
Distribution—export	FX	P	G			144.6	289.2	289.2		289.2
Foreign loan principal	FX	P	G			0.0	0.0	1,062.7		1,062.7
Foreign loan interest	FX	P	G			621.9	637.6	637.6		106.3
Fixed assets—F	FX	P	G	2,343.3						
Preproduction expenditures—F	FX	P	G	111.6						
Initial working capital—F	FX	P	G		64.5					
Imports (agriculture)	FX	P	G			623.6	689.6	680.1		680.1
Other real outflows	FX	G	P							(723.9)

TABLE 6.8b Distribution Summary, Other—CYP

Item				Year						
			SUM	1	2	3	4	5	...	10
Government	PR		G	0.0	(150.0)	(64.5)	29.9	1,465.6	432.3		2,947.4
Land development	PR	P	P	(150.0)	(150.0)						
Auxiliary materials	PR	G	P				145.8	238.6	230.4		230.4
Energy	PR	P	G				(80.3)	(89.7)	(88.9)		(88.9)
Corporate tax	PR	G	P				0.0	0.0	0.0		1,454.8
Dividends paid, FX	FX	P	G				0.0	(99.2)	(119.4)		(339.5)
Export sales	FX	G	P				1,677.9	3,355.8	3,355.8		3,355.8
Auxiliary materials	FX	P	G				(133.7)	(133.7)	(133.7)		(133.7)
Spare parts consumed	FX	P	G				(93.3)	(93.3)	(93.3)		(93.3)
Expatriate staff	FX	P	G				(72.5)	(72.5)	(25.0)		
Materials, services, insurance	FX	P	G				(9.6)	(9.6)	(9.6)		(9.6)
Materials, services, etc.	FX	P	G				(14.5)	(14.5)	(14.5)		(14.5)
Distribution—export	FX	P	G				(144.6)	(289.2)	(289.2)		(289.2)
Foreign loan principal	FX	P	G				0.0	0.0	(1,062.7)		(1,062.7)
Foreign loan interest	FX	P	G				(621.9)	(637.6)	(637.6)		(106.3)
Fixed assets—F	FX	P	G	(2,343.3)	(2,343.3)						
Preproduction expenditures—F	FX	P	G	(111.6)	(111.6)						
Initial working capital—F	FX	P	G	(64.5)		(64.5)					
Imports (agriculture)	FX	P	P				(623.6)	(689.6)	(680.1)		(680.1)
Other real outflows	FX	G	P								723.9
Equity NIC	FX	E	E	2,454.9	2,454.9						
Farmers	PR										
Farmers' surplus	PR	F	P		0.0	0.0	34.1	37.8	37.2		37.2
Workers							59.9	67.4	67.0		67.0
Unskilled labor	PR	W					97.6	109.1	108.1		108.1
Domestic content (agriculture)	PR	P	W				(37.7)	(41.7)	(41.1)		(41.1)
External sector	FX	G	E	(2,454.9)	(2,454.9)	0.0	0.0	99.2	119.4		339.5
Equity NIC	FX	E		(2,454.9)	(2,454.9)						
Dividends paid, domestic	PR	E	P		0.0	0.0	0.0	99.2	119.4		339.5

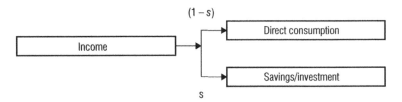

FIGURE 6.3 Disposition of Income Stream

discounted at the EDR of 10.3 percent. The IRR for "Economic impact including savings" is 10.9 percent. Savings have a positive impact on the project's economic performance.

Direct Consumption Impact

The portion of the project's distribution effect that is applied directly to consumption can be weighted to reflect the social policy priorities of decision makers. For each group the income involved is the remainder after deducting the portion saved (Figure 6.3).[24]

Weighting can be based upon the ratio of consumption for each group compared with the *base level of consumption*—that is, the level of per capita consumption at which income flow to a private individual is considered as valuable as income flow to the government.[25] At the base level of consumption, the result of government indifference is that marginal income increments (or decrements) are neither taxed nor subsidized.[26]

The relationship that can be applied is

$$P^{CONS} = \left(\frac{b}{c_i} \right)^n$$

where P^{CONS} = shadow price of consumption
b = base level of consumption
c_i = consumption level for group i
n = elasticity of marginal utility of consumption with respect to changes in per capita income

As a practical matter, n can be considered a parameter to be adjusted by decision makers to be applied to all projects within their jurisdiction. The parameter is normally limited to the range between 0 and 2. At a value of zero, income is not weighted. At $n = 2$ the government policy is highly egalitarian. For example, income to a group at one half the base level would be weighted four times that of the base level.

TABLE 6.9 Distribution Impact of Savings—CYP, US$(000)

	MPS	1	2	3	4	5	6	7	8	9	10
Project	0.5	1,197.5	(12.9)	(25.5)	208.2	(8.3)	(118.1)	(126.6)	179.9	213.9	384.7
Government	0.7	1,302.5	32.3	(63.7)	(836.9)	(329.9)	(395.5)	(448.7)	(1,085.1)	(1,217.0)	(1,697.5)
Workers	0.1	(105.0)	(45.2)	20.9	1,025.9	302.6	258.4	303.1	1,246.0	1,411.9	2,063.2
Farmers	0.3	0.0	0.0	6.0	6.7	6.7	6.7	6.7	6.7	6.7	6.7
External	—	0.0	0.0	11.3	12.5	12.3	12.3	12.3	12.3	12.3	12.3
		0.0	0.0	0.0	0.0	0.0	0.0	0.0	0.0	0.0	0.0
Total economic value of savings											
Project		1,618.5	(40.5)	(28.0)	799.7	136.5	(38.9)	(28.4)	870.1	1,000.4	1,564.0
Government		1,817.4	45.0	(88.9)	(1,167.8)	(460.3)	(551.9)	(626.1)	(1,514.1)	(1,698.1)	(2,368.5)
Workers		(198.9)	(85.5)	39.6	1,943.8	573.4	489.6	574.2	2,360.8	2,675.1	3,909.2
Farmers		0.0	0.0	7.1	8.0	7.9	7.9	7.9	7.9	7.9	7.9
External		0.0	0.0	14.2	15.7	15.5	15.5	15.5	15.5	15.5	15.5
		0.0	0.0	0.0	0.0	0.0	0.0	0.0	0.0	0.0	0.0

Parameters:

Marginal productivity of capital, q—%	12.0%
CRI—%	10.3%
NPV w/o adj	1,377.3
NPV w.adj	3,399.0

	1	2	3	4	5	6	7	8	9	10
Economic impact including savings	(12,448.6)	(1,398.3)	794.6	8,224.6	194.6	(319.0)	(159.8)	1,811.0	2,285.3	13,467.2

IRR	10.9%
NPV	399.9

Direct Consumption Impact—CYP   For the Cambria Yarns Project the parameter n is set at 0.5. This means that consumption of a group at one-fourth of the base level would be weighted twice its nominal value:

$$\left(\frac{1}{\left(\frac{1}{4}\right)}\right)^{0.5} = 2$$

Results of income distribution are shown in Table 6.10. "Total economic distribution value" is the sum of distribution effects of each classification, which are calculated from the proportion of income distortion flowing into direct consumption and weighted as previously shown in the shadow price of consumption formula. The total economic distribution value is added to the values in each period in Table 6.9 ("Economic impact including savings"), which consists of VEF plus savings impact). The result is shown in the line "Economic impact including distribution." When discounted at the EDR of 10.3 percent, NPV is 1,218.6 and the economic IRR is 12.3 percent (see Table 6.10). In other words, NPV and IRR at this level indicate the economic value of the project including both savings and direct consumption impacts.

Adjustment for Policy Goals

Decision makers may find it appropriate to adjust the results of economic analysis to account for the social value of resources, per se. Resources generated by the project may be considered *merit* goods if their production accords with social policy goals, or *demerit* goods if not. If the social value of project output is not fully reflected in the difference between the social value of income distribution effects and the efficiency value, the value of the project can be raised or lowered by adjustments to the net benefit values in each project period, from which economic NPV and IRR can then be determined. Assignment of merit and demerit values may be based upon considerations such as regional development, use of strategic resources, public health, job creation, industrial policy (general and sector), environmental goals, or other priority goals.

An example is the production of food products that have wide appeal but adverse health impacts. If the adverse consequences of consumption have otherwise not been taken into account in the analysis, demerits can be deducted. If the economic value of the output is x and its social value is considered to be 70 percent of x, a conversion factor of 0.7 would be applied to the value of output in each period and a new NPV calculated.

The practice of making this type of adjustment is necessarily highly subjective and open to question. Whether adjustments are economically

TABLE 6.10 Distribution Impact of Direct Consumption—CYP, US$(000)

	1-savings rate	Consumption to base level	Base level to consumption	Years									
				1	2	3	4	5	6	7	8	9	10
Project	0.5	2	0.50	1,302.5	32.3	(63.7)	(836.9)	(329.9)	(395.5)	(448.7)	(1,085.1)	(1,217.0)	(1,697.5)
Government	0.3	1	1.00	(45.0)	(19.4)	9.0	439.7	129.7	110.8	129.9	534.0	605.1	884.2
Workers	0.9	0.2	5.00	0.0	0.0	53.9	60.7	60.3	60.3	60.3	60.3	60.3	60.3
Farmers	0.7	0.6	1.67	0.0	0.0	26.4	29.2	28.8	28.8	28.8	28.8	28.8	28.8
External		—		0.0	0.0	0.0	0.0	0.0	0.0	0.0	0.0	0.0	0.0
Total economic distribution value				876.0	3.5	118.4	21.2	68.3	3.0	(15.5)	(61.4)	(83.5)	(144.2)
Project				921.0	22.8	(45.0)	(591.8)	(233.3)	(279.7)	(317.3)	(767.3)	(860.6)	(1,200.3)
Government				(45.0)	(19.4)	9.0	439.7	129.7	110.8	129.9	534.0	605.1	884.2
Workers				0.0	0.0	120.5	135.7	134.8	134.8	134.8	134.8	134.8	134.8
Farmers				0.0	0.0	34.1	37.7	37.2	37.2	37.2	37.2	37.2	37.2
External				0.0	0.0	0.0	0.0	0.0	0.0	0.0	0.0	0.0	0.0

Parameters:

n, marginal elasticity of consumption with respect to change in per capita income   0.50

Economic impact including distribution				(11,572.6)	(1,394.9)	913.0	8,245.8	262.9	(316.0)	(175.3)	1,749.6	2,201.8	13,323.0

IRR   12.3%

NPV   1,218.6

or politically inspired will always remain in doubt. Only if an adjustment system of this type is developed systematically and applied uniformly, and in a nonsubjective manner, are such alterations justified.

Sensitivity Analysis

For nonrevenue projects, economic analysis is likely to be the primary evaluation method, so it may be appropriate to consider the effects of uncertainties in both operating and economic parameters. Operational features that have both large impact and large variation in price should be selected for examination regarding sensitivity and risk, with selected parameter variations predicated on a combination of statistical information and informed opinion, rather than an arbitrary range. For economic sensitivity, effects of uncertainties in objective parameters (e.g., marginal propensity to save, shadow rate of foreign exchange) and a range of variations in subjective parameters (e.g., elasticity of the marginal utility of income, discount rate) should be examined to understand the range of possible outcomes. Even if sensitivity of subjective parameters is applied uniformly to all projects, the effect of variations may be useful information, particularly for marginally acceptable projects.

Sensitivity Analysis—CYP   Sensitivity analysis is carried out by observing the results of changes in the parameters through the likely range of values. In the Cambria Yarns Project, for example, the effect of variations in proportion of marginal income of the government devoted to savings (reinvestment) is shown in Table 6.11, with NPV determined at the EDR for the project (10.3 percent).

Final Economic Appraisal

As part of the appraisal process, calculated/estimated economic and social impacts of the project such as net economic benefit (economic NPV), IRR,

TABLE 6.11   Sensitivity of Economic NPV to Savings Rate—CYP, US$(000)

Percentage of Marginal Income of Government Saved/Invested	Economic NPV Including Savings Impact	Economic NPV Including Direct Consumption Impact
60	(1,294.1)	(49.1)
70	399.9	1,218.6
80	6,440.3	6,832.5

efficiency ratios, and contributions to other national or regional goals are compared with criteria and with other projects competing for scarce resources. Economic appraisal is a component of the general appraisal of the project, discussed at length in Chapter 8.

VALUE-ADDED

The purpose of value-added analysis (VAA) is, in principle, the same as that of other approaches, particularly if attention is focused on the project's impact on national income. The sum of all value-added (VA) generated in production processes in the country is closely related to national income (see Figure 5.2), which flow into consumption and savings. National income has been a traditional measure of national prosperity. Therefore, the value-added approach to calculation of a project's economic effects as a measure of its contribution to national objectives is a logical concept. The method described herein does not account for scarcity of resources consumed or generated by the project, nor does it inherently deal with externalities. Market prices are applied throughout, which has the virtue of being linked to national accounts (almost invariably compiled at market prices). This approach to economic analysis for project selection is more intuitive and easier to understand than methodologies based on analysis of market distortions. If value-added analysis is performed using shadow or accounting prices the result should be similar, if not identical, to ECBA at the level of economic efficiency. However, it then is subject to the same uncertainties as ECBA.

Value-Added Components

Value-added generated by the project can be divided into (1) wages and salaries and (2) what may be termed *social surplus*, the excess of VA after wages and salaries are taken into account. It includes profits paid out to shareholders (dividends),[27] interest to lenders, rents to owners of property employed by the project, and taxes transferred to the government.

From the point of view of the project, wages and salaries are a cost factor, but from the national perspective they contribute to national income. The elements of VA determine how the value created is distributed among members of society. National decision makers might consider the project favorably if a large proportion of the VA is in the form of wages and salaries. However, if the national savings rate is low, a greater proportion of VA in the form of profits and interests might be favored, as the savings rate (and consequently investment) for recipients would likely be higher than for wage earners. Domestic wages and salaries and social surplus contribute to national income at the project level.

At a basic level, as included in national accounts, VA can be determined for a period of operations from actual or projected accounts of an enterprise. VA content can be derived from the relation of profit to revenue and costs of the project:

$$P = O - M - I - W - S$$
$$P + W + S = O - M - I$$

where P = profit
S = surplus (other "costs," e.g. rents, interest, taxes)
W = wages and salaries
O = output value or revenue
M = material inputs (intermediate goods and services)
I = investment (capital consumption or depreciation for a period)

Both the left and right sides of this equation (second form) represent ways to calculate the VA. On the left side it can be expressed in terms of profit plus wages and salaries plus other cost elements. On the right side VA can be considered as the value of output, net of intermediate inputs and investment. Profit and other cost elements are generally aggregated as *social surplus*.

These relationships are expressed as follows:

$$VA_P = W + S + P = O - M - I$$

where VA_P = value-added produced by the project

In the national accounts, value-added is invariably calculated at market prices. For the project, the value of output is the domestic market price or the export price converted to domestic currency at the official exchange rate. The values for inputs are the domestic purchase price or the import price, as the case may be.

VA and National Income

VA for the project can be related to national accounts, as a means of determining its contribution to the national economy. The aggregated value added created by all producers of goods and services in the economy essentially amounts to income for all groups and individuals.

As shown in Figure 6.4, gross domestic product (GDP) is the most inclusive form, consisting of the value of all final goods and services produced

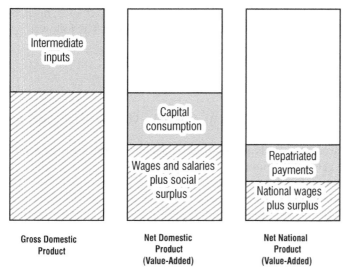

FIGURE 6.4   Levels of Value-Added

in the country during the year. GDP reduced by capital consumption (depreciation) is the net domestic product; when further reduced by payments to foreign nationals (repatriated payments), the result is the net national product (NNP). NNP at factor cost (reduced by indirect taxes) is equivalent to net national income (NNI), which is the aggregate of *value-added* for all producers in the country.

At the national level:

$$NNI = GDP + FI - CC - IT = GNP - CC - IT$$

where NNI = net national income
GDP = gross domestic product
GNP = gross national product
CC = investment or capital consumption
FI = net factor income from abroad (positive or negative)
IT = indirect taxes less subsidies

NNI consists of the wages and salaries plus other forms of income (social surplus) accruing to all citizens of the country.[28] If VA is calculated for a particular period, the investment or capital consumption component CC is usually represented by depreciation (plus amortization of intangible assets) for the period; in the dynamic method of calculation (temporally panoramic, discounted at the EDR) the actual value of asset investment might be used instead, at the point in time when it is acquired. At the project level, in each of the project operating periods $j = 1, 2, \ldots n$, this translates as follows:

$$VA_j = O_j - (M + CC + RP)_j = W_j + S_j$$

where $RP =$ repatriated payments

For consistency with the definition of NNI, O_j would be net of indirect taxes.

Intermediate inputs (goods and services) consumed by the project are deducted from the value of output to properly attribute VA to other producing entities and to avoid double counting.[29]

For a particular period, NNVA can be calculated by substituting the depreciation for the period in lieu of investment outlay for a representative period (e.g., full production level):

$$VA_j = O_j - (M + D + RP)_j$$

where $D_j =$ depreciation, period j

Value-Added Redistribution

The content of VA is distributed and redistributed in essentially three stages: primary—wages and salaries, profits, interest (all of them paid in the production process); secondary—through the financial system and budget (taxes, subsidies, government expenditure); and final—investment and consumption.

Wages and salaries are spent, saved, or paid to the government in the form of taxes. Social surpluses, such as dividends to shareholders (distributed profits) and reserves, interest payments to lenders, taxes to the government, and rents, find their way into public and private consumption and investment. Normally savings are channeled through financial institutions into investment that is the basis for future income and consumption.

Reserves and expansion funds are used directly by the enterprise for future investment. All of the VA is ultimately channeled into either savings/investment or consumption. Both contribute to the national economy—spending into immediate consumption and savings/investment for future consumption.

Value-Added Stages

Value-added is created at each of the various stages of integration of a final product. The illustration of Figure 6.5 shows three stages of production

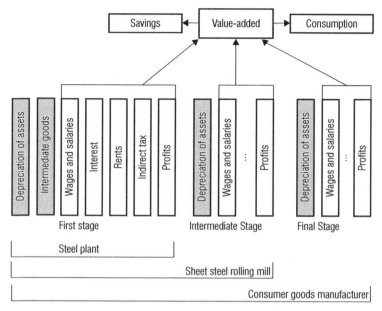

FIGURE 6.5   Value-Added in Stages of Product Integration

for a consumer good fabricated of steel: the steel mill, the rolling mill (to produce sheet steel), and the consumer goods manufacturer. The steel mill produces ingots as its final output, with a contribution of VA to the economy. Ingots are an input to the rolling mill, which produces sheet steel with its VA contribution. The sheet steel, in turn, is an input to the producer of consumer goods, with VA created at that level.

Each stage creates its own VA, the value of output less intermediate inputs and investment (represented by depreciation for a particular period). An intermediate input from a lower to a higher level is deducted from the higher stage in determining VA, as it represents output attributable to the lower stage. In this way the total of VA contributed by each producer of goods and services is essentially equivalent to the gross national product (GNP), as illustrated in Figure 5.2.

Decomposition of Value-Added

To determine VA attributable to the project, greater accuracy is achieved by departing from its conventional definition applicable to the system of national accounts in which intermediate inputs are fundamentally excluded (to include them would amount to double counting at the national level).

However, in project analysis some intermediate inputs may contain their own VA, so that the full value of an intermediate input is not necessarily excludable.

Decomposition of VA (see Figure 6.6) is a useful way to develop a more accurate estimate of the VA contribution rather than deducting the full value of all intermediate inputs (including investment). The value of output can initially be broken down into VA, local intermediates, and imports. Imports clearly do not contribute to national income and so can be deducted directly. The local intermediates can be further investigated for VA content by breaking them down in the same manner. Once again the imported component of the intermediate can be deducted immediately. If decomposition proceeds through several stages, ultimately local intermediate inputs will reduce to the vanishing point so that the value can be expressed in terms of VA and imports.[30]

However, this approach is applicable only if production of the input is attributable to the existence of the project, in other words, incremental production. If "Peter" (another enterprise or other present consumer) is "robbed" to pay "Paul" (this project), thereby reducing availability of the input to the other entity, then its VA is already accounted and cannot be credited to this project. In this case the entire value of the intermediate would be deducted.

A formal approach to determining VA for a project, which includes the impacts of linkages, is provided by Chervel and le Gal.[31] In a system

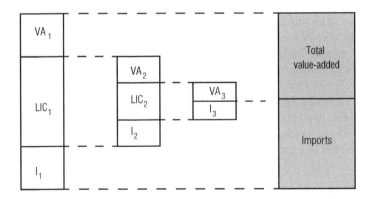

VA = Value-added
LIC = Local intermediate components
I = Imports

FIGURE 6.6   Decomposition of Value-Added

of matrixes, intermediate inputs are decomposed so that ultimately, for all practical purposes, only value-added and imports remain.

NPV of VA

The project is designed and appraised for a finite number of project periods (years) to the planning horizon. In a manner very similar to financial analysis and ECBA, net present value (NPV) is a means of incorporating VA created over different periods of time into a single aggregate indicator. The VA created in each project period to the planning horizon is determined.

NPV of VA is determined by adding discounted values of the VA for all periods from project inception to its termination. This includes phases of planning, construction, operation, and decommissioning (when applicable). Discount factors based upon the EDR are used to calculate discounted values for each period, which are then summed to determine the NPV of VA. Discounting can be applied to total VA for each period or to any or all of the components into which it is divided. In some of the indicators discussed subsequently, the discounting method is applied separately to VA components (e.g., wages and salaries, distributions to profit earners). In practice, the EDR is a parameter usually adjusted by decision makers according to the availability of investment resources.

$$NPV(VA) = \sum_{j=1}^{n} VA_j df_j$$

Value-Added Criteria

In addition to value added per se, another criterion is that the VA generated should at least equal the wage bill. If not, the project's social surplus is negative—that is, the value generated is less than the value of labor required for its production.

$$\sum_{j=1}^{n} VA_j df_j \geq \sum_{j=1}^{n} W_j df_j$$

where W_j = wages and salaries, period j

The test can be applied at market or accounting prices.[32] If the present value of VA is greater than the present value of wages and salaries (including benefits), the project is acceptable on this basis; if not, the project may be rejected because it does not stimulate improvement in national income.

Distribution of VA

Value-added generated by the project accrues to various groups and geographical regions; this pattern of value-added *distribution* is a project characteristic. At issue is how the distribution pattern accords with policy. Social groups are identified accordingly. The share of value-added for each group can assist in determining how the project compares with alternative investment opportunities in regard to priorities:

- Wages and salaries plus fringe benefits to wage earners.
- Profit distributions (dividends) to domestic shareholders, interest on private capital, rents for private owners, and fringe benefits.
- Taxes paid to the national treasury, interest on loans from public banks, profits paid to state-owned shares, rents and insurance premiums received by the state.

! Distribution ratios can be determined for a representative period and/or for the entire economic life of the project at nominal values or on a discounted basis, either at market or accounting prices. The ratios can be determined as follows:

$$DB^X = \frac{VA^X}{VA}(100)$$

where DB^X = distribution benefit (percent), group X
VA^X = value-added, group X

The most meaningful assessment of distribution is the employment of a numerator that is discounted *value-added* for the group and a denominator that is discounted *value-added* for the project. Similar distribution ratios can be developed for regions of the country—for example, less developed and more developed according to per capita income or another suitable criterion.

Value-Added and Accounting Prices

In the national accounts of every country, flows are recorded at market prices.[33] One of the advantages of calculating VA effects of a project at market prices is that the results can be directly linked to national accounts. Appraisal is simplified by comparing project impacts with components of economic indicators such as gross domestic product (GDP) or national income.

Not all of the VA as measured at market prices is actually attributable to the project. Virtually every project interacts with the rest of the economy. Resources consumed have an opportunity cost; resources generated contribute to the economy to the extent of their economic or social values. Each project inevitably encounters constraints on markets and resources that call into question the use of market prices for assessing its VA contribution. To cite just one example, if the VA of the project includes skilled labor that is in short supply so that jobs otherwise done by these workers have to be outsourced, the wages and salaries paid to these workers cannot realistically be included in the income component of VA attributable to the project because there are offsetting economic costs. Such interactions and constraints would affect most, if not all, resources generated and consumed by the project.

The result is value-added attributable to the project that takes into account its interactions with the rest of the economy, and distribution effects that are not directly measured by the proportion of value-added accruing to social groups at market prices.

If accounting prices are employed in the calculation of VA, the process would be similar to the approaches explained in "Economic Pricing Principles" and "Shadow Prices of Primary Resources" in Chapter 5. One difference would be in determining the accounting price of labor, since wages and salaries are a component of VA but a cost in the ECBA method. For example, if the CF for labor in ECBA is 0.6, the CF for VA would be 0.4. In other words, 40 percent of wages are excluded as economic cost in ECBA (i.e., *included as benefit*), but included as economic benefit in VA.

SUPPLEMENTARY INDICATORS

In addition to basic economic indicators, others can be determined that reflect the degree to which development objectives are fulfilled. These indicators are applicable for both cost/benefit and VA methods of analysis. Basic and supplementary indicators can be weighted and combined into a single measure of economic acceptability.

Employment Effect

This indicator measures the jobs created per unit of investment. Direct and indirect employment for host country workers should be considered. Indirect employment is the sum of increases or decreases in employment for linked upstream and downstream projects—that is, those whose existence is directly related to the project under consideration. The numerator is the employment in the various categories indicated: total employment, employment of unskilled workers, direct workers, and indirect workers. The denominator is the amount of investment in the project—the original investment in fixed assets, preproduction expenditures, and working capital.

$$Z_e^x = \frac{J\,O^x}{I}$$

where Z_e^x = employment ratio, jobs created per unit of investment (or other scarce resource)

JO = number of job opportunities

I = investment

x = representation of either total jobs, unskilled jobs, direct jobs, or indirect jobs

Foreign Exchange (FX) Effect

Foreign exchange is employed or generated by the project as part of financing of investment, as receipts for exports, payments for imports, and as repatriation of earnings and dividends. The FX effect can be determined in nominal terms (for a representative project year) or at its discounted value. In either case, FX flows for each project period (inflows minus outflows) are determined from project inception to the planning horizon. Direct and indirect (linked project) flows and impacts from import substitution or export diversion are included.

$$PV(FX) = \sum_{j=1}^{n} \left(FI_j - FO_j \right) df_j$$

where $PV(FX)$ = present value of net foreign exchange flow

FI_j = foreign exchange inflow

FO_j = foreign exchange outflow

In the dynamic version of this indicator, net FX for each period is discounted at the EDR, and then summed to determine its present value. A positive net flow indicates that the project contributes to the availability of FX. This indicator is relevant only for a country with systematic problems in its foreign obligations and inadequate foreign exchange reserves.

International Competitiveness

International competitiveness is measured as the amount of foreign exchange generated per unit of domestic resources used in production. An export-oriented project should be internationally competitive—net foreign exchange generated should exceed the value of domestic resources employed to produce it.

Flows from exports and imports (inputs and outputs, including capital and other foreign exchange flows—for example, repatriated payments) and the corresponding domestic resources consumed in production is determined for each period, discounted at the EDR. The result is an indicator of competitiveness:

$$IC = \frac{\sum\limits_{j=1}^{n} \left(FI_j - FO_j\right) df_j}{\sum\limits_{j=1}^{n} DR_j df_j} \geq 1$$

where IC = measure of international competitiveness
       DR_j = domestic resource inputs, period j

Numerator and denominator are expressed in the same units, either in foreign exchange or in domestic currency. In the former case, foreign exchange flows are converted to the equivalent domestic currency value. The use of accounting prices provides a better (more realistic) measure of competitiveness. Foreign exchange is converted at the shadow exchange rate and domestic resources priced at their respective accounting prices to reflect real cost to the economy.

The project is considered internationally competitive if the ratio is equal to or greater than 1 (unity). This means that the value of foreign exchange generated is at least equal to the value of domestic resources employed. The cutoff rate may be set at less than unity to promote exports, so long as the criterion is uniformly applied to all projects. In case of ranking, projects with higher international competitiveness are accorded priority.

If foreign and local components are expressed respectively in foreign and local currencies, the reciprocal of this relationship is the effective *exchange rate* (number of local currency units per unit of foreign exchange) for the project. This can be compared with the market or shadow exchange rate as a measure of project efficiency in the project appraisal process.

Relative Efficiency

Relative efficiency is similar to a profitability indicator, measuring benefits produced per unit of scarce resource employed. The numerator is the present value of net benefits of the project (ECBA) or value-added in each period from inception to the planning horizon, discounted by the EDR. The denominator is the present value of the scarce resource, such as capital investment, foreign exchange (net foreign exchange outflow), and labor (wages, salaries, and fringe benefits paid to scarce labor). In the latter case, only values related to skilled labor are usually of interest, and to semiskilled and unskilled only if one or both is also scarce.

$$E_{SR} = \frac{NPV}{PV_{SR}}$$

where E_{SR} = relative efficiency of scarce resource
SR = scarce resource
PV_{SR} = present value of scarce resource

NOTES

1. There may be bases for socioeconomic appraisal other than consumption. For example, if the country is concerned mainly with a growth objective, uncommitted income might be the basis for selecting the discount rate. There may be still other fundamental social objectives, such as employment, balance of payments, and national security. The economic discount rate would be selected on the basis of a single or multiple national objectives. Methods of multi-objective optimization have been developed, in which deviations from weighted objectives are minimized, such as goal programming in linear systems.

2. In his chapter "Discount Rates" (*Cost Benefit Analysis*, R. Layard and S. Glaister, eds., second ed., Cambridge University Press, 1994), Joseph E. Stiglitz argues that the appropriate social discount rate might vary from project to project, based upon the impacts of each (e.g., distribution).

3. In his research working paper prepared for the World Bank, "The Social Discount Rate: Estimates for Nine Latin American Countries" (2008), Humberto Lopez suggests that the social discount rate increases with the rate of economic growth, but is somewhat dependent on the project's planning horizon.

4. Stiglitz (see note 2) identifies the producer rate of interest (the rate at which firms can borrow or lend), consumers' marginal rate of substitution or consumer rate of interest (amount of income required at time t to compensate for a decrease in income at time $t + 1$), or the social rate of time preference (related to the rate at which future utility is discounted) as possibilities for the EDR, but dismisses all of them, or even a weighted average, as a theoretically satisfactory solution. He suggests that only by considering critical sources of market imperfections in each particular setting can the correct discount rate be determined.

5. According to one model, the CRI is theoretically determined as $CRI = ng + p$; n is the elasticity of marginal utility of consumption with respect to change in per capita income; g, the annual growth of average per capital income; and p, pure time preference. Because the values of n and p are subjective, the formula for a shadow discount rate is not very useful. If there is a credible social process revealing implicit valuations (weights), then these parameters gain in objectivity. However, easier said than done.

6. For the Cambria Yarns Project, the basis for export prices is CIF; international transport (including cargo insurance) plus domestic transport and handling to the port (exports) and domestic markets is included as part of operating cost, so the border price for exports is effectively FOB (CIF *minus* international transport cost) *minus* transport and handling from plant to port.

7. The lease payments are intended as economic rent, to cover site development cost for the project; if forgone benefits in other applications is greater than generated by the project, the balance would be considered a subsidy; if lower, the excess would be a tax (transfer payment), in either case with a distribution effect.

8. Sales of cotton yarn to domestic textile producers results in incremental production, and not import substitution. The relevant price is considered textile producers' willingness to pay. If, instead, these sales resulted in diminished imports (import substitution), the relevant price would be the border price—that is, CIF plus domestic handling and transportation costs.

9. In the economic analysis tables, farm operations are separated for clarity even though they are internalized for the purposes of economic analysis. The net effect of raw cotton transactions (as shown in Table 6.1) is the composite of *outflow* for "Raw materials" (e.g., 3,394.6 in year 3) and *inflow* in "Real agriculture flows, output" (e.g., 2,459.0 in year 3). The net effect in year 3 is $2,459.0 - 3,394.6 = -935.6$, which represents the forgone revenue from sorghum production.

10. All such figures are in US$(000).

11. This treatment responds to the growth of GNP as the criterion for economic optimization, rather than GDP, as the difference is net factor income from abroad. In this case the payment of dividends to foreign nationals decreases the project's effect on GNP.

12. The project pays dividends to foreign shareholders in foreign exchange at the official exchange rate. It buys undervalued dollars from the government, at the official exchange rate.

13. A tax holiday is granted to the project by the government, which in some circumstances might be considered a subsidy.

14. For items with a VDR of zero, mainly financial flows, it may be necessary to use the financial value as the basis for calculating the foreign exchange distribution effect (e.g., the foreign content of dividends paid).

15. This approach is similar to that of John Hansen in UNIDO's *Guide to Project Appraisal* (Vienna: UNIDO, 1986), but with significant differences, particularly regarding effects of income distribution.

16. An alternative treatment of dividends to domestic shareholders would be to consider profit earners as a separate domestic social group rather than part of the external sector.

17. The foreign partner, NTC, accepts a share of equity with an adjustment for the shadow exchange rate (SER), and dividends are paid accordingly. The agreement is for an 80 percent share rather than 81.5 percent justified by the SER (see Table 4.1).

18. This is the approach employed in the Cambria Yarns case. An alternative is to treat foreign dividends as financial flow with zero VDR; the flow would be treated as a distribution effect in which the project loses and the external sector gains. There could be an additional FX distribution effect if the SER differs from the OER.

19. Distribution of the foreign exchange distortion attributable to differential cost of agricultural imports is shown as affecting the integrated project rather than farmers, who directly contract for the purchase of these inputs. The assumption is that the project benefits from lower costs of agricultural inputs than would be the case without currency exchange through the central bank, which covers the premium on foreign exchange.

20. The cost of imported capital items in the economic context is taken into account as debt service on the foreign exchange loan with which they were procured, included as part of real flow; there is no other imposed or structural distortion except for the overvalued local currency. This approach is predicated on availability of the foreign exchange loan to this project exclusively.

21. According to J. Weiss, *Practical Appraisal of Industrial Projects: Application of Social Cost Benefit in Pakistan* (Vienna: UNIDO, 1980), page 33: "A distinction is drawn between the savings and consumption changes resulting from a project.... instead of adjusting the total income changes for different groups to take account of their existing income levels, only the changes in consumption have been revalued in this way. Therefore, the distribution weights involved in this (part of) appraisal are consumption weights and not income weights." In the ECBA method described in this chapter, it is assumed that savings flow into investment, producing a future consumption stream.

22. Ibid., 33–34: "In case studies all government income and private savings are given a weight of 1.0 (savings are . . . not adjusted to a consumption equivalent), essentially on the admittedly dubious assumption of rational allocation of resources by the government." According to the UNIDO *Guide* (see note 15), page 65 (footnote): "This guide, unlike the original Little-Mirlees and UNIDO methods, takes into account the differences between both government and private consumption and savings." This is the approach followed herein, on the assumption of nonoptimal allocation of resources by the government and private sector to the project planning horizon.

23. Parth Dasgupta and Amartya Sen, *Guidelines for Project Evaluation* (Vienna: UNIDO, 1972), 177, gives an expression for the infinite sum over time of increments of consumption.

24. Weiss, *Practical Appraisal*, 143–145.
25. I. M. D. Little and J. A. Mirrlees, *Project Appraisal and Planning for Developing Countries* (London: Heinemann Educational Books, 1974), 238–239. Although these are consumption weights, the use of income distribution values should not constitute a significant distortion.
26. In selecting income at the level that is neither taxed nor subsidized as the base level, the assumption is that fiscal policies are consistent with the essential needs of the economy. If this were clearly not the case, some other means of determining the base level would be necessary. For example, the average or median household income might be a better base level as it would reflect the societal norm.
27. In both shadow pricing and the VAA method of economic evaluation, surpluses that are not distributed (i.e., not paid out as dividends), are assumed to remain within the enterprise for reinvestment, representing the potential for deferred consumption. In a general economic context, *social surplus* is sometimes defined differently as the total of consumer and producer surplus. The consumer surplus is a benefit to consumers by not paying what some consumers would be willing to pay, as defined by the demand curve. The producer surplus is the amount that producers benefit by selling at price higher than that at which some producers would be willing to sell, as defined by the supply curve.
28. Net domestic product (NDP) = GDP – capital consumption = Wages + Surplus + Indirect taxes. Net national income (NNI), which comprises aggregate income of households, businesses, and government, excludes indirect taxes from NNP. In other words, NNI = NDP + Factor income from abroad – Indirect taxes.
29. Intermediate inputs are similarly treated in national accounts such as GDP, NNP, NNI.
30. The technical procedure is similar to the one described for decomposition of product value into traded and nontraded components.
31. M. Chervel and M. Le Gall, *Manuel d'évaluation économique des projets: la méthode des effets* (Paris: Ministère des Relations Extérieures, 1984).
32. This approach to VA can most readily be related to national accounts. However, it does not take into account interactions of the project with the rest of the economy, which would involve a form of shadow, or accounting, prices that better reflect the actual economic impact of the project. Use of accounting prices would provide results close, if not identical, to the ECBA approach at the level of economic efficiency.
33. Standard economic indicators such as GDP have serious deficiencies because they measure only market transactions. Aside from uncounted off-the-books transactions and unproductive expenditures that are counted (rebuilding facilities devastated by natural disasters, security related to crime, higher medical costs from increasing illness rates), some economists seek a better way to measure the effects of human activity on public welfare. To enhance awareness of its economic cost, some cities and towns charge individuals for depositing municipal waste according to weight or volume rather than covering the cost

only through taxation. Putting a market price on carbon emissions from coal-fired power plants is a means of better reflecting the economic cost of energy. As an aid in industrial project design, a system for life cycle assessment with full ecological accounting has been developed at Ohio State University (see www.resilience.osu.edu/CFR-site/eco-lca.htm).

REFERENCES

Asian Development Bank. 1997. *Guidelines for the economic analysis of projects.* Manila: Asian Development Bank.

Brent, Robert J. 2001. *Cost benefit analysis in developing countries.* Cheltenham, Glos, UK: Edward Elgar Publishing.

Chervel, M., and M. Le Gall. 1984. *Manuel d'évaluation économique des projets: la méthode des effets.* Paris: Ministère des Relations Extérieures.

Chervel, M. 1987. *Calculs économiques publics et planification: les méthodes d'évaluation de projet.* Paris: Publisud.

Dinwiddy, C., and F. Teal. 1996. *Principles of cost-benefit analysis for developing countries.* London: Cambridge University Press.

Fabre, P. 1997. *Financial and economic analysis of development projects.* Luxembourg: European Commission, Methods and Instruments for Project Cycle Management.

Lopez, Humberto. 2008. The social discount rate: Estimates for nine Latin American countries. Policy Research working paper 4639. Washington, D.C.: World Bank.

Pearce, D. W., and D. Ulph. 1995. A social discount rate for the United Kingdom. Norwich, UK: Centre for Social and Economic Research on the Global Environment (CSERGE), working paper 95-01.

Stiglitz, Joseph. 1994. Discount rates. In R. Layard, and S. Glaister, eds., *Cost benefit analysis,* 2nd ed. London: Cambridge University Press.

Ward, W. A., and B. J. Deren. 1993. *The economics of project analysis: A practitioner's guide.* Washington, D.C.: World Bank.

Weiss, D. 1978. Economic evaluation of projects: A critical comparison of a new world bank methodology with the UNIDO and the revised OECD Approach. Berlin: German Development Institute. Online version 2002, at http://www.sciencedirect.com/science.

Weiss, J. 1980. *Practical appraisal of industrial projects: Application of social cost benefit in Pakistan.* Vienna: UNIDO.

Wiener, D., and M. Chervel. 1985. Le calcul économique de projet par la méthode des effets. Collection documents pédagogiques, no. 4. Paris: Ministère de la Coopération.

CHAPTER 7

Investment Decision under Uncertainty and Risk

Project analysis is essentially a forecasting exercise—every prescribed operating feature of the design is a forecast that is inevitably subject to uncertainty, the fundamental determinant of the degree of risk when decisions are acted upon. Greater uncertainty in critical project design features connotes greater risk in the outcome of the investment decision—that is, how closely the design performs according to expectations, and how accurate are predictions of the behavior of the external environment.

Uncertainty surrounds every phenomenon—physical, economic, political, or otherwise. Scientists and engineers employ the concept of *tolerance* to deal with uncertainties in their models and variables and recognize that no theory or model can ever be *proved*. Even human perceptions are limited by tolerance or error in sensory apparatus, so that nothing that crosses the mind is known with absolute certainty. Risk results from a decision made under conditions of uncertainty.

A perception of the configuration of an enterprise that does not exist is required, as well as a prediction of how it is to function and interact with its external environment. The outcome is subject to variability that can be favorable or unfavorable. By studying project characteristics, potential risks associated with the design and its forecasts can be identified, leading to quantitative and qualitative assessments and an appropriate framework for the investment decision.

FORECASTING

Forecasting is the process of estimating or projecting future states or values. In regard to market response, for example, a forecast is an attempt to determine demand and sales for the project, which depend upon estimates of market share and timing of market penetration. Some issues for the forecaster: Is the forecast worthwhile? Will the results influence the decision? What factors enter into the forecast? How do they interact? Are they endogenous (within control of the project) or exogenous (outside the decision system)? What is the quantity and quality of information available concerning these factors? What degree of accuracy is desirable and what is the best and most cost-effective way to achieve it? What might be the consequences of not forecasting?

To produce a forecast, a model is required—quantitative, qualitative, or a combination. A model is an abstraction and necessarily incomplete, built upon a limited number of independent variables that explain the behavior of one or more dependent variables, to be employed with discretion. In constructing a model for demand forecasting (dependent variable), key internal and external variables that affect demand are identified, including controllable (essentially internal to the project) and less controllable (essentially external) factors.[1] Demand is predicated on the *future states* of these independent variables, which must be predicted to arrive at an estimate of demand.

Some forecasting methods are primarily quantitative—most or all of the model variables have numerical values that are drawn from historical data or that are future-oriented, with variables assigned values based upon the expertise and vision of the analyst and/or consultants. Other models are essentially qualitative—more descriptive than numerical. A summary of forecasting methods is shown in Figure 7.1.

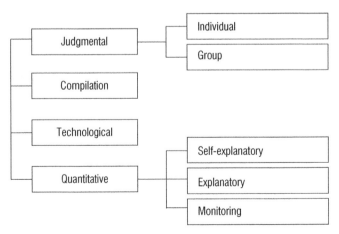

FIGURE 7.1   Forecasting Methods

Judgmental Methods

Judgmental methods are futuristic approaches to forecasting, relying on the forecaster's command of qualitative and quantitative aspects of the project feature (e.g., demand for project output). They can be predictions of individual experts with considerable experience in the sector of interest, predicated on a particular marketing approach and on predicted market developments. The expert basically projects a scenario describing the role of the project and the conditions that will prevail to the project's planning horizon. In one approach, the scenario or future state is posited and the forecaster describes those steps necessary to realize the scenario as a test of its validity. Group methods can be employed, particularly for an existing company contemplating an investment project—committees of experts, sales force estimates, panels of executive opinion. The *Delphi method* is an iterative approach in which each member of a panel of experts is provided access to the opinions of the others in several rounds until something like a consensus is reached. The idea is to avoid the bandwagon effect of majority opinion that might occur in a workshop setting.

Compilation Methods

Compilation forecasts are predicated on acquisition of data concerning related industry or economic variables rather than a complex of independent variables. The forecast depends upon a compilation of information from clients or consumers who will use the product, generally applied to intermediate goods (raw materials and components).

A *consumption coefficient* is a technological parameter based upon the intermediate or end-use product for which the planned product will be an input—for example, demand for cement or steel in metric tons can be related to the volume of new construction in terms of space or level of investment. A gas turbine project designer needs to know how many and what capacity of power plants will be constructed over the next few years to provide an estimate of demand. Demand for automobiles can be estimated by determining consumption coefficients for the public (e.g., cars per 1,000 inhabitants by income level), for industrial units, and for government agencies. The actual automobile population is subtracted from the total to estimate current demand.

The *market buildup* approach relies on estimates of the rate of expansion of demand and market saturation level. A compilation of demand data provides an estimate of the rate of growth. The new capacity is more readily accommodated if the product is in the growth phase of its life cycle. Risk increases as market saturation is approached.

Technological Methods

The future course of systems development is the basis for *technological forecasting*. Validity depends upon the astuteness of the analyst regarding the dynamics of technology: how systems will develop to require new products; what features of new products will be in greatest demand because they are most effective or efficient; what the interactions will be between product innovations.

System dynamics seeks to understand whether the better mousetrap will provide advantages for consumers from which benefits will accrue to the project. Knowledgeable individuals, usually with technical or scientific expertise, attempt to understand the complex interrelationships between advancing technology and the external and internal environments. How will telecommunications, for example, be carried out in the future? What kinds and what volume of information will be exchanged, and between whom? What communications media will be employed? Which components will the system comprise? What types of organizations will be in a position to provide goods and services? Understanding these issues provides the basis for developing a forecast of demand.

Trend extrapolation involves analysis of historical and current market developments to predict future direction. The extrapolation may not rely so heavily on future market forces, perhaps because the product trend has a high level of momentum—future developments appear inevitable. During the growth phase of an innovative product that has responded well to a societal need, the trend is perhaps more reliable than analysis of market forces. The approach is to study visible movements in the industry over time—the direction and shape of movements in the future, and the extent to which the technological trend will continue. A perceptive analyst would have been able to discern the trend toward higher-level languages and less involvement of users in the formulation of computer program and coding instructions; the trend toward graphic and vocal interfaces in communications would have been anticipated.

Cross impact forecasts are based upon how developments in other industries influence the sector of interest. International trends in manufacturing and trade have an impact on demand for mobile communications. The development of glass fiber bundles for imaging and communications had a cross impact on the copper mining industry (because of copper's use in electrical wiring).

Morphological analysis is a systematic way of considering all possibilities within a market or industry, a method of identifying and investigating possible relationships or configurations in the underlying system. The name derives from *morphology*, the study of form and structure (from the Greek *morphe*, meaning shape or form). System parameters are ordered and assigned values, which are combined and recombined into new arrangements to understand the market or industry's structure and possible configurations and niches for a new entrant. Promising configurations are identified for further study by assigning efficiency and other weights.[2]

Quantitative Methods

Most quantitative models are formulated with variables for which historical information is available. Forecasts are based on the assumption that the future behavior of the market or other phenomena will be much like the past. The problem is to identify the independent variables and how they are related.

Other quantitative models can be built upon mathematical relationships between variables that arise from the vision of the analyst. They do not rely on historical data, although for stochastic (probabilistic) models of this type, variability distribution might be based on historical information. For example, if a visionary stochastic model is constructed concerning revenue forecasts, the historical pattern of price variability might be applied. Quantitative models are tested when possible, and in all cases are used for extrapolating, or forecasting, the future.

Self-explanatory models assume that the phenomena (e.g., demand or sales) are strictly time-dependent and not dependent upon relationships with other variables. No explanatory system is attempted. The problem is to ascertain which mathematical function best describes how the dependent variable varies over time.

Explanatory models are mathematical structures that describe relationships between dependent and independent variables. The problem is to discover or otherwise determine the mathematical form that best *explains* the relationship. Although these methods provide descriptions of relationships between variables, they are not truly explanatory in the sense that they explain mechanisms of the relationship. Association is not causation. Confidence in these models can be strengthened by combining them with analysis of the mechanisms that describe how the dependent variable is affected by the independent variables (e.g., hypothesis testing).

A major determinant of consumption levels is consumer income,[3] influencing the portion of budgets that households are willing allocate to a product. Demand for medicines, for example, may be related to personal income in addition to the status of the population's health. Product consumption levels usually are positively correlated with income levels of consumers, although some products are negatively correlated, such as consumption of inexpensive foods by lower-level income groups.

Monitoring involves tracking signals that are associated with changes in the phenomena of interest, but that do not explain the relationship. There may be an explanatory mechanism, but the basic forecasting model for demand or other project parameters does not deal with it. Tracking signals can be used ex ante to determine whether the forecasting model is inconsistent with actual values and trends—that is, if demand is systematically higher or lower than values predicted by the forecasting model.[4]

RISK—DEALING WITH UNCERTAINTY

Forecasts of the external business environment and its effects on demand, production, and sales are approximations: Historical data provides an indication of a past trend, but usually cannot be confidently extrapolated into an uncertain future, and expert opinion can be faulty. Some project parameters have patterns of variability that are inherently uncertain—that is, they can only be predicted statistically. Under conditions of uncertainty, risk enters the picture only when a decision is made; it is a function of the particular choice among alternatives.

Uncertainty and its associated risk is an underlying factor in virtually every project element, concerning both information underlying its design and the conditions in which it will function. The potential for risk abounds in any project environment, as decisions are based on information that is inherently imprecise. Some of the areas particularly subject to uncertainty are prices (patterns, inflation, and escalation); technology trends; estimates of plant productivity; time and cost of construction and start-up; changes in the political, social, and business environment.

Risk is a factor in markets, which almost invariably react negatively to uncertainty. Whenever normal business conditions are threatened by economic, social, or political instability, investors tend to reduce exposure, with good reason. Normally business performance suffers, although opportunities exist even under conditions of general business adversity.

Risk analysis is an essential part of project development. The incidence of adverse conditions has consequences that range from annoying to fatal. Murphy's Law predicts that if anything can go wrong, it will. Fortunately, many risk factors can be estimated and even quantified, so that they can be avoided or at least mitigated. Analysis involves considering the consequences of variability of design parameters (individually and in combination) within ranges determined either from experience or from statistical information about project elements (e.g., markets, technical features, financial and economic variables). The worst-case scenario may yield unacceptable results, but its likelihood has to be taken into account in the investment decision.

Measures to avoid, mitigate, or spread risk may be included in the plan. Ultimately, the perception of operational risks must be compatible with the risk tolerance of stakeholders. Building the risk factor into project analysis leads to better decisions with more secure predictions of how the project investment will perform.

The methods of analysis described here pertain primarily to *project* risk, and not expressly risk related to the macroeconomic situation or financial markets. For bundles of projects or mega-projects, more advanced techniques of risk analysis may be required.

Concepts of Risk

As a general rule, risk connotes danger, the possibility that something will happen to threaten the economic position or status of the project. The following are conceptions of risk that may prevail in the minds of stakeholders:

- *Chance of ruin.* The possibility that oncoming changes in economic, political, or social conditions will cause the project to collapse—that the external environment will become so hostile that the project cannot survive—may be of concern.
- *Possibility of loss.* In some cases it is not so much a fear of collapse as the possibility of suffering a loss that is of concern. The enterprise can survive as a viable entity, but perhaps the rates of return will be less than expected, with attendant reduction in value of the enterprise.
- *Variability of return.* A wide range of possible occurrences or fluctuations (e.g., in rates of return) pose an element of risk. When performance is highly variable, markets respond in kind. In fact, markets have adopted a quantitative indicator to deal with variability in performance and to assess investment risk—β (beta)—which measures the movement in share value of the enterprise relative to the overall market. During economic upturns and declines, for enterprises with high β, change in value is more pronounced than market averages.
- *Probability of an undesirable outcome.* A general view of risk is the probability of an undesirable outcome, according to objective or subjective criteria.

Operational Risk

Some assets such as facilities, raw materials, machines, and skills of individuals can only be fully productive if matched to other assets of a special kind (*asset specificity*). For example, a particular aluminum production line can work efficiently using bauxite ore with specific percentages and types of hydrous aluminum oxides; a power plant can achieve full productivity if coal of a specific calorific value is used as fuel. These installations require specialized inputs to guarantee efficient (and competitive) production. If planned suppliers fail to provide the requisite ore or fuel, the project might incur *switching costs*,[5] meaning that production could continue but at a higher cost level. If the supplier is in a monopolistic position vis-à-vis the project in the relevant cost range, price forecasts have to take into account its predicted behavior.

Uncertainty related to these types of supply situations carries the *possibility* of higher materials, services, and transaction costs than those in the preinvestment study. An approach to mitigating these uncertainties is to modify the relationship (contractual or otherwise). If there exists a high risk of *opportunistic behavior* by a principal supplier, some type of strategic response is warranted, either acquisition (*vertical integration*), finding substitutes (materials or sources), or, if those are not possible, reconsidering the viability of the project. With acquisition, supply transactions are internal to the project, mitigating to some extent possible unacceptable price changes, but additional financing is needed to cover the investment in the supplier's operation, and the project is also confronted with possible inefficiencies related to inexperience in managing the new unit.

The influence of unexpected changes in prices can be checked with sensitivity analysis. However, the source of possible variations in *behavioral risk* may have little to do with ordinary fluctuations in variables related to other risk calculations. An additional reason for separating these type of risks related to *behavior* is that they are more suitably addressed with *scenario analysis*. Tools for risk analysis should not only produce quantitative assessments, but also relate variability in projected performance to behavioral factors in the external environment and consequently to formulate possible countermeasures.

Perspectives on Financial Risk

Financial stakeholders in the project might adopt any combination of the following perspectives on risk:[6]

- The investment in isolation (the investor is concerned only with project risk).
- Risk for the investment portfolio of the enterprise (e.g., management is responsible for overall performance, and therefore concerned with risk for all enterprise assets).
- Stakeholder diversification (a stakeholder with all its eggs in one basket is exposed to risk of not diversifying).

- Risk of contingent claims against the enterprise (e.g., claims of creditors that depend upon the future course of events, such as payments of principal and interest to bondholders only if the company's earnings are sufficient to cover payments).
- Change in market values of claims against the enterprise (e.g., debt instruments) if the basis for determining risk is altered (e.g., downgraded credit rating).
- Contribution to risk for the economy: Government policymakers might view the project in the context of overall economic risk (only if it has major economic impact); associated with correlation with the economic portfolio (see the later subsection "Portfolio Diversification") might be of concern.

Dimensions of Risk

Stakeholders are likely to have differing attitudes toward risk: There are risk-taking, risk-neutral, and risk-averse individuals and institutional cultures. One measure of the response to potential gains from the project is utility,[7] the physical and psychological satisfaction derived from additional wealth.

Marginal utility is the satisfaction derived from the next unit of wealth. For a risk-averse individual, the marginal utility of additional income decreases with additional wealth—a loss of one unit of wealth has more impact on satisfaction than a gain of one more unit; for the risk-neutral individual, the loss of one unit of wealth is weighted equally with a gain of one unit; a risk-taker has an increasing marginal utility—the next unit of additional wealth is valued higher than a loss of one unit.

Risk-reward tolerance usually varies among potential project investors or investment groups. One way of looking at this is the *certainty equivalent*, which is defined as the certain (or guaranteed) reward at which an investor is indifferent between accepting it and a possibly higher but risky reward based upon the investor's utility curve, a measure of satisfaction derived from a marginal unit of wealth. It can also be defined as the maximum amount an investor is willing to pay for an expected return with particular risk characteristics. It is, in effect, the value of the expected return minus the risk premium.

Stakeholders' attitudes toward risk affect design of the project structure, attracting financing and other types of support, and planning and promotion. The relationship between risk and potential reward is an important criterion. Most investors are risk-averse—conservative about the possibility of losing capital. If a means can be found to minimize or at least alleviate risk, it is more likely that financial backers will be identified in the project promotion process; only when risks are reduced to a satisfactory level will potential collaborators agree to bring the project into existence.

Investors are concerned with risks associated with meeting investment criteria (rate of return, NPV, payback), loss of capital, or portfolio risk.[8] The lender is concerned with default on the loan and seeks to mitigate or eliminate the possibility of such an eventuality. The guarantor has the ultimate responsibility for covering default in debt service and seeks to hedge these risks. Regulatory agencies seek to avoid risk of misallocating scarce investment resources.

The dimensions of risk are variability and time. Risk generally increases when *activities and events are projected over longer periods*. The further out in time, the greater the uncertainty in conditions and outcomes. When historical information reveals a pattern of variability, risk appears to be greater. Regularity in periodic or cyclical variations seems more predictable and connotes less risk than random variability that exists in markets and in economic and political systems.

Project risks[9] involve the likelihood and degree of unacceptable deviations from predicted operational characteristics that are the basis for the investment decision. Risks can be categorized to clarify the analytical framework:[10]

- *Business risk*. The probability of not meeting targets (e.g., implementation schedule and costs, sales levels, production schedules, operating costs) is affected by how well the implementation project and the enterprise created are designed and managed.
- *External risk*. Threats may be present in the commercial or wider environment, such as the possibility of political instability with adverse impacts on business and capital markets. Industries move in and out of favor of governments, which sometimes encourage with incentives, profit repatriation, and protection, and at other times are more restrictive, even to the extent of confiscating project assets.[11] Competition is often a major commercial risk.
- *Price level or inflation risk*. General inflation and escalations in prices of project inputs affect both investment costs and operating margins. Inflation increases financing costs in domestic capital markets, with rates generally adjusting to compensate lenders for lower value of receipts. Inflation risk affects lease or buy decisions: With fixed lease payments, inflation tends to increase attractiveness as risk is partly transferred to the leasing agency.
- *Interest rate risk*. Rising interest rates affect the cost of capital: Short-term rates affect financing costs for working capital; long-term rates, particularly when floating-rate instruments are in the debt structure, have an impact on debt service.

- *Exchange rate risk.* When currency exchange is controlled, usually the local currency becomes overvalued, creating the possibility of devaluation and consequent higher prices for imports. An unfavorable balance of payments also carries the risk of devaluation relative to trading partners, which adversely affects the cost of imported intermediates (and makes exports more attractive). Devaluation also increases the level of debt service in domestic currency when there is foreign currency exposure.
- *Marketability (of security) risk.* Shareholders are subject to the vagaries of the market, as prices of their holdings vary according to factors related to the general business climate and project performance. The inverse relationship between market value and interest rates in fixed-income credit markets adversely affects the value of these types of securities held by the enterprise when rates are rising. The possibility of government intervention is another factor; if exchange restrictions are imposed, foreign currency-denominated instruments may lose value.

QUANTITATIVE RISK ASSESSMENT

Risk can be assessed quantitatively and/or qualitatively, commensurate with the forecasting approach employed. Quantitative risk assessment, estimating the probability of an unacceptable outcome, can be applied either to forecasts of performance indicators extrapolated from historical data or to future-oriented predictive models. Qualitative risk assessment is applicable for descriptive scenario forecasts.

Sensitivity Analysis

Sensitivity analysis is a means of analyzing the effects of variations in selected project variables that have significant implications for project performance and associated risk.

Variables included in the analysis (e.g., availability and cost of raw materials, labor, energy supplies; elements of the marketing concept; implementation delays) are selected according to two simultaneous criteria: those that are *subject to large uncertainties* (variability) and that also have a *large quantitative impact.* Using only one of these criteria, say uncertainty, could result in expenditure of resources to study items that have only minor impact. Similarly, it is not particularly useful to perform sensitivity analysis for variables that have a large impact on performance indicators but that are not likely to vary significantly.

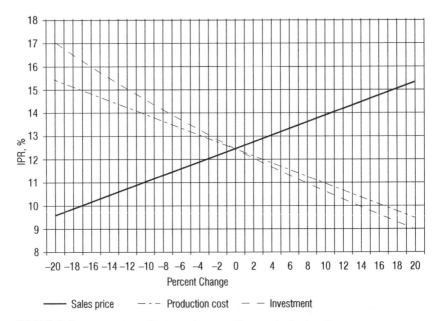

FIGURE 7.2 Sensitivity of IRR to Percent Changes in Project Parameters

To determine critical variables, funds and resource flows are examined to identify investment, revenue, and cost items that have the greatest impact,[12] which can then be studied for potential variability (e.g., quantities and prices) from forecasts. The mechanisms of variability need examination so that operational features that impact upon performance indirectly are understood and taken into account in variability estimates.[13] Values are assigned to potentially critical variables corresponding to pessimistic, normal, and optimistic[14] scenarios, and corresponding performance indicators calculated (e.g., IRR, NPV, breakeven, profit, ratios, payback period).

Figure 7.2 illustrates the kind of relationship that can be developed for the effect on a performance indicator of deviations of project parameters from nominal projected values. In this graph the effect of deviations from the expected investment, sales price, and production cost on internal rate of return (IRR) are shown. The parameters are varied through a range of values above and below the nominal values, and the resultant percentage change in IRR is calculated for each.

In this example, IRR is highly sensitive to investment, and only slightly less sensitive to sales price and production cost. IRR moves in the same direction as deviation in sales price, but opposite to investment and production cost. Similar graphs can be generated for any other static or dynamic performance indicator.[15] Sensitivity, as indicated by the slope of each curve (percentage change in indicator per percentage deviation of parameter), usually varies over a range of deviations in the parameter.

Probability Distribution and Risk

Many commercial and industrial phenomena can be described statistically, and probability of occurrence of a range of parameter values can be determined.[16] Analysis of periodic historical sales of a commodity (and many other phenomena) can be analyzed to ascertain relationships between variables. Distributions can be described mathematically and statistical parameters derived that can be used to estimate probability of occurrence. For example, analysis may reveal that the probability of sales below a minimum acceptable level of 10,000 tons (the risk of not meeting the sales target) is 10 percent.

Patterns of variability for each parameter differ in regard to magnitude, frequency, and project phase. The relationship between deviation patterns for critical variables is of some importance in assessing risk—for example, whether or not critical variables are highly correlated (usually move in tandem). The probability-adjusted or expected value of an indicator, is determined by assigning probabilities to possible values of the variables. In the following example, possible reactions of a competitor to the enterprise as a new entrant and its implications for profitability are shown. The probability of each reaction and its impact is estimated. Each of the alternative reactions would affect sales revenues and costs and require implementation of counterstrategies, which in turn would affect profits for the enterprise. The result is a weighted average profit, as illustrated in the following table:

Possible Reaction	Probability	Profit (Percent)	Weighted Profit
No reaction	0.1	20.0	2.0
Price competition	0.4	18.5	7.4
Marketing	0.3	19.0	5.7
Price and marketing competition	0.2	17.5	3.5
Most likely outcome			18.6

The results indicate that the most likely outcome in regard to competitor reaction is profit of 18.6 percent. The probability of 19 percent or greater is 40 percent (0.3 + 0.1). If the cutoff rate is 18 percent, there is about a 20 percent risk of not achieving the goal (only if the competitor employs price reduction and promotion).

Identifying critical variables, their probable values, and the impacts and timing of likely deviations from the forecast is needed to assess risk—for example, timing of a predicted drop in sales prices, during start-up or after the payback period, and how it would affect project performance. For analysis of multiple variables, stochastic (probabilistic) models may be applied, using distribution functions for each. Stochastic simulation uses the Monte Carlo method, in which random values are assigned to each variable and the corresponding performance indicators are determined, providing a statistical distribution (probability of occurrence) for the indicators.[17] In this way the likelihood that a performance indicator such as internal rate of return (IRR) or net present value (NPV) meets or exceeds the criterion can be estimated with a specified degree of confidence. The usefulness of stochastic models for investment decision making is limited by the accuracy and confidence in the model,[18] and is practicable only for larger projects.

The *variance* is the average squared deviation from the mean. Squaring is employed to deal with deviations that are above the mean (positive) and below it (negative). The *standard deviation* (SD) is the square root of the variance; it is the most common measure of dispersion of values. A relatively large standard deviation connotes greater risk. A *confidence interval* is the range of values of a variable that fall within limits defined by the probability of occurrence. For example, the 90 percent confidence interval for a variable that has a 5 percent probability of exceeding 20 and a 5 percent probability of being below –10 is –10 to 20. This means that there is a 10 percent chance that the variable will have a value less than 10 or greater than 20.

Cumulative probability can be used as a measure of risk, the sum of probabilities that the phenomenon will have unacceptable values. A *continuous probability distribution* is shown in Figure 7.3. The ordinate (vertical axis) is the probability of occurrence of the phenomenon (e.g., NPV, IRR, profit). The abscissa (horizontal axis) is the corresponding value. The curve shows the probability of occurrence for each value. For a continuous distribution it is possible only to determine the probability of a finite interval of values. The principle described applies also to discrete distributions.

For a stakeholder criterion—a minimum profit, IRR, or NPV that is acceptable—any value below that level is unacceptable. The measure of risk, therefore, is the likelihood of performance below the criterion. This is represented by the cumulative probability (sum of probabilities of occurrence) below the criterion, or minimum acceptable outcome.

If the probability distribution is known, the area under the probability curve below the minimum acceptable outcome can be determined. Standard probability distributions are applicable to many phenomena. For example, if the distribution is normal (Gaussian), probability tables[19] can be used to find the number of standard deviations between the mean and the minimum acceptable level and the probability of a value below the minimum. Statistical

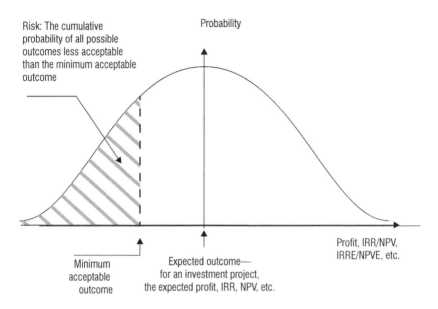

FIGURE 7.3 Cumulative Probability Distribution

parameters can also be derived from historical data applicable to the project (e.g., price history of significant inputs). An example of quantitative risk assessment related to cotton prices is provided on our web site, in discussion of the Cambria Yarns Project.

The *coefficient of variability* is the ratio of standard deviation (e.g., of NPV) to expected value. This indicator perhaps is more meaningful as an indicator of risk than the SD alone as it measures variability relative to expected value. If NPV is 1,000 and SD 10, risk is not very great. For the same SD with NPV of 100, risk is obviously much more significant. If the distribution is normal, one standard deviation on each side of the expected value represents a probability of about 68.3 percent—in other words, there is a probability of about 68.3 percent that the NPV will actually be between ±1 SD of the expected value.

For example, in the Cambria Yarns Project, if the coefficient of variability for NPV(I) equals 1, the SD equals the expected value of 5,950 (expressed in thousands of US$ in the financial tables). A negative value of NPV indicates that the project is financially unacceptable. The probability of occurrence of a negative value can be found as follows (illustrated in Figure 7.4), assuming that NPV(I) is normally distributed:

$$z = \frac{5,950}{5,950} = 1.00$$

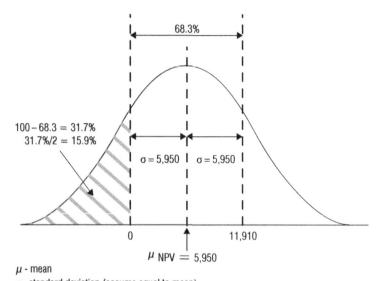

μ - mean
σ - standard deviation (assume equal to mean)

FIGURE 7.4   Cumulative Probability and Risk

where z is the number of standard deviations from the mean. In other words, a reduction of NPV(I) by 1.00 SD would reduce it to zero. From the Gaussian (normal) distribution tables, the area under the (symmetrical) distribution curve outside of ± 1 SD is about 31.7 percent (100 − 68.3). The probability of a value below zero, or the risk of a negative NPV(I), would be about 15.9 percent, as shown in the figure.

As a practical matter, determining statistical variability and risk associated with key indicators requires knowledge of probability distributions of underlying variables (those on which the indicator is dependent). If such variables can be identified, and their probability distributions determined, multivariate analysis techniques can be employed to determine the probabilistic relationship.[20] Another approach to risk assessment associated with key indicators is discrete probability analysis, as illustrated in Appendix 7.1. Expert opinion would normally be the basis for probability estimates of discrete outcomes for independent variables.

Breakeven

The breakeven point (e.g., sales quantity as a percentage of production capacity) is a measure of risk; breakeven close to capacity leaves little margin for error and indicates a high level of risk. *Breakeven* can be determined either on the basis of profit or cash flow. At the breakeven point (BEP), costs are just covered by revenues. An operating loss results if the sum of fixed and variable costs exceed revenues (profit basis) or outflows are not covered by inflows—in other words, a cash deficit occurs if outflows exceed inflows (cash basis).

Breakeven values are computed for a product or defined product mix. If price (rather than quantity) is the variable affecting revenue, the breakeven point defines the price at which revenues equal costs. For multiple products, the sales volume at breakeven consists of a combination of products and prices, but no single breakeven price. The analysis can be based upon linear and nonlinear cost and revenue relationships. Assumptions upon which standard (linear) breakeven can be determined are as follows:

- Variable production and marketing costs are a linear function of (proportional to) production level or sales volume.
- Fixed operating costs are the same for every volume of sales.
- Sales prices for a product or product mix are the same for all levels of output (sales); the ratio of quantities in a product mix is constant.

The standard formula for BEP on a cash basis for an operating enterprise is:

$$BEP_Q = \frac{FC - \text{Depreciation}}{\text{Unit contribution}}$$

where BEP = breakeven point
FC = fixed cost (numerator is fixed cash outflow)
Unit contribution = price minus variable cost per unit

The cash basis for breakeven is considered more appropriate for project planning than the standard profit indicator because liquidity for a fledgling enterprise is such a critical issue. For project planning, the cash flow plan can be used instead, where fixed costs are represented by the fixed cash outflow. Figure 7.5 shows the relationships on a cash basis between revenue (cash inflow), fixed cost, and variable cost.

Breakeven, CYP *Fixed costs* are defined in the operating cost statement, Table 2.13. In the breakeven example of Figure 7.5, general and administrative expenses (G&A) and marketing are also considered completely fixed (to simplify presentation of the concept—not strictly in accord with the fixed-variable designations in Table 2.13). Note that for the cash basis

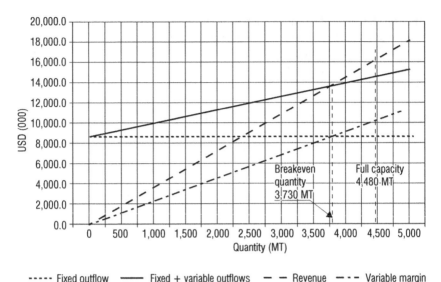

FIGURE 7.5 Breakeven

fixed expenditures replace fixed costs, depreciation is excluded, but debt service is included. Although principal payment on the loan is not a cost, it is included as an element of cash flow when determining cash-based breakeven.

In this example, factory costs are considered completely *variable* (again, to simplify). If operations are above the breakeven point the enterprise generates a positive cash flow; if below, an operating deficit results. The relative slopes of cost and revenue curves and the position of the equilibrium point in relation to total capacity can identify potential weaknesses in the project design.

The BEP is shown in the lower area as the intersection of the variable margin or total contribution (R minus V, or the difference between revenue and variable cost) and the fixed cash outflow (FC). In this case the BEP is 3,730 MT with a capacity of 4,480 MT, or about 78 percent of full capacity. The BEP occurs where the contribution line crosses the fixed cash outflow line. Another way of viewing the relationship in the upper area is the intersection of (FC + V) and R. This follows from the relationship at BEP (Q_{BEP} = quantity at breakeven; p = price; uv = unit variable cost):

$$FC + V = R$$
$$FC = (R - V) = (p - uv)Q_{BEP}$$

For multiple (*n*) products:

$$FC = \sum_{j=1}^{j=n} \left(p_j - uv_j \right) Q_{BEP,j}$$

BEP can be determined mathematically (for a single product) in terms of quantity, sales revenue, and percent of full production:

$$BEP_Q = \frac{FC}{(p - uv)}$$

$$BEP_{Sales} = \frac{FC}{1 - uv/p} = \frac{pFC}{(p - uv)}$$

$$BEP_\% = \left(\frac{FC}{R - V} \right)(100)$$

where
p = price
uv = unit variable cost
$(p - uv)$ = unit contribution
R = revenue at full production
V = variable cost at full production capacity

The measure of risk is the closeness of BEP to planned production. If BEP quantity of production is low (e.g., 50 percent of capacity), there is considerable buffer to accommodate adverse operational results—lower than expected sales or higher than expected investment or operating costs. When BEP is close to production capacity (e.g., 90 percent or greater), the project has greater risk of operating loss.

If the criterion is avoidance of an operating deficit, sensitivity analysis with respect to one or more variables indicates the degree of risk by considering their probable ranges, which can be selected on the basis of risk tolerance. For example, if the acceptable level of risk is 15 percent, the 70 percent confidence interval for the variable (assuming the probability of 15 percent above and below the range) is examined (assuming a symmetrical distribution). Figure 7.6 shows the effect of variations in sales prices for the confidence interval for sales price (+20 percent to –10 percent), with corresponding BEPs (other variables might be similarly examined singly or in combination, e.g., sales quantity, fixed cost, variable cost).

The price multiplier of 0.9 (10 percent price drop) brings BEP almost to the planned production level, so the risk of an operating loss based upon price change is approximately 15 percent.

	Situation 0 (design)	Situation 1 (price up 20%)	Situation 2 (price up 10%)	Situation 3 (price down 10%)
Price multiplier	1.0	1.2	1.1	0.9
Production capacity	4,480	4,480	4,480	4,480
Fixed outflow $US(000)	8,575.7	8,575.7	8,575.7	8,575.7
Price, US$(000)/MT	3.63	4.36	3.99	3.27
Unit variable cost, US$(000)/MT	1.33	1.33	1.33	1.33
Variable margin US$(000)/MT	2.30	3.03	2.66	1.94
BEP (metric tons)	3,730	2,835	3,221	4,429
BEP/production	83.3%	63.3%	71.9%	98.9%

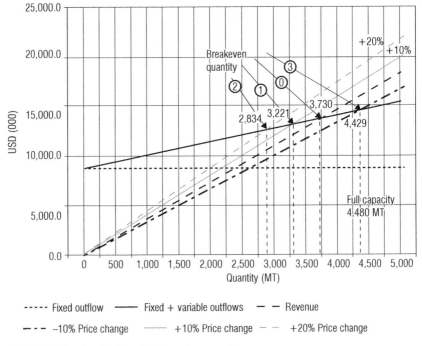

FIGURE 7.6   Sensitivity of BEP to Revenue Change

The result of breakeven analysis depends upon the structure of revenues and costs. BEP differs for periods from start-up to full capacity as finance and other fixed costs and production cost coefficients change with time and experience.

Payback as a Measure of Risk

Events in the future are characterized by greater uncertainty than the present, so they are inherently more risky than current or near-term events. Therefore, to recover the investment in a short time frame is a risk-avoidance measure. A short payback period connotes less risk for the project and investors (see Chapter 3 for a discussion of payback and related financial concepts, including net present value or NPV and hurdle rate).

The payback period is the time, measured from project commencement, necessary to recover initial investment from operating surpluses. Payback can be determined in nominal terms or in discounted form. The latter is more conservative as it will almost invariably show a longer payback period. The discount rate for the dynamic payback is the hurdle rate for the project.

Only investors can define a satisfactory payback period. Five-year plans for existing companies are common, indicating low confidence in estimates beyond that time frame. Managers of enterprises in industrialized countries typically limit their planning to three to five years. These ranges might indicate practical limits for the payback period for investors interested in this means of risk avoidance.

Short NPV

A similar approach to risk avoidance is *short NPV*. Time as an element of risk enters into this approach to risk avoidance. Rather than calculate NPV to the planning horizon,[21] the calculation is limited to a number of years based upon investor preference. Results beyond the point in time for which uncertainty appears to be too great for comfort are ignored. Short NPV is the sum of present values of net flow, using the hurdle rate, up to and including the last period to the shortened planning horizon. The horizon selected depends upon risk tolerance, the industrial sector, and the general economy.

The result should be similar to dynamic payback. In fact, if dynamic payback and short NPV are calculated for total investment, the dynamic payback should occur at approximately the same number of years for which the short NPV would be zero. If the investor's time frame for calculating short NPV is smaller, the outcome will usually be unacceptable (negative short NPV).

QUALITATIVE RISK ASSESSMENT

Qualitative approaches to forecasting inherently include assessment of risk. Descriptions of future scenarios are seldom proposed with an air of certainty (as are quantitative indicators of future performance on occasion). Qualitative risk assessment is more readily comprehensible than quantitative assessment, and for this reason more frequently employed.

Systematic analysis of the economy, social and political systems, and capital markets by knowledgeable individuals is required to predict the future and to understand the major elements of risk and their consequences for the project. The secular or long-term trend of the economy in general, and the industry of interest in particular, are areas to be studied, including the effects of driving forces that will tend to increase or decrease the rate of change.

Performance of economies and particular industries are often cyclical. Some industries are decidedly synchronized with the economic cycle (e.g., consumer durables). Other industries that are more attuned to the pace of technological development follow their own cycles. The ascendant phase of the cycle is more propitious for launching a project than the descendant phase. There is always the question of the extent to which the current cycle will follow past patterns.

RISK MANAGEMENT

Undertaking the project exposes stakeholders to the inherent risk of uncertain outcomes in their investment decisions. To cope with risk, project stakeholders have basically two options (not necessarily mutually exclusive): to seek insurance against identified risks or to engage in active risk control or *risk management*. Hedging instruments are a form of insurance that can be employed in a limited number of situations; access may be a problem, as these instruments may not be available in the markets of some developing countries. Government investment promotion agencies may provide guarantees against some risks, particularly to promote foreign direct investment.[22] Management alternatives are avoidance, mitigation, or spreading risk. The main instrument of the *avoidance* strategy is to invest (or finance) only when the expected returns are higher than the cost of capital plus the risk margin. *Mitigation* involves control or reduction of the forces behind risk—for example, deciding to produce a key input rather than depend on an unreliable supply chain. Risk can be *spread* by agreement (contracts) between classes of investors, lenders, suppliers, and guarantors.

Risk management can be employed in regard to the *investment portfolio*, with risk spread over a number of investments, selected according to risk profile (see the subsection "Portfolio Diversification"). As a practical matter, only entities with control of relatively large amounts of capital can employ this strategy. Financial institutions usually manage risk by employing risk-spreading and hedging mechanisms (see the subsection "Hedging with Derivatives").

Risk management is incorporated into the project design through strategic planning that seeks to enhance opportunities and to reduce threats (see Chapter 1, the subsection "Strategic Project Planning").

Some risk-avoidance measures are identified earlier in this chapter. In these approaches, conservative criteria for performance indicators are selected, such as a low percentage BEP, or a very limited duration for calculating short payback or NPV, in which all data beyond a selected number of years is ignored. Other measures to reduce, avoid, or spread risk for investors are as follows.

Risk Premium

The hurdle or cut-off rate for a project can be increased with a *risk premium*. This raises the barrier, in effect demanding of a project a higher return for its inherent risk or for the risk in the operating environment. If the project is to be financed from capital markets, the cost will generally reflect the level of risk in the particular industrial sector and/or environment.

When the project is to be financed with sponsor's equity, the normal expectation or hurdle rate can be adjusted upward to account for general and sector risk. Of the determinants of the hurdle rate, the risk premium is the discretionary factor (see the "Cost of Capital" section in Chapter 4. Increasing the discount rate will have the effect of reducing the value of NPV, perhaps to the point of driving it to a negative value so that the project would be rejected.

In the following example, at the nominal 10 percent discount rate, NPV is positive (+66) and the project appears acceptable. When a risk adjustment of 5 percent is added to the discount rate (10 percent + 5 percent), NPV is negative (–27). If the risk premium is justified by the state of the economy or by the nature of the venture, the project should be rejected.

	Period						
	1	2	3	4	Discount rate, percent	10	15
Period flow	– 1,000	350	450	500	NPV	66	– 27

Portfolio Diversification

Diversification of investments is a strategy for minimizing risk. Projects are selected for investments that are dissimilar in volatility pattern compared with those already within the investment portfolio. The strategy is appropriate for fairly large and established investors or groups with an investment portfolio, but is rarely an option for new or small-scale investors. One mechanism that can be employed for determining the appropriate mix is the capital asset pricing model (CAPM).[23]

The project is evaluated with reference to other holdings of the investor or group. The basic idea is to construct the portfolio so that all the eggs are not in one basket. A parameter of CAPM is β, a measure of volatility and an indicator of the relationship of project risk to that of the general market or portfolio. The model finds an acceptable risk premium over the risk-free return: Essentially, the risk premium increases if the project characteristics are aligned with the rest of the portfolio because this does not add to diversification. A lower premium (or negative premium) is added if there is greater divergence between project characteristics and the portfolio.

Hedging with Derivatives

The values of derivative financial instruments are based upon an underlying commodity or security. Relatively small financial resources can be used to leverage large amounts of the underlying units. Hedging involves the use of derivatives to buffer potential losses; mechanisms may not be widely available in all countries, but futures contracts on commodities or currencies can be an important tool for risk management where accessible. In futures trading a premium is paid, very much like an insurance policy, to ensure delivery at a set price. In commodity-related projects (inputs or outputs), the use of commodity futures is a very important hedging approach.

If the project expects to require commodities in the future (inputs), it can lock in the price by *buying* futures (the right to exchange local currency for commodities at a specified price). If the price rises before the time that the commodity is required, the increase in the value of the future will basically match the increase in the commodity price. The project can also *sell futures*, to effectively lock in a sales price (revenue). If the sales price falls, the premium received for the futures basically matches the decrease in the sales price so that the revenue is approximately equal to what would have been obtained had the price remained the same.

Completion Contract

The project can ensure a guaranteed minimum level of performance by arranging a completion contract, usually with intervention of third parties or other insurance mechanisms. Completion contracts can cover construction or delivery of goods and services (e.g., a contract with clients to purchase plant output, with suppliers to provide inputs, or with contractors to ensure construction within budget).

RISK IMMUNIZATION FOR FINANCIERS

Financing of projects in unstable economic and political environments is often a problem that can only be solved by immunizing financiers from risk. Attention to the concerns of financiers and how they may be alleviated is often essential for securing credit.

Guarantees

The most common form of coverage is *collateral*, pledges by the borrower of assets that will come under the control of the lender in case of default. Sometimes the assets of the project can represent all or part of the collateral. Fledgling enterprises are seldom in control of many valuable assets. Sometimes project sponsors have to pledge personal possessions, such as land, homes, and other things of value.

The guarantee is another common form of risk coverage for lenders. Third parties are called upon to provide backing for the project, assurances to lenders that the debt will be serviced, or that output will find a market. In some cases the government will back debt with its full faith and credit.[24]

For a large-scale project, a major international finance group may be asked to join as a project lender, which enhances the confidence of the investment community (even if only a small part of the project is covered). The loan originates with a major development bank (e.g., IFC), which may resell a portion of the loan to a commercial syndicate. It is possible to include local businesses, banks, and the host government of the lender or development banks in the finance package.

Direct guarantees are commitments by third parties (individuals or institutions) to ensure the project's compliance with commitments. The guarantor agrees to back up the lender in case of default, in some cases with collateral. The type of guarantee depends upon the financing institution. A government guarantee is sometimes required for multilateral financing.

Lending institutions tend to try to maintain conservative portfolios. They generally prefer to extend credit to secure clients or to clients who can obtain the backing of secure guarantors. Even development banks seek to minimize risk of defaults on servicing of debt. The guarantor may agree to act as the customer of last resort, taking control of unsold product inventory and maintaining the revenue stream so that debt can be serviced.

Other Risk Coverage for Lenders

Some guarantees are indirect—the guarantor does not pledge to cover debt service, but rather provides other forms of backing to enhance lender confidence. For example, the guarantor may consent to an *agreement covering project output* to ensure set payments sufficient to cover debt service and contingencies. The agreement could include transfer of assets of the defaulting project to the lender. Price supports by the host government for project output may be included.

In a *contingency contract* the borrower and/or guarantor agree to take specific action under triggering conditions, such as failure to comply with the production plan or other management shortcomings. This can involve liquidation of assets or other means of raising funds to cover the debt service.

Lenders will sometimes respond favorably to *comfort letters*—endorsements of the project sponsors, as borrowers, by entities with substantial resources at their disposal that are far in excess of the amount of the loan—short of an ironclad guarantee, but implying that support will be offered as a last resort. A creditworthy, respected individual or entity states, in writing, its intention to monitor the project closely, to allow use of its name in connection with the project, and to do all it can to ensure success of the project.

A *conversion right* grants to the lender the right to assume ownership of the project under specified conditions. A *completion contract*, mentioned earlier, also has relevance for the lender, guaranteeing that the project will operate according to specifications (i.e., a determined quantity of output of prescribed quality at specified cost, by a given date, and for a specified duration).

Insurance premiums can be paid to insurance companies or agents to cover assets or against default or adverse business conditions. Coverage for most risks is usually difficult to obtain. Some governmental or quasi-governmental entities such as the U.S. Overseas Private Investment Corporation (OPIC) or the Multilateral Investment Guarantee Agency (MIGA) provide coverage for political risk. The package can be structured to provide coverage for adverse consequences of default, delays, or increased costs attributable to actions of the host country.

A recent innovation is the *credit default swap* (CDS), a form of insurance. In the context of project finance, the buyer of a CDS pays a premium for effectively insuring the underlying debt instrument, and receives a lump-sum payment in case of default. The seller receives monthly payments from the buyer for the duration of the contract. In case of default, the seller has to pay the buyer the amount agreed in the contract. In this context the project would normally be asked to buy the CDS in favor of the lender, who would be compensated in case the project defaults. In other words, the buyer of the CDS pays a premium in return for credit protection; the seller guarantees the creditworthiness of the instrument. The risk of default is transferred from the holder of the fixed-income security to the seller.[25]

A *cross default clause* in a loan contract provides that in case of default, all other loans from the same institution are also in default. This provides some risk reduction for lenders, as other projects of the individual or group for which loans are outstanding to the institution may be able to provide some degree of coverage.

Some *risk-spreading* devices are discussed in Chapter 4 in the subsection "Innovative Financing." Floating-rate instruments shift some or all of the rate risk to the borrower. Syndicated loans spread participation and risk among a number of financial institutions. Lenders can add premiums to riskier parts of the portfolio to compensate for some percentage of defaults.

INTERNATIONAL INVESTORS AND RISK

Investors who are not nationals of the host country are generally averse to change; as noncitizens, they are unfamiliar with the terrain and seek to have a stable platform from which to operate. They tend to be wary of international and domestic economic and political uncertainty.

Larger international enterprises are more likely to accept the risk of concentrating on the project's domestic market, rather than being dissuaded by the need for market diversification of smaller enterprises. To engage in a small (relative to the rest of the portfolio) project with greater risk than their basic business and investment portfolio is not so threatening. Local partners are usually expected to share risk by exposing their own capital resources and to provide or support new equity requirements and liability for any new debt incurred for the project.

Given their presence in unfamiliar terrain, international investors will be more inclined to seek to alleviate risk than those more familiar with the territory. They may seek support from prestigious international co-investors and financiers to help in securing credit from international banks and export credit agencies, or one or more co-investors (e.g., international institutions), either foreign or local, to cover part of the investment package. They may try to find investment structures that reduce immediate financial risk (e.g., joint ventures, management contracts with options to buy shares later), and usually insist, as a condition of their participation, that insurance be provided to protect their assets (e.g., through OPIC) or another form of insurance such as credit default swaps.

To satisfy risk concerns of foreign partners, existing enterprises may have to be restructured so that the new investment is applied to segregated attractive assets only, with the nonperforming assets sold or liquidated.

APPENDIX 7.1: DISCRETE PROBABILITY ANALYSIS—MULTIVARIATE

If the probabilities of discrete values of *independent variables* can be determined, the probability of any combination is the product of the individual probabilities. In the following example, the value and the probability of occurrence are shown of two independent project variables (X = price and Y = production cost) for the pessimistic, likely, and optimistic scenarios, in which case there are 9 (i.e., 3 × 3) probability outcomes for the dependent variable (e.g., NPV). With three underlying variables, the number of probability outcomes would be 27 (i.e., 3 × 3 × 3).

NPV is calculated for each combination of the two parameters, and the probability of each combination is calculated as the product of the individual probabilities of the two parameters. For example, the probability of X = 150 and Y = 300 is (0.4)(0.3) = 0.12 or 12 percent. The sum of probabilities in all cells = 1 (certainty).

The probability of negative NPV can then be estimated by summing the probabilities in each cell (combination of the two parameters) for which the NPV is negative. This will be the probability of an unacceptable outcome. The probability of NPV < 0 (not acceptable) = 0.06 + 0.08 + 0.06 + 0.15 = .35 or 35 percent.

	X	Pessimistic	Likely	Optimistic
Y		100 / 0.30	150 / 0.40	250 / 0.30
Pessimistic	500 / 0.20	−1,000	−800	−600
		(0.06)	(0.08)	(0.06)
Likely	400 / 0.50	−150	700	1,850
		(0.15)	(0.20)	(0.15)
Optimistic	300 / 0.30	1,200	975	3,000
		(0.09)	(0.12)	(0.09)

If the variables are not independent—that is, they are correlated to some extent—the approach should be somewhat different. The probability distribution should take into account tandem movements of the variables.

NOTES

1. External factors, or variables, although nominally outside control of the project, are *uncontrollable* only in a general sense; labor supply, for example, can be affected by the project's organizational structure, job descriptions, and training capacities. Similarly, internal variables are not completely *controllable* as they must accommodate conditions outside the enterprise.

2. See Erich Jantsch, *Technological Forecasting in Perspective: A Framework for Technological Forecasting, Its Techniques and Organization* (Paris: OECD, 1967), 11.3.6, page 174 www.jstor.org/pss/3008658. Jantsch applies morphological research to technological forecasting, identifying the techniques as "the most systematic approach to the generation of new technological information." The principles of morphological research were developed by Fritz Zwicky, astrophysicist at California Institute of Technology, as a method for studying relationships in a complex, nonquantifiable system. See F. Zwicky, *Discovery, Invention, Research—Through the Morphological Approach* (Toronto: Macmillan, 1969); and F. Zwicky and A. Wilson, eds., *New Methods of Thought and Procedure: Contributions to the Symposium on Methodologies* (Berlin: Springer, 1966).

3. The word *consumer* is not intended to connote passive acceptance of what the market has to offer. The term is used only as an efficient way to identify *users* of goods and services of the enterprise (who are likely discerning) and *producers* in another context.

4. The tracking signal can be determined as the ratio of cumulative error (sum of deviations between actual and forecast values over the forecasting periods) to the mean absolute deviation. The tracking signal can be positive or negative, determined by the value in the numerator. A limiting value determines when the forecast is out of control. For an example of the use of tracking signals, see Muhammad Al-Salamah, "Tracking Signal in Forecasting," http://faculty.kfupm .edu.sa/SE/salamah/tracking_signal_in_forecasting/tracking_signal_in_forecasting .htm.

5. Switching costs are costs associated with changing from one supplier to another, which can be tangible or intangible. Some types of costs are incurred in switching to a new supplier are contract termination penalties, setting up new supply channels, learning costs (e.g., new logistics and cognition), possibly new equipment and installations, and new forms of risk.

6. See N. Seitz and M. Ellison, *Capital Budgeting and Long-term Financing Decisions*, 3rd ed. (Harcourt Brace Jovanovich, 1999), 354–355.

7. See J. B. Cohen, S. M. Robbins, and A. E. Young, *The Financial Manager* (Columbus, OH: Publishing Horizons [NIP], 1986), 21.

8. The capital asset pricing model (CAPM) is a method of managing project risk with respect to the investment portfolio of sponsors; see Cohen et. al., *The Financial Manager*.

9. Risks may be categorized in a number of ways. One type of breakdown is as follows: lack of experience of sponsors in similar projects; misinterpretation

of data; bias in the data and in its assessment; changing external economic environment invalidating much of the usefulness of past experience; and errors of analysis. See A. J. Merrett and A. Sykes, *The Finance and Analysis of Capital Projects*, 2nd ed. (London: Longman, 1974), 143.

10. Each type of project has its own particular set of risk factors. Private-public partnerships (PPP or BOT) have four fundamental risk factors:

    1. Risk regarding completion of construction (exceeding cost limits, time delays, acquiring timely permits, lack of needed infrastructure, *force majeure*, etc.)

    2. Operating risk (insufficient demand, return on investment, payment delays, maintenance, *force majeure*, etc.)

    3. Political risk (direct or indirect expropriation, construction of competing public project, taxation, changes in relevant laws, political transformations, strikes, riots, etc.)

    4. Financial risk (debt service, refinancing, changing interest rates, loss of liquidity, exchange rate). See B. Esty, "Poland's A2 Motorway," Teaching Note 5-202-031 (Cambridge, MA: Harvard Business School, 2002).

11. Risk in the host country is usually associated with the economic/political situation—for example, outstanding foreign debt in relation to domestic product, balance of payments, and monetary and fiscal policies.

12. Sensitivity analysis is not usefully applied to the entire range of system components; some might meet the criteria—a particular class of machinery or construction item, for example. Sales price, rather than quantity, might be the major area of uncertainty. Analysis of variability of the parameter is the best way to determine the appropriate range for sensitivity analysis.

13. Statistical estimates of variances and confidence intervals for critical variables are needed for quantitative assessment of risk. Mechanisms of variation are another factor to be investigated, if possible (if not, educated guesses will have to serve). Some variables are particularly volatile, such as transportation (which is influenced by demand and energy costs), and supplies and products in speculative or highly competitive markets. Qualitative analysis of variances is applied to nonquantitative aspects of the project design, such as effectiveness of marketing strategy or political trends.

14. Better-than-expected project performance, although not a threat to project success, is included to understand the range of possibilities.

15. Sensitivity is expressed in absolute terms (e.g., 50 units of NPV per 1 unit of sales price); as percentages (e.g., 10 percent change in NPV per 1 percent change in price); or, as shown in Figure 7.2, absolute change in indicator per magnitude (percent) deviation in independent variable (sales price, investment, or production cost). Sensitivity is usually not constant with respect to percent deviation in the variable. In the example shown, the zero percent (0) deviation represents the expected value; at the expected sales price the IRR is 12.4 percent. If the sales price drops by 10 percent, IRR reduces to 11 percent.

16. Most statistical analysis related to risk assessment can be performed using commercial software such as SAS/STAT, which operates on data sets to provide

statistical parameters. Spreadsheets such as Excel have many statistical features that are useful for risk analysis.

17. Probability and sensitivity analysis involve a considerable amount of computations; computer simulation is usually required.

18. One problem is the independence or correlation of variables—for example, the cost of nitrogen fertilizer production depends upon energy costs, while its market price depends on supply and demand as well as production costs. Identifying correlations between variables is necessary for applying a stochastic model to assess risk (and its implications for investment, production, and marketing strategies).

19. Parameters of standard distributions (e.g., mean, standard deviation, and variance) can be found in many texts on mathematical statistics—for example, P. G. Hoel, *Introduction to Mathematical Statistics*, 5th ed. (John Wiley & Sons, 1984); or W. J. Dixon and F. J. Massey, *Introduction to Statistical Analysis*, 4th ed. (McGraw-Hill, 1984).

20. For more extensive treatment of statistical methods, see G. J. Kress and John Snyder, *Forecasting and Market Analysis Techniques: A Practical Approach* (Westport, CT: Quorum Books, 1994); or T. Lucey, *Quantitative Techniques* (London: DP Publications Ltd., 1982). Techniques for assessing project risk include Monte Carlo simulation, multivariate analysis, and decision tree analysis. Proprietary methods, including software packages, are available from a number of consulting firms.

21. The planning horizon is not necessarily the expected project life. The planning period may be controlled by other factors, such as diminished confidence of stakeholders in projections beyond a certain time frame or standard planning interval for the sponsoring enterprise.

22. Foreign investors, in particular, may be concerned with risks identified with the country—the political situation and state of the economy—considering indicators such as the relationship of foreign debt to GDP. Government guarantees may be necessary to encourage investment, covering, for example, value of investment, currency conversion, or profit repatriation.

23. See Cohen et. al., *The Financial Manager*. An application is included in Appendix 3.1.

24. The Overseas Private Investment Corporation (OPIC) in the United States and the European Investment Fund (EIF) in the European Union are two examples of government-sponsored agencies that guarantee loans for investment projects in developing countries. Each of these organizations has its own criteria for eligibility and loan terms. OPIC requires at least 25 percent equity by a U.S. company and a debt-to-equity ration no higher than 60/40.

25. The CDS market now is greater than that of the underlying debt covered, indicating the degree of speculation associated with these instruments. As there is uncertainly about the owner of a CDS at any time, there is also some uncertainty that the buyer will be compensated in case of default on the underlying credit agreement.

REFERENCES

Bowerman, B., R. O'Connell, and A. Koehler. 2004. *Forecasting, time series and regression: An applied approach*. 4th ed. Florence, KY: Cengage Learning.

Cliff, L. D. 2000. *Risk-based capital: Regulatory and industry approaches to capital and risk*. Reprint. Darby, PA: Diane Publ.

Dixon, W. J., and F. J. Massey. 1983. *Introduction to statistical analysis*. 4th ed. New York: McGraw Hill.

Esty, B. 2002. Poland's A2 motorway. Teaching note 5-202-031. Cambridge, MA: Harvard Business School.

Jantsch, Erich. 1967. *Technological forecasting in perspective: A framework for technological forecasting, its techniques and organization*. Paris: OECD. http://www.jstor.org/pss/3008658.

Kress, G. J., and J. Snyder. 1994. *Forecasting and market analysis techniques: A practical approach*. Santa Barbara: Greenwood Press.

Lucey, T. 1988. *Quantitative techniques*. 3rd ed. London: DP Publications, Ltd.

Makridakis, S. 1998. *Forecasting: Methods and applications*. 3rd ed. New York: John Wiley & Sons.

CHAPTER 8

Project Appraisal

A t all stages of development, appraisal is a process of comparing expected performance and other characteristics with stakeholders' criteria. Study and design provide a conceptual project model describing interactions with the environment, performance indicators, and associated risks. At any stage of the process, stakeholders need to assess whether to continue to the next stage—either with analysis of greater depth or, at the final stage, the decision on whether to go ahead with the investment. Successful investment of capital resources is almost always supported by reasoned justification, whether or not apparent. However, compact reasoning by a seasoned and successful investor or other stakeholder, underpinned by accumulated experience (that often looks like intuition), can be a useful adjunct to more formal appraisal.

Appraisal is essentially a continuous process starting from project conception, with increasing depth and formality as the project approaches the decision point. As design adjustments suggested by feedback from stakeholders, suppliers, and clients are incorporated into the plan, interim reports can be issued noting changes from previous versions. As a practical matter, changes can be compiled over a period of time (e.g., monthly, quarterly) before issuing interim reports, except when a particular change vastly alters the configuration or prospects. Documenting changes can be a daunting task if they take place too frequently.

The outlook of prospective stakeholders is determined by their assessment of how effectively their scarce resources are to be employed: for investors, their capital; for lenders, their pool of funds; for guarantors, institutional integrity; for licensors and regulators, social capital. Reward versus risk is a salient concern of all, but it is a subjective matter.[1] In the final analysis, decision makers will determine how complete a picture of the project they deem necessary: a feasibility/optimality study, or a compilation of information, preliminary and advanced formal studies in some or all areas, intuition, and subjective judgment.

MACRO-MICRO APPRAISAL

Appraisal can be carried out from the point of view of the project as an independent commercial entity, or as it relates to the wider domain that includes the socioeconomic and environmental setting in which it is to operate. In virtually all cases, to a degree commensurate with the size of the project and the scope of its impacts, appraisal advisedly takes the wider domain into account.

As a stone dropped into a pond, an investment project creates ripples beyond the confines of its *commercial domain*—clients, suppliers of goods and services, workers, financiers. Its effects extend beyond those limits and reverberate in the surrounding community (see Figure 1.1 in Chapter 1), effects that are both *internal* and *external* in the sense of not directly affecting the flow of resources and funds into and out of the enterprise. At the micro (project) level, the sponsor's primary concern for the project as a business opportunity is almost invariably supplemented with some concern for wider impacts if only to satisfy licensors and regulators. An appraisal issue is to what extent and how removed from the project these external ripples should be considered—in other words, what are the limits of the project's relevant *wider domain* (see Figure 1.1).

The range of issues to be addressed in the appraisal process has been identified to a large extent during the formulation and design phase. However, for appraisal to be effective, it has to be independent and not constrained by preconceptions of what is applicable and what is not.

Socioeconomic and environmental criteria can be applicable at the micro or macro level. Some criteria relate to conditions at the site, others to regional, national, or even international conditions, depending upon the magnitude and range of impacts.

At the *micro* level, the fundamental issue is *whether the proposal is a good project for the sponsor:*

- Is entrepreneurship available to energize and to retain momentum in the face of obstacles to implementation and growth? Or is it spread too thin to effectively spearhead the project?
- Is the project potentially bankable? Is backing sufficient for financiers to provide the necessary long- and short-term credits?
- Does the project make the best use of the sponsor's resources or can they be used in some other activity to better advantage?
- Is there possible conflict, from the present to the planning horizon, between project and corporate objectives?

At the *macro* level, two types of questions arise, one from the investor's viewpoint and the other from society's. The first is *how the macro environment conforms to project needs:* What are the threats and synergies?

The extent of concern for external impacts depends upon the nature of the project. A relatively small project, with little regional or national impact, may cover the ground by simply setting up a process that informs the public and solicits feedback that leads to acceptance or accommodation; this is probably all that appraisal needs to cover in the investment decision process. Issues of concern for projects that are either large enough or otherwise strategically significant may be dictated by licensing authorities or by prudent consideration of long-term compatibility with local, regional, and national goals.

The second is *whether the project makes sense for the region, country, or in the context of international economy* (depending upon the range of impacts).[2] The justifiable level of appraisal is commensurate with the size and impact of the project and the orientation of stakeholders. Implications for the world economy might be of concern for a major project financed by an international development agency; for relatively small projects, feedback from local political authorities and community leaders may provide sufficient information. In a more general sense, the basic socio-economic issue is whether resources committed to the project are efficiently allocated in regard to macro criteria:

- Is allocation of resources to the project consistent with regional, national, or international development goals (e.g., providing economic improvement, positive distribution effects, technological advance, security)?
- Will the project have positive impact on macroeconomic indicators (e.g., GNP, balance of payments, trade balances, national revenue streams, the global economy)?
- Is the economic rate of return criterion satisfied, at least equal to the social discount rate?
- Is the project ecologically sound and compatible with aspirations for maintaining a healthy physical environment?

Other issues: (1) whether the project is designed to operate in a reasonably sustainable mode so that its presence does not compromise future economic prospects; and (2) whether the project design is consistent with social aspirations and environmental constraints as expressed in statutes and regulations, or by expressions of concern by those affected by its existence, and how it otherwise contributes to or detracts from society's needs. Issues of possible concern are identified in Chapter 1, Appendix 1.1.

SWOT ANALYSIS

An appropriate basic framework for appraisal is SWOT analysis—identification and evaluation of internal strengths and weaknesses, and external opportunities and threats—which should be progressively applied at each development stage and from the point of view of the particular evaluator.[3] While this analysis is most conventionally applied to the commercial domain, it is equally applicable to the wider domain, as described in Chapter 1.

Strengths and Weaknesses

Strengths are the internal factors that provide an advantage over competitors (or alternative applications of resources). This may include such things as prior experience of the sponsor or a proven market in a related line of goods or services; or a patented process of manufacture, superior in quality to the competition. *Weaknesses* are characteristics that fall short of desirable internal project features, such as limited availability of experienced management personnel, or lack of a secure line of short-term credit. Security and reliability—the extent to which adequacy of internal features can be predicted with a high degree of confidence—are measures of strength. If strong features predominate, and operational criteria are otherwise met, the project is worthy of implementation. Weak features have to be hedged in some way so that their potential adverse consequences are averted.[4]

Opportunities and Threats

Opportunities are propitious external conditions, existing or foreseen—for example, rapid economic growth in the region with demand for the project's output enhanced by higher levels of income or incentives offered by regional authorities. *Threats* are external impediments to project success, such as imminent introduction of an attractive and competitive substitute product, or lack of suitable infrastructure (or the prospect of inadequate maintenance) at the selected site. Examples of opportunities and threats that warrant examination are as follows:

Opportunities	Threats
Economic growth	Economic decline (recession)
Growth sector	Market saturation
New markets	Diminished availability of resources
Cost push (sellers' inflation)	Degraded image
Propitious regulatory change	Adverse regulatory change
Fortuitous political change	Hostile political change
Weakening competition	Strengthening competition
Availability of renewable inputs	Reliance on depleting resources

- *Economic growth rate.* "The rising tide lifts all boats" (except for those with a hole in the bow) in a growing national economy. With economic recession the situation is reversed.

- *Sector growth rate.* Growth in the project's industrial sector is fortuitous—increasing demand may be a response to improvements in product technology or changes in lifestyle. If the sector is cyclical (i.e., demand for the product follows the general economic cycle), entry during the ascendant phase is less risky, in contrast to the situation where the market is at or near saturation.

- *New markets.* Market opportunities can arise from newly established international trade agreements, technological innovations, or advancements in transportation technology or packaging.

- *Change in resource availability.* Accessibility to needed resources can be threatened by supply tightness (unforeseen constraints on production resources), depletion (inaccurate estimates of natural deposits), or contamination (upstream discharges to clean water necessary for the production process).

- *Cost-push*, or *sellers' inflation*, results from increases in factor costs not being matched by increases in productivity. The opportunity arises for more efficient processes to replace older technology. The project has the advantages of (1) not having to contend with, and possibly replace, older but still serviceable equipment; (2) advances in technology; and (3) learning from the mistakes of older (in terms of service) competitors.

- *Image.* The image of an existing enterprise can be damaged by a project (venture) that fails to meet expectations—that is, if the new product is not well accepted by the market or if the venture places strains on operations or profitability, whereby access to capital sources or credit can be adversely affected. Unacceptably adverse social or environmental impacts may bring on greater regulatory pressures.

- *Regulation and deregulation.* Regulation implies a degree of market protection, but usually at the expense of controls that may negatively affect profits. Deregulation opens opportunities for access to markets and pricing strategies (but enhances prospects for risky behavior of competitors).

- *Political change.* Pending changes in the political environment can be opportunities or threats, more or less favorable to the project investment. Sectors can be opened or closed, profit repatriation liberalized or restricted, foreign direct investment encouraged or restricted.

- *Competition.* Competitors may be strengthening their positions and increasing market share through such means as new and better management, improved technology, innovative marketing strategy, or image enhancement. Opportunity arises from weakening competition (e.g., loss of competent management, liquidity problems, marketing fiascos).

- *Renewable inputs.* The opportunity for access to renewable, as opposed to reliance on nonrenewable or depleting, resources makes the project more attractive in terms of sustainability and also in regard to eliciting favorable responses from regulators and the general public.

STAKEHOLDER PERSPECTIVES

Each project participant (stakeholder) has particular criteria, interests, and priorities. Even within an investment group, individuals may not view the project in the same way. A young investor may look for long-term results while an older investor seeks more immediate but also safer returns. Investors, financiers, regulators, licensors, guarantors, suppliers, promotion agencies, and the general public all have private or public interests to be served. Even if a project study report is geared to a general audience, appraisal is very specific.

Issues of primary, secondary, or tertiary interest to each stakeholder can be arranged in a matrix indicating the degree of concern, but *they cannot be identified categorically*. The following table illustrates a possible breakdown of the varying interest levels of participants for project features (it may not be representative of all projects):

	Investor	Financier	Regulator	Guarantor	Supplier	Citizen
Market	2	1	0	1	2	0
Technology	2	0	0	1	1	0
Financial						
Return	2	1	0	1	1	0
Liquidity	2	2	0	2	2	0
Debt service	2	2	0	2	1	0
Economic	1	0	2	0	0	1
Environment	1	0	2	0	0	2

2 = Highly interested; 1 = Mild interest; 0 = Not interested.

Issues relevant for each stakeholder are project-specific. Any of the issues listed in the discussion of the content of an appraisal study (see the later section "Appraisal Report") can be of greater or lesser relevance for any stakeholder.[5] As a general rule, investors are interested in the rate and timing of financial benefits; financiers, in the reliability of debt servicing; regulators, in the degree to which local, regional, or national objectives are served; guarantors, in the degree of risk of having to cover obligations; and suppliers, in the project's viability as a long-term client. All participants realistically have some level of interest in all aspects of the project: If investors sneeze (expected profitability not achieved), financiers may catch the flu (suffer default on the loan).

Risk

An overriding consideration in appraisal is the element of risk. To be appropriately applied, criteria should be risk-adjusted either through formal statistical means[6] or by estimates from knowledgeable experts. Most people are risk-averse, seeking to minimize threats, although some gravitate to the challenge of difficult hurdles (risk analysis is covered in depth in Chapter 7).

The major issue to be addressed is whether identifiable risks are within tolerance, which varies for each stakeholder. Risk pervades the entire project design—the business model, financial arrangements, technology, and project design. Consequences can involve the need for additional investment; a liquidity crisis; higher-than-expected production, marketing and finance costs; or lower-than-expected production, sales volumes, and sales prices. Identifying relevant elements and levels of significant risk allows each stakeholder to decide if the likelihood of an undesirable outcome is acceptable.

Risk concerns differ for public- and private-sector projects. In the private sector, risk assessment is closely linked to profits or cash flow for investors. For public-sector projects, risk is more associated with providing the intended services within budgetary constraints. Lenders for projects in both sectors are generally concerned primarily with service of their loans.

Conflicting Views of Venture Partners

Foreign and local partners usually have decidedly differing viewpoints concerning the price of participation—that is, what proportion of total equity is to be provided by each partner for a share of the enterprise. Role-playing in this kind of encounter, taking the position of the partner, is a good way to resolve these kinds of issues. For the local partner, the foreign counterpart is looked upon as an individual or group for whom paying more for participation than would be expected of a local investor is rationalized by the partner's affluence or covetousness regarding local markets. The foreign partner regards the local partner as the beneficiary of business acumen and resources; confidence in the abilities of the local partner is tempered by its relatively weak position: "If they were competent, they would be wealthier (more successful)." Major issues of concern to local venture partners include these:

- Does the project offer potential for complementary benefits for partners' enterprises (e.g., incremental cash flow, market research, management contracts)?
- Are there benefits related to technology transfer and know-how (technological enhancement, attractive lump-sum and royalty payments)?
- Will there be improvements in supply chains for other partner operations—greater and more reliable channels, quantities, lower prices?
- Does the project offer possibilities for securing or opening new domestic or export markets?

Prospective foreigner investors, unfamiliar with the culture and history of the host country, are more inclined than local investors to be concerned with political, economic, and social issues, such as these:

- Political stability and orderly transition of political power, conducive to a healthy business climate.
- Economic trend (growth rate), as it affects prospects for political stability, strong domestic demand, availability of domestic credit, and prospects for future earnings.
- Monetary policy: Inordinate expansion carries the threat of domestic inflation; contraction in the money supply may create problems of credit availability and higher interest rates.
- Fiscal policy: expenditures that reflect economic need rather than special interests, consistent with revenues to avoid overstimulation with inflationary consequences.
- Trade policy: Unrestricted trade is regarded favorably if inputs are imported and for exported products; restrictions on competing imports may be regarded favorably, at least in the short term.
- Trade balance: A favorable balance is conducive to free currency exchange and avoidance of overvalued local currency vis-à-vis currency of the foreign partner.
- Accounting standards: how accurately the domestic partner's balance sheet reflects actual values of assets and liabilities.
- Legal system: promulgation of laws and jurisprudence; transparency of procedures; uniformity of application.
- Social legislation and evolution: Its history and development are of concern; if properly conceived and administered, the social welfare program

can be regarded favorably as a contributor to a healthy and educated population and political stability.

- Labor climate and availability: Inadequate economic distribution mechanisms with potential for labor unrest may be regarded unfavorably. Existence of legal and administrative worker protections may be viewed favorably as potentially enhancing qualities of the work force. Heavy-handedness with regard to workers by political authorities is generally regarded as a serious problem. A highly skilled and plentiful workforce reduces problems of recruitment and training.
- Demographics—numbers, growth rates, age and income distribution—and migrations that affect markets as they relate to demand (e.g., urban populations of middle-class consumers); however, a very high rate of population growth can be an economic and social destabilizer.
- Financial system: efficiency, consistency, transparency, regulation in the banking system; efficient, transparent, and regulated capital markets.
- Foreign direct investment (FDI) policy: a supportive attitude as expressed by administrative and legislative actions; liberal policy toward currency convertibility and repatriation of profits; transparency and promptness of review by regulatory and licensing authorities of investment proposals.
- Infrastructure: communications, transport, energy, and other infrastructure services important for project operations; compatibility and/or integration with infrastructure features in the investor's home country is a consideration (e.g., communications systems).
- Living conditions: quality of conditions for sponsors, managerial staff, and work force; community facilities (e.g., recreation, education).
- International profile—foreign relations and domestic practices of the country: harmonious membership in the international community; participation in normal, unfettered, and fair trade relations; adoption of internationally acceptable legal and judicial standards; protection of intellectual property rights.

APPRAISAL REPORT

An appraisal report, in which issues of significance are reviewed and evaluated from the perspective of each participant, is virtually essential for rational decision making, based upon the project study and other information available to the appraiser. If prepared by a consultant, the project is to be appraised according to criteria of project sponsors, or the audience that project sponsors wish to address (financial institutions often order such reports before granting loans). *Alternative reports* may be required, as interests and criteria of participants differ substantially. It is possible to address the concerns of all participants in a single report, in which special concerns of one or another are highlighted.

Outline of Appraisal Report

A suggested general outline for an appraisal report follows (relevant portions of the project design/study should be referenced in each area):

- *Purpose.* What is the intent of appraisal? Who is the client, what is the scope, and what are the perspectives? The scope, for example, may be limited to determining whether a joint venture proposal is workable and in the local partner's interests.
- *Project background.* This section describes the project origins, participants, and relationships with other institutions.
- *Analysis.* Consistent with its purpose, the analysis compares project performance characteristics with stakeholder criteria, and illuminates any other areas that warrant attention in the view of the appraiser.
- *Conclusion.* Taking all the preceding factors into account, the report should contain a statement regarding the overall acceptability of the project according to stakeholder criteria (investor or other participant) and the project's compatibility with other activities and goals.

Appraisal: Issues to Be Addressed

In general, the appraisal report (1) identifies critical design and operating characteristics in each of the following areas, and (2) explains whether there are plausible strategies to achieve desired outcomes and to control or manage associated risks.

Business/Operating Plan

- Is the proposed project concept plausible and doable? Are general and marketing strategies suitable for achieving project goals? Is the project design (e.g., marketing concept, technology, capacity, location) consistent with the strategy and availability of required resources?
- Is the macroeconomic environment propitious? Are expanding markets supported by general economic prosperity, or are there other supportive conditions that are independent of the economic cycle?
- Does the project align with institutional or personal preferences and commitments? Is its degree of alignment conducive to eliciting

approbation and support of key individuals and organizations, and building image or prestige (high visibility) important to stakeholders?
- Is the project compatible with other investments, operations, missions, interests, abilities?

Commercial/Market

- *Product characteristics, life cycle.* Does the nature of the product or service respond to the needs and/or demands of potential consumers? Is its position in the anticipated life cycle propitious for investment (i.e., not imminently obsolescent or subject to substitution)?
- *Market for product/service.* Does market study demonstrate that there is *sufficient demand* for goods and services to be produced?
- *Sound marketing strategy.* Is the marketing plan logical and workable? Is there a *need to be filled* and a viable plan to fill it? Is the information infrastructure adequate for carrying out the marketing plan? Will the plan work in the proposed environment, considering the likely counter-measures of competition?
- *Realistic sales projections.* Are the sales projections based upon a realistic assessment of the target market? Are estimates of market share and penetration attainable? Are sales prices realistically estimated?
- *Viable distribution plan.* Is there a workable system for delivering project output to the market that will continue to the planning horizon?

Engineering and Technology

Technical issues that deal primarily with physical viability are relevant to concerns of all participants—the body of the enterprise has to function adequately for the mind to be effective:

- *Production at competitive costs.* Can the technology produce the planned output at competitive costs?
- *Process technology.* Is the necessary technology available? Is further development required to demonstrate that it can function effectively under operating conditions, at least at the pilot or prototype stage?
- *Sustainable under operating conditions.* Will the technology be able to function over the long run under conditions at the plant site? Will the project adversely affect prospects for future investments? Are parts and services available?
- *Quality demanded by market.* Does the process ensure the quality demanded by the market? Are the qualities of available inputs adequate to meet product standards? Will quality standards result in a higher than acceptable proportion of rejected output?

- *Reliable inputs to planning horizon.* Is sufficiency of materials and other inputs ensured over project life? Are supplies and their price estimates reliable?

Organization, Personnel, Management

This section concerns the facilities and systems that compose the physical entity, which cannot function effectively without adequate structure and direction.

- *Competent entrepreneurship.* Is there a competent entrepreneur to provide leadership—an individual or group within the organization with the necessary vision, intelligence, energy, and commitment to overcome obstacles that are surely going to appear?
- *Competent management.* Have people with necessary managerial skills been identified with the capacity to build and operate the enterprise?
- *Execution capability.* Is the organization capable of executing necessary functions? Is the structure appropriate? Are all functions allocated within the structure to maximize synergies and minimize interferences? Does the structure provide the functions and interactions necessary to execute implementation, operations, and marketing plans?
- *Personnel availability.* Is the project reasonably assured of personnel being available or who can be trained, *within acceptable costs,* to staff administrative, marketing, and production functions? Are there sufficient technical personnel (engineers and skilled technicians) available? Will competition for their services be an insurmountable problem?

Financial

Financial appraisal concerns profitability, liquidity, and adequacy of available capital to finance the project.

- Do projected revenues and operating costs provide acceptable profit margins? Do cash returns meet minimum expectations (NPV, IRR)? Is payback acceptable? Does expected breakeven provide an adequate safety margin? Are other indicators satisfactory in relation to criteria?
- Is the magnitude of investment within capital constraints? Are sources of finance identified and committed to supplying the necessary capital to cover the initial investment during planning and implementation phases?
- Are adequate financial resources available for all operating periods to the planning horizon? Will there be sufficient domestic currency and foreign exchange to meet financial operating needs over the life of the project? Does the financial plan demonstrate that there are adequate financial resources from internal and external sources to cover all

periods of operations (and decommissioning when necessary)? Is the project capable of servicing loans, and with what level of security? What is the likelihood of default considering project resources, experience, and guarantees?

- How sensitive are financial indicators to uncertainties in the information base upon which the project design is predicated, to inflation and relative price changes, and to changes in the business environment (e.g., competitors, consumers, markets, supplies, and public policies)?

- Is the financial structure acceptable? Does the financial structure satisfy the criteria of investors, lenders, and guarantors? Are the provisions of equity and debt financing satisfactory in terms of liquidity and risks of inflation and fluctuations in interest and exchange rates?

Lenders

Issues particularly relevant for lenders include:

- Does the study indicate adequate coverage of debt service and other financial obligations to the planning horizon?

- Is the project compatible with the lender's portfolio structure and with institutional experience (types of projects successfully financed)?

- Does it conform to development objectives (particularly for an institution mandated to promote economic development along specified lines)?[7]

- How will the project affect client relations (e.g., interests of preferred clients)?

- Is the magnitude of investment appropriate? Is it large enough to warrant syndication? If the loan is relatively small, is the cost of administering the loan too great?

- Is there potential for indirect gains—that is, benefits to be derived from additional activities of linked projects?[8]

Wider Domain

The project must operate within constraints of the external environment —regulatory, statutory, and in some cases socially responsible approaches to its physical, economic, and sociocultural dimensions. Whether or not the project is subject to licensing by a regulatory or statutory authority with specific economic and social criteria to be satisfied, it is prudent to assess compatibility with relevant elements of the wider domain as described in Chapter 1. For example, if unregulated degradation of the physical environment would occur as a consequence of the project, sponsors should at least be aware of the effects on their criteria if it became necessary to alleviate the problem (e.g., impact of cost of mitigation on profitability or payback). For some impacts only qualitative assessment may be possible (see Chapter 7).

Economy

- Is there possible conflict, from inception to the planning horizon, between the project and regional, national, or international goals?
- Is the project in conformance with policies, statutes, and regulations governing the type and pace of industrial development?
- How will the project contribute to the economy, to distribution and other economic goals?
- Will the project make efficient use of economic resources, and are there better alternative uses of the main inputs?
- Is the project consistent with other national priorities (e.g. security, trade, clean environment)?

Social and Cultural Milieu

- Is the project compatible with cultural mores and traditions? If not, are there plausible ways to overcome consequences?
- Are there social consequences, such as displacements of populations or degradation of the quality of life, that have not been adequately resolved?

Environmental Issues

- Do emissions and effluents to be generated by the process exceed regulated standards? If so, are there measures of mitigation to bring emissions to acceptable levels?
- Are the impacts on habitats acceptable to regulatory authorities? Are inhabitants likely to object to emissions if they are not yet aware of the impacts? What measures are included in the plan for dealing with public opposition?
- Are product features environmentally acceptable? Does operation or use of the product or its disposal create environmental impacts that may be of concern to users, to the general community, or to national authorities?
- In the absence of emissions standards, do impacts indicate the likelihood of future regulatory actions? Does the nature of the process or product cause concern about regulatory actions that might require design modifications? What impact will anticipated regulation have on the project in terms of capital expenditures and modifications to operations and costs?

■ Are there sustainability issues? Is the project capable of continuing operations over the long run without encountering resource constraints or unacceptable cumulative ecological, social, or economic impacts?

Risk Assessment

Have risks been identified concerning the project's internal features and interactions with its commercial and wider domains, and satisfactory plans included to eliminate, mitigate, or spread risk so that the probability of failure is within acceptable limits?

Appraisal, CYP   The range of issues to be covered in an appraisal report for the CYP are selected from those identified in the preceding list. Major risks to be scrutinized with care include transportation of finished goods to the port; transition of farmers from sorghum to cotton production; and price fluctuations for output (see CYP on our web site). The strategy of utilizing the foreign partner's (NTC) existing distribution network and aggressive pricing is an area of concern. From the commercial perspective, the project appears to be satisfactory in terms of return on investment and equity, and also for each of the partners (NPV in US$000), including sensitivity to expected variations in parameters.

	Hurdle Rate (%)	NPV	IRR
Investment	8.6	5,947.5	12.4
Equity	12.0	1,971.3	15.3
CIL	12.0	314.5	14.7
NTC	12.0	1,656.7	15.4

The economic impact of the project appears to be favorable: when distribution effects are taken into account. NPV in terms of the accounting unit (consumption relative to the base level, in US$000) is a positive 1,218.6, IRR at 12.3 percent compared with the economic discount rate (EDR) of 10.3 percent. At the economic efficiency level, i.e. without distribution, the project appears unacceptable economically, with NPV negative ($-2,999.1$) and $IRR_{VEF} = 5.8\%$, considerably less than the EDR. Major risks from the socioeconomic point of view include increase in environmental degradation from cotton production in the area and the rate of transition to more sustainable agriculture; and possible retaliation from providers (exporters) of yarns to domestic textile producers.

CAVEATS FOR THE APPRAISER

Some familiar themes ripple through the history of investment project development gone awry:

- *Wrong timing:* trend of the sector in decline; economy in the descent phase of the necessary cycle; product in the late stages of product life; lateness in regard to activities of competition; too long a delay for repair/modernization investment; commencement of project implementation before funds have been secured.

- *Nonoptimal financing:* cost of capital too high (e.g., greater than the return on capital); excessive debt service load during the early part of the operations phase; failure to consider the cost of capital for the total financing package (e.g., fees, discounts, and commissions); too heavy reliance on debt financing with insufficient internal funding; heavy taxation resulting from poorly timed financing charges or depreciation.

- *Insufficient working capital:* absence of a secure line of credit to cover needed cyclical working capital requirements (particularly foreign exchange); inadequate financing for expanding operations.

- *High leverage:* too high reliance on debt for the capital structure, leading to excessive debt service and risk of default.

- *Overestimated market potential:* unrealistic estimates of market size and the ability to capture market share; assumptions on capturing market share without a workable strategy, with attendant overestimation of the revenue stream.

- *Underestimated capital cost:* assumptions about pricing of capital goods and production inputs based upon current conditions that may not prevail over the life of the project.

- *Underestimated competition:* assumption that competition will stand still in the face of a new player; lack of awareness of potential countermeasures that may thwart the best-laid plans.

- *Planned capacities inconsistent with market:* possible acquiescence to capacity promoted by equipment suppliers that is unrelated to demand and market potential.

- *Unidentified sources of skilled personnel:* assumption of availability of suitably skilled personnel; local managers and technicians lacking experience in the industry, or skills necessary to deal with the advanced technology selected.

- *Inadequate infrastructure:* deficiencies in support services and infrastructure.[9]

- *Project design alternatives:* insufficiently studied alternative solutions (e.g., regarding environmental protection or mitigation); unjustified reliance on early design concepts rather than accumulated information; inadequate attention to market, technology, and financial alternatives.
- *Location and site selection:* based on noncommercial (e.g., political) preferences.
- *Ineffective planning:* expansion too rapid; problems of implementing new technologies overlooked.

NOTES

1. Assume, for example, that a project requires an investment of 100 (a numerical measure of the necessary resources). One project may have a reward of 100 with a probability of 50 percent, and a 50 percent probability of no reward, while another with the same investment requirement may have a reward of 75 with a probability of 90 percent, and a 10 percent probability of no reward. Which is the better choice? The answer will not be the same for all decision makers (see Chapter 7).
2. This assessment generally requires a form of economic cost/benefit analysis (ECBA) in conjunction with an environmental impact assessment (EIA).
3. Project features are rarely distinguishable as purely internal or external. An essentially internal feature (e.g., corporate culture) is inevitably linked to the external environment (e.g., mores, cultural practices of host community).
4. Indicative of adverse consequences of unanticipated weakness is the usually severe adverse reaction in capital markets to an unpleasant negative surprise (e.g., lower than expected earnings); confidence is shaken in the ability of management to understand the intricacies of the business.
5. An appraisal report will naturally focus on those issues of primary concern to the stakeholder who commissioned it.
6. If project data is suitable for statistical analysis, criteria can be measured against confidence intervals for indicators, derived from statistical treatment of project parameters.
7. For development finance institutions, the project's impact on development objectives (e.g., national income and distribution impacts, measured with economic cost/benefit analysis) may be of primary concern.
8. Potential for indirect gains may determine financing decisions of commercial banks.
9. As an example, a coffee processing plant was constructed that required large quantities of electrical power without accounting for the distant location of the nearest substation (and associated cost to build a transmission line).

REFERENCES

Amachree, S. M .O. 1988. *Investment appraisal in developing countries*. Farnum, Surrey, UK: Ashgate Publishing, Ltd.

Chong, Gin. 2007. How to appraise investment projects. *Journal of Corporate Accounting and Finance* 19 (2) (December).

Dayananda, D., S. Harrison, and R. Irons. 2003. *Capital budgeting: Financial appraisal of investment projects*. London: Cambridge University Press.

Overseas Development Administration. 1989. Appraisal of projects in developing countries: A guide for Economists/HM3587. 3rd ed. Norwich, UK: HMSO Books.

CHAPTER 9

Implementation Planning and Budgeting

A s part of the investment decision process, a preliminary implementation plan provides a foundation for estimating the schedule and cost of bringing the project to fruition. Information derived from this plan—the magnitude and timing of investment—is a principle determinant of the project's viability. Although not as precise and detailed as more advanced postinvestment decision planning, this step greatly reduces the chance of major divergences between the plan and the actual costs and schedules of the construction/enterprise formation process, which can be anywhere from unpleasant to catastrophic.

Once sponsors decide to go ahead with the project, implementation planning—detailed design, procurement of machinery and equipment, construction of facilities, and formation of the enterprise—is the next logical step. The schedule of implementation and related expenditures is of importance regarding both capital availability and effects on performance indicators to be measured against stakeholder criteria. Careful and accurate formulation of the preliminary plan (prior to, and as necessary information for, the decision) is a prudent investment of design/study time and resources, even in the early stages, when uncertainties are greatest.

Investors need assurance that their profitability and payback estimates will not be less favorable than expected as a consequence of cost overruns. Delays might jeopardize loan agreements. Lenders need to plan their disbursement and retrieval of principal, interest, and fees, as commitment fees for undisbursed funds are usually less than the interest that would be collected, which would affect their rate of return and cash flow projections. Other possible adverse consequences include abrogation of contracts for personnel services, capital equipment, and material suppliers.

The *investment project* is the entire process of conceiving, promoting, planning, and constructing the enterprise. The decision to go ahead signals the start of implementation. An implementation schedule—a compilation of all activities and events leading to the completed plant being ready for operations and to the formation of the functional enterprise—is an integral part of investment design/study, and provides essential information for the investment decision: the flow and timing of resources and expenditures.

Implementation is, in effect, a separate project, or subproject, with a narrow focus. Planning and managing implementation, in turn, is divided into areas or sub-subprojects that may be managed separately—creation and activation of the operating organization, and construction, activation, and commissioning of the plant and ancillary facilities to prepare them for production—a good idea with or without a turnkey construction contract, and always well coordinated with overall project management.

The implementation subproject (see Figure 1.3) consists of activities and events from the time of the investment decision to commencement of operations. Its goals can be viewed as intermediate objectives in the larger project context. Necessary resources, both human and material, are to be mobilized to complete all tasks in the proper sequence so that the result is an organization ready to function and a plant that is ready to operate according to specifications.

The implementation project has a start date, determined by the time it takes to organize after a decision to go ahead, and a completion date, the time when the plant will be ready to commence commercial operations. It is conducted under fiscal and time constraints derived from the preliminary budget and schedule developed during the preinvestment phase and upon which the investment decision was predicated. The budget and schedule are based upon estimates of activities and resources required to create the functioning enterprise. To satisfy performance criteria, expenditures have to be either reasonably consistent with estimates or adjusted to the satisfaction of stakeholders. Completion delays may significantly diminish the attractiveness of the project as an investment opportunity.

IMPLEMENTATION PLANNING

The two levels of implementation planning are (1) a preliminary plan developed in the early stages prior to the investment decision, and (2) a more detailed project implementation plan after the decision has been made to invest and to go ahead with construction.

Preliminary (Preinvestment) Implementation Plan

As part of the project study and as input for the investment decision, a preliminary implementation plan is needed for budgetary purposes. It deals with issues associated with constructing and commissioning the plant—quantities and timing of material, personnel, and financial needs. Activities are usually more aggregated and approximated than for post-decision planning. Of particular concern at this preliminary stage are the duration of implementation and resource requirements (i.e., timing, quantities, and types of capital required during each project period).

The plan describes the process from the investment decision to the state of the enterprise at the termination of the implementation project—the steps necessary to assemble and activate facilities, organizations, systems, and materials to achieve operational status.

The preliminary plan does not require the breadth and depth of detail of the postdecision plan (the project implementation plan, described next) but it needs to be sufficiently accurate and consistent with it to predict timing of major activities and events, to plan resource flows (e.g., financial), and to support the investment decision. It is usually prepared from secondary information (plans of similar existing enterprises) or by an experienced consultant in the field.

Project Implementation Plan

After the decision to invest, a detailed project implementation plan (PIP) is prepared by the implementation team. The design of the PIP and how well it is executed have major implications for performance of the enterprise. The plan comprises a network of phased, interrelated activities and events (some of which may be concurrent) necessary to complete the project. Their timing and interrelations define phasing of personnel and material resource needs, which in turn defines budgets, timing and magnitude of disbursement plans, and funding requirements. The degree of compliance with the plan affects how well performance criteria are satisfied. Delays or overruns have consequences for project liquidity and can also adversely affect financial and economic rates of return.

The PIP is derived from the design/study that defines basic project parameters. Its purpose is to guide the implementation project to completion, according to schedule and budget, and to indicate need for corrective actions when deviations from the plan are encountered. The PIP, describing activities and events in a logical order and sequence, covers two essential areas: company formation and the construction and commissioning project. The plan needs to be updated as work progresses.

The PIP consists of dovetailed and interlinked activities and events that must be completed to create a functioning enterprise, from the point of the investment decision to initial production. Its scope is similar, if not identical, to the preliminary implementation schedule from the project study, the difference ideally being of depth rather than breadth. However, despite due diligence, divergences between the two plans are likely, the result of factors unforeseen during preliminary planning. This is why price and quantity contingencies are sometimes added to the nominal investment package.

If the implementation period is very long (e.g., a construction period of two, three, or more years), budgets may need to be reviewed for inflation and escalations. Monitoring the relationship of estimates in the preinvestment study to actual costs incurred during the implementation phase is a means of detecting cost overruns and assessing their implications for liquidity, finance requirements, and profitability.

PROJECT MANAGEMENT

An implementation project of virtually any size requires good management skills to bring the project to fruition after a go-ahead decision with the greatest likelihood of success (on time and on budget). An organization is to be created and/or a manager assigned (depending upon project size and complexity) whose mission is to plan, execute, monitor, and control the project. The team initially consists of a core group—the project manager and support staff—with responsibility to develop the PIP. Once the plan is reviewed and accepted by project sponsors, the implementation team can be filled out—staff assembled and provided permanent or temporary facilities to carry out their work.

After approval of the PIP by project sponsors, the team is assigned responsibility and authority to carry out the plan and to negotiate agreements with suppliers, contractors, and consultants. Knowledge of conditions at the site and a broad understanding of the working environment are virtually essential for project leadership. Awareness of the commercial setting, socioeconomic conditions, and the ecology of the region or site facilitates good decision making.[1] All the pieces in the puzzle must fit together—failure of any one may jeopardize the project. For example, efficient port facilities that are important for the project design may be available but ineffective if the highway to the port is badly maintained (perhaps because the highway authorities are inexperienced, understaffed, or underpaid).

Management responsibility and authority from conception to the planning horizon can be divided essentially into three levels: sponsors/investors; general contractor for the construction project; and a number of subcontractors who usually carry out much of the work of building the plant, assembling, and installing the production facilities.[2]

Level 1: Project Development

Authority: Sponsor/investor.

Responsibilities: Profit and loss for the entire investment project—implementation, enterprise formation, operations, decommissioning (when applicable).

Activities:
- Appointment of the implementation team.
- Originating and appraising the project concept.
- Project design and feasibility/optimality studies.
- Preliminary engineering and selection of technology.
- Technology acquisition and transfer.
- Project finance—securing equity and debt to cover financial needs.
- Investment decision.
- Detailed design and engineering specifications (usually by engineer consultant).
- Site acquisition.
- Enterprise formation:
  - Business (operations) plan.
  - Organization design, human resources planning, legal and regulatory procedures.
  - Organization setup (e.g., recruitment, training, and orientation of key management, administrative, and marketing personnel).
  - Recruiting and training personnel for preproduction activities.
  - Licensing and other authorizations.
  - Legal procedures necessary to formally establish the enterprise.
  - Activating the enterprise (e.g., enterprise management, administration, preproduction marketing, promotion).
- Construction project oversight.
- Operations—management of the enterprise.
- Decommissioning (when applicable):
  - Planning.
  - Dismantling and disposal contracting.
  - Acceptance of restoration by governing authority.

Level 2: Construction Project (CP) Management

Authority: General contractor (GC).

Responsibilities: Building the plant and financial control of CP.

Activities:

- Management and coordination of construction project—planning, budgeting, monitoring, and control.
- Design of CP implementation scheme.
- Detailed engineering design and supervision.
- Selection and supervision of subcontractors, consultants, and suppliers.
- Preparation of tender documents, tendering, evaluation of bids.
- Negotiations and award of contracts.
- Site preparation.
- Construction works (buildings, outdoor works).
- Equipment installation and operations documentation.
- Quality management.
- Purchase of materials and supplies for test runs and for initial stocks.
- Recruitment and training of production personnel.
- Plant commissioning, start-up, and initial production.
- Arranging certification process.
- Arranging final acceptance tests.

Level 3: Execution

Authority: Contractors and subcontractors.

Responsibilities: Performing specified tasks and financial control of subcontracts.

Activities:

- Supplementary designs and drawings related to subcontract responsibilities.
- Equipment manufacture and delivery.
- On-site erection.
- Quality monitoring.
- Commissioning jobs (work units).

What are the abilities and characteristics of a good manager? The answer is probably culture-dependent to some extent. However, some characteristics are universally desirable, and the absence of one or more may be an indicator of managerial shortcomings:

- Leadership—delegating, communicating, coordinating. Autocratic control is not leadership; at times difficult decisions must be made at the top, but a true leader understands the benefit of delegating authority and responsibility, of communicating the goals and objectives throughout the organization, and coordinating activities of subordinates by avoiding overlapping responsibilities and uncertain channels of communication and decision making.

- Understanding the virtues of good planning and control. Planning sets the course, and monitoring confirms either that the course is being followed or, if not, that corrective action is necessary.
- Recognizing knowledge and talent and how it can best be applied—matching skills and abilities to the challenge of the job. Improper use of human resources can be counted as part of the waste stream, the same as unnecessary consumption of physical resources.
- Balancing requirements and resources, particularly skilled and talented people in great demand. Balancing the application of human and physical resources with the tasks at hand requires keen insight and comprehensive understanding of what is happening.
- People skills—rapport. A good manager understands people and their inherent human nature—the hopes and fears that are part of every psyche. Empathy and rapport are needed to keep staff in a cooperative frame of mind.

Consequences of Inadequate Planning and Management

Competent management is essential for successful project implementation, and its absence invariably leads to detrimental time delays and cost overruns. If project implementation is to be managed by the sponsor or project staff, capabilities have to be assessed realistically. Do these people really have the skills and knowledge to plan and execute? If not, an outside consultant-contractor is needed with appropriate management experience, to be included as part of project cost estimates. In a turnkey project, contractors and suppliers have to be selected with similar care. Prior history of successful implementation of similar projects is usually mandatory.

What are some of the consequences of inadequately addressing the need for competent management of implementation?

- *Escalation in cost of resources.* Construction delays resulting from improper planning and management can escalate the cost of resources, particularly in an inflationary environment, diminishing the attractiveness of the project.
- *Excessive consumption of resources.* Delays tend to increase consumption of resources—for example, construction personnel are less efficiently employed when activity durations are lengthened.

- *Higher financial costs.* Time is money—financial costs (interest) compound rapidly with implementation delays.
- *Losses in sales revenue.* Prolonged construction and commissioning schedules delay start of production with attendant loss in anticipated sales and profits.

Project Adjustments

During the course of the implementation project, change is inevitable. As the project progresses, some targets are unmet, others require adjustment. A criterion for selection of managers is the ability to adjust to changing conditions, unfazed by perceptual or emotional perturbations. These factors have to be taken into account even in the preinvestment planning phases of the project, which will affect the investment decision.

CONDUCTING THE IMPLEMENTATION PROJECT

The implementation project is most effectively carried out with competent management utilizing the best tools available to assist in planning and execution. It can be separated into several subprojects, such as site work and infrastructure, building construction, production facilities, and enterprise formation. In any case, all subprojects have to be coordinated under general management.

The manager or management team, whether enterprise staff member(s) or under contract, generally reports directly to project sponsors. Construction projects usually require approval of political authorities (zoning and land use regulations) and other authorizations (e.g., building permits, licenses from environmental authorities).

Appointing the Management Team

The management team directs the construction project, headed by a member of project staff, a consultant acting on behalf of the sponsors, or a manager assigned by the lead contractor of a turnkey project. The team manages the entire project or divides it into segments, each to be managed by an individual or group subordinate to general management. For large projects some of the tasks are subcontracted (e.g., detailed engineering, supervision of construction and installation).

Planning, Budgeting, Monitoring, and Control

Managing the construction project is similar, in most respects, to other management challenges, but there are differences. Many of the relationships that need to be developed are short-term and often one-time, more like an infatuation than a marriage. A definite termination date is in sight from the beginning.

A management contract, or scope of work, defines objectives, timetable, and compensation. The first task for the manager is to understand the project, through orientation by project sponsors and digesting all documented information (e.g., history and genesis).

The structure of the management team—positions, responsibilities, and relationships—is developed and clarified with job descriptions. Personnel not available from the sponsoring organization need to be recruited and oriented to the project. An indispensable step is specifying, for all team members, lines of authority and communication (how information is to be disseminated, how directions are to be handed down, how recommendations are to be handled).

Project Management Cycle

Project management can be considered as a cyclical process, as illustrated in Figure 9.1. Actually there are two cycles. In the primary loop, goals and objectives are set. For plant construction and commissioning this is clear—build the plant within allotted time and within budget. Activities are planned to complete the job, and the necessary resources mobilized. The project is then implemented—that is, constructed and commissioned. The secondary cycle deals with measurement and control. Progress is monitored using instruments that measure indicators of performance, which are

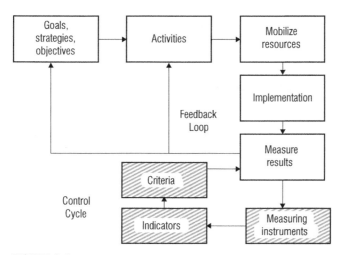

FIGURE 9.1 Management Cycle

compared with criteria (e.g., resource utilization versus budgets, time allot-ted for an activity versus time to complete). Deviations trigger corrective action (feedback loop). One of the major responsibilities of management is to keep the ship on course, which may entail adjusting goals and objectives (if monitored information indicates such a need), but more likely requires adjusting activities. This is one of the severe tests of management skill.

Construction Project Planning

The techniques of project planning apply to the actual construction project. However, during the preinvestment phase, when the question is whether to undertake the project, a preliminary plan is needed for determining the implementation time frame and for estimating project costs; although nec-essarily less detailed and precise, it provides vital information for decision makers.

Construction project planning and budgeting involves the follow-ing steps:

- Determine the tasks (activities), on- and off-site, necessary to complete the project.
- Determine the logical sequence of activities and events.
- Prepare a time-phased implementation schedule, positioning all the ac-tivities appropriately in time, allowing for adequate duration to com-plete each activity.
- Determine the resources needed to complete the activities and to cover the corresponding costs.
- Prepare an implementation budget and cash flow to ensure availability of adequate funds throughout the project.
- Document all data (start and completion dates of activities, resources consumed).

During the actual construction project, the following activities are car-ried out:

- Periodically compare forecasts and budgets with actual results.
- Revise plan and update budget accordingly.

Activities (Work) Breakdown Structure

Identifying and describing all activities that must take place to com-plete construction and plant commissioning is facilitated with an *activity breakdown structure* (ABS), a systematic method for defining construction project components and how they are related. Constructing a building, for example, requires a series of steps, each of which may consist of a series of activities for completion—for example, construction of the foundation, framing, and exterior; installation of roofing and piping. Each of these in turn involves a sequence of tasks. Breaking down the entire construction and commissioning into tasks or activities is the purpose of the ABS, which should also include estimates of human and material resources needed for each activity.

Creating the ABS is a useful endeavor in preliminary planning stages and necessary for a detailed PIP after commitment to investment. The early effort is based upon educated approximations; detailed analysis relies on firm job estimates. The same procedures are employed in either case, the level of depth increasing as the decision point is approached:

- *Organize jobs into manageable units.* The ABS decomposes major jobs into a series of tasks or activities necessary to complete the project, in the form of a network, with a more detailed breakdown of tasks in each stage. Jobs are defined (what is to be accomplished) so that they are manageable and encompass the entire scope of necessary effort from the investment decision to the operating plant.
- *Analyze precedence requirements.* Commencement of one job may be contingent on completion of other jobs. The precedence requirements are identified—that is, which jobs must be completed before others can begin (e.g., laying the foundation of a house must precede the construction of the walls). A job may also be a precedent for the start of other jobs.
- *Time to complete.* The time to complete each task is estimated. The entire construction schedule for the project is dependent upon the time required to complete each job and how they are sequenced.[3]
- *Resource requirements to complete each job or activity.* This includes both human and material resources, as well as information requirements prior to commencement or during the job. This is necessary to plan procurement, for cost estimating, and to clarify information flow.

Table 9.1 shows a simplified example of an activity breakdown listing all tasks and subtasks necessary to complete construction and enterprise formation. This kind of chart can be developed using specialized project planning and management software or a standard spreadsheet program.[4] Jobs are coded for coordination with related jobs in the same category. Job length, in days (or hours, weeks, months) to complete, is estimated from discussions with contractors or from experience. Job precedence is indicated—all jobs or tasks that must be completed before each job can be

TABLE 9.1 Activity Breakdown Structure—Job Length, Precedence, and Resources

Task ID	Tasks	Duration	Start	Finish	Predecessors[1]	Successors[2]	Skilled Labor, PM[3]
1	Organize project team		10/10/2XX1	11/9/2XX1			
2	Recruit members	21 days	10/10/2XX1	10/30/2XX1		3,5,19	0
3	Project team training	10 days	10/31/2XX1	11/9/2XX1	2	5	0
4	Construction project		11/10/2XX1	8/17/2XX2			
5	Detailed design	30 days	11/10/2XX1	12/9/2XX1	2,3	6,7,14	0
6	Equipment and machinery procurement	120 days	12/10/2XX1	4/8/2XX2	5	16	0
7	Site preparation	14 days	12/10/2XX1	12/23/2XX1	5	8,9	5
8	Outdoor installations	10 days	12/24/2XX1	1/2/2XX2	7		6
9	Building foundations	8 days	12/24/2XX1	12/31/2XX1	7	11,12	2
10	**Construct buildings**		1/1/2XX2	5/30/2XX2			
11	Administration	90 days	1/1/2XX2	3/31/2XX2	9	13,16	9
12	Plant, warehouse	150 days	1/1/2XX2	5/30/2XX2	9	13,16,14	12
13	Finish site preparation	10 days	5/31/2XX2	6/9/2XX2	11,12	15	1
14	Recruit production staff	62 days	5/31/2XX2	7/31/2XX2	5,12		0
15	Production staff training	10 days	8/1/2XX2	8/10/2XX2	14	17	0
16	Install machinery and equipment	60 days	5/31/2XX2	7/29/2XX2	11,12,6		10
17	Plant commissioning	7 days	8/11/2XX2	8/17/2XX2	15,16		
18	**Enterprise formation**		10/31/2XX1	4/23/2XX2			
19	Recruit management team	90 days	10/31/2XX1	1/28/2XX2	2	20,22	0
20	Recruit personnel (admin, mkting, pers., proc., etc.)	60 days	1/29/2XX2	3/29/2XX2	19	21	0
21	Train personnel	15 days	3/30/2XX2	4/13/2XX2	20	23	3
22	Legal (documentation, registration)	21 days	1/29/2XX2	2/18/2XX2	19	23	0
23	Activate enterprise	10 days	4/14/2XX2	4/23/2XX2	21,22		4

[1]Predecessor activities must be completed before commencement of the subject activity, each of which may have its own precedence requirements; some may have "slack," that is, can be scheduled over a time span—earliest start (ES) to latest finish (LF)—greater than its expected time for execution, without affecting the completion date.

[2]Successor activities can start only after completion of the subject activity. Activities without slack are in the critical path (CP). Activities that can be scheduled over a time span from earliest start (ES) to latest finish (LF) involves slippage of the completion date.

[3]This is one example of a resource requirement, unskilled labor for each activity in person-months (PM). Peak resource requirements can be "smoothed" over time by moving activities within the time frame from earliest start (ES) to latest finish (LF). Use of project management software such as MS Project facilitates this process.

started (predecessors), and those that can only be started upon completion of each job (successors). In Table 9.1, only the earliest start and finish dates are shown. Columns could be added for the latest start and finish times that are derived from network analysis (see later subsection). Resource requirements for each task are defined. In the example, only skilled labor is shown, but similar data for all major resources (materials, equipment, and other facilities) can be included in the analysis.

Responsibility Matrix

After completing the ABS, assignment of responsibility for tasks can be organized systematically in the form of a responsibility matrix—essentially a device for assigning members of the team and other individuals and organizations to specific tasks. An example is shown in Appendix 9.1. The matrix includes the following information:

- *Jobs and functions* necessary for completion of implementation from the ABS are listed on the vertical axis, including actual construction jobs and all ancillary activities that enter into the creation of the enterprise.
- *Assignment of responsible personnel:* Members of the team and other individuals and organizations are assigned responsibility for completing each of the tasks and functions.
- *Level of responsibility* can be assigned using a coding system. For example, A = general responsibility; B = operating responsibility; C = specific responsibility; D = must be consulted; E = may be consulted; F = must be notified; G = must approve.

Implementation Scheduling

Scheduling of project activities is intended to ensure that all the requisites for successful operations—construction, delivery and assembly of equipment, recruitment and training of operating personnel, and delivery of production inputs—are completed prior to start-up. A study of climatic history and variability helps to anticipate conditions that may hamper and delay the construction work on-site, providing a basis for probability estimates of time of completion.

The ABS provides information on which activities (tasks) are precedent for other activities, which defines sequence and relationships. The schedule can be developed as follows:[5]

- Determine the logical sequence of events without concern for duration of each task. Positioning of some tasks is obvious: Detailed engineering

must necessarily precede construction and installation; company formation must be completed before the assignment of staff. Other tasks may
need more analysis before they can be positioned correctly.

■ Analyze how specific tasks are to be undertaken, which will normally
reveal that some can be subdivided into subtasks; detailed engineering,
for example, is the result of the coordinated effort of several groups of
architects and engineers.

■ Tasks and subtasks must be properly timed to show their interdependence with other tasks, namely precedents (completion of another task
necessary before this task can be started) and those for which the task
is precedent (this task must be completed before another task can be
started). Once the order and relationships are determined, the nature of
each task can be studied to determine its duration.

Activity scheduling determines the duration of the construction project,
and of resource and financial requirements as a function of time. In preliminary stages, for relatively simple projects, activities can be laid out primarily
on a Gantt chart with time intervals on the horizontal axis and activities
on the vertical axis.[6] Time spans for all major activities are indicated with
bars for each on a time scale showing their temporal relationships, their
start and end dates, and the number of days (or hours) required to complete the job. This chart can also be used as a management device if prepared using project management software or a spreadsheet program, with
updates showing number of days remaining to complete the job and time
overruns.

An example is shown in Figure 9.2 (generated by MS Project software)
based upon earliest starts for each job. The slack (range of time that the job
start could be delayed without affecting overall project completion) can be
indicated for each noncritical job (in respect to timing). In this example the
numbers adjacent to each job are the assigned duration. Jobs that are on
the *critical path*—that is, those for which there is no slack—are shown with
shading. Delay in completion of jobs without slack (critical path) delays
completion of the entire project.

For more complex projects a network approach with greater detail in
the activity breakdown structure (ABS) can be employed.[7] Simplified critical
path methods can be employed for relatively small projects even without
resorting to a computer, although use of project planning and management
software greatly facilitates the process.[8] By whatever means, the implementation schedule, plan, and expenditures are reviewed periodically to detect
discrepancies with investment and implementation estimates upon which
the investment decision was predicated.

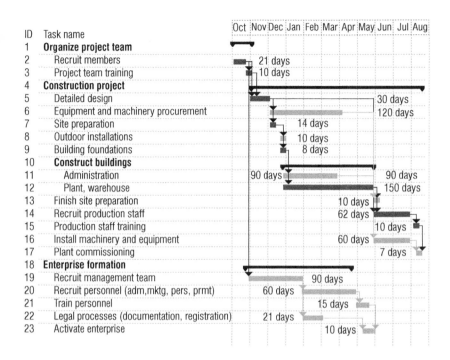

FIGURE 9.2 Gantt Chart
Source: MS Project (Microsoft Corp.).

Network Analysis

Network analysis can be used to develop the implementation schedule, indicating the proposed start and duration of each activity and the overall start and completion dates, and to determine the *critical path*, the particular sequence of jobs that defines the amount of time necessary for completion. All jobs on the critical path have no slack—any delay in completion will affect the project termination date. One advantage of using a computer program is that it makes determination of resource consumption and timing easier and more precise.

Even for a relatively complex project, a program may not be necessary in preliminary stages, when the network is simplified and jobs are in more aggregated form. The example in Figure 9.3 is based upon the ABS of Table 9.1. Jobs are arranged in a network as shown, respecting all precedence requirements. The jobs are coded (1, 2, 3, etc.) and the number of days for completion of the job indicated (e.g., job 9 needs 8 days or 64 working hours for completion).

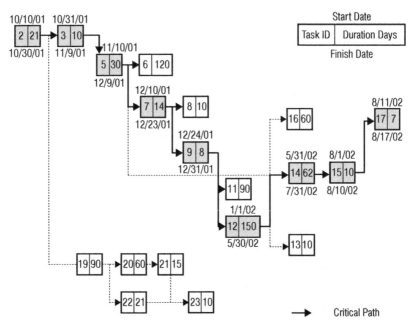

FIGURE 9.3   Network Analysis

Detailed planning has to reflect local work regulations, for example, the specific work week in the host country. In some countries the work week is six days with shortened hours on the sixth day. The project completion date has to reflect not only technical requirements but also regulations on working conditions. For example an activity requiring 1600 work-hours to complete with a 5 day work-week (40 hours/week) would require about 9.3 months, whereas with the 5.5 day work-week the job could be completed in about 8.5 months.

Technical requirements of some jobs don't allow for work breaks (e.g., casting concrete foundations), which might entail overtime work with higher investment cost.

The network diagram is generated in a forward and backward pass. In the forward pass the *earliest start* and *earliest completion* for each task are determined. Any job can start only on the earliest date of completion for all jobs that must precede it. For example, the earliest start (ES) for job 14 (5/31/02) depends on the earliest completion of job 12 (5/30/02). The earliest finish (EF) for job 14 is 7/31/02, because it takes 62 days to complete.

The backward pass provides the latest start (LS) and latest finish (LF) for each job. Starting from the overall completion date determined in the forward pass, the latest start and completion dates are determined (bottom of block). These dates are not shown in the example.

The *critical path* is the series of jobs that defines the time to complete implementation. Once the forward and backward passes are completed, the ES, EF, LS, and LF are known for each task; those for which the ES and EF are identical to the LS and LF, respectively, are in the critical path—namely, jobs for which there is no slack time. If they are not completed on schedule, the completion date for the entire project is delayed. In the example the jobs that exhibit these conditions are jobs 2, 3, 5, 7, 9, 12, 14, 15, and 17. The total time to complete is the sum of the individual job completion times. The only way that an earlier completion date can be realized is to shorten the time to complete one or more of the critical path jobs: Any delay in the completion of these tasks will delay the completion of the entire project. Jobs not in the critical path (i.e., those with slack) can be accomplished in less time than the interval between ES and LF and can be scheduled for any period between these dates. If job durations are changed, however, those in the critical path may change. Figure 9.4 is a portion of a network diagram generated by planning software.

Resource issues affect scheduling of noncritical jobs. Jobs with slack time can be shifted so that resources assigned to them are available in other critical areas. The cost estimate for the project is the total cost of all jobs

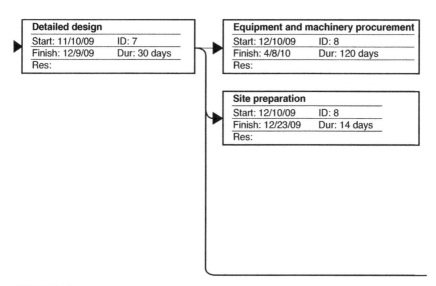

FIGURE 9.4 Network Diagram
Source: MS Project (Microsoft Corp.).

necessary to complete it. For this reason, one way to determine the cost and timing of the implementation plan is to assign all necessary resources to jobs and then do cost and timing analysis from this information.

In practice, a network analysis is rarely static. It should be updated periodically as new information on job completions becomes available.

Resource Analysis

The requirement for any particular resource can be analyzed by plotting the requirement associated with each job or task on a spreadsheet or bar chart.[9] The chart shows the timing of the job and the number of units of the resource needed for the job. The total requirement for the resource for any period (e.g., month) is the total for all jobs.

Skilled labor resources for the example are shown in Figure 9.5. Demand for the resource over time is dependent upon the scheduling of jobs. Shifting the timing of jobs with slack to any time between the ES and LF dates is a way to smooth the demand for any resource. Job 6, equipment and machinery procurement, for example, could be postponed as much as 64 days (see Figure 9.3 and Table 9.1) without affecting the completion date.[10] This allows some flexibility in scheduling so that the maximum demand for resources can be diminished to some extent. The program assumed here is the earliest start (ES) for each job (other alternatives could be assumed for all but the critical path jobs).

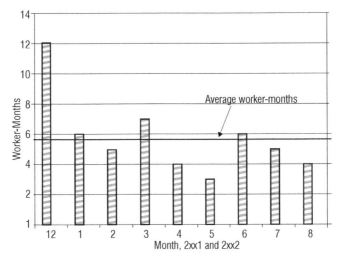

FIGURE 9.5   Balancing Resource Requirements over Time

The same type of analysis is performed for each scarce resource. The approach is useful for estimating the application, timing, and cost for *all* resources—for example, classes or skills of workers (management, technical, factory workers), materials, and financing.

In the example used here, the number of skilled worker-months in any month varies from 12 to 3. It is usually efficient to balance resources to a more uniform utilization. Shifting job schedules within the slack period is an iterative process that can be handled most easily with computing facilities. For smaller projects it can be done with a spreadsheet, or even manually, with a little patience. The objective is to achieve a more uniform resource demand so that costs can be minimized. Ideally the number of workers-months per month would be the average shown (about 6), but there inevitably is some variation in labor demand.

Engineering—Basic for Project Study, Detailed for Implementation

In the preinvestment phase, preliminary engineering design and analysis are part of project study (the information base for the decision) and usually provide a point of departure for postdecision detailed engineering. Basic engineering is performed for the project study, and more detailed engineering once the project is accepted for implementation. For relatively small projects, preliminary engineering designs and specifications may be sufficiently detailed, with little or no refinement needed for the implementation project. In most cases, detailed engineering is undertaken only after the decision is made to invest, as the cost is considerably greater than the simplified and aggregated information developed for a decision. The engineering effort typically necessary for construction and commissioning comprises detailed plans for designs of buildings and outdoor works, site preparation, refinement of technology to be employed in production, procurement of machinery and equipment, plant layout, materials handling, planning and scheduling construction of plant and ancillary facilities, preparation of flow charts, waste processing, and supervision of construction and commissioning.

Technical documentation precedes the start of construction and installation: plans, drawings, three-dimensional models, descriptions, equipment lists (e.g., quantities, prices, sources), and operations and maintenance manuals. Design and performance specifications are needed to serve as benchmarks for plant commissioning demonstration tests. Documentation follows standards that are comprehensible to sponsors, to the team, and to current and future operating personnel.

The time and cost for detailed engineering is included in the investment package as part of the cost of implementation. In some industries, engineering costs can be estimated using factors based upon similar projects; in any case, they are dependent upon the complexities of the process and site but should be in proportion to the magnitude of the investment package. Rarely should engineering costs exceed 5 percent of the investment.

Contractors, Consultants, and Suppliers

Seeking comprehensive competitive tenders for goods and services from several national and international suppliers of demonstrated reliability and with good delivery capacity is conducive to controlling construction costs. The implementation team has to study the qualifications of contractors, consultants, and suppliers prior to tendering, eliminating from contention those that do not meet minimum standards, such as experience in the business, history of on-time deliveries, and integrity. Cost estimates for the time and effort to carry out competitive bidding are budgeted as part of the implementation project.

Land Acquisition

Acquisition of land may be complicated by negotiations with local authorities for infrastructure improvements, for which allocation of costs is usually an issue. An *option to buy*, conveying the right to purchase under specified conditions, is a means of securing access to desirable sites without actual purchase. The option may grant access to the site. Execution of the option by the project can be contingent on infrastructure improvements, such as timely installation or upgrading of roads to withstand traffic loads during construction and operations; extension of existing rail lines; and installation of interim and permanent energy, water lines, and telecommunication facilities. Although environmental issues are usually resolved prior to investment, some issues may carry over into the postinvestment phase. Execution of the option to purchase the land can be contingent on acceptance by authorities of an environmental impact assessment (EIA) and an environmental impact statement (EIS). The cost of an option is usually not a large percentage of site cost.

Procurement of Materials and Services

Arrangements for delivery of production materials are included in the PIP. A survey of domestic suppliers' facilities ensures their ability to deliver specified quality and quantity of materials in accordance with the supply schedule. For imported goods, supplier-to-plant transfer constraints are studied to resolve transit problems before shipping commences.

The complement of spare parts normally supplied with machinery and equipment usually is adequate to support production only for a limited time. The PIP includes provisions for procurement of spare parts and maintenance materials, taking into account relatively high consumption in early stages when production workers and maintenance technicians are relatively inexperienced.

Scheduling of agricultural inputs takes into account crop development activities and cultivation periods. If the crop has not been previously grown commercially in the area, test cultivations are advisable during the project study phase so there is reasonable assurance of agricultural viability—sustainable yields and harvesting schedules on a commercial scale under actual field conditions—prior to the decision to invest. Contracts with agricultural suppliers need to include guarantees from preemption by alternative buyers.[11] Quality specifications for agricultural input to the project are also important, such as water content of tomatoes or sucrose content of sugar beets or cane.

Construction and Installation

Infrastructure capacity and delivery schedules for plant equipment factor into the sequence of site development, construction of plant and buildings, outdoor works, and installations. Location and capacities of storage facilities (open-air and warehouses) have to be coordinated with material flow schedules. Expediting deliveries of equipment and materials (diligent follow-up) is a likely requirement for the implementation team, which may also need to assist some suppliers and contractors to interpret technical specifications and work procedures.

Plant Commissioning

Plant commissioning is the process of assuring completeness and operating capability of the plant, and transition to operational status. The commissioning process depends upon the type of agreement negotiated between project sponsors and contractors (see the "Contracting" subsection later in this chapter).

Testing the plant and facilities under representative operating conditions is the principle objective. Acceptance should be predicated on demonstrated performance in accordance with quantity and quality specifications:

- *Preoperational checks*—a final examination by contractors to ensure that all equipment and facilities are properly installed and connected prior to operating trial runs.

- *Trial runs*—preliminary operation of the equipment to identify unforeseen problems of design, installation, and connection prior to performance tests.
- *Performance tests*—operation of plant and equipment under partial- to full-load conditions, of sufficient duration and intensity to ensure compliance with specifications.
- *Acceptance and take-over*—agreement by the implementation team to accept the plant after review of performance tests and a thorough plant inspection by project personnel; transition of operational responsibility from contractors to project personnel.

Acceptance is predicated on the ability of enterprise personnel to operate the plant under normal operating conditions, ideally without assistance from consultants or other temporary personnel. Even if expatriate experts or other consultants are required in the early stages, part of their commission is to adequately train local staff to the level of self-sufficiency. Normally the plant is not taken over by project personnel until it has operated for some time at full production level, with local staff fully in control of the process.

Commissioning and start-up stages can be utilized as an opportunity for hands-on training. Maintenance technicians and plant operating personnel can be trained earlier, perhaps at the suppliers' plant or in specialized training institutes. A labor contingent is required during commissioning and start-up, and included in the PIP and budget. A supplies program covers materials and services inputs consumed during this preoperational phase.

Enterprise Formation

The project is intended either to form a new enterprise or to extend or modify an existing operation. Positions and responsibilities of management, administrative staff, supervisors, and production workers are defined; a marketing organization is set up to prepare the market for the new products (preproduction marketing); and a purchasing function is established to secure project inputs and factory supplies. Personnel are recruited and trained as needed for commissioning, who are then prepared to assume operating responsibility from start-up, with the added benefit of greater productivity and efficiency during early plant operations.

Legal Process, Registration, and Authorization

The legal framework for the new enterprise is set up and integrated with that of the sponsoring entity, if applicable. Local, national, bilateral, or international statutes, rules, and regulations applicable to enterprise formation need to be assimilated by the team to understand the scope and significance of legal issues. Legal assistance usually is necessary to draw up articles of incorporation or partnership agreements, and to study and advise on statutes, regulations, and customs in the host country (in the case of foreign direct investment) and for any other countries in which operations may be planned. The objective is to prepare the enterprise charter and complete legal approval and registration procedures.

Company formation generally involves the following steps:

- Signing a letter of intent between business partners (if applicable) to establish an enterprise. If the venture commences in an exploratory mode, prior to the decision to invest, one of the issues may be joint preparation of a project study.
- Agreement between the partners on financial arrangements and drafting of documents required by authorities.
- Formal application to authorities.
- Official approval and registration of the new enterprise.

Formation of a limited liability enterprise, particularly for a joint venture or foreign direct investment (FDI), may take several months, with expert assistance required. Costs of formation (part of preoperational capital expenditures) depend upon its type and size and regulations in the host country (and perhaps in the home countries of partners) for establishing a new venture. Possible cost elements include publication of company by-laws; appointment of a board of directors, as well as their meetings and travel costs; appointment and orientation of management; setting up bank accounts; duties and taxes related to formation; and legal assistance.

Governmental Approvals

Approval is usually required to import technology, machinery, and equipment, and some inputs (e.g., processed materials, parts and components, and services), particularly where foreign exchange controls are in effect. Time and effort required to process and obtain necessary approvals should be included in the PIP and budget. This might be a lengthy process, particularly for foreign investment; several months may be necessary for import approvals.

Activation

The implementation team may be assigned responsibility for activating the enterprise—that is, setting the entity and its functions into motion, in preparation for operations. The structure proposed during the study phase may require adjustment indicated by subsequent information and events. At appropriate points in the implementation phase, the enterprise organization is developed and staffed, through recruitment and training. The inclusion of activities and events concerning enterprise formation in the PIP ensures that the enterprise is fully functioning at start-up. Typically, senior management personnel are members of the implementation team and appoint line managers (if applicable), who then proceed to organize functions for which they are responsible. Production and maintenance personnel needed for commissioning the plant usually carry over into the production phase, although additional personnel may have to be recruited and trained for normal production levels (e.g., more shifts added to attain full production level).

Part of organization development is creating and staffing marketing and sales functions. Marketing and promotion and procurement functions have to be up and running well in advance of commencing normal operations. Activities include designing and undertaking an advertising campaign, setting up distribution channels and sales facilities (e.g., showrooms, workshops, special equipment), training sales personnel and dealers in the distribution network, and establishing procurement channels. Activation should be timed to ensure the level of marketing necessary to secure market access from commencement of production and sales.

Estimate of Implementation Project Costs

Expenditures for the implementation project—resources employed in carrying out enterprise formation, and in managing the construction and commissioning project—are part of the initial investment package (preoperational expenditures) and are usually treated as capital investment to be amortized.

Standard costs can be found in published references—for example, associations of architects and engineers maintain data on unit labor requirements and rules for calculating fees for architectural and engineering services (based upon the type and scope of the project and the work). Other cost items, such as housing, transport, legal fees, and duties, may require local surveys. Adding price and physical contingencies (judiciously) accounts for the inevitable surprises in actual versus estimated costs. Under inflationary conditions, prices can be projected for the most likely time frame for project implementation, and further adjusted if the project start is delayed.

Contracting

As part of the project development process, much of the work and other services are normally provided by other individuals and organizations under contracts with consultants, engineers, architects, construction companies, suppliers, and financing institutions. There are usually legal dimensions in contracting, some or all of which may require professional expertise—negotiating, evaluating bids and awarding contracts for machinery, equipment, and installation; construction; and technology acquisition (see the later subsection titled "Standards").

The time interval between invitation for bids and final award of contracts can be specified in the bidding process. Delivery from the time of award, specified in procurement agreements, may range from a few months for relatively simple plant and equipment to one or two years or more for more complex installations. Synchronizing ordering and delivery schedules with construction and erection minimizes capital tie-up. It is worth the team's effort to try to anticipate problems related to the transfer and delivery of construction and plant equipment to avoid undue delays. It is not too early to address these issues during the project study phase. The purpose is to clarify costs and problems of execution (and to provide a guide for the implementation team)—for example, conducting simulation of transport stages for bulky or heavy machinery and equipment. The sequence of deliveries reflects lead times and delivery schedules for imported and domestic equipment. Lead times for domestically procured equipment in some developing countries may be greater than for imports.

The PIP includes provisions for determining shipping and transport routes (supply chains and distribution channels), and details about commercial and customs documents required according to local statutes and regulations. There may be a need to plan interim warehousing of machinery, equipment, and supplies prior to installation.

Quality Control and Testing

The plan includes quality control inspections, if appropriate, at the supplier's plant. Specifying test requirements (e.g., duration and test conditions) in the contract documents with clarity and detail (e.g., a statement of test objectives, test procedures, performance criteria and conditions, obligations of parties) avoids claims and disputes. Testing by an independent consultant enhances impartiality (but independence from the supplier needs to be confirmed). Approval of test results is normally a condition for release of payment to the supplier.

Testing is of equal importance for the project—an unsatisfactory result implies delayed start-up of plant operation and production. Even compensation from a performance bond has marginal value compared with production losses that may result from equipment delivery delays. As a condition of sale, a successful performance test needs to be backed up with a warranty for a specified period, with terms of repair or replacement (e.g., venue, cost). Provisional acceptance of performance test results is followed by final acceptance after expiration of the warranty period.

Construction Management

Management of the construction project (CP) or subproject inevitably involves relationships with other individuals and organizations commissioned to do the work of building and activating the plant facilities, usually under contract. Figure 9.6 illustrates three possible arrangements regarding procurement and contracting. The sponsor, or a designated investment project (IP) leader, may elect to do direct contracting with equipment suppliers and construction companies. Prior experience in procurement and contracting is an important criterion for selection of the IP leader.

A more common arrangement is to place responsibility for the construction project in the hands of a general contractor (GC), which appoints its own management team to organize and direct detailed construction planning, construction, and commissioning. The contract between the IP leader and the GC has to spell out in detail the design of plant and facilities (complete engineering drawings), the schedule for completion of stages of

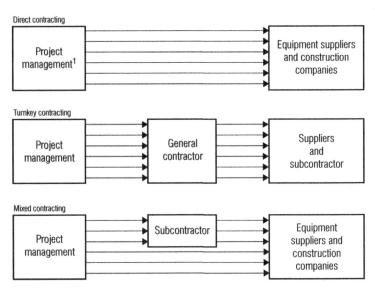

[1] *Project management* refers to either the investor or a designated investment project manager.

FIGURE 9.6   Construction Contracting
Source: Suggested by Andrzej Mlotkowski.

construction, the budget and payment schedule, and, most important, operating specifications as the basis for final performance testing. Incentives and penalties may be included in the contract between the IP leader and the GC or other contractors regarding project completion.

Another possibility is a mixture of subcontracting and direct contracting between the IP leader and suppliers/construction enterprises. For example, site preparation may be handled separately from the construction contract, through a subcontract with an earthmoving company, while the plant is constructed under contract to a builder. There may also be separate subcontracts for equipment procurement and installation, or any other activity within the scope of the CP.

A typical sequence for the CP is shown in Figure 9.7. After the investment decision, in many countries there is a need for authorization to proceed from licensing authorities, which may include an economic development agency, local and regional planning boards, environmental protection agency, utilities boards, and the like. Upon receipt of all necessary approvals, the IP manager usually commissions a consulting engineer to draw up detailed plans and specifications for all plant and facilities (i.e., civil works, buildings, production system, materials handling, quality control). In most cases the consulting engineer becomes the agent for the IP, monitoring the process

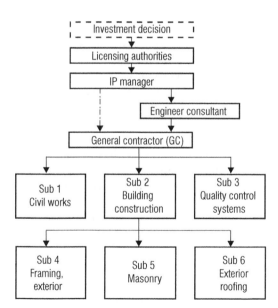

FIGURE 9.7 Contracting Sequence
Source: Suggested by Andrzej Mlotkowski.

to ensure compliance with design specifications. A GC is usually selected, with responsibility for the entire CP, but some aspects may be controlled directly by the IP manager, such as recruitment and personnel training.

A system of subcontracts is usually negotiated between the GC and/or IP for specific segments of the CP. In the illustration, the GC negotiates separate subcontracts for civil works, building construction, and for the production and quality control systems with other enterprises specializing in these areas. The building subcontractor, in turn, negotiates subcontracts with providers of special construction facilities and services. Ultimately, the GC is responsible for the performance of subcontractors at all levels.

Turnkey Projects A common arrangement for the construction project is a turnkey project, which can be designed to achieve varying levels of operational status. The project might also include transfer of technology (see later subsection) involving conveyance of design and operating information, with construction responsibility in the hands of the technology provider or managed by an engineering and construction company with monitoring by project staff:

Level	Added Components
Standard	Plant design, materials, operating documents, start-up
Extended	Technical assistance
Product-in-hand	Product to quantity and quality specifications
Market-in-hand	Execution of marketing plan, securing of markets
Joint venture	Equity, usually short-term

In the standard project configuration, the provider supplies the engineering designs for the plant, descriptions of material input requirements, documentation (procedures), operating instructions, and supervision of plant start-up. In an extended turnkey project, technical assistance may be provided over a period designed to ensure compliance with performance specifications. At the level of product-in-hand, the provider intervenes to the point of producing a guaranteed product quality and production rate. Market-in-hand provides assistance to the point of securing markets for project output. A joint venture project involves equity participation by the provider for a fixed time interval or by agreement regarding compliance with performance specifications.

Contract Standards

The Fédération Internationale des Ingénieurs-Conseils (FIDIC), or the International Federation of Consulting Engineers, has standardized conditions for construction contracts (e.g., build-operate-transfer [BOT] and its variants) and turnkey projects that are available through subscription. FIDIC is also a source for model contracts for engineering consulting and for joint ventures. FIDIC publishes a model contract used by multinational development banks (such as the International Bank for Reconstruction and Development—The World Bank) in their projects.

The International Organization for Standardization (ISO) is a source for procurement specifications. The ISO maintains about 250 technical committees that review and publish engineering standards for a wide range of technologies, equipment, materials, components, and services. Standardization in design specifications at all levels is particularly important for attracting foreign direct investment (FDI) for the project.

Technology Acquisition and Transfer

Technology acquisition is usually a part of the implementation project. A legal agreement is the foundation for describing the terms of transfer (e.g., patent rights, restrictions on exploitation, level of transfer, brand names, trademarks, copyrights, financial and economic matters, training), particularly if the provider seeks equity participation. Technology transfer can be related to virtually any operational dimension—product, process, machinery and equipment, procurement, marketing, distribution. The acquisition schedule should be included in the PIP and costs included in the implementation budget and preoperational expenditures. Some of the items specified in the transfer agreement include royalties and lump-sum payments, documentation, and training.

IMPLEMENTATION BUDGET

The implementation team has the responsibility for managing the flow of funds and resources during the implementation phase, which entails assembling information on receipts (capital inflows) and expenditure of resources related to enterprise formation and activation, management of the implementation project, procurement of machinery and equipment, site development, building construction, and plant commissioning. Funds and resource flow plans are necessary for management purposes. Some of these responsibilities may be delegated to other entities—for example, a general contractor, as shown in Figure 9.7.

In the most detailed form (possibly developed to some extent prior to the investment decision, depending upon project size and complexity), estimates are linked to the resources employed in planned activities and tasks, as developed in the ABS and network analysis. After all resources are assigned to jobs (activities) and the costs of jobs have been calculated, the total cost is the sum of costs for all jobs. Alternatively, resources can be listed by item, unit, and total cost, and then summed. In one manner or another, the timing of investment inflows and outflows has to be estimated. In preinvestment planning, this information is necessary for financial appraisal; during the actual implementation, it is essential for project management.

Costs of resources to be utilized during the implementation phase, and of all capital inflows (monetary and in-kind), are included in the PIP and the implementation budget (financial plan) for implementation activities (as previously described) and for other capital expenditures. Appendix 9.2 is a checklist of items to be included in the implementation project as pre-production expenditures, in addition to expenditures for machinery, equipment, installations, site development and construction, and personnel costs. Estimating methods are more thoroughly discussed in Chapter 2, in the subsection "Preoperational Expenditures."

APPENDIX 9.1: SAMPLE RESPONSIBILITY MATRIX FOR A PORTION OF A PROJECT

Table 9.2 demonstrates the matrix of roles and responsibilities in a sample implementation project.

APPENDIX 9.2: CHECKLIST OF PROJECT IMPLEMENTATION COSTS

Preparation of Project Implementation Plan (PIP)

- Personnel costs (management, staff, engineering).
- Travel and communication expenses.
- Ancillary equipment, such as computers, photocopiers.
- Printing supplies.

Project Management

- Salaries, wages, and benefits of management staff.
- Rent and operation of offices, vehicle expenses, living quarters.

TABLE 9.2 Responsibility Matrix

Project Element and Function	Product Line Manager											Technical Director				Director of Manufacturing			
	Managing director	Product line manager	Project manager	Project engineer	Project controller	Marketing manager	Export manager	Contract administration manager	Installation manager	Field project manager	Coordination manager	Technical director	Prototype manager	General studies manager	Other technical managers	Director of manufacturing	Plant manager A	Plant manager B	Project manufacturing coordinator
Prepare proposal	F	A	B	C	C	D	D	C	D		E	E				D	E	E	
Approve proposal	G	A,G	G			D	D	D	D		E	E				D	E	E	
Negotiate contract		A,G	B	E	E			C											
Sign contract	A,B	D	E					C											
Plan and control project		A	B	C	C			C											
Design and develop prototype		A,G	A,G	B	B							E	C	C	C	E			D
Control product configuration		E	A	B	B			D			E	E				E			D
Control product quality			A	B				D								E			D
Negotiate agreements	A	A	B,G			D	D	D		F	D	E	D	D	D		D		D
Conduct project evaluation meetings		A	B	D	D		D	D		D	E	E	D	D	D	E	E	E	D
Report and maintain contacts		D	B	E	F	D	E	E	E	E	E	E	E	E	D	E	E	E	D
Conduct design review	F	F	B	C	E			E	E	E	E	E	E	E	D	E			E

Relationship code: A = general responsibility; B = operating responsibility; C = specific responsibility; D = must be consulted; E = may be consulted; F = must be notified; G = must approve.

Source: Adapted from Russell D. Archibald, Managing High Technology Programs and Projects (Hoboken, NJ: John Wiley and Sons, 2003).

- Travel and communications.
- Printing and photocopying.
- Legal assistance.

Enterprise Formation—Organization Buildup

- Salaries, wages, and benefits of managers and administrative staff.
- Salaries and wages of staff and labor during implementation phase.
- Recruitment costs (advertising, recruitment services).
- Rent and leasing fees for offices, training facilities, vehicles, living quarters.
- Finance costs, duties, taxes, fees.
- Legal and consultant fees.
- Travel and communication expenses.
- Allowances for expatriate staff.
- Training fees (local and abroad), including travel and subsistence.
- Business connection costs (e.g., hospitality).
- Training documentation and training material (if not part of supplier contracts).
- Capital issue expenses.
- Registration and incorporation fees.
- Printing and incidentals expenses.
- Public relations expenses.
- Underwriting commissions.
- Brokerage fees.
- Insurance.
- Preproduction marketing and promotion (and other operations departments).
- Salaries, wages, and benefits of marketing and sales personnel.
- Advertising development, media.
- Establishing distribution network, including special equipment.
- Training sales personnel and dealers.
- Travel.
- Printing public relations materials.
- Communications.

Construction and Commissioning Project: Supervision and Coordination of Construction, Installation, Testing, Trial Runs, Start-up, and Commissioning

- Salaries, wages, and benefits of site staff.
- Costs of local and foreign experts and consultants.

- Rents (living quarters, offices).
- Erection, operation, and camp maintenance.
- Process and auxiliary materials and factory supplies for test runs, performance testing, and initial production.
- Utilities costs during construction, performance testing, and initial production.
- Interim warehousing off-site.
- Spare parts and maintenance.
- Insurance premiums during project implementation.

Detailed Engineering: Design of Process, Equipment, and Civil Works

- Salaries, wages, and benefits of engineering staff.
- Engineering consultant fees.
- Rent and operation of offices, vehicle expenses.
- Travel, transport, communication, subsistence.
- Site and laboratory tests.
- Legal assistance.

Procurement of Machinery and Equipment

- Production machinery
- Ancillary production equipment
- Materials handling equipment
- Service equipment (electrical, water, etc.)

Buildings and Installations

- Construct buildings
- Install machinery, production equipment, and ancillary facilities
- Construct site facilities (waste treatment, roads, electrical, gas, water supplies, etc.)

Tendering and Evaluation of Bids, Negotiations, and Contract Awards

- Salaries, wages, and benefits for procurement staff.
- Printing of tender documents, drawings, and specifications.
- Travel and other related expenses.
- Stamps, duties, and fees.
- Quality control inspections (local and abroad).
- Duties and taxes during the implementation period.
- Equipment transport costs, unloading and handling charges.
- Communications.

Technology Acquisition and Transfer

- Lump-sum payments (royalties are usually operating expense).
- Transfer of know-how, including training.
- Travel and communication expenses.
- Consulting fees.
- Testing, technology assessment costs.
- Detailed process engineering.

Financial Costs during Construction

- Interest during construction (term loans, current bank accounts).
- Fees (e.g., commitment).

Temporary Facilities Required for Construction

- Site engineering office.
- Temporary supplies of power, water.
- Temporary access, storage facilities, site security (e.g., fencing).
- Construction workshops.
- Recreational facilities.

NOTES

1. Carryover of members of the team facilitates the transition from implementation to production, particularly management, technical, and supervisory personnel.
2. This concept of project management structure is attributable to Dr. Andrzej Mlotkowski, based upon his practical on-site experience.
3. Suppliers of plant equipment may be able to provide information concerning duration and content of installation and commissioning activities. Shipping or forwarding companies can provide information on transport activities—duration, handling of documents, and customs clearance procedures.
4. Microsoft Project is a software package designed for implementation planning and monitoring, which facilitates scheduling of jobs and resources. Table 9.1 is essentially the output available from this program.
5. This work is facilitated using a project planning and management software package, such as Microsoft Project.
6. A Gantt chart, showing bars on a time scale representing the duration of tasks, is a useful device at any stage of implementation, for both planning and control, and is available in project planning software.
7. Two network analysis programs are Critical Path Method (CPM), developed by the DuPont Company, and Program Evaluation and Review Technique (PERT), developed by the U.S. Navy.

8. A number of project planning software packages are available in addition to Microsoft Project, including Intuit Quickbase, @task, Project Kickstart Pro, and Project Manager.

9. This type of analysis is facilitated with the use of project planning and monitoring software (see previous footnotes identifying some available packages).

10. Job 6 (machinery procurement) can start as early as 12/10/01 and takes 120 days. The earliest date for delivery of the machinery is 4/8/02. The only job that needs to be completed before plant commissioning is job 16 (installation of machinery), which takes 60 days and which must be completed before job 17 (plant commissioning) with ES/LS date of 8/11/02. The total number of days between 4/08/02 and 8/10/02 (the day before mandatory start of commissioning) is 124. Subtracting the number of days for job 16 leaves 64 days of slack. In other words, job 16 could be postponed 64 days without affecting completion of the project. This information would be provided automatically with project scheduling software such as Microsoft Project.

11. Failure to do so may result in hauling personnel staring at empty fields rather than at ripening crops to be harvested.

REFERENCES

Gray, Clifford F., and Erik W. Larson. 2005. *Project management.* New York: McGraw-Hill.

Heerkens, Gary, and Roger A. Formisano. 2001. *Project management.* New York: McGraw-Hill.

Kerzner, Harold. 2009. *Project management: A systems approach to planning, scheduling, and controlling.* Hoboken, NJ: John Wiley & Sons.

Meredith, Jack R., and Samuel J. Mantel. 2005. *Project management: A managerial approach.* Hoboken, NJ: John Wiley & Sons.

Marsh, P. D. V. 1974. *Contract planning and organization.* New York: UNIDO.

Project Management Institute. 2010. *Project management: A guide to the project management body of knowledge.* 4th ed. Newtown Square, PA: PMI.

UN Industrial Development Organization. 1975. *The initiation and implementation of industrial projects in developing countries: A systematic approach.* New York: UNIDO.

About the Authors

LECH KUROWSKI

Lech Kurowski is an economist with over 25 years of experience in investment projects analysis. He has been involved in both performing investment studies and analyzing investment proposals prepared by consulting companies, for governments and individual investors in more than 40 countries in Europe, Asia, and Africa. He has applied his accumulated experience in a number of training programs on financial and economic appraisal of projects. He provided consultations mainly to industry-related projects, but was also involved in infrastructure projects (industrial parks), in education, and in adaptation of historical buildings and historical ensembles to self-sustained operation in contemporary conditions while preserving their historical values.

During his professional career Dr. Kurowski cooperated with several international organizations in providing advice to governments of their member countries—among others, United Nations Industrial Development Organization (expert and longtime staff member), World Bank, and OPEC Fund for International Development. He has also been involved in the preparation of the economic analysis approach applied by the government of China.

At present he is a professor of economic analysis at the Wroclaw University of Economics in Wroclaw, Poland.

DAVID SUSSMAN

David Sussman has served as consultant to medium- and small-scale enterprises throughout the world, with concentration in Latin America. He has conducted more than 50 workshops and seminars in industrial investment planning and project appraisal for managers, consultants, and bankers in Europe, Asia, Africa, and the Americas, dealing with issues such as project planning, market analysis and marketing strategy, engineering design of product and process, financial and economic analysis, project financing, implementation planning, and promotion.

He served as operations manager for a small-scale enterprise, training company staff in production and management. He has also served as a planner and director of nonprofit public service enterprises. He is a licensed professional engineer with further specialization in management science.

He was responsible for most of the important systems design and developed many of the concepts used in the project analysis approach of the U.N. industrial development organization, having served as a consultant for over 20 years. He has also served as a consultant for other international development organizations, such as the UN Development Program, International Executive Service Corps, ACDI/VOCA, the Asian Development Bank (IBRD affiliate), and Technoserve, Inc.

Mr. Sussman has also developed financial management systems for public and private sector organizations using standard commercial software. He has extensive experience working with cooperative enterprises. He performed a study of the economic structure of a savings and loan operation, was director and financial planner for a food cooperative, and designed financial management systems for a savings and loan/agricultural production cooperative in Latin America and for agricultural cooperatives in Paraguay and Ghana.

His published items include the following:

- "Training Course in Preparation and Appraisal of Industrial Investment Projects"—principal editor and contributor, UNIDO, 2000.
- Contributor to UNIDO's *Manual for Preparation of Industrial Feasibility Studies*, 1995.
- *Users' Guide and Case Study Manual* for the COMFAR project analysis software, 1995.

Index

Printed and bound by CPI Group (UK) Ltd, Croydon, CR0 4YY

16/04/2025

14658444-0004